WITHDRAWN

The History of British Women's Writing, 1690–1750

The History of British Women's Writing
General Editors: **Jennie Batchelor** and **Cora Kaplan**

Advisory Board: Isobel Armstrong, Rachel Bowlby, Carolyn Dinshaw, Margaret Ezell, Margaret Ferguson, Isobel Grundy, and Felicity Nussbaum

The History of British Women's Writing is an innovative and ambitious monograph series that seeks both to synthesize the work of several generations of feminist scholars, and to advance new directions for the study of women's writing. Volume editors and contributors are leading scholars whose work collectively reflects the global excellence in this expanding field of study. It is envisaged that this series will be a key resource for specialist and non-specialist scholars and students alike.

Titles include:

Caroline Bicks and Jennifer Summit (*editors*)
THE HISTORY OF BRITISH WOMEN'S WRITING, 1500–1610
Volume Two

Ros Ballaster (*editor*)
THE HISTORY OF BRITISH WOMEN'S WRITING, 1690–1750
Volume Four

Jacqueline M. Labbe (*editor*)
THE HISTORY OF BRITISH WOMEN'S WRITING, 1750–1830
Volume Five

Forthcoming titles:

Elizabeth Herbert McAvoy and Diane Watt (*editors*)
THE HISTORY OF BRITISH WOMEN'S WRITING, 700–1500
Volume One

Mihoko Suzuki (*editor*)
THE HISTORY OF BRITISH WOMEN'S WRITING, 1610–1690
Volume Three

History of British Women's Writing
Series Standing Order ISBN 978–0–230–20079–1 hardback
(*outside North America only*)

You can receive future titles in this series as they are published by placing a standing order. Please contact your bookseller or, in case of difficulty, write to us at the address below with your name and address, the title of the series and the ISBN quoted above.

Customer Services Department, Macmillan Distribution Ltd, Houndmills, Basingstoke, Hampshire RG21 6XS, England

---

The History of British Women's Writing, 1690–1750

Volume Four

Edited by

Ros Ballaster
Professor of Eighteenth-Century Studies, Faculty of English Language and Literature, Mansfield College, Oxford University, UK

First published 2010 by
PALGRAVE MACMILLAN

Palgrave Macmillan in the UK is an imprint of Macmillan Publishers Limited,
registered in England, company number 785998, of Houndmills, Basingstoke,
Hampshire RG21 6XS.

Palgrave Macmillan in the US is a division of St Martin's Press LLC,
175 Fifth Avenue, New York, NY 10010.

Palgrave Macmillan is the global academic imprint of the above companies
and has companies and representatives throughout the world.

Palgrave® and Macmillan® are registered trademarks in the United States,
the United Kingdom, Europe and other countries.

ISBN 978–0–230–54938–8   hardback

This book is printed on paper suitable for recycling and made from fully
managed and sustained forest sources. Logging, pulping and manufacturing
processes are expected to conform to the environmental regulations of the
country of origin.

A catalogue record for this book is available from the British Library.

A catalog record for this book is available from the Library of Congress.

10   9   8   7   6   5   4   3   2   1
19 18 17 16 15 14 13 12 11 10

Transferred to Digital Printing in 2011

Contents

Series Preface

One of the most significant developments in literary studies in the last quarter of a century has been the remarkable growth of scholarship on women's writing. This was inspired by, and in turn provided inspiration for, a post-war women's movement which saw women's cultural expression as key to their emancipation. The retrieval, republication, and reappraisal of women's writing, beginning in the mid-1960s, have radically affected the literary curriculum in schools and universities. A revised canon now includes many more women writers. Literature courses that focus on what women thought and wrote from antiquity onwards have become popular undergraduate and postgraduate options. These new initiatives have meant that gender – in language, authors, texts, audience, and in the history of print culture more generally – is a central question for literary criticism and literary history. A mass of fascinating research and analysis extending over several decades now stands as testimony to a lively and diverse set of debates, in an area of work that is still expanding.

Indeed so rapid has this expansion been, that it has become increasingly difficult for students and academics to have a comprehensive view of the wider field of women's writing outside their own period or specialism. As the research on women has moved from the margins to the confident centre of literary studies it has become rich in essays and monographs dealing with smaller groups of authors, with particular genres and with defined periods of literary production, reflecting the divisions of intellectual labour and development of expertise that are typical of the discipline of literary studies. Collections of essays that provide overviews within particular periods and genres do exist, but no published series has taken on the mapping of the field, even within one language group or national culture.

A History of British Women's Writing is intended as just such a cartographic standard work. Its ambition is to provide, in ten volumes edited by leading experts in the field, and comprised of newly commissioned essays by specialist scholars, a clear and integrated picture of women's contribution to the world of letters within Great Britain from medieval times to the present. In taking on such a wide ranging project we were inspired by the founding, in 2003, of Chawton House Library, a UK registered charity with a unique collection of books focusing on women's writing in English from 1600 to 1830, set in the home and working estate of Jane Austen's brother.

JENNIE BATCHELOR
UNIVERSITY OF KENT

CORA KAPLAN
QUEEN MARY, UNIVERSITY OF LONDON

Acknowledgements

This one is for the many women who have shared their passion for women's writing with me over many years: from animated discussions when I was a doctoral student with the Oxford feminist theory reading group (Jeri Johnson, Dianne Chisholm, Stephanie Flood, Karen Van Dyck, Lynne Hancock especially) to colleagues and students at the University of East Anglia and Oxford University while I have been in academic employment.

I have been honoured to work as supervisor, course tutor or examiner with a number of doctoral students who have constantly revised my opinions and opened my eyes to new materials and ways of reading them: Rebecca Bullard, Melanie Bigold, Debbie McVitty, Caroline Rozell, Elizabeth Scott-Baumann, Alice Eardley, Jennifer Batt, Claudine Van Hensbergen, Taylor Walle, Lisa Anscomb, Sarah Salih. Finally, I hope this collection will match the quality of many other tributes to the inspirational supervision and friendship of a scholar too rarely acknowledged for her contribution to the discovery, dissemination and understanding of women's literary activity in the eighteenth century: Professor Marilyn Butler.

Notes on the Contributors

Sharon Achinstein is Reader in Renaissance English Literature at Oxford University and a Fellow of St Edmund Hall, having previously taught at the University of Maryland and at Northwestern University. She has published essays on women writers, including Elizabeth Singer Rowe, Mary Astell, and Mary Mollineux, and has authored *Literature and Dissent in Milton's England* (2003). She co-edited (with Elizabeth Sauer), *Milton and Toleration* (2007), and is currently preparing an edition of Milton's divorce tracts for the forthcoming *Complete Works of John Milton*.

Ros Ballaster is Professor of Eighteenth-Century Studies at Oxford University and Fellow in English at Mansfield College. She has written and published extensively about women's writing of the eighteenth century. Her first book was *Seductive Forms: Women's Amatory Fiction 1684–1740* (1992). Her most recent publications addressed representations of eastern cultures in eighteenth-century England: *Fabulous Orients: Fictions of the East in England 1662–1785* (2005 and winner of the Rose Mary Crawshay Prize from the British Academy) and an accompanying anthology *Fables of the East* (2005).

Melanie Bigold is a Lecturer in English at Cardiff University. She is currently working on two projects. The first, a forthcoming book on *Women of Letters: Manuscript Culture in an Age of Print*, looks at the writing lives of Elizabeth Singer Rowe, Catharine Trotter Cockburn, and Elizabeth Carter. The second project, begun on a SSHRC fellowship at the University of Toronto and as a Plumer Visiting Fellow at St Anne's College (Oxford), is a study of critical biography and the afterlife of lives in the eighteenth century. The primary focus of the project is George Ballard's important history of learned women, *Memoirs of Several Ladies* (1752) and his manuscript archives.

Toni Bowers is Associate Professor of English at the University of Pennsylvania, where she teaches British literature, cultural studies, and gender studies. The author of more than thirty articles and reviews, she has also written two scholarly books, *Force or Fraud: British Seduction Stories and the Problem of Resistance, 1660–1760* (forthcoming, 2010) and *The Politics of Motherhood: British Writing and Culture, 1680–1760* (1996).

With John Richetti, she has edited a new classroom adbridgment of Samuel Richardson's *Clarissa* (2010) and with Tita Chico she is co-editing a collection of new scholarly essays entitled *Seduction and Sentiment in the Atlantic World, 1660–1800* (forthcoming Palgrave, 2011). She is currently at work on a study of the metaphors that enabled the Union of England and Scotland in 1707.

Jill Campbell is Professor of English at Yale University. She is the author of *Natural Masques: Gender and Identity in Fielding's Plays and Novels* (1995). Her edition of Fielding's *The Author's Farce* is now available in *The Broadview Anthology of Restoration and Early 18th-Century Drama*. She is currently completing a book on satiric portraits and self-representations of Lady Mary Wortley Montagu, Lord Hervey, and Alexander Pope.

E.J. Clery is Professor of Eighteenth-Century Literature at the University of Southampton. Her publications include *The Feminization Debate in Eighteenth-Century England: Literature, Commerce and Luxury* (Palgrave Macmillan, 2004), *Women's Gothic from Clara Reeve to Mary Shelley* (2000), and *The Rise of Supernatural Fiction, 1762–1800* (1995).

Christine Gerrard is Lecturer in English at the University of Oxford and Fellow in English at Lady Margaret Hall. She is a specialist in political writing of the period 1660–1760, and eighteenth century poetry, particularly women's poetry. She is the author of *The Patriot Opposition to Walpole, 1725–1742* (1994), and *Aaron Hill: The Muses' Projector, 1685–1750* (2003). Her work as an editor includes *Eighteenth Century Poetry: An Annotated Anthology* (with David Fairer, 1999, 2nd edition, 2004), *A Companion to Eighteenth Century Poetry* (2006), and *The Complete Correspondence of Samuel Richardson*, vols 1–2 (2009). She is currently researching and writing a book on literature in the reign of George I (1714–27).

Moyra Haslett is Senior Lecturer in English at Queen's University, Belfast. Her previous publications include *Byron's Don Juan and the Don Juan Legend* (1997), *Marxist Literary and Cultural Theories* (Palgrave, 2000) and *Pope to Burney, Scriblerians to Bluestockings* (Palgrave, 2003). She is currently completing an edition of Thomas Amory's *The Life of John Buncle, Esq* (1756), for the 'Early Irish Fiction' series (2011) and is also working on a monograph on representations of female community in the long eighteenth century.

Kathryn R. King teaches English at the University of Montevallo where she is Advisor to the Vice President of Academic Affairs on Academic Initiatives. She is the author of *Jane Barker: A Literary Career* (2000) and co-editor with Alexander Pettit of Eliza Haywood's *Female Spectator* (2002). She has published articles on eighteenth-century women writers in numerous books and journals, among them *RES, ELH,* and *Eighteenth-Century Life*. She is Eighteenth-Century Section Editor for the online journal *Literature Compass* and is currently writing a political biography of Haywood.

Shawn Lisa Maurer is Associate Professor of English at the College of the Holy Cross in Worcester, Massachusetts, where she has also served as Director of Women's and Gender Studies. Her publications combine a focus on women writers with attention to the historical construction of gender, in particular masculinity, across a variety of genres, including periodical literature, fiction, and drama. She is the author of *Proposing Men: Dialectics of Gender and Class in the Eighteenth-Century English Periodical* (1998) and has edited Elizabeth Inchbald's *Nature and Art* (2005). She is currently at work on a study of adolescence and the novel in the eighteenth century.

Karen O'Brien is Professor of English Literature at the University of Warwick. She is the author of *Women and Enlightenment in Eighteenth-Century Britain* (2009) and *Narratives of Enlightenment: Cosmopolitan History from Voltaire to Gibbon* (1997), and is the editor of volume II (1750–1820) of the forthcoming *Oxford History of the Novel*.

Jane Shaw is Reader in Church History at Oxford University and Dean of Divinity and Fellow of New College, Oxford University. She has published widely in the field of eighteenth-century history, including *Miracles in Enlightenment England* (2006). She is Co-Director of The Prophecy Project at Oxford University, which looks at the work of the late eighteenth-century prophet, Joanna Southcott, and the prophetic thinkers and movements that came out of her writings, and she has just completed a history of the Panacea Society, an early twentieth-century Southcottian, millenarian group in England (forthcoming, 2011).

Jane Spencer is Professor of English at Exeter University. Her first book was *The Rise of the Woman Novelist: from Aphra Behn to Jane Austen* (1986). She edited a selection of Aphra Behn's drama (*The Rover and Other Plays*, 1995) and her *Aphra Behn's Afterlife* (2000) addressed the reception and influence of Behn's work in eighteenth-century England. Her latest book was *Literary Relations: Kinship and the Canon, 1660–1830* (2005) and she is currently working on a study of attitudes to and representations of animals in the eighteenth-century in Britain.

Kate Williams writes historical biographies and on eighteenth and nineteenth-century history and culture for newspapers. She is revising her doctoral thesis to be published as *Stolen Pleasures: Richardson and Amatory Fiction*. She has published articles in books and journals on eighteenth-century fiction.

Chronology

List of significant works by British women writers 1690–1750 by year of appearance.

- All works in italics are publications unless otherwise indicated (by reference to performance date or manuscript circulation).
- Most works are only mentioned on first publication/appearance unless there is particular significance to later appearances (such as a prestigious 'collected works').
- Works which are first published by authors who were composing largely in the period before 1690 are omitted from this list unless they carry particular significance in the period under discussion.
- I have excluded works by British women writers in languages other than English, most notably editions of Latin texts.

1690   Mary Evelyn, *Mundus Muliebris: or, The Ladies Dressing-room Unlock'd, and her Toilette Spread*, posthumously published by her father, John Evelyn

1691   Barbara Blaugdone, *Account of the Travels, Sufferings and Persecutions of Barbara Blaugdone*

       Joan Vokin, *God's Mighty Power Magnified: As Manifested and Revealed in his Faithful Handmaid Joan Vokins*

       Alicia D'Anver, satirical poem entitled *Academia; or, The Humours of the University of Oxford* went on sale in Oxford

1692   Anne Conway, *The Principles of the most ancient and modern Philosophy*

       Joan Whitrow, *To King William and Queen Mary, Grace and Peace, The Widow Whitrow's Humble Thanksgiving to the Lord*

1693   Alicia D'Anver, *The Oxford-Act. A Poem*, further satirical poem attacking Oxford University

       Catherine Cockburn, 'Olinda's Adventures', published anonymously in *Letters of Love and Gallantry*

1694   Mary Astell, *A Serious Proposal to the Ladies* and *Letters Concerning the Love of God*

       Elinor James, *Mrs James's apology because of unbelievers* (broadside pamphlet)

Jane Lead, *The Enochian Walks with God* (and she founds Philadelphian Society)

One number of the periodical *The Athenian Mercury* dedicated to Elizabeth Rowe's poems (also in 1695)

Joan Whitrow, *The Widow Whiterows Humble Thanksgiving for the Kings Safe Return*

1695   Catharine Trotter, *Agnes de Castro: A Tragedy* opened at Drury Lane

Elizabeth Bathurst, *Truth vindicated by the faithful testimony and writings of Elizabeth Bathurst*

Elinor James, *Mrs. James's Reasons that Printing may not be a Free-Trade* (broadside in response to lapse of Licensing Act)

Jane Lead, *The Laws of Paradise* and *The Wonders of God's Creation Manifested*

She Ventures and He Wins (comedy) by 'Ariadne' performed at Lincoln's Inn Fields

1696   Delarivier Manley, *The Royal Mischief* at Lincoln's Inn Fields and *The Lost Lover* at Drury Lane performed and *Letters written by Mrs. Manley* published allegedly without her consent.

Judith Drake, *An Essay in Defence of the Female Sex*

Elizabeth Singer Rowe, *Poems on Several Occasions*

Jane Lead, *A Message to the Philadelphian Society,* and *The Tree of Faith* and *Fountain of Gardens*

Damaris Masham, *A Discourse concerning the Love of God*

Mary Pix, *The Inhumane Cardinal* (novel) published. Plays *Ibrahim* (tragedy) and *The Spanish Wives* (farce) performed at Drury Lane

Joan Whitrow, *To the King and Both Houses of Parliament* (broadside delivered into hands of William III)

Elizabeth White, *The Experiences of God's Gracious Dealing with Elizabeth White*

M. Marsin, *The Near Approach of Christ's Kingdom*

1697   Mary Astell, *Serious Proposal Part II*

Joan Whitrow, *Faithful Warnings, Expostulations and Exhortations, to the Several Professors of Christianity in England, as well those of the Highest as the Lowest Quality*

Jane Lead, *A Revelation of the everlasting Gospel-Message*

Mary Pix, *The Innocent Mistress* (comedy) and *The Deceiver Deceived* (comedy) performed at Lincoln's Inn Fields.

The Unnatural Mother, comedy written 'by a Young Lady' performed at Lincoln's Inn Fields.

Five tracts by M. Marsin published this year: *All the Chief Points Contained in the Christian Religion; Rehearsal of the Covenant by Moses; The Womans Advocate; A Clear and Brief Explanation*; and *The Figurative Speeches: by which God has veiled his Secrets.*

1698   Catharine Trotter, *Fatal Friendship* (verse tragedy) performed at Lincoln's Inn Fields

Jane Lead, *Messenger of an Universal Peace*

Mary Pix, *Queen Catharine* (tragedy) with epilogue by Catharine Trotter performed at Lincoln's Inn Fields

M. Marsin, *Truth Vindicated against all Heresies*

Elizabeth Tipper, *The Pilgrim's Viaticum: or, the Destitute but not Forlorn* (a poetry collection)

1699   Jane Lead, *The Ascent to the Mount of Vision* and *The Signs of the Times*

Mary Pix, *The False Friend* (tragedy) performed at Lincoln's Inn Fields

M. Marsin, *Two Sorts of Latter-Days, Proved from Scripture*

Frances, Lady Norton sees into publication the works of her deceased daughter, Grace, Lady Gethin under title *Misery's Virtues Whetstone. Reliquiae Gethinianae.*

Ann Docwra (Quaker), *An Apostate-Conscience exposed*

1700   Ann Docwra, *The Second Part of an Apostate-Conscience exposed*

The Female Advocate; or, a Plea for the Just Liberty of the Tender Sex by a 'Lady of Quality' named as 'Eugenia'; responds to John Sprint's misogynist wedding-sermon, published 1699 as *The Bride-Woman's Counsellor*

Mary Pix, *The Beau Defeated* (comedy) performed at Lincoln's Inn Fields

Mary Astell, *Reflections upon Marriage*

Susanna Centlivre, *The Perjur'd Husband* (tragicomedy) performed at Drury Lane

The Nine Muses or, Poems written by Nine several ladies upon the Death of ... Dryden (includes poems by Sarah Fyge, Delarivier Manley, Sarah Piers, Catharine Trotter, Mary Pix)

Elizabeth Thomas publishes single elegy on John Dryden *in Luctus Britannici* as by a 'Young Lady'

Margaret Fell, *Epistle against uniform Quaker Costume*

Jane Lead, *The Wars of David*

M. Marsin, proto-feminist Bible commentary *A Full and Clear Account the Scripture gives of the Deity*

Catharine Trotter, *Love at a Loss* (comedy) performed at Drury Lane

1701   Mary Lady Chudleigh, *The Ladies Defence* in response to John Sprint's sermon (see 1700)

Catharine Trotter, *The Unhappy Penitent* (tragedy) performed at Drury Lane

Mary Pennyman, *Some of the Letters and Papers which were written by Mrs Mary Pennyman, relating to an Holy and Heavenly Conversation*

Mary Pix, *The Double Distress* and *The Czar of Muscovy* (both tragedies) performed at Little Lincoln's Inn Fields.

Jane Wiseman, *Antiochus the Great* (tragedy) performed at Lincoln's Inn Fields

M. Marsin, feminist tract *Good News to the Good Women* and *Two Remarkable Females of Womankind* and *An Answer to Dr Whitby, proving the Jews are not to be called into the gospel of the Christian Warfare*

Anne Finch's Pindaric ode 'The Spleen' published anonymously in Charles Gildon's *New Collection of Poems on Several Occasions*

1702   Jane Lead, *A Living Funeral Testimony*

Mary Mollineaux, *Fruits of Retirement, or Miscellaneous Poems* (posthumous)

Susanna Centlivre, *The Beau's Duel* and *The Stolen Heiress* performed at Lincoln's Inn Fields

Elinor James, *May It Please Your Lordships* (broadsheet welcoming Anne to the throne)

Catharine Trotter, *A Defence of the Essay of Human Understanding, written by Mr. Lock*

1703   Susanna Centlivre, *Love's Contrivance* (comedy) performed (anonymously) at Drury Lane

Mary Lady Chudleigh, *Poems on Several Occasions*

Mary Davys, *The Amours of Alcippus and Lucippe*

Mary Pix, *The Different Widows* (comedy) performed at Lincoln's Inn Fields

Sarah Fyge Egerton, *Poems on Several Occasions* with commendatory verses by Mary Pix and Susanna Centlivre

1704   Mary Pix, *Violenta; or, The Rewards of Virtue turn'd from Boccace into verse* (verse tale)

Mary Astell, *Moderation truly Stated* and *An Impartial Enquiry into the Causes of Rebellion and Civil War in this Kingdom* and *A Fair Way with the Dissenters*

1705   Mary Astell, *The Christian Religion, As Profess'd by a Daughter of the Church of England*

Catharine Trotter, *A Poem on His Grace The Duke of Marlborough's Return from his German Expedition*

Delarivier Manley, *Secret Memoirs ... from the New Atalantis*

Susanna Centlivre, *The Busie-Body* and *The Man's Bewitched* (both comedies) performed at the Haymarket

Mary Astell, *Bart'lemy Fair, or an Enquiry after Wit*

8 July 1709–31 March 1710   *The Female Tatler*, periodical with female eidelon(s), published thrice weekly

1710   Mary Lady Chudleigh, *Essays upon Several Subjects in Prose and Verse* dedicated to Princess Sophia of Brunswick

Susanna Centlivre, *A Bickerstaff's Burying* (farce) performed at Drury Lane and *Marplot in Lisbon* (comedy) performed at the Haymarket

Margaret Fell, *A Brief Collection of Remarkable Passages* including 14-page autobiography

Elinor James, *Mrs James Prayer for the Queen and Parliament, and Kingdom too*

Delarivier Manley, *Memoirs of Europe*

1711   Delarivier Manley, *Court Intrigues* (revised version of *Lady's Pacquet*) and four pamphlets: *A True Narrative of What Pass'd at the Examination of the Marquis de Guiscard* and *The Duke of M—h's Vindication* and *A True Relation of the Several Facts and Circumstances of the Intended Riot and Tumult on Queen Elizabeth's Birth-Day* and *A Learned Comment on Dr Hare's Sermon*

Elizabeth Stirredge's autobiography written for her children, *Strength in Weakness Manifest*, published posthumously by Quaker woman publisher, Tace Stowle.

1712   Susanna Centlivre, *The Perplex'd Lovers* performed without its Whig epilogue which had not received a licence

Elinor James, verse broadside *This Day Did God ...*

1713   Jane Barker, *Love Intrigues*

Anne Finch, Countess of Winchilsea, *Miscellany Poems, on Several Occasions*

Elizabeth Elstob, pamphlet compilation *Some Testimonies of Learned Men, in Favour of the Intended Edition of the Saxon Homilies*

1714   Delarivier Manley, *Adventures of Rivella* and two pamphlets: *The Honour and Prerogative of the Queen's Majesty Vindicated* and *A Modest Enquiry into the Reasons of the Joy Expressed ... upon ... the Report of the Queen's Death*

Susanna Centlivre, *The Wonder, a Woman keeps a Secret* (comedy) performed at Drury Lane

Frances, Lady Norton *A Miscellany of Poems, Compos'd, and Work'd with a Needle, on the Backs and Seats &c. of Several Chairs and Stools*

Mary Kettilby's executrix published her *A Collection of Above Three Hundred Receipts in Cookery, Physick and Surgery; for the use of all good wives, tender mothers, and careful nurses*

Sarah, Lady Piers, *George, for Britain*, a poem

Elinor James, *This Day Ought Never to be Forgotten, being the Proclamation Day for Queen Elizabeth*

1715 Jane Barker, *Exilius* in *Entertaining Novels*

Elizabeth Elstob, *Rudiments of Grammar for the English-Saxon Tongue* and *An Apology for the Study of Northern Antiquities* published together

Susanna Centlivre, *A Gotham Election* and *A Wife Well Managed* (two farces) published (not performed for political reasons)

Lady Mary Wortley Montagu composes six 'Eclogues' between February and following July

Elinor James, *Mrs James's Thanks to the Lords and Commons for their great sincerity to King George*

1716 Lady Mary Wortley Montagu, three pirated 'Town Eclogues' appeared in *Court Poems*

Susanna Centlivre, *The Cruel Gift* (tragedy) performed at Drury Lane

Mary Davys, *The Northern Heiress, or the Humours of York* (comedy) performed at Lincoln's Inn Fields

Mary Monck's poems published posthumously with others of her circle by her father under title *Marinda: Poems and Translations upon Several Occasions*

1717 Susannah Hopton, *A Collection of Meditations and Devotions* (posthumous). Included *Daily Devotions* of 1672 and *Meditations and Devotions on the Life of Christ* and *An Hexameron*

Susanna Centlivre, *An Epistle to the King of Sweden, from a Lady of Great-Britain*, a poem answered by Mary Davys with *An Answer from the King of Sweden to the British Lady's Epistle*

Delarivier Manley, *Lucius, the first Christian King of Britain* performed at Drury Lane

1718 Susanna Centlivre, *A Bold Stroke for a Wife* (comedy) performed at Lincoln's Inn Fields

Lady Mary Wortley Montagu, edited letters dated between 3 August 1716–1 November 1718 which make up her manuscript travel book about European and Middle Eastern travel, her *Embassy Letters*

Jane Barber translated Lenten meditations from unknown Fenelon source as *The Christian Pilgrimage* with 14 psalms

Mary Hearne, *The Lover's Week* dedicated to Delarivier Manley

1719 Eliza Haywood, *Love in Excess* part 1 (two vols)
Elizabeth Lady Wardlaw has 'fragment' of ancient ballad of 'Hardyknute' privately published in Edinburgh.
Mary Hearne, *The Deserters*. Republished 1720 with *Lover's Week* as *Honour the Victory and Love the Prize*

1720 Eliza Haywood, *Love in Excess* part 2 (two vols)
Penelope Aubin, translation from Robert Challes's *The Illustrious French Lovers*
Eliza Haywood, translation from Boursault's 'Ten Letters from a Young Lady of Quality' as *Letters from a Lady of Quality to a Chevalier* (published by subscription)
Susanna Centlivre's autobiographical poem *A Woman's Case*
The Epistles of Clio and Strephon, letters and poems between Martha Fowke and William Bond
Delarivier Manley, *The Power of Love in Seven Novels*

1721 Penelope Aubin, *Strange Adventures of the Count de Vinevil* and *The Life of Madam de Beaumont* and (edited) Gomberville's *Moral Virtue Delineated* and *Doctrine of Virtue*
Eliza Haywood, *The Fair Captive* (tragedy) performed at Lincoln's Inn Fields
Jane Madan's 'Abelard to Eloisa' written in response to Pope's 'Eloisa' (published 1728)

1722 Eliza Haywood, *The British Recluse* and *The Injur'd Husband*
Penelope Aubin, *The Noble Slaves* and *The Life and Amorous Adventures of Lucinda* and translation of Pétis de la Croix's *Life of Genghizcan the Great* and Mme de Beaucour's *Life of the Countess de Gondez*, *The Adventures of the Prince of Clermont*
Susanna Centlivre, *The Artifice* (comedy) performed at Drury Lane
Lady Lucy Herbert, *Several Excellent methods of hearing Mass*
Elizabeth Thomas, *Miscellany Poems* (reprinted 1726 as *Poems on Several Occasions*)
Lady Mary Wortley Montagu, *A Plain Account of the Innoculating of the Small-Pox*, anonymously, and as 'by a Turkey merchant'

1723 Jane Robe, *The Fatal Legacy* (tragedy translated from *La Thébaïde* by Jean Racine) performed at Lincoln's Inn Fields
Jane Barker, *A Patch-Work Screen for the Ladies*
Penelope Aubin, *Life of Charlotta Du Pont*
Eliza Haywood, *A Wife to be Lett* (comedy) performed at Drury Lane; *Idalia; Lasselia* and *Works* (3 vols)

1724 Mary Davys, *The Reform'd Coquet* published by subscription

Eliza Haywood, *The Masqueraders; The Fatal Secret; The Surprize; The Arragonian Queen; La Belle Assemblée* (vol. 1) translated from Mme de Gomez *Les Journées Amusantes; Memoirs of a certain Island adjacent to Utopia* (vol. 1); *Memoirs of the Baron de Brosse* (vol. 1); *The Tea-Table* (35 nos in periodical form); *Poems on Several Occasions* and *Works* (vol. 4) and *Secret Histories, Novels and Poems* (4 vols)

Mary Caesar begins journal (to 1741)

Elizabeth Harrison, 'A Letter to Mr. John Gay, on his Tragedy call'd "The Captives" '

Elizabeth Tollet, anon, *Poems on Several Occasions*

1725   Mary Davys, *Works* (2 vols published by subscription)

Eliza Haywood, *Memoirs of a Certain Island Adjacent to the Kingdom of Utopia* (vol. 2); *The Tea-Table* (part 1 as a vol. under her name); *The Lady's Philosopher's Stone*, translation from Louis-Adrien Duperron de Castera; *The Unequal Conflict; Fatal Fondness; Mary Stuart, Queen of Scots;* and *Secret Histories, Novels and Poems* (second edition)

Delarivier Manley, *A Stage-Coach Journey to Exeter*

1726   Jane Barker, *The Lining of the Patch-Work Screen*

Penelope Aubin, *The Life and Adventures of the Lady Lucy* and *The Illustrious French Lovers* (a translation)

Eliza Haywood, *The Mercenary Lover; The City Jilt; Reflections on the Various Effects of Love* (part 1); *The Distress'd Orphan; The Secret History of the ... Court of Caramania; Letters from the Palace of Fame; Cleomelia*

Catharine Cockburn (nee Trotter), *A Letter to Dr Holdsworth,* and also wrote 'Vindication of Mr. Locke's Christian Principles' in response to Holdsworth (not published until her posthumous *Works* of 1751)

1727   Mary Davys, *The Accomplish'd Rake*

Eliza Haywood, *The Fruitless Enquiry; Philidore and Placentia* (2 vols); *The Perplex'd Duchess*

Mary Herberts, *The Adventures of Proteus, &c., a Sett of Novels*

Arabella Plantin, *Love Led Astray* and *The Ingrateful* published in *Letters to the Lady Wharton*

Elizabeth Boyd ('Louisa'), *Variety, a Poem, in Two Cantos*

1728   Penelope Aubin, *The Life and Adventures of the Young Count Albertus*

Elizabeth Singer Rowe, *Friendship in Death, in Twenty Letters from the Dead to the Living*

Mary Barber, *A Tale, Being an Addition to Mr. Gay's Fables* (poem) published anonymously in Dublin

Elizabeth Hanson, *An Account of the Remarkable Captivity of Elizabeth Hanson* published in Philadelphia

Elizabeth Thomas, *Codrus; or, the Dunciad Dissected* (satire on Pope)

Eliza Haywood, *The Agreeable Caledonian* (Part 1); *Irish Artifice, or the History of Clarina* published in *The Female Dunciad*; *The Disguis'd Prince*, translation (Part 1)

1729   Eliza Haywood, *Frederick, Duke of Brunswick-Lunnenburgh* performed at Lincoln's Inn Fields and dedicated to Frederick Lewis, Prince of Wales; *The Fair Hebrew*

Penelope Aubin, translation *The Life of the Countess de Gondez*

Elizabeth Rowe, *Letters on Various Occasions* (vol. 1 of *Letters Moral and Entertaining*)

1730   Penelope Aubin, *The Humours of the Masqueraders*

Elizabeth Thomas, *The Metamorphosis of the Town*

Eliza Haywood, *Love-Letters on All Occasions*

1731   Elizabeth Thomas, *Pylades and Corinna* (vol.1), posthumous

Elizabeth Rowe, *Letters Moral and Entertaining* (vol. 2)

1732   Elizabeth Thomas, *Pylades and Corinna* (vol. 2)

Elizabeth Boyd, *The Happy Unfortunate; or, the Female Page: a Novel*

Elizabeth Rowe, *Letters Moral and Entertaining* (vol. 3)

Mary Chudleigh's letters to Elizabeth Thomas 1701–03 published in *Pylades*

Mary Davys, *The False Friend* (altered from 'The Cousins' in 1725 *Works*)

Anne Viscountess Irwin, country-house poem to her father, *Castle-Howard*

1733   Lady Mary Wortley Montagu, anon, *Verses address'd to the Imitator of Horace*

Mary Chandler, *Description of Bath; a Poem, in a Letter to a Friend*

Eliza Haywood (with William Hatchett), *The Opera of operas* performed at the Haymarket

Mary Masters, *Poems on several Occasions*, published by subscription

1734   Jean Adam, *Miscellany Poems*, published at Glasgow

Lady Mary Wortley Montagu, lampoon on Swift *The Dean's Provocation for Writing the Lady's Dressing-Room, A Poem*

Eliza Haywood, translation *L'Entretien des Beaux Esprits*

Anne Dutton, *A Narration of the Wonders of Grace, in verse*

1735   Mary Barber, *Poems on Several Occasions*, published by subscription and dedication to Lord Orrery by Jonathan Swift (who also helped to edit the work)

Charlotte Charke, *The Carnival* (farce) performed for her benefit at Lincoln's Inn Fields, and *The Art of Management, or Tragedy Expell'd* (topical farce) performed at York Buildings

Elizabeth Cooper, *The Rival Widows* (comedy) performed at Covent Garden

Anne Dutton, *A Discourse upon walking with God: in a letter to a friend*

Sarah Chapone, *Hardships of the English Laws in Relation to Wives*

1736   Eliza Haywood, *The Adventures of Eovaai*

Elizabeth Rowe's *Philomela; or, Poems by Mrs. Elizabeth Singer (now Rowe)* (without author's permission) and *The History of Joseph* (8-book biblical epic; 2nd edn with 2 further books in 1737)

1737   Lady Mary Wortley Montagu, *The Nonsense of Common-Sense* (periodical, 16 December 1737 to 14 March 1738)

Elizabeth Rowe, posthumous *Devout Exercises of the Heart*

Elizabeth Blackwell, *Curious Herbal* (weekly parts and then vol. 1)

Elizabeth Cooper, *The Muses Library* – anthology of English poetry, reissued 1741

Sarah Stone, *A Complete Practice of Midwifery*

1738   Elizabeth Carter, *Poems upon Particular Occasions* (limited number of copies published for friends and family) and scholarly edition of translation of Jean-Pierre de Crousaz's commentary on Pope's 'Essay on Man': *Examin*

Frances Seymour, Countess of Hertford, *The Story of Inkle and Yariko* with a companion piece of verses

Elizabeth Rowe, *Devout Exercises of the Heart*

1739   Mary Collyer, poem *The Woman's Labour; an Epistle to Stephen Duck*

Penelope Aubin, *A Collection of Entertaining Histories and Novels* (posthumous)

Elizabeth Carter, *Sir Isaac Newton's Philosophy Explained for the Use of the Ladies,* translated from Francesco Algarotti

Elizabeth Rowe, *Miscellaneous Works in Prose and Verse,* posthumous collection edited by her brother-in-law, Theophilus Rowe

Laetitia Pilkington, *The Statues; or the Trial of Constancy* (narrative poem)

Elizabeth Blackwell, *Curious Herbal* (vol. 2)

Elizabeth Boyd, *Don Sancho* (ballad opera) published with *Minerva's Triumph, A Masque*

'Sophia' (poss Sophia Fermor), pamphlet *Woman not Inferior to Man*

1747 Lady Mary Wortley Montagu, *Six Town Eclogues with some other poems* (without the author's knowledge)

Elizabeth Teft, *Orinthia's Miscellanies; or, a Complete Collection of Poems*

Sarah Fielding, *Familiar Letters between the Principal Characters in David Simple* (by subscription)

Catharine Trotter Cockburn, *Remarks upon ... the Nature and Obligations of Virtue*

Charlotte Lennox, *Poems on Several Occasions*

Eliza Haywood, translation from Prévost *Memoirs of a Man of Honour*

1748 Mary Leapor, *Poems upon Several Occasions* (posthumous)

Teresa Constantia Philips, *Apology for the Conduct of Mrs T.C. Philips* (monthly instalments into 1749)

Laetitia Pilkington, *Memoirs* (vol. 1, Dublin and London 3 months later)

Anne Dutton, *Letters on spiritual subjects*

Eliza Haywood, *Life's Progress through the Passions; Epistles for the Ladies* (from 15 November planned serial monthly; ran to 12 books through to 1750)

1749 Sarah Fielding, *The Governess; or, the little Female Academy; Remarks on Clarissa*

Elizabeth Moxon, *English Housewifery, Exemplified in above four hundred Receipts*

Eliza Haywood, pamphlet *A Letter from H— G— , Esq.; Dalinda, or the Double Marriage*

Laetitia Pilkington, *Memoirs* (vols 2 and 3, Dublin)

1750 Hannah Snell, *The Female Soldier*

Mary Jones, *Miscellanies in Prose and Verse*

Charlotte Lennox, *Life of Harriot Stuart*

Anne Dutton, *A Brief Account of the gracious dealings of God, with a poor, sinful, unworthy creature*

Sarah Scott, *History of Cornelia*

1755 Elizabeth Tollet, posthumously published *Poems on Several Occasions* (most written 1720–50)

Introduction

Ros Ballaster

Against the charms our ballocks have
   How weak all human skill is
Since they can make a man a slave
   To such a bitch as Willis!

Whom that I may describe throughout,
   Assist me, bawdy powers;
I'll write upon a double clout,
   And dip my pen in flowers.

Her look's demurely impudent,
   Ungainly beautiful;
Her modesty is insolent,
   Her wit both pert and dull.

A prostitute to all the town,
   And yet with no man friends,
She rails and scolds when she lies down,
   And curses when she spends.

Bawdy in thoughts, precise in words,
   Ill-natured though a whore,
Her belly is a bag of turds,
   And her cunt a common shore.

John Wilmot, Earl of Rochester 'On Mrs Willis'
(c. September 1680) [1]

Stella and Flavia every hour
Unnumbered hearts surprise:
In Stella's soul lies all her power,
And Flavia's in her eyes.

More boundless Flavia's conquests are,
And Stella's more confined:
All can discern a face that's fair,
But few a lovely mind.

Stella, like Britain's monarch, reigns
O'er cultivated lands;
Like Eastern tyrants, Flavia deigns
To rule o'er barren sands.

Then boast, fair Flavia, boast your face,
Your beauty's only store:
Your charms will every day decrease,
Each day give Stella more.

Mary Barber, 'Stella and Flavia' (1734)[2]

The contrast between these two poems acts as a means of measuring the distance travelled in conceiving of the figure of woman in literary culture from the late seventeenth to the mid-eighteenth century. Both poems are written in regular quatrains of alternate rhyming tetrameter and trimeter. Rochester's is a libertine poem in which woman is the ground of a perverse creativity; Sue Willis was a prostitute on the fringes of Charles II's court circle. The poet depicts himself as deriving his writing ink by dipping his 'pen' in menstrual blood (the 'flowers' of the poem) gathered in a clout (a clout is a fragment of clothing, here a towel used for sanitary purposes). Rochester's is a mocking inverse pastoral: the poetic speaker of Edmund Spenser's pastoral poem of 1579, *The Shepheardes Calendar*, is named Colin Clout (the term can also be used to refer to a piece of earth) and his poetry is the product of his unrequited love for a simple shepherdess. For Rochester's aristocratic speaker and Spenser's peasant songster the female body is the earthly source of masculine creativity and form.

Mary Barber, wife of a Dublin woollen-draper whose *Poems on Several Occasions* was published by subscription in 1734 with the support of Jonathan Swift and his circle, presents a contrast between two women rather than a creative dynamic between male poetic speaker and female love/lust object, but here too the issue is the extent of the female object's power to promote creative activity. Flavia is all surface and Stella all depth; the former commands with her eyes and the latter with her 'soul'. Barber too is making a compliment in imitating an earlier poet, here Jonathan Swift's verses to his friend, Esther Johnson, whom he terms 'Stella' and whom he consistently represents as a virtuous as well as practical muse by contrast with the superficiality of other women; Swift is in turn imitating the courtier poet Philip Sidney's *Astrophel and Stella* (composed in the 1580s and first published in 1591).[3] The paradox in Barber's poem is that although Stella's charms are private and confined, they grow on people and are productive whereas Flavia's flashy and extensive public charms prove 'barren'.

In the poems of both Rochester and Barber we have seen that a link is forged between the reproductive powers of the female body and the representational, productive powers of the poet. But also in both cases a perverse form of creative stimulation is set against an authentic potentiality. Willis's body produces a bag of turds rather than a 'child' (poem) – her procreation with men does not result in a living organic body. Flavia's charms generate tyranny whereas Stella's produce culture and civility. However, in Barber's poem a virtuous female influence is invoked by a female poet publishing under her own name as a source of creative – and national – energy, whereas in Rochester's such a potential influence is only invoked by its absence, by a male poet whose work circulated only in manuscript and was identified with its author by the very 'bawdy powers' it consistently summoned.[4] The contrast between these poems is to some extent a construct for the purposes of argument: there are of course earlier and later poems in which female virtue is associated with national and civic identity, and poems in which pride and female promiscuity are associated with a degenerative culture. However, the period to which literary historians often refer as the 'long eighteenth century' (from the 1660 restoration of the Stuart monarchy through to the late eighteenth century and the death of the last Hanoverian George in 1830) is increasingly identified with shifts in the ways that gender is thought and represented and especially with the idea of a culture that comes increasingly to *value* rather than *denigrate* a process of feminization, privatization, and inwardness associated with women. Notable in the contrast between these two poems is the shift from an aristocratic metaphor of private waste to a bourgeois language of public trade. Rochester's speaker tells us that Willis 'curses when she spends' – spending refers both to orgasm and to the spending of money, presumably earned in Willis's case through the trade of prostitution;

Stella by contrast ensures she has something to 'trade' with and her trading activity is the generative ground of a stable limited monarchy (a popular image of Hanoverian rule), whereas Flavia squanders wealth in her pursuit of the empty profits of seizing territory associated with the wasteful eastern tyrant. The significance of the increasing dominance of a language of trade in the late seventeenth and eighteenth centuries to the opportunities for representation by and of women is returned to at many points in this volume and is further elaborated upon below.

This introduction seeks to outline the ways in which we think about the relations between gender and literature in the years 1690 to 1750. It has been persuasively argued that gender becomes a significant and independent *category* in this period, if not always through stable use of the term itself. The influential historian Thomas Laqueur has argued that some time in the eighteenth century there is a shift from a one-sex model (whereby the female body is understood to be an inferior version of the male body on a hierarchical scale) to a two-sex model (female and male bodies are understood to be different and opposite).[5] Political historians and literary critics have argued that this 'division' of the sexes is coterminous with other 'divisions' of knowledge and identity – emergent distinctions of public and private, divisions of places of work and home, divisions of politics into oppositional parties rather than a hierarchy of monarch and state. The distinction between gender (a performance of certain acculturated characteristics) and sex (biologically-determined characteristics of the body) is one among a number of conceptual distinctions being forged in this period in the process of moving from absolutist to more mixed and complex modes of conceiving government, whether of person or state. As a result of this shifting and separation of categories and ascription of new significance to apparent differences, readers need to be wary of assuming that when writers represent sexual difference they are primarily concerned with issues of gender and sexual difference: they may equally be using gender as a representational structure that allows them to explore ideas of networks of difference, competition, power. As in the case of the poems above, to read them literally is to fail to recognize that the women described in these poems are the ground or instance of an opportunity to consider the social role and aesthetic prerogatives of the poet, male or female. However, the representation of gender should not be *reduced* to a mere metaphor for something else. The poems by Rochester and Barber are also, if not equally, 'about' the roles women are given in society, an understanding of the importance of women to culture and sociability.

In what follows this introduction pays attention to the specific character of the period under discussion which gives rise to our understanding that culture becomes increasingly 'feminized' in this period, if not always to the political or practical advantage of women. First I summarize the arguments about the feminization of eighteenth-century culture and take a look at the genres associated with feminine and masculine genders in the period. Second I look at two specific and possibly interlinked developments: the emergence of a proto-feminist politics grounded in the still new continental rationalism of Descartes, and the emergence of party as the defining distinction of state politics often expressed in terms of gendered conflict especially by women who wrote and published their work for partisan ends. Finally I return to the issue of the signifying role of the 'feminine' to elaborate further the influential valence of the governing language of 'trade', a language that informs the growing sense of writing as a form of professional career. This new sense of the professional and trading nature of the writing career offers to women (whose 'influence' is increasingly defined by their 'domestic' removal from the professions) both new challenges and new opportunities (this is the period in which we see women define themselves as pursuing careers in writing, whether through the medium of print or manuscript, or both).

1 A feminization of culture

'Gender' is performed by both men and women. However, it is a measure of precisely this differentiating, opposed 'division' that is being invented at precisely this juncture in European history that 'gender' is only visible when the marker of difference – that is, a woman – is present. This is particularly clear in Restoration and early eighteenth-century Britain when masculinity requires redefinition in the aftermath of the convulsions and decimations of a civil war. In a century haunted by the fear of a repetition of such conflict trading relations came to be increasingly valued over military conquest, sociable interaction and polite conversation over contestation and polemic, domestic virtues over civic pride.[6] Michael McKeon charts a larger transformation in the move away from political absolutism across the seventeenth century in Europe toward more contractual ways of thinking about the relation between subject and state. 'Modernity', according to his reading, is marked by the making explicit what has been previously been tacit and the attendant process of making categories that have previously only been seen as *distinct* into *separate* and *opposed* categories. He identifies a concomitant shift away from conceiving of identity in terms of political loyalty or subjection to an external and given authority in this period to conceiving of identity in terms of social relationship and self-consciousness or inwardness. This new conception, he suggests, can be best represented through valorizing the figure of the private woman, estranged from political agency and responsibility but conjuring moral power in the household: 'the wholesale deprivation of women in the polity makes it possible to imagine a different kind of subjecthood, one not of the political but of the ethical subject'.[7]

Two areas of development are particularly significant for our thinking about the changing literary scene for women in this period. First, the growth of print culture as a medium for the circulation of literary writing and the opportunities it opened up for men and women of the less privileged classes to make a living by writing across a variety of genres; until the late seventeenth century probably only the stage could allow a writer to live through the public presentation of his or her written work. Second, the development of Cartesian philosophy and Baconian empirical science in Europe which stressed the importance of challenging what is seen as 'customary' and looking at real lived experience and the capacity of subjects to reason as a measure of human value. This makes possible the emergence of a feminist discourse about women's capacity to reason (if not at this stage claims for suffrage or political 'equality' for women).[8]

2 Gender and genre

This period sees the growth of print culture alongside the continuation of a thriving culture of social authorship in manuscript. Print gives women and lower-class men new opportunities, but we should not assume that we will encounter women's writing only in print form in this period – a number of gifted writers continue to circulate their materials in manuscript and at least claim not to have sought print fame: for example Lady Mary Wortley Montagu who protests in a letter to her daughter Lady Bute written from Italy on 10 October 1753, 'upon my word, I had never printed a single line in my life'. 'Sure no body', she continues:

> ever had such various provocations to print as my selfe. I have seen things I have wrote, so mangle' d and falsify'd, I have scarce known them. I have seen Poems I never read, publish'd with my name at length, and others, that were truly and singly wrote by me, printed under the names of others. I have made my selfe easy under all these mortifications by the reflection I did not deserve them, having never aim'd at the Vanity of popular Applause.[9]

It is the case though that where women do publish they are more likely to do so in the genres of the pamphlet, petitions, and visionary writing than in turning to drama and the novel. A number also took advantage in the growth of the periodical press to submit for publication individual poems under classical and other pseudonyms, such as Elizabeth Carter whose poems appeared for many years from 1734 onwards under the name of 'Eliza' in the *Gentleman's Magazine*. However, the vast majority of writing by women (and men) that has come down to us, whether in manuscript or print form, is devotional writing in the shape of memoirs, diaries, spiritual autobiographies, and published prophecy. This is partly because the Quaker movement, in which women enjoyed a measure of power, especially with regard to the preservation of written records, had a conscious policy of preserving manuscript and print materials.[10] But also of course because piety was an expected part of women's daily domestic regime and often involved the maintenance of a regular record of prayer and devotion and because women could claim that their public speech was authorized by the pressing communicative need of a greater masculine force, that of God. Two chapters of this volume pay particular attention to the religious context of women's writing: Sharon Achinstein considers the energy associated with the dissenting movements of the period and especially the literary and theological legacy of John Milton's *Paradise Lost* (1665/1668). Jane Shaw looks at the different forms – especially the contrast between rationalist and visionary modes – that piety and devotion took in women's religious writing in the period of relative toleration of differences within the Christian religion after 1690 in Britain.

Not least in religious texts – as the pervasive example of *Paradise Lost* attests – this is a period where the distinction between literary and non-literary writing is not always clearly made. However, within the genres we now consider more obviously 'literary' there are gender divisions that operate quite significantly. Some genres are associated with female and male voice/writing more powerfully than others. Powerful gender-marked oppositions dictate many of the expectations around genre in some of the key writings of the period: most obvious is masculine epic versus feminine romance: the new popularity of the form of the mock-epic marks its departure from the 'true' chivalric/martial epic by often concerning itself with 'feminine' things such as the boudoir, make-up, and shopping. Equally, the term 'novel' is often used pejoratively to refer to the short prose tales of love and seduction by women before the advent of mid-century male novelists such as Samuel Richardson and Henry Fielding and male appropriation of the mode – significantly through claims that it might rival the epic (the chapter in this volume by Kate Williams on the rise of the novel elaborates this process). There are some instances of genre with high cultural status where female voice is important. For example, the lyric of complaint about lost or abandoned romance derived from Ovid's *Heroides* is associated with a powerful if mourning female voice and this in turn informs and resonates in the tales of seduction and betrayal narrated by Eliza Haywood and Penelope Aubin.[11] Women in this period experiment in virtually every form of writing that their male contemporaries do. Criticism of their doing so did not always deter women, but it is true that where women are venturing into a high cultural form associated with men they often do not seek to see such works circulate in print. Women were less often deterred from *writing* by sexual double standards or attacks on their virtue than they were from *publishing* the works they penned. Lady Mary Wortley Montagu writes court satires as potent and sexually cruel as those of John Gay (with which they were often confused) in the 1710s and sees them circulate widely in manuscript form (and manuscript circulation can reach as many readers as a print run in this period). Women who are not concerned about their sexual reputation cheerfully enter into the print market on equal terms with men: Susannah Centlivre and Mary Pix in the drama and Eliza Haywood later in the novel. Being accused of sexual publicity because one acknowledged literary products as female-authored was an occupational hazard for the jobbing female writer but so long as she earned money by turning herself into a literary curiosity she rarely admitted to being concerned.

3 Gender and sexual/party politics

The second development significant for women's ventures into literature is the influence of rationalist and empirical philosophy which makes possible an enquiry into 'custom' and the presentation of the assumption of women's inferiority to men as a matter of custom rather than proven truth. This period sees the emergence of a discourse by women which is recognizably feminist in the works of writers such as Mary Astell, Mary Lady Chudleigh, and Elizabeth Thomas. A specific language of female rationalism emerges on the heels of the Cartesian revolution ('I think therefore I am'). These writers claim that women have an equal capacity to reason as men and thus should not be debarred from education and kept in ignorance. Here is Astell at her polemical best:

> The Incapacity [of Women], if there be any, is acquired, not natural; and none of their Follies are so necessary, but that they might avoid them if they pleas'd themselves. Some disadvantages indeed they

labour under, and what these are we shall see by and by and endeavour to surmount; but Women need not take up with mean things, since (if they are not wanting to themselves) they are capable of the best. Neither God nor Nature have excluded them from being Ornaments to their Families and useful in their Generation; there is therefore no reason that they should be content to be Cyphers in the World, useless at the best, and in a little time a burden and nuisance to all about them.[12]

Astell and her fellow feminists do not argue for women to have the vote (suffrage is a very limited privilege in this period and not recognized as an especially significant measure of political influence) but they do argue that the relationship between husband and wife is one of contract rather than natural hierarchy. These writers engage with (and sometimes support) the major French and English philosophical writings of their day. Especially important in these discussions is John Locke as a philosopher of human understanding and the leading spokesperson of ideas of contractual over patriarchal government.

These writers do not, however, always agree with John Locke. In her published essay *Reflections on Marriage* (1700) Astell deftly and ironically exposes the hypocrisy in Locke's contract theory of government, with its argument that the relation between ruler and subject is contractual, renegotiable, and entitles the subject to depose the king should he prove despotic and not act in his subjects' interests, and his assertion of the 'natural' rights of the husband to tyrannize over the wife, indeed his view of the husband as recompensing himself for the loss of power in contracting into civil society by wielding authority over women:

> [...] if Absolute Sovereignty be not necessary in a State, how comes it to be so in a Family? or if in a Family why not in a State; since no Reason can be alledg'd for the one that will not hold more strongly for the other? If the Authority of the Husband so far as it extends, is sacred and inalienable, why not of the Prince? [...] [I]f Arbitrary Power is evil in itself, and an improper Method of Governing Rational and Free Agents, it ought not to be Practis'd any where; Nor is it less, but rather more mischievous in Families than in Kingdoms [...]. *If all Men are born free,* how is it that all Women are born slaves?[13]

Astell is thus no reforming radical in terms of her theories of state politics; indeed she was a stalwart defender of the established Stuart monarch, James II, in the 1688 Glorious Revolution and suspected of Jacobitism thereafter.

Feminism in this period is not necessarily associated with reform and progressive ideologies as it is in our own time. Women on both sides of the party divide, Whig and Tory, make similar cases about the need to challenge custom and to allow women the advantages of a literate (if not classical) education. This is not to say that class and party could not *divide* women against each other and it did. Some of the most significant women writers of the period are propagandists for party or sects and often take their female counterparts in opposed positions to task. Delarivier Manley in her Tory scandal novel, *The New Atalantis*, of 1709, makes explicit targets of Whig writers such as Susannah Centlivre and Mary Pix (respectively accused of political toadyism and plagiarism) and spends much of the novel attacking the Whig maid of honour, Sarah Churchill, Duchess of Marlborough who wielded influence over Queen Anne. Just as their male contemporaries did, women often used parables and narratives about embattled female virtue or decadent female sexuality to pass political comment on what they saw as the corruption or exploitation of their culture or nation.

4 The trade in women: issues of representation

New attention to the ubiquity and power of women has to do with the shift to a society which is re-evaluating commerce: from a view of commerce as a marginal activity when power lies in the hands of a landed aristocracy to a view of commerce as an activity central to the modern state, its empire, and its culture. Femininity has historically functioned as a trope in writing for the foreign and decadent, and it is revamped in the eighteenth century to be associated with commerce in the shape of allegorical figures such as lady Credit whom Daniel Defoe represents in his journal, the *Review* of Tuesday 14 June 1709 as a despotic power and an 'invisible phantom':

> She tyrannizes over youth, beauty, virtue, estate; she makes honest women whores, and whores honest women. By her the homely get husbands, while all men shall shun the fair; if she forsake the honestest woman in the world, nobody will touch her; if she covers the most scandalous behaviour, it passes for virtue; the spouse deceived by her takes a prostitute, and swears she was a virgin; demonstration will hardly confince against her evidence; and a whole life of virtue won't repair the injury she does, whre she falls off.[14]

But what is significant at this moment is that the negative language attached to a consumerist femininity is now being contested by a positive language which associates trade with the virtues of prudence and economy. Indeed that same positive discourse begins to see the pursuit of luxury goods as a central part of a thriving economy. In other words trade starts to be associated with virtue rather than decadence and corruption. Behaviours associated with women and with the feminine start to gain credit in themselves: sociability, exchange, commerce, procreation. Conservative satirical writers such as Pope see a feminized culture as a sign of decline, but republican Whigs such as Joseph Addison and Lady Mary Wortley Montagu and later Daniel Defoe can present it as a sign of increased civilization and civility.

Let us conclude this survey with two further contrasting quotations, both concerned with the figure of woman in relation to trade. The lines from the first canto of Alexander Pope's 1714 five-canto version of the *Rape of the Lock* have become a favourite of eighteenth-century literary historians because they perform so miraculously this equation of a commercial trading culture with feminine decadence, luxury, and wasteful inauthentic consumption. Belinda is an inverted version of the epic hero preparing himself for battle; his squire helps him don his armour and he makes sacrifices to propitiate the gods. Belinda stands at her toilet preparing with the aid of her maid to dress her body, hair, and face in readiness to play cards at court. The god she worships, however, is her own image in the glass and the offerings made are goods from foreign trade to enhance her own beauty. These goods are laid out with military precision for her consumption and exploitation. Pope's mock-heroic mourns the loss of epic values and their replacement with the trivial and the superficial, the turning of ethical values into purely consumerist ones:

> And now, unveil'd, the *Toilet* stands display'd,
> Each Silver Vase in mystic Order laid,
> First, rob'd in White, the Nymph intent adores,
> With Head uncover'd, the *Cosmetic* Pow'rs.
> A heav'nly Image in the Glass appears,
> To that she bends, to that her Eyes she rears;
> Th'inferior Priestess, at her Altar's side,
> Trembling, begins the sacred Rites of Pride.
> Unnumber'd Treasures ope at once, and here
> The various Off'rings of the World appear:
> From each she nicely culls with curious Toil,
> And decks the Goddess with the glitt'ring Spoil.

This Casket *India*'s glowing Gems unlocks,
And all *Arabia* breathes from yonder Box.
The Tortoise here and Elephant unite,
Transform'd to *Combs*, the speckled and the white.
Here Files of Pins extend their shining Rows,
Puffs, Powders, Patches, Bibles, Billet-doux.
Now awful Beauty puts on all its Arms;
The Fair each moment rises in her Charms,
Repairs her Smiles, awakens ev'ry Grace,
And calls forth all the Wonders of her Face;
Sees by Degrees a purer Blush arise,
And keener Lightnings quicken in her Eyes.[15]

Defoe by contrast is not concerned with the activities of the high society lady and her maid but rather with those of the prostitute and the bourgeois wife (reminding us of Rochester's presentation of Sue Willis in his argument that prostitution is a form of wasteful expenditure of a powerful resource). Defoe seeks to promote commercial prudence through encouraging marriage and childbirth in women – in other words his speaker aims to make women's compulsion to trade and to seek financial advancement into a source of virtue rather than corruption:

> The great Use of Women in a Community is to supply it with Members that may be serviceable, and keep up a Succession. They are also useful in another Degree, to wit, in the Labour they may take for themselves, or the Assistance which they may afford their Husbands or Parents. It will readily be allowed, that a Street-walking Whore can never answer either of these Ends: Riot and Diseases prevent one, and the Idleness which directs her to this course of life incapacitates her for the other [...].
>
> Some Remedy might be apply'd to this by our Laws giving more Encouragement to Matrimony. What if some Immunities attended that State, some Exemptions from Taxes, or the like? or what if the old *Roman* Law, entitling the Parents of three or more Children to certain Privileges, were put in force among us, or something grounded upon that Hint? I am perswaded, such Encouragements to Virtue would have a better Effect than all the Whippings, *Bridewels*, and *Work-Houses*, which are invented as Discouragements to Vice.[16]

In both texts though there is a surprising turn. The ideological drift is not quite sustained. Pope may be decrying consumerist femininity but he does make it both magnetically attractive and magical. The playful, productive use of the couplet suggests that a new consumerist femininity might be enlivening and diversifying the epic tradition rather than stultifying it. Defoe attempts to make the case for a prudential economy but the incentives for prudential virtue are financial rather than moral: exemption from taxes and privileges under the law. In both cases then the claim to prefer moral incentives to the attractions of commodity culture and financial advantage is not quite borne out by the rhetoric of the text. The figure of woman has become a kind of 'shorthand' for the new world of commerce, consumption, and exchange (whether positively or negatively) valenced in these texts.

It is the female body and its (re)productive potential which we find reproduced repeatedly in writings of this period by both men and women; often portrayed as an irritant and impediment in the pursuit of epic or heroic values, but equally frequently standing in the place of the failed epic or hero with new compensations and charms. The figure of woman proves a special force of fascination in those new modes of the period: the novel, the periodical, the mock-epic.

What relation did women writers have with these images of women and men? As we have seen, this period is significant in a number of ways for the history of women's writing: it sees the beginnings of a discourse of 'enlightened' feminism, the response by women writers to the Cartesian and natural scientific revolutions of the later seventeenth century, and attempts by women (as writers and publishers) to exploit the transformations in literary culture attendant on the establishment of new financial institutions (the founding of the Bank of England, the stock market, and capitalist print). Special attention is given in this volume to the sense of a transforming culture at the end of one century and the beginning of another. The experimentalism of women's writing is drawn attention to, in the new forms of the 'novel' and the 'periodical' but also in more established genres that are changing with their circulation in the print as well as manuscript market. Pastoral and georgic poetic modes are reconfigured in urban forms for satiric ends in a mode such as the town eclogue but they are also deployed to imagine the utopian possibilities and ethical problems of expanding trade and empire. Learned translation and transmission enjoy new marketing possibilities as evidenced by the success of Elizabeth Elstob's Anglo-Saxon translations and Elizabeth Carter's dissemination of Newtonian thought. Religious and devotional poetry and prose are used to disseminate and cement the ties of sectarian communities such as the Quakers and the Philadelphians as well as to display the individual's piety in public.

Contributions to this volume demonstrate that women were engaging in forms old and new in ways that sought to shape and transform rather than simply reflect or respond to the aesthetic initiatives of their male contemporaries. Consequently, we have organized the volume according to key debates and themes, rather than by chronology or by specific writers or writers' coteries. Nevertheless, as much space as possible has been given to individual women writers or coterie groups. This is one of the earliest periods in which we can begin to recognize women as enjoying 'careers' as writers, enjoying public success (whether through print or manuscript circulation), name recognition (whether of a consistent pseudonym or, more rarely, their given names), and sometimes indeed living by their writing. Contributors have been encouraged to use two or more writing careers of women as exempla in the course of their essays and to give as much space as possible to close attention to critical texts. They have also ventured value judgements on the quality and significance of individual writers' works and their contribution to the discourse/context in which the chapter is placing them. Three literary 'careers' surface in a number of chapters and the reader can trace the influence and standing of these women through that process: Lady Mary Wortley Montagu (largely unpublished but nevertheless a fine and influential practitioner), Eliza Haywood (strikingly her opposite, always a presence in print and yet a shadowy biography), Mary Astell (still the most gifted polemicist as well as important voice of rationalist feminism of her generation).

The volume falls into four sections. 'Debates' focuses the reader's mind on three debates which are central to the period and significant in the history of women's writing: woman's place (the contributions of Mary Astell, Lady Mary Chudleigh, Elizabeth Thomas and others produce the first recognizably 'feminist' counter-discourse in this period), luxury (women are seen as the major stimulants for and consumers of the luxury trade), country and city (the urban metropole is a place of risk and opportunity for women as writers but women are also reshaping in interesting ways their relationship to the 'retirement' associated with the country, imagining the country as a place of female authority and labour).

'Transformations' looks closely at women's agency in and responses to key aesthetic transformations/movements of the period: the politics and aesthetics of dissent, and especially the engagement with John Milton's *Paradise Lost*; the Scriblerian project – the importance of women as correspondents, aesthetic ideals, and as negative stereotypes in the writings of Alexander Pope, John Gay, Jonathan Swift, and Henry Fielding, and also the responses of women in print and manuscript to Scriblerian writings; and the 'licensing' (as William B. Warner terms it) of the novel as a genre in the mid-eighteenth century at the hands of Samuel Richardson and Henry Fielding.[17]

'Writing modes' concentrates on women's entry into the major literary modes other than the novel and poetry which receive fuller attention elsewhere in this volume. It provides perhaps the most significant essay of the volume on the vexed issue of the differing status and significance of manuscript and print 'publication' in the period. Kathryn King provides an introduction to the area in which there has been most energetic critical and bibliographical work in recent years ('the history of the book') and illustrates the importance of considering women's writing and involvement in diverse literary cultures in constructing new histories about the extent to which the economics of the 'book' determine the nature and quality of literary writing. Three chapters in this section pay attention to three different genres to which women made especially significant contributions in this period: the periodical, the drama, and learned letters.

'Worlds of feeling' concentrates on the two generic areas in which women write and publish prolifically in the period: poetry and the novel. Rather than offering separate chapters on each genre, however, the section focuses on the shared cross-generic project in this period of modelling a critical reader open to but also suspicious of feeling. The transformations already charted that led to a new stress being placed on the responsibility of the individual to govern or let play his or her passions make 'feeling' an issue of urgent and chattering debate in the eighteenth century. Women, no doubt because of the expectation that they take responsibility for the management of feeling in domestic spaces, are understood to be particularly responsive to feeling, and the worlds of emotional interaction depicted in literary texts revolve around female characters and speakers. Three chapters address the representation of religious love, erotic love, and companionship/friendship in writing by women. Structuring the section this way enables a continuing focus on the growth of collaborative modes of writing (between women and between men and women) and the significance of ideas of relationship/correspondence to the shaping of a new aesthetics in which women were increasingly understood to be major participants.

The book concludes with a critical review of works about women's writing in this period, starting with the earliest attempts to anthologize and map women's writing in the late eighteenth century and concluding with an evaluation of the editorial and critical enterprises of the present day. Readers will also find a full bibliography and (in the preliminary pages) a chronology of women's writing designed to support the understanding we trust this volume will further.

Notes

1. *The Complete Poems of John Wilmot Earl of Rochester*, ed. by David M. Veith (New Haven: Yale University Press, 1968), pp. 137–8.
2. In *Eighteenth-Century Women Poets: An Oxford Anthology*, ed. by Roger Lonsdale (Oxford: Oxford University Press, 1989), pp. 124–5. See also *The Poetry of Mary Barber (?1690–1757)*, ed. by Bernard Tucker (Lewiston: Edwin Mellen, 1992).
3. On Swift's poems to Stella, see Ros Ballaster, 'Jonathan Swift, the *Stella* poems', in *A Companion to Eighteenth Century Poetry*, ed. by Christine Gerrard (Oxford: Blackwell, 2006), pp. 170–83.
4. See David M. Vieth, *Attribution in Restoration Poetry: A Study of Rochester's Poems in 1680* (New Haven: Yale University Press, 1963).
5. Thomas Laqueur, *Making Sex: Body and Gender from the Greeks to Freud* (Cambridge, MA: Harvard University Press, 1990).
6. See Philip Carter, *Men and the Emergence of Polite Society in Britain 1660–1800*, Women and Men in History Series (London: Pearson Education, 2001).
7. Michael McKeon, *The Secret History of Domesticity: Public, Private and the Division of Knowledge* (Baltimore and London: Johns Hopkins University Press, 2005), p. 150.
8. See Rebecca Mills, ' "That Tyrant Custom": The Politics of Custom in the Prose and Poetry of Augustan Women Writers', *Women's Writing*, 7 (2000), 391–409.
9. *The Complete Letters of Lady Mary Wortley Montagu: Volume III: 1752–1762*, ed. by Robert Halsband (Oxford: Clarendon Press, 1966), p. 39.
10. See Suzanne Trill, 'Religion and the Construction of Femininity', in *Women and Literature in Britain 1500–1700*, ed. by Helen Wilcox (Cambridge: Cambridge University Press, 1996), pp. 46–51 on 'Quaker Women's Writing'.
11. See Ros Ballaster, *Seductive Forms: Women's Amatory Fiction from 1684 to 1740* (Oxford: Clarendon Press, 1992), especially chapter 2, 'Amatory Fiction and the Construction of the Female Reader', pp. 31–68.
12. Mary Astell, *Mary Astell's A Serious Proposal to the Ladies: Parts 1 and II*, ed. by Patricia Springborg (London: Pickering and Chatto, 2007), Part I, p. 10.
13. Mary Astell, 'Preface' to *Reflections upon Marriage*, 3rd edn (1706), in *The First English Feminist: 'Reflections upon Marriage' and other writings by Mary Astell*, ed. by Hilda Smith (Aldershot: Gower, 1986), p. 76.
14. Daniel Defoe, *The Best of Defoe's Review: An Anthology*, ed. by William L. Payne (New York: Columbia University Press, 1951), p. 119.
15. Alexander Pope, Canto I, *The Rape of the Lock* (1714), in *The Rape of the Lock and Other Poems*, ed. by Geoffrey Tillotson, vol. II of the Twickenham Edition of the Poems of Alexander Pope, 3rd edn (London: Methuen and Co, Ltd., 1962), ll. 121–44, pp. 155–7.
16. Daniel Defoe, *Some Considerations upon Street-Walkers. With a Proposal for lessening the present number of them. In two letters to a Member of Parliament* (London, 1726), pp. 6–7.
17. See William B. Warner, *Licensing Entertainment: The Elevation of Novel Reading in Britain, 1684–1750* (Berkeley: University of California Press, 1998).

Part I
Debates

1
Woman's Place

Karen O'Brien

The period 1690–1750 was one in which the place of women in the moral, intellectual, and social life of the nation was discussed and debated as never before. This intensified interest in the place of women had many sources and significances. It was partly an effect of the spectacular developments in physical science and philosophical epistemology in the early Enlightenment. It was closely related to the often turbulent religious controversies of this period within and outside the Anglican communion. These were in turn part of the broader political and cultural response to the Glorious Revolution of 1688–69, and the political and civil rights and (limited) religious toleration enshrined in the revolution settlement. As well as the response to national political events, there were also important continental influences, notably those of French Cartesian philosophy and the culture of the French aristocratic salons. Greater engagement in philosophical, theological, political, and scientific writings with the question of women took place in the context of a rapid expansion of print culture. This brought increased circulation of new genres such as periodicals, novels, and semifictionalized memoirs and autobiographies, many of which drew attention to women as analytical and imaginative subjects, and, above all, as writers themselves.

The issue of women's place and role also gained greater prominence as a social theme, one that established the coordinates that would continue to govern the discussion of women until well into the nineteenth century. By the end of this period, there emerged a new understanding of women as having social, as well as familial and biological, roles to play, including roles as writers (however controversially), as consumers of writing and of other goods, and as shapers of the nation's distinctive social tone. This entailed a re-evaluation of women's education, not just for the sake of their spiritual salvation, or to make possible the participation of a few women in elite, learned culture, but for the wider benefit that educated women might bring to the community. It was further shaped, to an increasing extent, by fictional portrayals of women, in the new realist and domestic novels, as moral agents operating within a recognizably modern and broad social milieu. Attention to the capacities and education of women was also undoubtedly drawn by the presence, for the first time in nearly a hundred years, of female monarchs, Queen Mary II and then Queen Anne, as well as the exceptionally prominent political role played by Anne's close friend Sarah, Duchess of Marlborough. Yet the legal and economic status of women remained at best unchanged, or even deteriorated.[1] After the first decade of the eighteenth century, debates about the place of women began to lose much of the sharp sense of political analogy that characterized those of the seventeenth to early eighteenth centuries. Advocates for greater civil, educational, and intellectual equality for women, though not self-consciously shaping a feminist counter-discourse, had to contend not only with traditional forms of misogyny but also with a new set of 'pro-woman' commonplaces that paid patronizing deference to women's 'polishing' effect on social 'manners': as, for example, Mary Lady Chudleigh's poem *The Ladies Defence* (1701) in which the protagonist Melissa challenges not only the woman-hater Sir John Brute but also the modern gallant Sir William Loveall who pays homage to the benign influence of the sex. Patronizing praise of 'the sex' was not uncommon at this time. Chudleigh had before her the example of William Walsh's *A Dialogue Concerning Women, Being a Defence of the Sex* (1691), written as an elaborate compliment to a learned female addressee, and later dismissed as an insincere and 'labour'd Common Place Book' by Judith Drake in her *Essay in Defence of the Female Sex* (1696).[2]

The notion of women as guardians and shapers of manners and morals steadily gained ground during this period, although it was not until later in the century that writers set out what they saw as the deeper economic and historical reasons for female influence. As the notion of women's influence upon manners and morals steadily took hold, it became increasingly difficult for male, and especially female, advocates of equality to make the case for greater female freedom and opportunity on the basis of women's natural desires. The literary libertinism of writers of amatory and scandal fiction such as Aphra Behn, Eliza Haywood, and Delarivier Manley met with increasingly hostility.[3] This was paralleled, in Britain as on the continent, by the decline of intellectual *libertinage*, a mode of discourse that had, in the case of writers such as Pierre Bayle, approached questions of female sexuality with a rare degree of scepticism and freedom from prejudice.[4] Mandeville's writings, including *The Fable of the Bees* (1714, 1723), *A Modest Defence of Publick Stews* (1724), and his *Enquiry into the Origin of Honour* (1732), brought this libertine tradition from the continent to eighteenth-century London.[5] Yet in England, his works, with their frank and sympathetic acknowledgement of the way that society perverts female sexuality, were deemed far less acceptable than those of the man he sought to refute: Lord Shaftesbury, with his view of man's natural propensity for virtue in social life. Few writers were happy with Shaftesbury's religious views, but they found ways to adapt his harmonious account of the integration of private and public moral actions in a well-balanced state to the case of women, and thereby to make women's personal moral behaviour a matter of value and significance for the good of the country.[6] Between 1690 and 1750 such moralized discourses of female moral behaviour, the private sphere, and nationhood were only beginning to take what would be their distinctive, later eighteenth- and nineteenth-century form.

1 High politics and the politics of the family

Women writers of this period inherited a rich and politically resonant language of gender controversy. Since the Renaissance, women and pro-women writers had articulated the problem of women's subjection and lack of civil identity in terms of the household as a mirror and microcosm of the state. The household was understood as a model of the male-governed state in which women owed a quasi-political obligation to their husbands.[7] This way of discussing domestic relations took on an intensely party-political flavour following the Exclusion Crisis of 1678–81, and throughout the period from the Glorious Revolution to the political controversy over the succession to Queen Anne. The structuring vocabularies of dynastic and political debate ('non-resistance', divine right, 'passive obedience', arbitrary power, privileges, rights, and prerogative) certainly saturated gender wars in drama and prose romance, and they were, as Rachel Weil has shown, manipulated by writers of all political persuasions for a variety of pro- or anti-female ends.[8] On the Restoration stage, female characters spoke of their husbands' arbitrary power, and husbands of their wives' disobedience and rebellion.[9] In plays by Whig playwrights, young heroines claimed freedom of choice in marriage on the grounds of their liberties as Protestant subjects, while in Tory fictions and plays, such as those of Behn or Manley, adventurous women defended their privileges on an analogy with male aristocratic political entitlement, and exposed male disloyalty to women as part and parcel of Whig disobedience to legitimate royal authority.[10] The language of civil liberties permeated these gendered exchanges. In John Vanbrugh's *The Provoked Wife* (1697), for example, the protagonist Lady Brute debates with her would-be lover the 'just Causes' for marital infidelity and whether her husband's cruelty releases her from her 'duty', while her lover equivocates that 'where Laws dispense with Equity, Equity should dispense with Laws'.[11] At the heart of the political debate over the dynastic succession to Charles II, James II, and Anne, was the question of the duty to obey: when can a person in authority legitimately command obedience, where does that authority reside (God, the consent of the governed?), and what is the nature of that obedience ('passive', or conditional upon respect for one's rights?) Such questions resonated strongly with the traditional patriarchal notion of a wife's duty to love, honour, and obey. The Tory and Jacobite doctrine of 'passive obedience' (which held that it was not lawful to resist the monarch or his/her representatives) was highly current and widely criticized during the 1690s to 1710s. Women writers, in particular, made great play of the disparity between the Whigs' constitutional ideas of natural equality and conditional obedience in the political domain, and their expectation of total female obedience in the domestic realm. As Chudleigh's Melissa complains, men who were Whigs in the coffee house were usually still Tories in the bedroom:

> Passive Obedience you've to us transfer'd,
> And we must drudge in Paths where you have err'd:
> This antiquated Doctrine you disown;
> Tis now your Scorn, and fit for us alone.[12]

Lady Mary Wortley Montagu, in her letters from Turkey of 1716–18, makes ironic play of the disparity between the 'principle of *passive-obedience*' which, she says, guides her conduct as an ambassador's wife, and her Whig distaste for Ottoman political despotism (a warning, she writes, to the 'passive-obedient men' among the English Tories and Jacobites).[13] Sarah Fyge Egerton's poems angrily expose the ways in which the ideas of custom and patriarchy that traditionally prescribed women's obedience to men have been supplemented by new legal and political requirements to obey: 'Then comes the last, the fatal Slavery; / The Husband with insulting Tyranny / Can have ill Manners justifi'd by Law'. Although the subjection of women may be more extensive than ever, Egerton asserts that there is scope for women to assert a new civil right, that of the freedom to write better than the men: 'We will our Rights in Learning's World maintain; / Wits Empire, now, shall know a Female Reign'.[14]

The rhetorical presentation of women's learning and writing as a politicized right of resistance was reiterated many times during this period. For instance, Elizabeth Thomas, a poet in Chudleigh's circle, argued for women's right to learning on the basis of England's 'gracious *Laws* that give such *Liberty*':

> Most mighty *Sov'reigns* we submit,
> And own ye Monarchs of the Realm of *Wit*:
> But might a *Slave* to her Superiours speak
> And without *Treason* Silence break,
> She'd first implore your royal *Grace*,
> Then humbly thus expostulate the Case [for female learning].[15]

The most sophisticated and extensive female intervention in the public debate about obedience came from Mary Astell in her *Some Reflections upon Marriage* (1700, but particularly the third edition of 1706 with its new preface). Written during the bitter political controversies of the latter part of William III's reign, Astell's work is a brilliant, double-edged consideration of the obligation to obey authorities both political and domestic. She makes the model of authority in the household (inescapably, if not rightfully, absolute in her view) a testing ground for Whig constitutional models of authority in the political sphere. She shows up the speciousness of the Whig idea of conditional obedience to a political contract by citing men's customary expectation of passive obedience from their wives, despite the fact that the marriage contract is, outwardly and legally, a matter for their voluntary consent:

> if the Matrimonial Yoke be grievous, neither Law nor Custom afford her [the wife] that redress which a Man obtains. He who has Sovereign Power does not value the Provocations of a Rebellious Subject, but knows how to subdue him with ease, and will make himself obey'd; but poor People, who groan under Tyranny, unless they are Strong enough to break the Yoke, to Depose and Abdicate, which I doubt wou'd not be allow'd of here. For whatever may be said against Passive-Obedience in another case, I suppose there's no Man but likes it very well in this.[16]

Despite her apparent Tory pessimism, Astell is not like the conciliatory Clarissa in Pope's *The Rape of the Lock* (1717), advising women to accept situations they cannot change and advocating orthodox Anglican obedience to higher political and domestic powers.[17] Rather, she implies that real authority can never belong to man, even when it is dressed up as a 'social contract', but is only delegated to him by God, and that the best course of action for a woman is to preserve her moral autonomy by staying single: 'For Covenants betwixt Husband and Wife, like Laws in an Arbitrary Government, are of little Force, the Will of the Sovereign is all in all.'[18] Among Astell's male Whig targets, in the later editions of the *Reflections* and in her subsequent works, was John Locke. This was partly because, in the *Two Treatises of Government* (1689), Locke had famously attacked traditional patriarchy in favour of a voluntary and provisional social contract; but still more, as Mark Goldie has shown in the most important recent article on Astell's work, because of Locke's religious politics and his explicit assertions of women's natural subjection to men.[19]

Astell has often been read as an early and prescient critic of the inherent sexism of the political liberalism that Locke is credited with inventing. Carole Pateman notably, has criticized Locke's idea of the social contract for his implicit exclusion of women from the contracted polity, and for thereby subordinating women, not to the law of the father, but to 'men as men, or to men as a fraternity'.[20] Goldie has shown that it may not be entirely plausible to read Astell's *Reflections* as a critique of Locke's denial of citizenship to women, but that her probing exploration of the household/state homology, though not explicitly aimed at Locke, certainly served to remind readers of the 'double standard' of domestic tyranny and political liberty advocated by a number of Whigs.[21] More generally, there is evidence to support Pateman's broader insight that a conceptual shift did take place in this period which gradually de-politicized the role of wife and daughter, and emphasized the priority of women's femininity over their household status.[22] Although many who wrote about women's predicament did so in terms of the asymmetries of political and domestic liberty, others elaborated Locke's separation of the civil and private spheres in a different way by seeking to give moral and cultural content to the notion of female privacy. As Sarah Prescott has argued, a number of Whig women writers of the early eighteenth century, such as Elizabeth Singer Rowe and Mary Davys, deliberately drew attention to their virtue, Horatian retirement, and provincial location (away from the centres of political power) and amateurism, both enriching and de-politicizing the domestic sphere in the process.[23]

2 The Cartesian case for equality

Locke's *Two Treatises* shared a broader early Enlightenment preoccupation with the problem of equality.[24] For Locke, political equality and primitive gender equality (as he saw it) ends with the advent of the state, but what always remains is a basic equality of mental capability enabling all human beings to gain a knowledge of God and their duties to him. In this respect, Locke had a lasting impact on those wishing to argue, throughout this period, for women's equal intellectual capacity, and for their entitlement to education as a means of furthering their knowledge of God. And in this respect, if in few others, Locke's influence converged with that of continental Cartesians who built a case for female intellectual equality on the basis both of Cartesian method (the setting aside of traditional prejudice in order to begin one's intellectual enquiries) and Cartesian models of mind (in which the mind is not shaped or limited by bodily characteristics, including biological sexual difference). In France, learned women drew inspiration from Descartes's philosophy and used their conversational and writing skills to further the campaign against male prejudice of all kinds.[25] In Britain, Cartesianism found its way into gender debate via the theological writings and circle of the clergyman John Norris, which included Chudleigh, Thomas, and Astell (Egerton was also an admirer).[26] Norris argued that it is reason that enables us to see the true, perfect form of things that can otherwise only be imperfectly glimpsed through the senses. For him, this knowledge and the process of rational knowing, impelled by the will and by the love of God, are accessible to all truly thoughtful men and women.[27] Norris discussed these ideas in detail with Astell, and their correspondence was published as *Letters Concerning the Love of God* in 1695. After this, Astell explored this process of knowing in more detail in her *Serious Proposal to the Ladies, Part II* (1697).[28] She wrote this decidedly Cartesian work, she said, to help fellow women 'Disengage ourselves from all our former Prejudices' in order to achieve the highest intellectual apprehension of divine truth.[29] In a later work, Astell made it clear that this kind of mental emancipation, rather than emancipation in social or political structures, is the real and superior freedom open to women: 'true Liberty [...] consists in making a right use of our Reason, in preserving our Judgments free, and our Integrity unspotted, which sets us out of the reach of the most Absolute Tyrant'.[30]

Astell may not have chosen to make a case for female civil liberty on the basis of her feminist Cartesian rationalism, but it was certainly one that could, and had been made. Notably, the social and political dimensions of feminist Cartesianism were elaborated by the French philosopher Poulain de la Barre in a series of works in the 1670s, some of which may have been known to Astell herself.[31] In the most widely circulated of these works, *De L'Egalité des deux Sexes* (1673), Poulain marshals an array of historical and legal evidence against the common prejudice of mankind that women are naturally inferior to men. The case he makes is, partly, one for epistemological (and hence, spiritual) equality: women have the same ability and right to access the truth as men, whether worldly or metaphysical. But in setting aside traditional and false deductions of female inferiority from natural law, Poulain also makes the case for social and political equality for women who are, he writes, entirely capable of doing the same jobs and exercising the same power as men.[32] As his intellectual biographer Siep Stuurman points out, not only was Poulain an advocate for female equality, but also a pioneering analyst of the historical processes that had led to the subjection of women. Poulain was instrumental, in other words, in the forging of a radical Enlightenment social philosophy.[33]

The extent of Poulain's influence in Britain is not easy to ascertain. *De L'Egalité* was translated into English in 1677, and appeared in a different, unacknowledged translation 'By a Lady' under the title *Female Rights Vindicated* in 1758.[34] Among the more radical British thinkers of the late seventeenth to early eighteenth centuries, there were many who extended notions of male equality beyond moral equivalence to political parity, but only a few who followed Poulain in doing the same for women. The radical freethinker John Toland, a man well versed in continental philosophy, certainly shared Poulain's Cartesian impulse to expose 'prejudice' against women. In his *Letters to Serena* (1704), addressed to the learned Queen Sophie Charlotte of Prussia, he writes that 'whether the Exclusion of Women from Learning be the Effect of inveterate Custom, or proceeds from Designs in the Men, shall be no Inquiry of mine', and goes on to discuss a number of distinguished female scholars and the prejudice of men against them.[35] The essays contributed in 1709–10 by Mandeville to *The Female Tatler* bring together feminist Cartesian elements with probable borrowings from Astell, and possible influences from Poulain or Bayle.[36] Mandeville's two female writers – clever, unmarried sisters, Artesia and Lucinda – point out that women are just as capable as men of courage, justice, and all the heroic virtues, and that their achievements have been hidden from history by male historians: 'Since Men have enslav'd us, the greatest part of the World have always debar'd our Sex from Governing, which is the Reason that the Lives of Women have so seldom been describ'd in History.'[37] The sisters exemplify and argue for women's intellectual abilities, despite the tyranny of custom, and they echo Poulain's claim that women are capable of wielding political power: '[women were] design'd to advise and assist [men] in the Government of the Earth'.[38]

Cartesian and other rationalist arguments against male prejudice persisted well into the century. One of the most notable neo-Cartesian critiques of the gender order was *Woman Not Inferior to Man* (1739), a polemical work by an unidentified writer who called (probably) herself 'Sophia'. Modern historians have assumed that this work is a partial translation of Poulain, but it is in fact a free adaptation of his work written in a highly personal, female-identified voice (men, Sophia says, are 'stubborn brats').[39] Sophia's argument begins with the equality of rational capacity possessed by men and women, and then embellishes considerably the part of Poulain's work concerned with women's intellectual fitness for scientific enquiry and public office. The view that women cannot run the church, the government or the army, she argues, is the product of male prejudice: 'Why is *learning* useless to us? Because we have no share in public offices. And why have we no share in public offices? Because we have no *learning*.'[40] For a few years, Sophia's work had some currency, and was reprinted in 1743 and again in 1751 as the first part of a volume entitled *Beauty's Triumph*.[41] Sophia followed up this work with a second, *Woman's Superior Excellence over Man* (1740), a reply to a refutation of her original work entitled *Man Superior to Woman* by an anonymous male author. This second work gives a much clearer sense of her voice and personality, as she mounts a blistering, anecdote-laden attack on men's cruelty and coercion of women, and gives many examples of their usurpation of the 'rights and liberties of Women'. Sophia's colourful character-sketches include Hectorius who beats his virtuous wife ('plates, cups, knives or whatever things come first to hand, are the vehicles by which he conveys his ideas to her'), and Anarchus who 'when a-bed' is frequently to be found 'puking' on his wife.[42]

Sophia's identity has long been a mystery. Her two works have some similarities of theme and tone with the sixth number of Mary Wortley Montagu's *The Nonsense of Common-Sense* (1735) in which the latter argues that 'vulgar prejudices' against women's intellectual abilities must be dispelled, not least because they lead men to think that they can get away with 'treating the weaker Sex with a Contempt that has a very bad influence on their Conduct'.[43] The case for identifying her with Montagu is not strong, however, and, in other respects, one feels instinctively that, if a British woman at all, Sophia may have had some connection to the somewhat different circle of Sarah Chapone, which included Elizabeth Elstob,

George Ballard, Mary Delany, Samuel Richardson, and (indirectly) Astell herself. Sophia's trenchant tone and fund of stories about oppressed women strikingly resembles Chapone's *The Hardships of the English Laws in Relation to Wives*, published anonymously in 1735 and then partly reprinted in the *Gentleman's Magazine* that year. Chapone appeals to Parliament to amend the laws that give men, in effect, the power of life and death over their wives: 'I confess that I hardly believe it possible to reconcile these Laws with the Rights and Privileges of a free People. That there should be so great a Part of the Community [...] entirely deprived of their Liberty, or even of making Use of their Ingenuity and Industry to procure them a Subsistence.'[44] Chapone illustrates her argument with hair-raising stories of wives locked up, beaten, starved, and driven to suicide by their husbands with complete impunity. In exposing legal injustice, Chapone makes a number of (clearly strategic) concessions to traditional biblical and natural law arguments for female inferiority, and in this she does differ from the less compromising Sophia. Chapone also differs from Sophia in terms of social background, since Sophia's emphatic self-identification as 'A Person of Quality' in the first work is elaborated in the second when she describes her upbringing in the house of (what appears to be) a Catholic nobleman and failed politician (a profile that closely fits that of Chapone's intimate friend Mary Delany).[45] Unlike Chapone, Sophia concedes nothing to the idea of male intellectual superiority, citing 'Eliza' (clearly Elizabeth Carter) as a modern example of 'towering superiority of [...] genius and judgment'.[46] Carter herself tried unsuccessfully to find out who Sophia was, and subsequent attempted identifications of Sophia have remained, so far, inconclusive.[47]

3 Whigs, Locke, and the female Latitudinarians

In the works of writers as diverse as Mandeville, Astell, and Sophia, Cartesian influences and vocabularies certainly buttressed arguments against intellectual discrimination and, on occasion, for positive institutions for female education, such as Astell's *Serious Proposal to the Ladies* (1694) for an Anglican seminary for women. Defoe alluded to Astell (an 'Ingenious Lady') in the detailed plan he set out for a similar, more secular female academy in his *Essay upon Projects* (1697).[48] Astell's proposal was satirized by Richard Steele in *The Tatler* (the anti-female target of Mandeville's *The Female Tatler*).[49] It was also actively discouraged, most probably by Gilbert Burnet, the Bishop of Salisbury, not, as is often supposed, because he was opposed to female learning but because of what he saw as the High Church Tory flavour of her proposal.

He himself later suggested the creation of 'Monasteries without Vows' to give young women 'a due Measure of Knowledge and a serious Sense of Religion'.[50] Indeed, as Hannah Smith has shown, there were a number of male Anglican writers, in the late seventeenth to early eighteenth centuries, including Astell's acquaintance George Hickes, who supported the setting up of women's colleges of various kinds, often with a view to shoring up the Anglican Church at a time of crisis.[51] The issue of female education was, then, as subject to party-political and to High Church/Broad Church or 'Latitudinarian'/nonconformist religious debate as any other issue during this period. Indeed, many writings about women's place during this period were within the context of religious debate, and were part of a broader religious concern for moral regeneration and the reformation of manners.[52] Religious calls for a reformation of manners found a more secular echo, as Emma Clery has shown, in early periodicals such as *The Athenian Mercury*, with their call for reformed sexual ethics and gender relations.[53] Astell was a leading voice among High Anglicans, and Burnet was prominent among those actively instrumental in the formulation of a Whig, 'Latitudinarian' moral agenda, which included prescriptions for an educated female elite. The Latitudinarian wing of the Anglican Church endorsed the values of an undogmatic faith based upon reason and scripture, salvation open to all (as opposed to the elect only), religious toleration (within limits), and unconstrained, rational religious enquiry. Many of those broadly identified with this persuasion, including Locke, Burnet, and Locke's friend Damaris Masham, advocated and valued the participation of women in this process of enquiry. They were also engaged in the formulation of a practically-oriented ethics that sought to reconcile rational piety with the ideal of productive, socially useful daily life for women. Astell's support for legislation such as the Occasional Conformity Act of 1711 (curtailing the civil rights of Dissenters) and her intense dislike of Locke (whom she regarded as a religiously unorthodox Whig party hack) mark her opposition to the politics of the Latitudinarians. Astell's ideal of a purposive life for women also appeared, to her lower church contemporaries, somewhat other-worldly – although it should be said that Astell was also involved in practical schemes such as the founding of a charity school for girls in Chelsea. Masham, for example, while very much sharing Astell's commitment to female intellectual equality ('I see no Reason', she wrote, 'why it should not be thought that all Science lyes as open to a Lady as to a Man'), advocated a more practical social role for women as wives, educators of children, philanthropists, and philosophers.[54] Masham was the daughter of the leading Cambridge

Platonist theologian Ralph Cudworth and connected to Astell through her early friendship with Norris. By the mid-1690s, however, she had come under the personal and philosophical influence of Locke, and subscribed to his anti-Cartesian theory of knowledge as something that comes to us, not intuitively, but through sense impressions and the pleasure, reflective insight, and (ultimately) religious understanding we gain from the material world. In her *Discourse Concerning the Love of God* (1696), her anonymous reply to Astell and Norris's *Letters Concerning the Love of God*, Masham refuted their notion that it is through pure reason, and not through our senses, that we come to know God. This kind of epistemology, Masham argues, makes it 'impossible to live on the daily Commerce and Conversation of the World, and love God as we ought to do'.[55]

Astell supposed this work to be an attack on her by Locke, and she later offered an indirect but extended reply to both Masham and Locke in her major work *The Christian Religion* (1705).[56] At issue in these debates was the desire to establish philosophical and religious grounds for the claim of female rational equality. That claim gained lasting validity, as well as many detractors, in the eighteenth century. As late as the 1790s, Mary Wollstonecraft's arguments for female intellectual equality were anchored in her faith that God can be known through cultivated human reason.[57] Similarly, the Bluestockings' more conservative claims for public esteem for intellectual women had religious and political roots in their admiration for the work of the Latitudinarian theologian Joseph Butler.[58] Bridging the chronological gap between Masham and Astell, and the Richardson circle of the 1740s and the Bluestocking publications from the 1750s, came a leading female Latitudinarian thinker and interpreter of Locke, Catharine Cockburn, author of a *Defence of the 'Essay of Human Understanding', written by Mr. Lock* (1702). Prior to publishing this work, Cockburn (née Trotter) was a successful Whig playwright as well as a Catholic convert. Trotter sought, in her *Defence*, to show that Locke's epistemology provides a firm basis for a religiously sound ethics, as well as a valuable way of looking at morality from the perspective of the (male or female) moral agent.[59] Her work drew a favourable response from Locke and earned her the patronage of Gilbert Burnet and his highly intelligent wife Elizabeth. The Burnets encouraged Trotter's conversion from Catholicism to Anglicanism in 1707, and put her in touch with leading Latitudinarian theologians such as Samuel Clarke.[60] Her knowledge of Clarke and his work strengthened her belief in the rational accessibility of divine truth and the eternal difference between right and wrong. She continued to write works on religion and ethics up to her death in 1749, expressing her last-ing preoccupation with the natural benevolence of human beings, as opposed to their natural self-interestedness, as epicureans such as Mandeville saw it. She tried to establish that this benevolence, though springing from natural feelings, has an altruistic and rational basis: 'a disinterested benevolence and approbation of virtue are natural to man, and given him as the proper excitements to good actions. [...] for I take our consciousness of right and wrong to be the result of some percep-tion, that every rational mind necessarily has of the essential difference between good and evil [...]'[61] Cockburn clearly saw herself as correcting the influence of Shaftesbury's ideas of the innate 'moral sense' and his view that morality sprang from private feelings and instincts – ideas enjoying, in this period, a new lease of life in the work of the Glasgow-based philosopher Francis Hutcheson, and which subsequently deeply informed Scottish Enlightenment ideas of 'moral sentiments'. Although Shaftesbury was regarded as suspect on grounds of religious unortho-doxy, popular versions of his idea of the moral sense and of the basis of morality in sentiment permeated eighteenth-century culture, and, despite Shaftesbury's contempt for emotionally susceptible women, informed the creation of a whole new breed of virtuous, sentimental heroines in fiction.[62] Women novelists may have created their share of virtuous, Shaftesburian heroines, yet, as philosophers and religious writers, it is striking that they very rarely argued on the side of moral intuitionism, and tended to defend the notion of moral decision-making as, in the main, a rational process.

4 The rising respectability of the learned lady

Cockburn herself was much admired by the Bluestockings, and laid the ground for the kinds of respectability and success enjoyed by Carter, both for her poetry and her scholarship, and by Catherine Talbot for her religious writings.[63] By the mid-eighteenth century, a number of com-mentators were looking back on the period from the late seventeenth to the early eighteenth centuries as something of a heroic era for learned women. For instance, the antiquary George Ballard's *Memoirs of Several Ladies of Great Britain who have been celebrated for their writings or skill in the learned languages, arts, and sciences* (1752), which he published with help from Sarah Chapone, sought to put British women on a par with continental greats such as Anne Dacier or Anna Maria van Schurman. Ballard's *Memoirs* self-consciously reprised a long European tradition of works celebrating famous and talented women. Bathsua Makin's

An Essay to Revive the Ancient Education of Gentlewomen (1673), for example, contained a long list of great women in order to dispel the general prejudice that to educate women 'will make Women so high, and men so low, like Fire in the House-top, it will set the whole world in a flame'.[64] Mandeville in his essays for *The Female Tatler* drew heavily on Pierre Le Moyne's *The Gallery of Heroic Women* (1652, French original 1647) for his account of female worthies. By the late seventeenth century, Judith Drake considered the whole 'illustrious women' genre both tired and ineffective as a form of pro-female argument.[65] Yet, after Ballard, the genre enjoyed a revival enduring well beyond the end of the century.[66] Ballard's carefully researched biographical entries allowed his readers, and allow us, to see some of the emerging themes in female writing: among the many elite female authors of devotional writings, there are physicians (Anna, Lady Halket, Elizabeth Bury), linguists and translators (Elizabeth Bland, Constantia Grierson), and scholarly networks sustained by personal friendships but, also, increasingly, by print. Ballard himself had earlier become part of one of these networks through his rediscovery of the distinguished Anglo-Saxon scholar Elizabeth Elstob, formerly an active, publishing member of the pioneering group of Oxford Saxonists led by George Hickes (an early advocate of Anglican educational establishments for women, as we have noted). Ballard and Sarah Chapone rescued Elstob from the poverty and obscurity into which she had descended, and she spent her later days in the household of Margaret, Duchess of Portland, herself a remarkable collector, Bluestocking and long-time friend of Elizabeth Montagu.[67]

Ballard's *Memoirs* conveyed the scale of British women's achievement in literature, philosophy (albeit neglecting the Cambridge Platonist philosopher Anne Conway), devotional writing, and scholarship during and before the period under discussion here. However, despite the inclusion of amateur physicians, the *Memoirs* do not quite do justice to the extent of women's collaborative involvement in the practice and culture of science, particularly from the later seventeenth century. Margaret Cavendish, Duchess of Newcastle, appears as a somewhat isolated figure, and there is no entry for Lady Ranelagh (d.1691), the experimental scientist and sister of Robert Boyle. Yet, as we now know, the period from 1690–1750 was one in which women did engage with the new, Newtonian scientific culture, and were themselves invited to participate in that culture. That participation was invited by publications such as *The Ladies Diary* (from 1704), which provided lessons and set problems in mathematics, and Francesco Algarotti's *Sir Isaac Newton's Philosophy Explain'd for the Use of the Ladies* (1739, Italian original 1733), promoted by Lady Mary Wortley Montagu and translated by Elizabeth Carter.[68] Montagu herself was celebrated for introducing inoculation for smallpox to England. Newtonianism acquired the burnish of continental salon and court culture when Caroline of Anspach, the wife of the future George II, became actively involved in the dispute between Newton and Leibnitz about the invention of calculus and other matters. The many British readers of Voltaire learned of Emilie du Châtelet's major work on Newtonian physics and mathematics, initially through his acknowledgements of her contributions to his own works, such as the *Eléments de la Philosophie de Newton* (in the dedicatory epistle to the 1738 edition).[69] Subsequent generations of women scientists and women popularizers of science in Britain drew inspiration from the examples of Caroline of Anspach and the Marquise du Châtelet.[70]

5 Women and polite society

Natural philosophical subjects such as medicine, botany, and even astronomy formed part of a desirable repertoire of polite learning for many educated women. Polite learning was understood to be the kind of knowledge that could be profitably circulated in conversation, and that fostered sociability rather than scholarly isolation. Judith Drake, herself a physician, made a powerful case for the value of this kind of learning in women, contrasting it with the awkward, scholastic obscurantism of college-educated men. Moreover, she argued that modern civility is, or should be, the blending of the different intellectual styles of men and women through social contact:

> Almost all Men that have had a liberal, and good Education know, what is due to Good Manners, and civil Company. But till they have been us'd a little to Our [women's] Society, their Modesty sits like Constraint upon 'em, and looks like a forc'd Compliance to uneasie Rules, and Forms of Civility. Conversing frequently with us makes 'em familiar to Men [...][71]

Drake astutely anticipates the idea of mixed-gender polite sociability that would become so dominant from the early decades of the eighteenth century right up to the point, after the 1790s, when the withdrawal of the ladies after dinner started to be associated with Englishness and English manliness to be equated with taciturn stoicism rather than voluble sociability.[72] This wider cultural shift has been associated by historians with the rise of the 'bourgeois public sphere', in which politeness to and by women was understood both as a goal of sociability and as a means of refinement.[73] Increasingly, that refinement was understood as a historical process, and the 'freedom' of modern British women – allowed out at operas, public gardens, assembly rooms, and so on – was contrasted with the subjection of women in more primitive times. Paradoxically, the writings most often credited with promoting this culture of politeness, Addison and Steele's pioneering periodical, *The Spectator*, and Shaftesbury's philosophy, promoted a *re-privatizing* of women as a means of providing a domestic moral anchor for male civic and commercial interaction.[74] 'The Family is the proper Province for Private Women to Shine in', Addison insisted, while Shaftesbury worried that 'whatever *Politeness* [men] pretend to', adapting to the conversational style of women is 'more a Disfigurement than any real Refinement of Discourse'.[75] Even so, and however dubious its benefits for women, it is the case that eighteenth-century commentators took an ever-growing interest in the public sphere and the workings of civil society (as distinct from the realms of the household and the state). Economists looked at the female taste for fashion, not as a vice, but as a stimulus to demand and production.[76] Educational theorists, Locke foremost among them, approached the question of the education of girls with a view to what Locke called the 'Law of Fashion, or private Censure' which inevitably governs all those who step out into the world and 'which by a secret and tacit consent establishes it self in the several Societies, Tribes, and Clubs of Men in the World'.[77] Philosophers from Shaftesbury and Hutcheson to Hume and Smith discussed the moral capacities of women as a source, not of spiritual salvation, but of social cohesion. Women occupied an ever more prominent place in these emerging discourses of Britain's social self-analysis, and contributed actively to the reshaping of national 'manners' as educational writers, literary authors, historians, and scholars. These discourses paid increasing attention to the place and role of women in the progress and successful functioning of society. Many writers were complacent or unreflective in the way in which they associated that 'progress' with the growing public visibility and improved treatment of women by men, but they nevertheless fostered a sense of civil identity in women which women writers themselves were able to adopt and amplify.[78] Yet, in the longer run, this sense of civil identity came at the price of a depoliticized public understanding of the household, marriage, and the family, and was accompanied by a decreasing emphasis upon the rational capacities that women writers had asserted with such philosophical and polemic force in the late seventeenth and early eighteenth centuries.

Notes

1. See Amy Louise Erickson, *Women and Property in Early Modern England* (London: Routledge, 1993).
2. Judith Drake, *An Essay in Defence of the Female Sex* (London, 1696), p. 5. On Drake and the identification of the 'Beau' in her *Essay* as Walsh, see Hannah Smith's valuable, 'English "Feminist" Writings and Judith Drake's *An Essay in Defence of the Female Sex*', *Historical Journal*, 44 (2001), 727–47 (p. 746).
3. Ros Ballaster, *Seductive Forms: Women's Amatory Fiction from 1684 to 1740* (Oxford: Clarendon Press, 1992), pp. 198–211; Jane Spencer, *Aphra Behn's Afterlife* (Oxford: Clarendon Press, 2000).
4. David Wootton, 'Pierre Bayle, Libertine?', in *Oxford Studies in the History of Philosophy*, ed. by M.A. Stewart, 2 vols (Oxford: Oxford University Press, 1997), II, 197–226.
5. E.G. Hundert, *The Enlightenment's Fable: Bernard Mandeville and the Discovery of Society* (Cambridge: Cambridge University Press, 1994) and M.M. Goldsmith, '"The Treacherous Arts of Mankind": Bernard Mandeville and Female Virtue', *History of Political Thought*, 7 (1986), 93–114.
6. See Karen O'Brien, *Women and Enlightenment in Eighteenth-Century Britain* (Cambridge: Cambridge University Press, 2009), chapter 1, pp. 35–67.
7. See Constance Jordan, *Renaissance Feminism: Literary Texts and Political Models* (Ithaca: Cornell University Press, 1990), pp. 214–20; Margaret J.M. Ezell, *The Patriarch's Wife: Literary Evidence and the History of the Family* (Chapel Hill: University of North Carolina Press, 1987).
8. Rachel Weil, *Political Passions: Gender, the Family and Political Argument in England, 1680–1714* (Manchester: Manchester University Press, 1999).
9. Susan J. Owen, 'The Dramatic Language of Sexual Politics', *Restoration Theatre and Crisis* (Oxford: Oxford University Press, 1996), pp. 157–82.
10. Melinda Zook, 'Contextualising Aphra Behn: Play, Politics and Party, 1679–89', in *Women Writers and the Early Modern Political Tradition*, ed. by Hilda L. Smith (Cambridge: Cambridge University Press, 1998), pp. 75–94; Weil, *Political Passions*, p. 176.
11. Sir John Vanbrugh, *The Provok'd Wife, A Comedy* (London, 1697), pp. 56–7.
12. Mary, Lady Chudleigh, *The Lady's Defence: or, The Bride-Woman's Counsellor Answer'd* (1701), ll. 95–8, in *The Poems and Prose of Mary, Lady Chudleigh*, ed. by Margaret J.M. Ezell (Oxford: Oxford University Press, 1993), p. 18.
13. *Letters of the Right Honourable Lady M—y W—y M—e. Written during her Travels in Europe, Asia and Africa*, 3 vols (London, 1763), II, 1134, I, 19–20.
14. Sarah Fyge Egerton, 'The Emulation', in *Poems on Several Occasions, together with a pastoral* (London, 1703), pp. 108, 109.
15. Elizabeth Thomas, '*On Sir J-S- saying in a sarcastic Manner*, My Books would make me Mad', *Miscellany Poems on Several Subjects* (London, 1722), pp. 186, 182.
16. Mary Astell, *Reflections upon Marriage* in *Astell: Political Writings*, ed. by Patricia Springborg (Cambridge: Cambridge University Press, 1996), p. 46.
17. For this reading of Clarissa's speech, see Howard Erskine-Hill, *Poetry of Opposition and Revolution: Dryden to Wordsworth* (Oxford: Clarendon Press, 1996), p. 92.
18. Astell, *Some Reflections*, p. 52. An important account of this aspect of Astell's thought is Patricia Springborg, *Mary Astell: Theorist of Freedom from*

Domination (Cambridge: Cambridge University Press, 2005). This should be read alongside the recent collection of essays, *Mary Astell: Reason, Gender, Faith*, ed. by William Kolbrener and Michael Michelson (Aldershot: Ashgate, 2007). A complication of Astell's views on the expediency of passive obedience comes from Sarah Apetrei, '"Call No Man Master Upon Earth": Mary Astell's Tory Feminism and an Unknown Correspondence', *Eighteenth-Century Studies*, 41 (2008), 507–23.

19. Mark Goldie, 'Mary Astell and John Locke', in *Mary Astell: Reason, Gender, Faith*, ed. by Kolbrener and Michelson, pp. 65–81.

20. Carole Pateman, *The Sexual Contract* (Stanford: Stanford University Press, 1988), p. 3.

21. Goldie, 'Mary Astell and John Locke', p. 75. On Astell as a critic of Locke, see Ruth Perry, 'Mary Astell and the Feminist Critique of Possessive Individualism', *Eighteenth-Century Studies*, 23 (1990), 444–57 and Springborg, *Mary Astell*.

22. Ruth Perry's more recent *Novel Relations: The Transformation of Kinship in English Literature and Culture, 1748–1818* (Cambridge: Cambridge University Press, 2004) lends weight to Pateman's thesis about the rise of 'fraternal patriarchy' in this period.

23. Sarah Prescott, *Women, Authorship and Literary Culture, 1690–1740* (Basingstoke: Palgrave, 2003).

24. See, in general, Jonathan I. Israel, *Enlightenment Contested: Philosophy, Modernity, and the Emancipation of Man, 1670–1752* (Oxford: Oxford University Press, 2006), in particular chapter 21, 'The Problem of Equality'.

25. Erica Harth, *Cartesian Women: Versions and Subversion of Rational Discourse in the Old Regime* (Ithaca: Cornell University Press, 1992).

26. See Egerton's, 'To Mr. Norris, on his Idea of Happiness', in *Poems on Several Occasions*, p. 27.

27. On Norris and Astell, see E. Derek Taylor and Melvyn New's introduction to their edition of Astell and Norris, *Letters Concerning the Love of God* (Aldershot: Ashgate, 2005).

28. In part I of *A Serious Proposal to the Ladies* (London, 1694), Astell famously advocated a secular intellectual retreat for women.

29. Mary Astell, *A Serious Proposal to the Ladies, Part II: Wherein a Method is offer'd for the Improvement of their Minds* (London, 1697), p. 41.

30. Mary Astell, *The Christian Religion, As Profess'd by a Daughter of the Church of England* (London, 1705), p. 278.

31. On Astell's possible reading of Poulain, see Springborg, *Mary Astell*, p. 96.

32. François Poulain de la Barre, *De L'Eglité des deux sexes, discours physique et morale où l'on voit l'importance de se défaire des préjugez* (1674; repr. Paris: Fayard, 1984), pp. 72, 78.

33. Siep Stuurman, *François Poulain de la Barre and the Invention of Modern Equality* (Cambridge, MA: Harvard University Press, 2004), p. 2.

34. On editions and the reception of Poulain's work see Stuurman, *François Poulain de la Barre*, pp. 277–83.

35. John Toland, *Letters to Serena; containing, 1. The origin and force of prejudices...* (London, 1704), p. xi. See Justin Champion, *Republican Learning: John Toland and the Crisis of Christian Culture, 1696–1722* (Manchester: Manchester University Press, 2003), pp. 52, 169.

36. See M.M. Goldsmith's introduction to his edition of Mandeville, *By a Society of Ladies: Essays in The Female Tatler* (Bristol: Continuum, 1999), pp. 54–5.
37. Mandeville, *By a Society*, ed. by Goldsmith, p. 171. This echoes Astell, *The Christian Religion*, p. 137: 'Since Men being the Historians, they seldom condescend to record the great and good Actions of Women; and when they take notice of them, 'tis with this wise Remark That such Women acted above their Sex.'
38. Mandeville, *By a Society*, ed. by Goldsmith, p. 237.
39. *Woman Not Inferior to Man: or A Short and Modest Vindication of the Natural Right of the Fair-Sex to a Perfect Equality of Power, Dignity, and Esteem, with the Men. By Sophia, A Person of Quality* (London, 1739), p. 18.
40. *Woman Not Inferior to Man*, p. 18.
41. *Beauty's Triumph: or, The Superiority of the First Sex Invincibly Proved* (London, 1751).
42. *Woman's Superior Excellence over Man: or, A Reply to the Author of a Late Treatise* (London, 1740), pp. 10, 21, 59.
43. Lady Mary Wortley Montagu, *The Nonsense of Common-Sense*, no. vi, 24 January 1738, ed. by Robert Halsband (Evanston: Northwestern University Press, 1947), p. 25. The often repeated theory that Sophia was Sophia Fermor (1721–45) the daughter of the brilliant Henrietta Louisa Fermor, Countess of Pomfret (a friend of Lady Mary) seems implausible given her youth and the fact that she was on the continent at the time. See the note by 'Medley', *Notes and Queries*, Series 8, xi (1 May 1897), 348 which makes this identification.
44. *The Hardships of the English Laws in relation to Wives* (London, 1735), p. 47.
45. *Woman's Superior Excellence*, pp. 103–4.
46. Ibid., p. 47.
47. See E.J. Clery, *The Feminization Debate in Eighteenth-Century England: Literature, Commerce and Luxury* (Basingstoke: Palgrave, 2004), p. 139.
48. Daniel Defoe, *An Essay upon Projects* (London,1697), p. 286. Defoe's 'Academy for Women', was designed to educate women as intelligent companions for men ('in short, I wou'd have Men take Women for Companions, and Educate them to be fit for it', pp. 302–3).
49. *The Tatler*, ed. by Donald F. Bond, 3 vols (Oxford: Clarendon Press, 1987), I, 238–41; I, 439–40.
50. Gilbert Burnet, *Bishop Burnet's History of His Own Time*, 2 vols (London, 1724, 1734), II, 653.
51. Hannah Smith, 'Mary Astell and the Reformation of Manners in Late Seventeenth-Century England', in *Mary Astell: Reason, Gender, Faith*, ed. by Kolbrener and Michelson, pp. 31–47, especially pp. 36–7, 46.
52. Smith, 'Mary Astell and the Reformation of Manners', pp. 32–4.
53. Clery, *The Feminisation Debate*, chapter 2.
54. Damaris Masham, *Occasional Thoughts in Reference to a Vertuous or Christian Life* (1705) and *A Discourse Concerning the Love of God*, both in *The Philosophical Works of Lady Damaris Masham*, ed. by James G. Buickerood (Bristol: Thoemmes Press, 2004), p. 45.
55. Masham, *A Discourse Concerning the Love of God*, p. 121.
56. On this controversy, see Springborg, *Mary Astell*, pp. 58–68.
57. See Barbara Taylor, *Mary Wollstonecraft and the Feminist Imagination* (Cambridge: Cambridge University Press, 2003), chapter 3.

58. See the section 'Bluestocking Theology' in my *Women and Enlightenment in Eighteenth-Century Britain* (Cambridge: Cambridge University Press, 2009), chapter 1.
59. On Cockburn, see Anne Kelley, *Catharine Trotter: An Early Modern Writer in the Vanguard of Feminism* (Aldershot: Ashgate, 2002) and Martha Brandt Bolton, 'Some Aspects of the Philosophy of Catharine Trotter', *Journal for the History of Philosophy*, 31 (1993), 565–88.
60. On Clarke, see Isabel Rivers, *Reason, Grace and Sentiment: A Study of the Language of Religion and Ethics in England, 1660–1780*, 2 vols (Cambridge: Cambridge University Press, 1991, 2000), II, 15–16, 79–81.
61. Cockburn, *Remarks upon the Principles and Reasonings of Dr. Rutherforth's Essay* (1747), *The Works of Mrs. Catharine Cockburn*, 2 vols (London, 1751), II, 33.
62. See G.J. Barker-Benfield, *The Culture of Sensibility in Eighteenth-Century Britain* (Chicago: Chicago University Press, 1996), pp. 118–19.
63. See Kelley, *Catharine Trotter*, pp. 26–8. Catherine Talbot introduced Elizabeth Carter to Cockburn's works in 1751; see *A Series of Letters between Mrs. Elizabeth Carter and Miss Catherine Talbot*, ed. by Montagu Pennington, 2 vols (London, 1809), II, 49.
64. Bathsua Makin, *An Essay To Revive the Antient Education of Gentlewomen in Religion, Manners, Arts, and Tongues* (London, 1673), p. 3.
65. Smith, 'English "Feminist" Writings', p. 740.
66. See Ruth Perry's introduction to her edition of Ballard's *Memoirs of Several Ladies of Great Britain* (Detroit: Wayne State University Press, 1985).
67. On Elstob, see Kathryn Sutherland, 'Elizabeth Elstob', in *Medieval Scholarship: Biographical Studies on the Formation of a Discipline*, ed. by Helen Damico 3 vols (New York: Garland, 1995-2000), II, 59–73.
68. See Londa Schiebinger, *The Mind Has No Sex? Women in the Origins of Modern Science* (Cambridge, MA: Harvard University Press, 1989), p. 41.
69. See Judith P. Zinsser, *La Dame D'Esprit: A Biography of the Marquise du Châtelet* (New York: Viking, 2006).
70. See Patricia Fara, *Pandora's Breeches: Women, Science and Power in the Enlightenment* (London: Pimlico, 2005).
71. Judith Drake, *Essay in Defence of the Female Sex*, p. 141.
72. See Lawrence Klein, 'Gender, Conversation and the Public Sphere in Early Eighteenth-Century England', in *Textuality and Sexuality: Reading Theories and Practices*, ed. by Judith Still and Michael Worton (Manchester: Manchester University Press, 1993), pp. 100–15; Philip Carter, *Men and the Emergence of Polite Society: Britain, 1660–1800* (Harlow: Longman, 2000).
73. Jürgen Habermas, *The Structural Transformation of the Public Sphere: An Inquiry into a Category of Bourgeois Society*, trans. by Thomas Burger (Cambridge: Polity, 1989). And in Habermas's wake, for example, John Brewer, *The Pleasures of the Imagination: English Culture in the Eighteenth Century* (London: HarperCollins, 1997) and Lawrence Klein, *Shaftesbury and the Culture of Politeness: Moral Discourse and Cultural Politics in Early Eighteenth Century England* (Cambridge: Cambridge University Press, 1994).
74. See Kathryn Shevelow, *Women and Print Culture: The Construction of Femininity in the Early Periodical* (London: Routledge, 1989), and Barker-Benfield, *The Culture of Sensibility*, pp. 105–19.

75. *The Spectator*, ed. Donald F. Bond, 5 vols (Oxford: Clarendon Press, 1965), I, 349. See also I, 68; III, 465. Antony Ashley Cooper, Lord Shaftesbury, *Characteristicks of Men, Manners, Opinions, Times*, 2nd edn corrected, 3 vols (London, 1714), III, 186.
76. See Elizabeth Kowaleski-Wallace, *Consuming Subjects: Women, Shopping, and Business in the Eighteenth Century* (New York: Columbia University Press, 1997).
77. Locke, *An Essay concerning Human Understanding*, ed. by Peter N. Nidditch (Oxford: Clarendon Press, 1975), pp. 357, 353. On how girls are (often wrongly) socialized by their early education, see Locke, *Some Thoughts Concerning Education* (1693), ed. by John and Jean S. Yolton (Oxford: Clarendon Press, 1989), pp. 106, 210.
78. See Sylvana Tomaselli, 'The Enlightenment Debate on Women', *History Workshop Journal*, 20 (1985), 101–24 and Jane Rendall, *The Origins of Modern Feminism: Women in Britain, France and the United States, 1780–1860* (Basingstoke: Macmillan, 1985), chapter 1.

2
Luxury

E.J. Clery

1 Introduction: which luxury debate?

'Luxury' today is a poor, diminished term, mere advertising cant that barely registers on our intellectual radar. It is unrecognizable as the watchword that once played a decisive role in the mighty war of words fought over the establishment of free market capitalism and consumer culture. Over the past thirty years there has been a growing appreciation of its centrality to an understanding of eighteenth-century thought in every sphere. John Sekora, author of a seminal study of the *topos*, describes it as probably 'the greatest single social issue and the greatest single commonplace' in the period, while the historian Paul Langford goes further:

> A history of luxury and attitudes to luxury would come very close to being a history of the eighteenth century. There is a sense in which politics in this period is about the distribution and representation of this luxury, religion about the attempt to control it, public polemic about generating and regulating it, and social policy about confining it to those who did not produce it.[1]

And what was 'it'? According to the most basic definition, luxury was anything beyond what was necessary – an impossibly elastic category, as Bernard Mandeville, the notorious apologist for luxury, would argue.[2] But in its deployment the concept had vast ramifications, involving inherited classical and Christian codes of morality in collision with new economic imperatives. The management of social change, the maintenance of order, the interpretation of human nature itself, were all at stake.

What was the agency of women writers in this fundamental debate? The assumption has long been that they did not play any very essential role: Sekora's checklist of participants contains the name of not one woman; Christopher Berry's 1994 monograph, *The Idea of Luxury*, is equally unforthcoming. More recently new research has appeared on the engagement of women writers with the topic of luxury in the second half of the century,[3] but the question has never even been asked about the female authors of the preceding period. I want to suggest reasons for the difficulty in recognizing writings by women as interventions in debate about luxury and – by looking in some detail at the work of Mary Astell and Eliza Haywood (voices sharply divergent from each other as well as from better-known male contemporaries) – explore the idea that the inclusion of women writers must challenge our own established notions of the development of a single mainstream debate.

Constructions of sexual difference and the figure of 'woman' are crucial components in both the classical and Christian discourses on luxury, though they feature in different ways. In Christian representations luxury merges with 'luxuria', the deadly sin of lechery, personified as a woman. Eve is the original facilitator of luxury and 'Eve's curse' is the mark of women's particular association with excess and corruption, as well as with the punishment they entail. Among classical writers, luxury on the face of it appears a more political concept; a mode of explanation for the moral collapse of the *polis* in times of prosperity or excess. But invariably the analysis is conceived in terms of a decline into effeminacy; that is to say, citizens begin to show signs of the inner weakness, self-indulgence, and extravagance commonly attributed to women. The concern is primarily military. Prosperity makes men soft, undermining their courage, fortitude, and other heroic virtues, and incapacitating them for public service. The boundaries between the sexes weaken and, without this foundation, civilization comes crashing down. On a more pragmatic level, the devising of sumptuary laws specifically aimed at women's dress and manners are a recurrent symptom of moral panic both in the classical and pre-modern Christian eras.

This is a mere sketch of the complex conceptual schemas surrounding luxury. For much more fully worked accounts I refer you to the early chapters of Sekora and Berry, who both give some weight to the significance of gender in the two traditions. They also share the view that these early accounts of luxury, with their gendered tropes, are left behind at the start of the eighteenth century. This is thought to be true particularly of the Christian discourse. Sekora comments, 'The narrowly physical aspect of the concept – the "foule lust of luxurie" of Chaucer,

Spenser, and Shakespeare – was not one that eighteenth-century writers chose to emphasize', and adds 'their sense of luxury was more Roman than scholastic'. Likewise, what Berry calls the 'transition to modernity' involves a 'sea-change' that leaves behind the Christian paradigm and its sexual iconography. As for the classical polemic against effeminacy, although it remains ubiquitous in eighteenth-century discussions and representations, its survival is not thought worthy of note.[4]

Scholars of eighteenth-century luxury are generally agreed that in the course of the period a 'de-moralization' of the concept took place, and that this opened the way for the modern discourse of political economy, which seeks to demonstrate objectively the inherent logic and social benefits of economic growth. The 'modern' perspective first emerged in the upheavals following the Glorious Revolution of 1688, which involved a radical reformation of state finance in order to sustain new commitments to costly continental wars and the expense of a standing army.[5] Those excluded from power, old Whigs and country Tories, looked backward to the moral rhetoric of Roman historians and of Machiavelli's *Discourses* when denouncing government corruption and the erosion of civic virtue caused by the policies of ministers.[6] Supporters of financial innovation and the expansion of markets, predominantly Whig in sympathy and sometimes sponsored by government, began to evolve a more optimistic vision of luxury as an integral component of the successful body politic. If Adam Smith is the exemplar of this progression, then any writers anticipating his ideas are seized upon as supporting evidence of a general shift in attitudes towards an acceptance of luxury in the interests of national greatness: Hume, Johnson, Addison, and above all Mandeville – the genealogy is traced back as far as the 1690s, to Nicholas Barbon and Locke.

This narrative is of course a retrospective construction guided by conviction of the truth of economic rationality and the obsolescence of alternative viewpoints.[7] It does not, *ipso facto*, exclude women. The fact that gender as an organizing category is seen as redundant within the modernizing discourse on luxury is neither here nor there. But the narrative has simply failed to uncover any female interlocutor in the period 1690–1750. By contrast, the attention focused by social and economic historians on the 'new' luxury as it was unapologetically embraced by the elite and spread through the middle and even the lower ranks has revealed the importance of women as consumers. Although their part in trade and manufacture appears to have decreased, through shopping and the exercise of taste women were important participants in the expanding marketplace. By their attendance at masquerades, operas, pleasure gardens, and gambling parties, they contributed to the related expansion of a leisure industry.

Financial speculation, known in the eighteenth-century as 'stock-jobbing', was a widely condemned facet of luxury, seen as parasitical and prone to corruption; yet it too became an acceptable pastime among new groups, including women. Shares and bonds were a type of wealth which had yet to be regulated or taxed, and could be held by women independently of their husbands or male relations.[8] At the outset of the South Sea Bubble of 1720, with stock at £320 and rising, Mary Astell wrote to her friend Lady Ann Coventry: 'Even the Ladies as well as the Lords turn Stock-Jobbers, and have got the Cash out of the Citizens hands.'[9] Anne Finch, Countess of Winchilsea, made the same observation in her 'Song on the South Sea':

> Ombre and basset laid aside,
> New games employ the fair;
> And brokers all those hours divide
> Which lovers used to share.[10]

When the Bubble burst, Astell, having staked a sum intended to found a charity school for girls, was herself a loser, along with Lady Mary Wortley Montagu and thousands of others.

Women's freedom to get their fingers burnt in a stock market crash may be regarded as progress of a sort. The latest work by literary and cultural historians has begun to explore the way the ancient link between women and luxury continues in a secularized way in social commentary of the period, as women become, par excellence, consuming subjects or adepts of paper credit, citizens of a nation in which to participate in a money economy is to gain agency and a 'voice' through economic choices. At the same time there has been attention to the way in which women come to serve as emblems of this newly inclusive body politic, with its modern refinements and forms of consensus.

Nobody's Story: The Vanishing Acts of Women Writers in the Literary Marketplace, 1670–1820 (1994) by Catherine Gallagher, and *Authorship, Commerce, and Gender in Early Eighteenth-Century England: A Culture of Paper Credit* (1998) by Catherine Ingrassia were ground-breaking studies relating literature to early eighteenth-century arguments over economic change, with particular attention to gender.[11] Gallagher takes a series of case histories, including those of Aphra Behn and Delarivier Manley from our period, to show how the persona of the female writer became congruent with 'the discourse of marketplace exchange' and paved the way for a new kind of authorial identity. Ingrassia shows how Eliza Haywood's literary talents flourished in the modern world of paper credit, while she became for Alexander Pope an embodiment of the corrupting 'feminization of culture'.[12] In both works the 'feminine' construction of the modern economic subject is in its origins a negative one, drawn from the civic humanist discourse antagonistic to economic modernization and to luxury. Both critics acknowledge a debt to J.G.A Pocock, the great chronicler of civic humanist or 'neo-Machiavellian' thought, and to his compelling depiction of an androgynous *homo economicus*:

> Economic man as masculine conquering hero is a fantasy of nineteenth-century industrialisation (the *Communist* manifesto is of course one classical example). His eighteenth-century predecessor was seen as on the whole a feminised, even an effeminate being, still wrestling with his own passions and hysterias and with interior and exterior forces let loose by his fantasies and appetites, and symbolised by such archetypically female goddesses of disorder as Fortune, Luxury, and most recently Credit herself.[13]

However neither Gallagher nor Ingrassia explore the possibility of a female voice commenting on economic issues that is not co-opted by this identification between market capitalism and the feminine. It is perhaps telling that neither book features in the index the term 'luxury', with its inbuilt element of contestation. Female writers, according to these two accounts, may profit from the shift to a 'de-moralized' conception of luxury, but they do not reflect on or debate the changing definition of the term itself.

Other works, such as Laura Brown's *The Ends of Empire: Women and Ideology in Early Eighteenth-Century English Literature* (1993) and my own *The Feminization Debate in Eighteenth-Century England: Literature, Commerce and Luxury* (2004), look at the way 'the female principle' (Pocock's term), is deployed as a component of arguments over the ethics of capitalism, and in the latter case, there is an examination of the responses of women writers who found themselves utilized as emblems of modernity.[14] But again, there is little sense of women as active disputants in economic debate as it is commonly understood.

In spite of women's importance within commercial culture, then, and in spite of growing awareness of 'the feminine' as a point of articulation in economic discourse, as yet writings by women of the period as interventions in the debate on luxury are not on the map. At present, to posit luxury as 'the greatest single social issue', or as equivalent to eighteenth-century history itself, simply shows a new way in which women's writing can be marginalized. As so often in feminist scholarship, the procedure must be to ask whether the map itself needs changing. We need to raise the possibility that the problem is not women's failure to write within the ambit of the luxury debate; but that we are misrecognizing the luxury debate and what constitutes it. Once we begin to explore early eighteenth-century women's writing with the question of luxury in view, we may find that not only were women engaged in disputing the issue, but that what they said alters our picture of the eighteenth-century debate.

2 Mary Astell: 'Vertue is the only thing in fashion'

The 1690s saw an upsurge in arguments for free trade and the usefulness of luxury, rather surprisingly authored by Tories.[15] *Discourse of Trade* (1690) by Nicholas Barbon, *Discourses upon Trade* (1691) by Sir Dudley North, and *An Essay on the India Trade* (1697) by Sir Charles Davenant are all cited as milestones on the road towards a 'scientific' approach to political economy. The writers were men excluded from government office under William and Mary, who no doubt saw in the issue of protectionism a means of attacking the policies of the Whig government.

The key to their arguments is a newly instrumental justification of excessive wants and the acquisitive passions, gauged towards the promotion of British prosperity. Thus North affirms consumer aspirations as the fundamental basis of a growing economy:

The main spur to trade, or rather to industry and ingenuity, is the exorbitant appetites of men, which they will take pains to gratify, and so be disposed to work, when nothing else will incline them to it; for did men content themselves with bare necessities, we should have a poor world.[16]

This formulation may appear to give conceptual priority to consumption over production, but in fact it is underpinned by the ethos of production. Consuming desires should be permitted to flourish purely and solely to enable the political good of employment and trade. This is the new morality of luxury.

The Tory validation of the free market was one of the contexts in which Mary Astell's *A Serious Proposal to the Ladies* (1694) was written and published, and we can be sure, from the almost supernatural acuity with which she absorbs and analyses the political and philosophical arguments of the day, that she was well aware of the debating strategies being used by fellow Tories. In the Preface to *Moderation truly Stated* (1704), she later shows a ready familiarity with Davenant's opus, including his economic writings. The very first line of the *Proposal*, addressed to the female reader, acknowledges the topical interest in foreign trade and puts in question the instrumental argument for luxury:

> Since the Profitable Adventures that have gone abroad in the World, have met with so great Encouragement, tho' the highest advantage they can propose, is an uncertain Lot for such matters as Opinion (not real worth) gives a value to; things which if obtain'd, are as flitting and fickle as that Chance which is to dispose of them.

She then alludes to her own speculative venture, still in terms of profit and loss:

> I therefore persuade my self, you will not be less kind to a Proposition that comes attended with more certain and substantial Gain; whose only design is to improve your Charms and heighten your Value, by suffering you no longer to be cheap and contemptible.[17]

The incomplete syntax of the opening sentence, not unusual in Astell's writing or in print of this period generally, has a peculiar rhetorical force here. Presumably the original plan was to write, 'Since the Profitable Adventures that have gone abroad in the World, have met with so great Encouragement, I therefore persuade myself [...]' But the author has been waylaid by reflections on the delusory value of luxury commodities; reflections which perform the very deterioration into muddled inconsequence that they describe. She refers in the second part of the *Serious Proposal* (1697) to such seductions of the mind with fiscal precision as 'unaccountable Wanderings'.[18] The abortive proposition of the first sentence makes the promise of Astell's counter-offer, based on real value and sound sentence-construction, even more compelling.

Astell is intent on resisting the de-moralization of luxury and on restoring it to a moral framework, and yet she embraces economic schema of profit and loss. 'Value' and 'gain' are the dominant metaphors in Part I and the Introduction of Part II of the *Proposal*, as she attempts to persuade women to change their lives and improve their minds. To make the question of choice more vivid, she initially sets herself up in Part I in the manner of a projector, an economic adventurer in the Royal Exchange, and addresses the reader as a potential investor: don't buy shares in that scheme, try this one! 'I shall not need many words to persuade you to close with this Proposal.'[19]

What Astell is venturing could be described as a counter-economic discourse, an alternative theory of value which nevertheless operates in accordance with the logic of commerce. Her programme of otherworldliness is couched in terms of the material world and material interests ('Vertue is the only thing in fashion'). She adjures ladies to be 'so true to your Interest, as not to lessen your Empire and depreciate your Charms', and goes on to ask them, 'what it is that stops your flight, that keeps you grovelling here below, like *Domitian* catching Flies when you should be busied in obtaining Empires'. The expectation of the metaphysical aroused by 'flight', ends in the language of military conquest with connotations of trade, and the startling image of a feckless Roman emperor Domitian.[20] This is a point at which the language of sovereignty, the identification with an absolute monarch which Catherine Gallagher has observed as a feature of Tory women's writing, coincides with economic discourse.[21] Over and over again Astell returns to the problem of self-worth, of knowing one's own value, and of the danger of depreciation, and urges women to turn from outward luxury to inward profit-making and pleasure.

What is Astell's purpose in critiquing the values and redeploying the idiom of the emerging commercial order in the context of an address to women? The *Serious Proposal* is distinct from other feminist writings of the era, including Judith Drake's *An Essay in Defence of the Female Sex* (1796), in the sense that it is not a defence, and engages in little of the traditional knockabout invective regarding the relative merits of men and women. Instead it is 'seriously' critical of the present corrupted state of the majority of women. It offers them the means of reforming themselves from within in accordance with their 'true and greatest Interest'; that is to say, not by pursuit of 'Interest' in any worldly sense, but with a view to a higher, spiritual end. Like many a male author, Astell engages in a critique of her times via the figure of the fallen woman; unlike male social critics, she speaks directly to the woman herself, and draws up a plan not simply for her own recuperation, but for the moral regeneration of the body politic as a whole, with women as agents of reform. If an explanation is needed as to why Astell deals exclusively with women of the propertied classes, it could be found in this specific concern with the predicament of women in relation to luxury.

As Astell presents the problem, women stand in an especially degrading relationship to consumer culture. Their intense identification with trinkets and trifles is the result of their own reduction to the status of objects and commodities. Everything in their upbringing encourages them to collude in this state of affairs. They are denied the cultivation of mind that would encourage them to reflect upon and reject absorption in material pleasures. It is precisely because of this immersion in the dynamics of consumption, different in degree but not in kind from that of men, that the rejection of luxury *by women* represents the ultimate triumph, and that women are best qualified to bring about a general recuperation. Astell's point, that the link between women and worldly pleasures is contingent rather than essential (as male moralists would insist), is made clear in Part II of the *Serious Proposal*. This takes the form of a handbook for self-improvement which, aside from the introduction, is not gender-specific in its recommendations.

Thanks to Ruth Perry's excellent biography, we have a vivid picture of Astell's ascetic way of life: her opposition to luxury in practice was a matter of principle as well as necessity. It therefore comes as no surprise that she expects the ladies who inhabit the secular monastery, the central plank of her *Proposal*, to choose 'what Nature, not Luxury requires' in fulfilling their daily needs. Yet her general vision of the benefits of virtue and piety does not conform to the doctrine of self-denial. On the contrary, it is animated by the economic thinking displayed in the initial premise of the treatise: a maximization of pleasure, not a renunciation of it. 'True piety', she explains, is 'the most sweet and engaging thing imaginable [...] 'Tis in truth the highest *Epicurism* exalting our Pleasures by refining them.'[22] At one point she even attempts to claim 'Pleasures' entirely for heaven, distinguishing them from worldly 'Amusements'. But the distinction is not systematically sustained. Instead, Astell tends to emphasize continuities between the mundane and the spiritual. Her apprenticeship in neo-Platonic philosophy, carried out through correspondence with John Norris in the early 1690s, gave her the rhetorical tools to unite the human and the divine. As William Kolbrener has remarked, 'Synecdoche, a staple of an earlier metaphysical sensibility, underlies the worldview of *A Serious Proposal* where the proposed monastery is both "a Type and Antepast of Heav'n".'[23] The crucial difference is that mundane pleasures thrive on lack, in contrast to the perfect plenitude found in heaven; Astell is a subtle analyst of the psychology of 'unreal wants', the cycle of desire and disappointment.[24] But there are genuine equivalences too. She anticipates Mandeville in commending a regime of the passions lightly regulated from above. Not only pride and the desire for pleasure, but also ambition and the spirit of competition are given scope within her schema of religious virtue.[25]

At the start of the *Proposal* Astell dwells on the choice facing women as commodities within an exchange economy. A lady should refrain from throwing away her charms on 'vain insignificant men. She need not make her self so cheap, as to descend to court their Applauses [sic]; for at the greater distance she keeps, and the more she is above them, the more effectually she secures their esteem and wonder'. The proposal of the monastery is precisely designed to take women out of circulation, at a 'greater distance', in order to raise their value. Commentators have generally focused on the private salvation offered by the monastery, but Astell also points to public benefits: 'Having gained an entrance into Paradise themselves, thy wou'd both shew the way, and invite all others to partake of their felicity.' The residents will re-emerge to form the vanguard of a new spiritual enlightenment, disseminated by women's *reformed* conversation.[26] The monastery is 'a Seminary to stock the Kingdom with pious and prudent Ladies'. It is not surprising that Astell's instrumental vision of the enhanced exchange value of female virtue appealed powerfully to men like Daniel Defoe and Samuel Richardson, both sometime tradesmen with a commitment to the emergence of a moral commercial order.[27]

In these remarks on the place of luxury in Astell's thought, I have not tried to find a connection with other more familiar interpretations, which customarily make reference to Descartes, Hobbes, Locke, or the Cambridge Platonists. That attempt must be left for another occasion. But if any further evidence is needed of her abiding interest in luxury as a political issue and a social problem, it can be found in her later tracts dealing with topical controversies.[28] The celebrated Preface to her broadside *Moderation truly Stated* (1704) addressed to the economic theorist and Tory turncoat Charles Davenant, makes clear her detailed knowledge not only of his writings on trade and government financial policy but also of Machiavelli's *Discourses*, a foundational work for eighteenth-century discussions of luxury.[29] Here Astell is less interested in taking up a position in the debate than in observing, hilariously, the self-interested nature of anti-luxury rhetoric as ammunition for career politicians. In *Bart'lemy Fair: or, An Enquiry After Wit* (1709), however, she deploys it herself; her resources for dealing creatively with permutations of the new economic thinking appear finally exhausted. She rounds on the Earl of Shaftesbury and his patrician associates at the Whig Kit-Cat Club for their dissolute lifestyles, the breeding ground of their irreligion, invoking the most threadbare clichés of an 'Antient *English* Peerage' untainted by luxury. If Shaftesbury's *A Letter Concerning Enthusiasm* proposes, as Perry has suggested, 'a free marketplace of ideas', then Astell it seems has chosen to close up shop.[30]

3 Eliza Haywood: 'Love throws the fences down, and makes a gen'ral waste'[31]

From the appearance of her first prose fiction in 1719, *Love in Excess*, Haywood was hailed for her stirring depictions of desire; James Sterling's 1732 epithet, 'Great arbitress of passion', has frequently been cited since.[32] What critics today need to recognize, in order to get beyond the rather tiresome dispute over whether Haywood's work is political or escapist, is that passion is political and a fundamental category in discussions of luxury.[33] The reception of her fictions shows the continued currency of the 'pre-modern' sense of luxury cognate with lust, for good or ill; they are said to arouse 'luxuriant fire'; they amount to 'luxurious rants'.[34] Nicholas Barbon's famous defence of consumerism in his *Discourse of Trade* (1690) dwells on the desire that seeks its mate among material goods:

> Wares that have their Value from supplying the Wants of the Mind are all such things that can satisfie Desire; Desire implys Want: It is the Appetite of the Soul, and is as natural to the Soul, as Hunger to the Body. The Wants of the Mind are infinite, Man naturally Aspires and as his Mind is elevated, his Senses grow more refined, and more capable of Delight; his Desires are inlarged, and his Wants increase with his Wishes, which is for every thing that is rare, can gratifie his Senses, adorn his Body and promote the Pleasure and Pomp of Life.[35]

Barbon describes a romance, one that can have only a happy ending, involving limitless growth, enlargement, and refinement, with no conflict foreseen between pleasure and pomp, sensual gratification, and social prestige. I will argue that Haywood was in dialogue with this optimistic vision: she exposes the naivety of the 'romance narrative' implicit in progressivist economic discourse from the late seventeenth century onwards. Her insistence on the connections between desire, irrationality, and disaster was not only pertinent to the frequently tumultuous state of contemporary financial markets, but anticipates anti-rationalist accounts of capitalism in the present day.

Haywood began her writing career in the midst of a period of economic turmoil. J.G.A. Pocock has described the series of speculative disasters that marked the first decades of the eighteenth century as a series of 'psychic crises'. The Darien Scheme which bankrupted Scotland in 1699, the South Sea Bubble of 1720, and the French Mississippi Company which collapsed the following year, all exposed the terrifying reality that '[g]overnment and politics seemed to have been placed at the mercy of passion, fantasy and appetite, and these forces were known to feed on themselves and to be without moral limit'.[36] Haywood was to write directly on the South Sea Bubble in the conventional form of a political satire entitled *Memoirs of a Certain Island Adjacent to Utopia* (1724–25) directed against Walpole and his colleagues, accusing them of having profited from the misfortunes of others. But far more interesting are her novels written during and immediately after the boom and bust of the early 1720s with no ostensible reference to events, but closely related by their exclusive preoccupation with 'passion, fantasy and appetite'.

The first volume of *Love in Excess* was published in January 1719, the second in June of that year.[37] The third volume, published in February 1720, would have been written during the period of speculative frenzy around the Mississippi Scheme that had repercussions in markets throughout Europe, and the reception of the completed work would have coincided with the height of the South Sea share inflation, and must have added to the general sense current in the summer of 1720 of a nation in delirium. There is an economic idea implicit in the very title *Love in Excess*; a title in dialogue with other titles involving ratios of love. Congreve's *Love for Love* (1695) implies the ultimate restoration of balance characteristic of comic drama. Dryden's *All for Love: or The World Well Lost* (1678) measures love (described by its critics within the drama in terms of luxury) against a complex of worldly interest and militaristic public virtue. But in Haywood any notion of measure or calculation is abandoned. The freedom offered by the unfixed and as yet uncertainly functional novel form aids her in exploring the ruptures generated by excess.

In its workings the novel accords with Georges Bataille's principle of 'general economics': 'a society always produces on the whole more than is necessary to its subsistence, it disposes of a surplus. It is precisely the use made of this excess that determines it: the surplus is the cause of disturbances, changes of structure, and of its entire history.'[38] The priority Bataille gives to consumption, excess, and loss in his (anti-) economic theory makes it valuable, I would suggest, to scholars of the first bubbles and of the whole discursive field of luxury in the eighteenth century. This is not to say that the theory is without its problems; the anthropological accounts underlying Bataille's thesis are fraught with difficulty. But what Bataille does – and we may speculate that this is what Haywood's fiction is also doing – is to destabilize a mode of economic thought that presents consuming passions as containable and potentially productive and speculative crashes as deviations from the rule rather than endemic to the system.

Not for Haywood the neat equilibrium of the theory of countervailing passions. Her vision of excess is far distant from, for instance, the allegorical fiction of Addison's essay in no. 55 (Thursday 3 May 1711) of the *Spectator* illustrating the way in which luxury and avarice, two powerful tyrants at 'perpetual war', each aiming at 'Universal Monarchy over the Hearts of Mankind', eventually become weary of battles and 'resolved to live as good Freinds and Confederates, and to share between them whateer Conquests were made on either side'.[39] The love of pleasurable expenditure and the love of gain become mutually supporting. In Haywood's universe, love as a form of luxurious expenditure is entirely, recklessly prodigal; gloriously destructive. '*Love* is too jealous, too arbitrary a monarch to suffer any other passion to equalize himself in that heart where he has fixed his throne.'[40]

In *Love in Excess* the irreconcilability of the passion of love and other more mundane passions is explored through the main protagonist, the Count D'Elmont. Having won military honours, and thereby demonstrated his public virtue and conventional masculinity, he returns to Parisian high society. Indifferent to love himself, he quickly becomes an object of desire. He receives an anonymous declaration, decides to acquire a mistress for reasons of 'fashion', and proceeds to ruin the reputation of a young girl from a poor family and marry an heiress for money. It is not until the start of the second volume that love strikes. D'Elmont's former guardian, Monsieur Frankville, is dying and begs the Count to become guardian in turn to his orphan daughter Melliora. Even as the father takes his last breath, a spark is ignited between D'Elmont and Melliora. The narrator provides no moral perspective on this event, or any other; the narrative voice is amoral and fulsomely sympathetic to the plight of lovers, whatever their actions. It is left to Melliora to weigh up for the reader the impropriety of her new situation as ward of a married man whom she loves, and who quickly reveals his love for her.

This predicament culminates with a metatextual scene in which the Count discovers Melliora immersed in reading Ovid's *Epistles*, also known as the *Heroides*, notorious as a primer for the expression of female sexual passion. He accuses her of contradiction, since only a few days before she had condemned a recital of love poems. But she defends herself. She will not treat such books as 'preparatives for love' making the soul 'fit for amorous impressions' but instead use them to reinforce reason by endeavouring 'to retain in memory, more of the misfortunes that attended the passion of Sappho [one of the principal figures in Ovid's book, and an eventual suicide], than the tender, tho' never so elegant expressions it produced'. The discussion clearly pertains to the anticipated reception of Haywood's own amatory fiction, which features misfortune alongside erotic pleasure, but it cannot, on the basis of this episode, be taken as a rationalist validation of an ultimate moral purpose. Melliora is pressed to define how love might be united with reason, and describes a set of criteria – 'every circumstance must agree, parity of age, of quality, of fortune, and of humour, consent of friends, and equal affection in each other' – almost the reverse of her relationship to the Count, as he quickly points out. He rejects her injunction to 'think', and instead conveys his physical sufferings until she is unable to suppress her own bodily response: 'She heard his sighs, she felt his tremblings as he held her, and could not refrain shedding some tears, both for him and for her self, who indeed suffered little less.'[41] The outcome here and in the novel as a whole demonstrates the falsity of any notion that love can be regulated by rules of agreement or 'parity'. The truth of the passion of love lies in its excess, inimical to reason or even justice; for since love, even of the most illicit kind, is 'involuntary', it must be condoned. The argument is precisely analogous to Mandeville's amoral justifications of the acquisitive passions associated with luxury, which he claims are similarly implanted by nature. The difference between Haywood and Mandeville is that she is prepared to explore unblinkingly the disastrous results likely to ensue from an irrational pursuit of passion, while he clings to the fantasy of a higher, intelligible order arising from apparent anarchy.

The narrative voice in *Love in Excess* affirms love as a sovereign force again and again. It is described as the experience of the sublime, inexpressible and unrepresentable.[42] The susceptible reader is invited to identify with the elite band of true lovers and allow herself to be drawn into complicity with this valorization of ecstatic passion. The critic asks, to what end? Recently William Warner has suggested that Haywood teaches the individualist hedonism required by a burgeoning consumer culture.[43] Paula Backscheider has proposed that Haywood's works initiate women into the terms of their socialization by familiarizing them with 'use value, exchange value, and even cultural-commodity value'.[44] There is no doubt that her narratives exhibit the parallelism of amorous and acquisitive passions; and yet the elevated rhetoric of love that Haywood employs, the insistence on disinterestedness and unworldliness, must not be overlooked. The most curious and elusive strand in *Love in Excess*, not found in libertine representations, is the insistence on the heroism of love, defiant both of conventional calculations of right and wrong and prudential self-interest. This is the element that speaks to the 'psychic crisis' of an economic system gone mad.

In Haywood, the love story becomes a means of exploring the trauma of modern economic experience; the rhetoric of love, in all its rich variety, is brought to bear on problems of credit and loss. It may be possible to argue that she and other women writers form an avant-garde in this development; Defoe's *Moll Flanders* and *Roxana* are related to the phenomenon, but they lack the pathos of interiority found in Haywood. What is essential is that female experience should be at the heart of it.[45] In love, women are the paradigmatic gamblers, the investors liable to total bankruptcy. Men stand in for the dangerous opacity of the fluctuating market.

We have heard much of *homo economicus*, the exemplar of rational calculation, generally traced down to 1719 and the publication of *Robinson Crusoe*.[46] In the same year *Love in Excess* gives rise to his antithesis, a *femina economica*, manifesting the anti-economic principles of excess and waste. She demonstrates the value placed on love as a sacrifice which only a woman can perform to the full since only she can lose everything. The sacrificial function of the 'female ecstatic', a topic of interest within psychoanalysis, surrealism, and the work of Bataille,[47] is already identified by Haywood in her *Reflections on the Various Effects of Love* (1726):

> A Woman, where she loves, *has no Reserve*; she profusely gives her all, has not Regard to any thing, but obliging the Person she affects, and *lavishes her whole Soul*. – But Man, more wisely, keeps a Part of his for other Views, he has still an Eye to Interest and Ambition! As a certain Lady, who, 'tis to be suppos'd, has experience'd what she writes, somewhere affirms:
>> Women no Bounds can to their Passion set;
>> Love and Discretion in our Sex ne'er met.
>> Men may a cold Indifference, Prudence call,
>> But we to Madness doat, or not at all.[48]

She goes on to note that certain individuals may show characteristics of the opposite sex, 'but when any Instances of this kind happen, the Sexes seem to have exchang'd Natures, and both to be the Contradiction of themselves'. This last point is important for an understanding of the characterization of the Count d'Elmont and the young Frankville, Melliora's brother, in particular. Devotion to love has feminized them;

they lose all worldly ambition and live only for passion. Essentially, D'Elmont becomes a woman; perhaps at that moment when, after one of many failed attempts to force Melliora sexually, his soul mingles with hers in the ether while their bodies remain motionless below.[49]

Ultimately, Haywood does not sacrifice Melliora and the Count, but in the final pages the focus of the novel shifts to the scapegoat figure of Violetta and her pitiable death. Having accompanied D'Elmont, whom she loves, in time-honoured fashion in the garb of a male servant and been disappointed by his reunion with the lost Melliora, she expires with the other true lovers gathered round to witness her parting desire, addressed to the Count: 'forgive me heaven if it be a sin, I could wish, methinks, to know no other paradise than you, to be permitted to hover round you, to form your dreams, to sit upon your lip all day, to mingle with your breath, and glide in unfelt air into your bosom'.[50] The blasphemous eroticism of this proposition precisely indicates the kinship of luxury with death and dissolution.

4 Conclusion

At the end of this brief speculative sortie into uncharted territory, it would be a mistake to risk generalizations about the role of women writers in the luxury debate. I have identified, in the work of Mary Astell and of Eliza Haywood, two extensions to the field of the debate as it is currently described: respectively, a counter-economic discourse employing metaphors of value, profit and loss in anti-materialist contexts that establish a rivalry with the new utilitarian justification of luxury; and an anti-economic discourse that privileges loss over profit and detaches the passions from utility, redefining desire as a form of self-destructive idealism. How widespread such arguments were, and how specific to women writers, can only be determined by further research.

Even the most superficial review would establish that there is no unified 'women's position' on luxury. Women writers were divided by political affiliations, religious belief, status, location, and other accidents of birth and upbringing. On the other hand, if the evidence of Astell and Haywood is anything to go by, in their most original work, they seem to respond to the particularity of the connection between luxury and women or the 'feminine'. Giving the lie to claims made by recent intellectual historians, these authors maintain the Christian conception of Eve's guilt as a point of reference (though without endorsing it) well into the eighteenth century. As one might expect, they also show a heightened sensitivity to the way in which categories of gender operate within the discourse on luxury, testing out alternatives to the standard division between manly virtue and vicious effeminacy.

Those familiar with the Patriot attacks on Walpole in the 1730s, denouncing his encouragement of the socially corrupting monied interest to the detriment of landed property, may have been surprised by the lack of attention given here to female political writers who sought to intervene. This is an important area, but with regard to women's involvement in the luxury debate I would suggest that it represents something of an impasse, with a high proportion of imitative writing and other complicating factors. Mary Wortley Montagu, for instance, offers the interesting case of a woman whose family and social connections placed her in alliance with the court Whigs, while her intellectual formation directed her sympathies towards the ideal of republican virtue trumpeted by the Patriot opposition. Her anonymously produced political journal, *The Nonsense of Commonsense* (1737–38), the first ever authored by a woman, was directed against Bolingbroke's periodical *Commonsense*, but attempted to outdo him in civic humanist sentiment even while defending Walpole's policies. Numbers 2 and 9 both contain negative remarks on luxury. Eliza Haywood's political allegories, positioned in the opposition camp, contain passages that might have been written by Bolingbroke himself. *Adventures of Eovaai, Princess of Ijaveo. A Pre-Adamitical History* (1736) includes the figure of a republican rhetorician who expounds his views at length. However as Ros Ballaster has argued, this platform given to the arguments of the landed interest, including reflex anti-luxury polemic, is framed and distanced by the complexities of a narrative in which various forms of government are viewed and found wanting by the embattled princess.[51] In both cases, then, the woman writer seems to modify with caveats her apparent position. Elizabeth Montagu, aged 21, pinpoints the ambivalent relationship of women to the republican tradition in a letter to her friend and mentor, the Duchess of Portland, in 1741: 'Is it not a sad thing to be brought up in the patriot din of liberty and property, and to be allowed neither?'[52]

The implications of the most innovative women's writing on luxury are not restricted to the quarrels of the early Georgian governing class. As I have attempted to show, writings by Astell and Haywood throw into question, in their different ways, the teleological model of a gradual demoralization of luxury and acceptance of its socio-economic utility in a way that chimes with present-day critiques of economic discourse. In the light of our own, quite probably terminal, crisis of excessive consumption, attempts by historians of the eighteenth century to draw a line between 'new' luxury (stable, sustainable, enlightened, progressive) and 'old' luxury (excessive, corrupting, self-destructive) must appear misguided. To uncover the heterodox opinions of women of the past is to give historical weight to dissenting voices in the present.

Notes

1. John Sekora, *Luxury: The Concept in Western Thought, Eden to Smollett* (Baltimore: Johns Hopkins University Press, 1977), p. 66; Paul Langford, *A Polite and Commercial People: England 1727–1783* (Oxford: Oxford University Press, 1998), pp. 3–4.

2. See notably his 'Remark (L)', appended to the poem 'The Grumbling Hive', *The Fable of the Bees*, ed. by F.B. Kaye, 2 vols (1924; Indianapolis, Liberty Fund, 1988), I, 107–23.

3. Christopher Berry, *The Idea of Luxury: A Conceptual and Historical Investigation* (Cambridge: Cambridge University Press, 1994), p. 98. See for instance Elizabeth Eger, 'Luxury, Industry and Charity: Bluestocking Culture Displayed', in *Luxury in the Eighteenth Century*, ed. by Maxine Berg and Elizabeth Eger (Basingstoke: Palgrave, 2002), pp. 190–204.

4. Sekora, *Luxury*, p. 47; Berry, *The Idea of Luxury*, p. 98. J.G.A. Pocock in *Virtue, Commerce, and History* remarks that 'effeminate' is 'a term whose recurrence ought not to be neglected', though he too declines to investigate it as a central category (Cambridge: Cambridge University Press, 1985), p. 114.

5. P.G. Marshall, *The Financial Revolution in England: A Study in the Development of Public Credit 1688–1756* (London: Macmillan and New York: St Martin's Press, 1967); John Brewer, *The Sinews of Power: War, Money and the English State, 1688–1783* (New York: Alfred A. Knopf, 1993).

6. See Isaac Kramnick, *Bolingbroke and His Circle: The Politics of Nostalgia in the Age of Walpole* (1968; Ithaca: Cornell University Press, 1992); J.G.A. Pocock, *The Machiavellian Moment: Florentine Political Thought and the Atlantic Republican Tradition* (Princeton: Princeton University Press, 1975), pp. 423–506; J.G.A. Pocock, *Virtue, Commerce and History*, pp. 91–124.

7. This is not to say that the use of the model is crude or unreflective. Berry discusses the question of presentism, *The Idea of Luxury*, 101–2; and Berg and Eger refer to the process of gradual de-moralization as 'dialectical', *Luxury in the Eighteenth Century*, p. 7.

8. John Carswell, *The South Sea Bubble* (London: Cresset Press, 1960), pp. 10–11; Catherine Ingrassia, *Authorship, Commerce and Gender in Early Eighteenth-Century England: A Culture of Paper Credit* (Cambridge: Cambridge University Press, 1998), pp. 30–1.

9. Letter 26 March 1720 reproduced in Ruth Perry, *The Celebrated Mary Astell: An Early English Feminist* (Chicago and London: University of Chicago Press, 1986), p. 391.

10. *Eighteenth-Century Women Poets*, ed. by Roger Lonsdale (Oxford and New York, Oxford University Press, 1990), p. 26.

11. Catherine Gallagher, *Nobody's Story: The Vanishing Acts of Women Writers in the Literary Marketplace, 1670–1820* (Berkeley and Los Angeles, University of

California Press, 1994). Another useful account of the relationship of early fiction to the credit economy is Sandra Sherman, *Finance and Fictionality in the Early Eighteenth Century: Accounting for Defoe* (Cambridge: Cambridge University Press, 1996), esp. Chapter 1, which includes discussion of gender in the discourse of credit, pp. 14–54.

12. Gallagher, *Nobody's Story*, p. xiv; Ingrassia, *Authorship, Commerce and Gender*, p. 12.
13. Pocock, *Virtue, Commerce, and History*, p. 114.
14. Laura Brown, *The Ends of Empire: Women and Ideology in Early Eighteenth-Century English Literature* (Ithaca, New York: Cornell University Press, 1993) and E.J. Clery, *The Feminization Debate in Eighteenth-Century England: Literature, Commerce and Luxury* (Basingstoke: Palgrave, 2004).
15. Berry, *The Idea of Luxury*, pp. 102–25; J.A.W. Gunn, *Beyond Liberty and Property: The Process of Self-Recognition in Eighteenth-Century Political Thought* (Kingston and Montreal: McGill-Queen's University Press, 1983), p. 112.
16. Sir Dudley North, *Discourses upon Trade* (London, 1691), p. 27. See Jan de Vries's comment on this passage that it exhibits 'the new understanding, based on experience rather than theory, that consumer aspirations – the desire for luxury – formed a powerful wellspring of economic improvement. In fact, it led to what we would come to call economic development'; 'Luxury in the Dutch Golden Age in Theory and Practice', in *Luxury in the Eighteenth Century*, ed. by Berg and Eger, p. 44.
17. Mary Astell, *A Serious Proposal to the Ladies*, ed. by Patricia Springborg (Peterborough, Ontario: Broadview, 2002), p. 51.
18. Ibid., pp. 106–7.
19. Ibid., p. 52.
20. Ibid., pp. 57, 56, 57–8. The anecdote that the Emperor Domitian habitually passed his time catching and killing flies is taken from the Roman biographer Suetonius.
21. Catherine Gallagher, 'Embracing the Absolute: The Politics of the Female Subject in Seventeenth-Century England', *Genders*, 1 (Spring 1988), 24–39.
22. Astell, *A Serious Proposal*, p. 86; and compare p. 66, where Astell interestingly compares the pursuit of the pleasures of this world to investment in a leasehold property.
23. Astell, *A Serious Proposal*, pp. 97, 62; and see William Kolbrener, 'Astell's "Design of Friendship" in *Letters* and *A Serious Proposal, Part I*', in *Mary Astell: Reason, Gender, Faith*, ed. by William Kolbrener and Michael Michelson (Aldershot: Ashgate, 2007), pp. 49–64 (p. 62). It would be worth comparing the use of a new-Platonic idiom in the poetry of Astell's contemporary, Elizabeth Singer (later Rowe); for a discussion of her involvement in debate about modernity, see Clery, *Feminization Debate*, chapter 2.
24. See for instance Astell, *A Serious Proposal*, pp. 74, 92–3, 97–8.
25. Ibid., p. 53.
26. Ibid., pp. 50, 101 and see pp. 101–2. In this, Astell is to be differentiated from Judith Drake in *An Essay in Defence of the Female Sex* (1796), whose central aim is to demonstrate the value of female conversation *as it already exists*.
27. Astell, *A Serious Proposal*, p. 76. The idea of a Protestant nunnery is taken up by Defoe in *Essay on Projects* (1697) and by Richardson in *The History of Sir Charles Grandison* (1754).

28. In *Reflections upon Marriage* (1700), too, the dangers of luxury to women and the continuing inseparability of the question of luxury from gender and sexuality remained central issues.

29. There is evidence that the Preface was admired by contemporaries but it has received little recent comment. Mark Goldie misreads the neo-Machiavellian rhetoric, taken from Davenant, as her own; 'Mary Astell and John Locke', in *Mary Astell*, ed. by Kolbrener and Michelson, pp. 65–85 (p. 77).

30. Perry, *The Celebrated Mary Astell*, p. 227.

31. Epigraph to Volume II of Eliza Haywood, *Love in Excess*, ed. by David Oakleaf (Peterborough, Ontario: Broadview, 2000), p. 81.

32. James Sterling, 'To Mrs. Eliza Haywood on Her Writings' (1732), included in the appendix of Eliza Haywood, *Love in Excess*, p. 278.

33. See for instance Werner Sombart, *Luxury and Capitalism* (1913; New York: Ann Arbor, 1967) and Colin Campbell, *The Romantic Ethic and the Spirit of Modern Consumerism* (Oxford: Basil Blackwell, 1987).

34. 'To Mrs. Eliza Haywood, on Her Novel, called The Rash Resolve' (1724) and 'The Authors of the Town; A Satire' (1725), both by Richard Savage; Appendix of Haywood, *Love in Excess*, p. 272; see also, in the same volume, 'By an Unknown Hand, To the most Ingenious Mrs. Haywood, on her Novel, Entitled, *Love in Excess*', p. 83.

35. Nicholas Barbon, *Discourse of Trade* (London, 1690), p. 14.

36. Pocock, *Virtue, Commerce, and History*, pp. 113, 112.

37. See Patrick Spedding, *A Bibliography of Eliza Haywood* (London: Pickering and Chatto, 2004), p. 89.

38. Georges Bataille, *La Part maudite* (1967), cited in Jean-Joseph Goux, 'General Economics and Postmodern Capitalism', in *Bataille: A Critical Reader*, ed. by Fred Botting and Scott Wilson (Oxford: Blackwell, 1998), p. 197; compare H. Robert Hurley's translation, *The Accursed Share*, vol. I, *Consumption* (New York: Zone Books, 1988), p. 106.

39. *Spectator* no. 55, Thursday 3 May 1711, in *The Spectator*, ed. by Donald F. Bond, 5 vols (Oxford: Clarendon Press, 1965), I, 232–6, (p. 236).

40. Haywood, *Love in Excess*, p. 165.

41. Ibid., pp. 108, 109, 112.

42. Ibid., pp. 121–2.

43. William B. Warner, 'Formulating Fiction for the General Reader: Manley's *New Atalantis* and Eliza Haywood's *Love in Excess*', in his *Licensing Entertainment: The Elevation of Novel Reading in Britain, 1684–1750* (Berkeley and Los Angeles: University of California Press, 1998), chapter 3, esp. pp. 111–27.

44. Paula R. Backscheider, Introduction, *Selected Fiction and Drama of Eliza Haywood* (New York and Oxford: Oxford University Press, 1999), p. xxxii.

45. See, among many similar sentiments, the epigraph for Haywood's *The Rash Resolve* (1724) taken from Congreve: 'Woman is soft, and of a tender Heart, / Apt to receive, and to retain Love's Dart: / Man has a Breast robust, and more secure; / It wounds him not so deep, nor hits so sure'.

46. Ian Watt, 'Robinson Crusoe as Myth', *Robinson Crusoe*, Norton Critical Edition (New York: Norton, 1975), pp. 311–31.

47. See the Introduction to *The Bataille Reader*, ed. by Fred Botting and George Scott (Oxford: Wiley-Blackwell, 1997), pp. 12–13.

48. *Reflections on the Various Effects of Love*, in *Fantomina and Other Works*, ed. by Alexander Pettit, Margaret Case Croskery, and Anna C. Patchias (Peterborough, Ontario: Broadview, 2004), p. 115. The poem has no attribution, and is probably by Eliza Haywood.
49. Haywood, *Love in Excess*, p. 124. A number of critics have noted the way in which female characters are masculinized in the novel, see Juliette Merritt, *Beyond Spectacle: Eliza Haywood's Female Spectators* (Toronto: University of Toronto Press, 2004), chapter 2, pp. 25–44.
50. Haywood, *Love in Excess*, pp. 265–6.
51. Ros Ballaster, 'A Gender of Opposition: Eliza Haywood's Scandal Fiction', in *The Passionate Fictions of Eliza Haywood: Essays on Her Life and Work*, ed. by Kirsten Saxton and Rebecca Bocchicchio (Lexington, Kentucky: University of Kentucky Press, 2000), pp. 143–67.
52. Elizabeth Montagu, *The Letters of Elizabeth Montagu, with Some of the Letters of Her Correspondents*, ed. Matthew Montagu, 4 vols (London, 1809–13), I, 241. For an interesting discussion of Montagu's revisionist creation of a civic identity on the classical model, see Tania Smith, 'Elizabeth Montagu's Study of Cicero's Life: The Formation of an Eighteenth-Century Woman's Rhetorical Identity', *Rhetorica*, 26.2 (Spring 2008), 165–87.

3
The Country and the City

Christine Gerrard

Throughout the period 1690–1750 women poets wrote far more extensively about the country than they did about the city. Despite the rapid expansion of London during this period and women writers' increasing exposure to metropolitan opportunities for publication and print markets, no female poet embraced urban life with quite the same excitement or vigour as her male counterparts. Anne Finch's 'Ballad to Mrs Catherine Fleming in London', composed about 1718, recalls Swift's recent 'Description of a City Shower' (1710) and John Gay's *Trivia* (1716) in its vivid rendering of the 'jarring sounds in London streets' replete with street vendors and post bell, 'hurry, smoke, and drums'. Yet the liveliness of the street scene is invoked to supply an unfavourable contrast to the peace and solitude of the countryside, where the only sounds are whistling farmer's boys and distant sheep bells. The aural contrast shades into the moral (no need to lock one's door at night in the country) and then finally into the generic.

> Nor look for sharp satyrick wit,
>   From off the balmy plain:
> The country breeds no thorny bays,
> But mirth and love and honest praise.[1]

Finch associates the metropolis with wit and satire, and the country with affection and praise. She sees satire – what she describes elsewhere as 'clandestine spight' – as an urban form.[2] Its malice and aggression are male. Urban and rural experience are here polarized by gender and genre. As Paula Backscheider notes, the 'gendering of forms was deep in [women poets'] consciousnesses' and few women poets of the seventeenth and eighteenth century risked their reputations by the publication (or even private circulation) of satirical verse.[3] The vast majority of female verse in this period deploys poetic modes and forms characteristically connected to the countryside: the tradition of Horatian retirement verse emerging from royalist poetics of the Civil War, the country-house poem, the pastoral dialogue, the meditative 'night piece'. Such forms suited the themes we often associate with women's verse of the late seventeenth and early eighteenth century – female friendship, seclusion, rural tranquillity, divine contemplation. Yet we should not make the comfortable equation between the feminine and the conservative (either politically or poetically) that such associations seem to invite. Women poets such as Jane Barker, Anne Finch, Elizabeth Tollet, and Elizabeth Rowe, who developed a poetic language of inwardness, meditation, communion with nature, of solitude and sublimity, anticipated the mid-century poetic shift away from the urban wit and satire that had come to characterize the so-called 'Augustan' verse of the century's first four decades. And although many women poets produced conventional and unremarkable pastoral lyrics, the best of them – such as Anne Finch, Mary Leapor, Mary Collyer, Martha Fowke, beyond this period, Ann Yearsley – were extraordinarily alert to the nuances of genres and modes.

1 Pastoral and georgic experiment

In a period already characterized by its generic experimentation and subversion, women poets led the field. John Gay's *Shepherd's Week* (1714) reanimated tired pastoral clichés through its burlesque of the bucolic eclogue, replacing classical nymphs and swains with rude rustics; but the labouring poet Mary Leapor in 'Mira's Picture: A Pastoral' multiplies the ironies and disjunctions by making her own physical awkwardness and literary oddity the central subject as the swains Phillario and Corydon vie with each other to outdo the insults they can heap upon her. Although Swift and Gay had both experimented with the 'urban georgic' or 'town pastoral', it was arguably the sole woman poet associated with the circle, Lady Mary Wortley Montagu, who created the most unsettling tension between generic mode and content. The sophisticated world-weariness which bathes the *Town Eclogues* is utterly different from the freshness and innocence usually associated with pastoral eclogues. Both Montagu and Leapor experimented with the country house poem practised throughout the seventeenth and eighteenth centuries. Montagu mocks the capriciousness and indecision of Ralph Allen, Lord Bathurst, whose ever-changing country estate mirrors his latest whim in garden designer chic. Leapor's 'Crumble Hall', seen from a servant's perspective, takes on odd angles of vision (we first notice cobwebs and cornicing). Its absent master, interrupted vistas, and foregrounding of domestic detail destabilize both the conventional social hierarchy and the unbounded 'prospects' customarily associated with the form. Arguably women poets fail, or perhaps refuse, to 'command' the landscape in the way that male poets do. No female poet prior to Ann Yearsley in *Clifton Hill* (1785) writes a full-scale 'loco-descriptive' or georgic poem on a par with James Thomson's *The Seasons* (1730), John Philip's *Cyder* (1708), Richard Dyer's *The Fleece* (1757), or William Cowper's *The Task* (1785).[4] But some of the tasks of the georgic – a genre which bound together landscape and labour, country and city, in a patriotic vision of national greatness – were accomplished by the new wave of labouring class poets including the kitchen-maid Leapor and the washerwoman Mary Collyer. Leapor and Collyer start to configure the English countryside as a place of female agency and female labour, characterized by economic exchange and working relationships, rather than as an idealized retreat.

Important work by Carol Barash and Kathryn King, among others, has explored the coterie verse of late seventeenth-century royalist women poets such as Jane Barker and Ann Finch.[5] Bound together by a shared experience of exile and changed fortunes following the Glorious Revolution of 1688 which ousted James II from the throne, their poetry appropriated and developed the language of internal retreat, of rural solace, community, and friendship, found in the Cavalier lyrics of royalist poets such as Richard Lovelace and Robert Herrick. Barker, a Catholic born in 1652 to a family loyal to the Stuart cause, finally went into exile with James II's wife Mary of Modena in 1688. Her unpublished poems from the Magdalen College manuscript collection vividly map the horrors of the Cavalier experience of the Civil War onto the landscape. The very title of Barker's 'A Dialogue between Fidelia and her little nephew, Martius, as they walk in Luxembourg, disguised as a sherperdess or Country Maid' pushes the idea of pastoral disguise into more sinister territory than the conventional notion of courtier-turned-shepherd which underpins courtly pastoral. Pastoral disguise is a necessary subterfuge for the royalist on the run. Fidelia explains to her small nephew how her Cavalier family transformed themselves from aristocrats to peasants: they 'manage sheep and cows, / Instead of scarlet, Russet now they wore, / And sheep-hooks were the leading staves they bore'. Yet they find a retreat within the retreat, a 'little kind of Eden', 'well furnish'd with good fruit, fresh herbs, gay flowers, / Fountains and grass-plats'. It is 'free from court factions, and the discontents, / Which dayly rise in

Rebell Parliaments'. The death of Barker's parents and brother turn this Eden into hell; a desolate landscape sharpened by isolation and personal poverty.

> My flocks decay'd, my barns and houses fell,
> My lands grew barran, in fine nought went well,
> Thus helpless, friendless, destitute forlorn,
> 'Twixt debtors, creditors, and lawyers torn.[6]

Anne Finch, Countess of Winchilsea (1661–1720) also participated in what Barash describes as a royalist 'community of women telling stories about shared deprivation and loss'.[7] Like Barker (though an Anglican), Finch served Mary of Modena as a lady-in-waiting and remained loyal to James following the crisis of 1688. Finch and her husband Heneage also went on the run, finding refuge in the houses of various friends. After 1690 Jacobite charges against her husband were dropped and the couple lived a less troubled life in Eastwell Park, Kent, inspiration and setting for her 'Petition for an Absolute Retreat', first published in 1713. This famous poem's opening lines – 'Give me O indulgent Fate! / Give me yet, before I Dye, / A sweet, but absolute Retreat' – place it firmly in the 'happy man' Horatian tradition which shapes the most famous poem of the turn of the century, John Pomfret's *The Choice* (1701).[8] Like Pomfret, Finch requests a modest lifestyle based on 'plain, and wholesome Fare'. Yet this remarkable poem seems to owe less to Pomfret's prudent moderation than to the sensuality and emblematizing of nature's mystic book found in earlier Civil War poets, notably Marvell and Lovelace. Finch's account of the 'Figs (yet growing) candy'd o'er, / By the Sun's attracting Pow'r; / Cherries, with the downy Peach, / All within my easie Reach' (p. 36) echoes the seductions of Andrew Marvell's 'The Garden': 'The nectarine and curious peach, / Into my hands themselves do reach'.[9] Within this Edenic setting, both spiritual and sensual, Finch requests a partner ('since Heaven has shown / It was not Good to be alone', p. 39) who turns out to be another Eve rather than an Adam. The poem pays generous tribute to 'Arminda', Catherine Cavendish, Countess of Thanet, with whom the Finches took shelter soon after the events of 1688. In its interweaving of detailed natural description, biblical and classical reference, contemporary political events and personal tributes, the 'Petition' is at once deeply allusive and highly original. Like its more famous counterpart, the 'Nocturnal Reverie', the poem creates a personal space for meditation and reflection: 'Be no Tidings thither brought, / But Silent, as a

Midnight Thought, / Where the World may ne'er invade' (p. 34). Finch echoes Marvell's retreat into the woodland sanctuary of *Appleton House*, 'where the World no certain shot / Can make, or me it toucheth not'.[10] Yet the distractions that assault the speaker seem domestic and feminized rather than politicized – chitchat and gossip 'Of who's Deceas'd, or who's to wed' (p. 34).

The request of the 'Petition' for a space free from business and bustle, 'silent, as a Midnight Thought', is actualized in Finch's more famous 'Nocturnal Reverie'. The entire poem consists of one strikingly long, sinuous, and flexible sentence punctuated by a repetition of the opening phrase's refrain – 'In such a *Night*' – an echo of the elopement scene in Shakespeare's *Merchant of Venice* (V.i.1–3), 'In such a night as this / when the sweet wind did gently kiss the trees, / And they did make no noise'. Just as Jessica steals away from sleeping Shylock, so the speaker, along with the farmyard animals, finds a 'short-lived Jubilee [...] whilst Tyrant-*Man* do's sleep'.[11] It is possible to make too much of the gender implications of 'Tyrant-*Man*', but the poem emphasizes the empathy between female speaker and beasts of burden allowed to wander freely at night, the 'unmolested Kine' and the partridge calling to her 'straggling Brood' (ll. 34, 36). The poem seems at some level to reflect the frustrations expressed by so much women's writing of the period. Daily chores and 'household cares' do not permit space for creativity and thought. As the poem draws to a climax there is a moment of release when 'silent Musing urge the Mind to seek / Something, too high for Syllables to speak' (ll. 41–2). Yet this moment of almost visionary serenity is, like the animals' jubilee, short-lived. When 'Morning breaks, and All's confus'd again; / Our Cares, our Toils, our Clamours are renew'd, / Or Pleasures, seldom reach'd, again pursu'd' (ll. 49–51). The compliment to Anne Tufton, Countess of Salisbury, is almost casually slipped into the delicately realized nocturnal landscape, each item gradually coming into focus from its surrounding detail, as if thoughts of female friendship naturally unfold from the landscape itself.

> While now a paler Hue the *Foxglove* takes,
> Yet chequers still with Red the dusky brakes:
> When scatter'd *Glow-worms*, but in Twilight fine
> Shew trivial Beauties watch their Hour to shine;
> Whilst *Salisb'ry* stands the Test of every Light,
> In perfect Charms, and perfect Virtue bright.
>
> (ll. 15–20)

William Wordsworth's excision of lines 17–20, which he felt intruded on the natural description, changes the way we read the poem.[12] Finch's solitary musings can give rise to thoughts of female friendship, There is a notable absence of the heavy-handed moralizing that permeates other descriptive night-pieces such as Thomas Parnell's 'A Night-Piece on Death' (1721) and Thomas Gray's *Elegy Written in a Country Church-Yard* (1751).

2 Reading landscapes

A number of shorter pieces in the Wellesley Manuscript Poems show Finch's propensity for reading landscape allegorically and emblematically. The Jacobite-inflected fable, 'Upon an improbable undertaking' describes an oak blown down in a storm, mourned then replaced by a lesser foreign oak without root or branches. If only 'this Timber could maintain / Like what you've lost a stable reign'.[13] Women poets, like their male counterparts, imposed political readings upon the landscape. And yet Finch's landscape poems tend to invert or disrupt rather than reaffirm stable hierarchies of meaning. Whereas John Denham's *Cooper-Hill* (1642), Edmund Waller's *St James Park* (1661), and in turn Alexander Pope's *Windsor-Forest* (1713) drew on georgic and loco-descriptive traditions to celebrate or record significant events and recent traumas in national history through the unifying metaphors of the Thames or Windsor Forest,[14] Finch offers no secure vistas. The opening stanzas of her bold Pindaric ode 'Upon the Hurricane', written shortly after the Great Storm of 1703 wreaked devastation across the south of England, invert the catalogue of trees (pine, oak, beech) which such poems use in a metonymic way to celebrate the future greatness of British naval power. Even the ornamental Pine, 'who thought his Fame shou'd ever last, / When in some Royal ship he stood the planted Mast', is shattered by the winds.[15] The poem's apocalyptic overtones invite larger questions about fate and providence. Despite Finch's sly reference to the death by collapsing chimney stack of Richard Kidder, new Bishop of Bath and Wells, recent replacement for the popular non-juror Bishop Ken, the poem refuses to align 'The Great disposer's Righteous Will' with any political faction: 'Nor WHIG, nor TORY now the rash Contender calls' (ll. 188, 177). The poem draws on a Hobbesian image of nature in turmoil and man in a state of perpetual warfare,

> Free as the Men, who wild Confusion love
> And lawless Liberty approve,
> Their Fellow-Brutes pursue their way,

> To their own Loss, and disadvantage stray,
> As wretched in their Choice, as unadvis'd as They.

(ll. 204–8)

Finch's storm, annihilating Whig–Tory party-political distinctions, finds a humorous echo six years later in Swift's mock-bucolic 'Description of a City Shower', in which, soaked by city rain, 'Triumphant Tories, and desponding Whigs, / Forget their Feuds, and join to save their Wigs'.[16] The studied urbanity of Swift's street scene seems a world away from the violent Hobbesian world of Finch's ode, yet both are products of Queen Anne's England. Swift's poem was the first of many to accommodate urban experience to poetic form in new and sophisticated ways. Jonson's *The Famous Voyage*, a mock-heroic journey through a neo-classical underworld of filthy sewers and rubbish-strewn streets, established the parameters of a genre which re-emerged in Dryden's *Mac Flecknoe* and Pope's *Dunciad*. Swift's 'City Shower' registers a similar disgust in its closing triplet cataloguing the detritus of 'Drown'd Puppies, stinking Sprats, all drench'd in Mud', yet the speakers' deferential and considerate tone accommodates the possibilities of the city as locus of civil discourse, culture, and 'urbanity'.

The expansion of coffee houses and the publication of newspapers such as the *Guardian* and the *Tatler* (in which Swift first printed this poem) promoted a culture of middle-class 'politeness'. But coffee-houses were almost exclusively male, and this gendering of polite urban space made literary coteries meeting in private homes to read, discuss, and socialize also important. The Hill circle of the early 1720s, the best documented of these, was both urban and urbane. It met in Aaron Hill's house in Petty France, Westminster, and in lodgings in the Temple, home of Martha Fowke Sansom, one of the women writers, along with Eliza Haywood, whose talents the circle fostered. The circle's coterie and published writing mediates between town and country. Richard Savage's *Miscellaneous Poems* (1726), a showcase for the group's literary talent, features a number of poems addressing the theme of rural retreat, including John Dyer's experimental Pindaric version of *Grongar-Hill*. Poems by Dyer and Benjamin Victor depict their rural retreat 'completed' by the presence of Clio (Fowke), the object of fascination for many of the male members of the circle. Yet Fowke's 'Invitation to a Country Cottage' in the same volume strikes a different register. This down-to-earth self-portrait of the author at home in her rented Fulham cottage resists romanticization.

> Close to the Fire-side confin'd
> By the cold Fogs, and piercing Wind,
> Bless'd with my Dog, and Peace of Mind.[17]

Her companions are local rustics, valued for their honesty. The speaker enjoys games of cards without green baize tables and card-sharpers, the night's entertainment ending in country ballads which move 'natural Passions' and 'artless tears', rather than false displays of sensibility. 'O! come, my Friend, and see *one* place, / Where all Things wear an honest face'. In her autobiographical *Clio* (written 1723, published 1752), Fowke's cottage contrasts sharply with the sometimes seamy world of lodging houses, predatory men, gossip and scandal which characterizes London life for the literary woman.[18]

Implicit in the 'Invitation to a Country Cottage' is the contrast between urban artifice and country simplicity. Lady Mary Wortley Montagu's *Six Town Eclogues* play on the same antithesis through the ironic application of rural style to town manners. The early history of the poems' publication distinguishes them as a hybrid product of coterie manuscript culture and London print culture.[19] The manuscripts of the first three poems, reputedly written in collaboration with Pope and Gay, were hot property for the notorious publisher Edmund Curll, who pirated and published them in 1716 as 'Court Poems'. In his advertisement Curll stirred up publicity by announcing widespread coffee-house speculation over their authorship and hinting that they dealt with real-life snippets of court gossip (Lady Mary was very intimate with Hanoverian court circles). The six poems in the set, which Lady Mary simply called 'Eclogues', follow the pattern of Gay's burlesque *Shepherd's Week* by deploying Virgil's amoeban singing-contest form between rival nymphs or swains. The themes are not dissimilar – rivalry over love – but the contexts generate multiple ironies. In 'Thursday: Or, The Basset Table', Smilinda and Cardelia gossip over their love-affairs and gamble their equipages, coaches, snuff-boxes, and tooth-pick cases in an orgy of commodity fetishism that makes Pope's Belinda pale by comparison. The comedy arises from the close contiguity of the erotic and the inanimate.

> Then, when he trembles, when his Blushes rise,
> When Awfull Love seems melting in his Eyes!
> With eager Beats, his Mechlin Cravat moves:
> He loves! I whisper to my selfe, He loves![20]

The 'Mechlin Cravat' (a fashionable neck-tie) seems to have developed a love-life of its own. In 'Tuesday: Or, St James's Coffee-House' the smart beau Siliander recalls to Patch the peep-show disclosure of her Grace's breasts as she leans across the chair – 'While the stiff whalebone with the motion rose / And thousand Beauties to my sight expose' (ll. 66–7). The fashionable clothing functions as a metonym for feeling, signifying the emotional vacuity in the fashionable beau-monde which these poems remorselessly expose. Unlike the community of female writers and female friendships celebrated in Finch's work, the *Town Eclogues* expose a world of female rivalry and betrayal driven by economic pressures to marry well and above one's station. Montagu's poems draw on stereotypes of town and country still extant from the plots of Restoration comedy, in which 'country' equates with provincial boorishness and 'town' with the fashionable West End, with its parks, malls, and theatres. In 'Thursday: Or, The Basset-Table', Smilinda's hatred for Ombrelia stems from her creation's betrayal. Ombrelia, up from the country, was 'an aukard Thing when first she came to Town, / Her Shape unfashion'd, and her Face unknown, / She was my Freind' but now 'dares to steal my Fav'rite Lover's Heart' (ll. 60–2, 67). The 'country' figures in these poems only as the entrance or exit point for the stage of fashionable London life. 'Satturday: Or, The Smallpox', a poem often mined for biographical details of Lady Mary's own struggle with the damaging after-effects of smallpox, shows the 'wretched Flavia' longing for a pastoral retreat 'where Gentle streams will weep at my Distress' (l. 90), a world where she will no longer see or be seen, an escape from the remorseless specularity of the London scene.

3 New prospects

During the 1710s the worlds of 'Town' (the fashionable West End) and 'City' (the commercial East End) became inextricably enmeshed in the frenetic financial speculation that precipitated the South Sea Bubble. As Catherine Ingrassia has shown, women were heavily involved in speculative investments that allowed them to circumvent the usual restrictions of land and property ownership, and the unsettling effects of such activity are reflected in the numerous symbolic female representations of credit and unstable wealth, such as Addison's *Spectator* no. 3 (Saturday 3 March 1711), with its allegorical figure of Publick Credit, and James Milner's *Three Letters, Relating to the South Sea Company* (1720) depicting the Lady of the South Sea and the Lady of the Bank.[21] City chocolate-houses designed for female investors were set up. It is hard to find any evidence of women writers (let alone men) valorizing this kind of female enterprise. Anne Finch, Countess of Winchilsea's 'A Song on the South Sea' complains that

> With Jews and Gentiles undismayed
> Young tender virgins mix
> Of wiskers nor of beards afraid,
> Nor all the cozening tricks.[22]

The pious Mary Astell commented dryly of Lady Mary Wortley Montagu, whose speculation with Nicolas-François Rémond's capital caused a near scandal, 'we hear no more of Lady Mary Wortley's Wit, but of her Bargains'.[23]

Lady Mary did not seek solace in the country. Mistrustful of the easy sentimentalizing of country life, she mocks Pope's self-servingly elegiac lines on the two rural lovers struck down by lightning in the fields near Stanton Harcourt. Death may have been a kindness to the 'virtuous' pair:

> For had they seen the next Year's Sun
> A Beaten Wife and Cuckold Swain
> Had jointly curs'd the marriage chain.
> Now they are happy in their Doom
> For P. has wrote upon their Tomb.[24]

There is no extant poem by Lady Mary which treats the English landscape without irony: her best topographical poem comes from Constantinople, whose landscape inspires from her what promises to be an exotic version of Finch's 'Petition for an Absolute Retreat'. 'Give me, Great God (said I) a Little Farm / In summer shady and in Winter warm'.[25] The simplicity of the poem's opening lines gives way to an extraordinarily rich and sophisticated 'prospect' or loco-descriptive poem filled with closely realized natural detail ('the rich Jonquills their golden gleam display', l. 31) and a carefully built up landscape of foreground, middle-distance, and backdrop, 'In Distant views see Asian Mountain rise / And lose their Snowy Summits in the Skies' (ll. 40–1). Despite lingering upon the theme of ruins, Lady Mary is able to celebrate the civic and imperial history of the Ottoman Empire in a manner reminiscent of Pope's *Windsor-Forest*:

> The gilded Navy that adorns the Sea
> The rising City in Confusion fair,

Magnificently form'd irregular,
Where woods and Palaces at once surprise,
Gardens on Gardens, Domes on Domes arise.

(ll. 92–7)

This sense of harmony is entirely absent from her treatment of her friend
Ralph Allen's prospects and vistas in the 'Epistle to Lord Bathurst'.[26] The
poem gently mocks Allen's capriciousness (a stereotypically female characteristic in the verse of Pope and others) by showing the neglect which his
indecision imposes on his country estate. 'With Dirt and Mortar soon you
grow displeas'd , / Planting succeeds, and Avenues are rais'd' 'But scarce
the cold attacks your favorite Trees, / Your inclinations fail, and wishes
please' (ll. 13–14, 20–1). The poem speculates that Allen may be torn
between rural retirement and public duty as an MP in Westminster:

'Tis meanly poor in Solitude to hide,
Tho certain Pain attends the Cares of State,
A Good Man owes his Country to be great.

(ll. 28–30)

Yet Allen's civic ambitions are easily dissipated by the pleasures of the
town, including theatre and mistresses. The poem's humour only just
rescues it from becoming a scathing critique of the ineffectuality of the
English landowning classes.

Socio-economic status and gender are inevitably bound up with the
aesthetics of landscape description, whether in painting or in poetry.
The 'prospect' poem or scene, which incorporates a panoramic view of
the landscape, seems, until at least the end of the eighteenth century, to
be a predominantly male preserve. John Barrell argues that a high viewpoint 'creates a space between landscape and observer' and a generalized
view of the land that reflects a privileged economic bias associated with
the ideology of improvement.[27] For the male poet, the act of behold-
ing confers aesthetic ownership, and landscape poems often explicitly
substitute the satisfaction of looking for the satisfactions of owning,
a connection Addison makes in *Spectator* 411 (Saturday 21 June 1712):
'A Man of Polite Imagination [...] often feels a greater Satisfaction in the
Prospect of Fields and Meadows, than another does in the Possession.
It gives him, indeed, a kind of property in every thing he sees.'[28]
Dyer's *Grongar Hill* substitutes an 'ever-changing' series of vistas of the
'unpossess'd Delights I see' for property ownership.[29] Poetry written from

the perspective of the agricultural labourer often lies close to the ground: the speaker can neither afford nor enjoy such vistas. Ann Yearsley's later *Clifton Hill* undercuts its title's promised prospect by redirecting the gaze downwards to the flora and fauna struggling for survival, like the poet herself, in the harsh hilly landscape. The work of an earlier labouring poet, Mary Leapor, also seems to resist such commanding perspectives. Leapor, who worked as a maid at Edgcote House, the original of Crumble Hall, until a year before her death at twenty-four, solicitously invites the reader on a tour around the house and grounds, but at each turn we encounter an awkward staircase or dead wall.

> Would you go farther? – Stay a little then:
> Back thro' the Passage – down the Steps again;
> Thro' yon dark Room – Be careful how you tread
> Up these steep Stairs – or you may break your Head.
> [...]
> No farther – Yes, a little higher, pray:
> At yon small Door you'll find the Beams of Day,
> While the hot Leads return the scorching Ray.
> Here a gay Prospect meets the ravish'd Eye:
> Meads, Fields, and Groves, in beauteous Order lie.
> From hence the Muse precipitant is hurl'd,
> And drags down *Mira* to the nether World.[30]

The prospect of a prospect is cut short as we are plunged into the kitchen, with its steams, vapours, and toil, the hub and heart of the house's domestic economy. Leapor was commemorating with affectionate irony a way of life that was soon to vanish. Edgcote House, a large medieval house with a rich history, owned successively by Henry V, Thomas Cromwell, and Ann of Cleves, was pulled down two years after Leapor left by an owner bent on modern landscape 'improvements'. *Crumble Hall* reanimates the older tradition of country-house hospitality established in Jonson's *To Penshurst* (1616), which describes a house built not for 'envious show' but for comfort. Just as Penshurst stands at the centre of its rural economy, a microcosm of England in its interdependency of different social classes, so Crumble Hall has welcomed, accommodated, and fed around its enormous tables knights, friars, soldiers, peasants, and paupers alike. Everything within this rambling, Gothic house stuffed with the objects and detritus of centuries of occupation has a place, even the spiders and the sheep-ticks in the old mattresses, part of what David Fairer wittily calls the poem's 'Gothic eco-system'. The house's present owners remain almost invisible. The languid 'Byron', asleep over a pile of unread books, is only glimpsed through the library door, a landowner absent or withdrawn from his traditional roles. But it is difficult to read into this poem a sustained act of class warfare.[31] Leapor's tone is affectionately proprietorial.

The very act of caring for a house confers upon the servant a privileged aesthetic perspective. No one knows a house as well as someone who cleans and polishes it, and the poem beautifully details the fine carving and decoration unnoticed by those who walk by. Similarly rich detail goes into the sensually charged kitchen scenes, ruled over by

> *Sophronia* sage! Whose learned Knuckles know
> To form round Cheese-cakes of the pliant Dough;
> To bruise the Curd, and thro' her Fingers squeeze
> *Ambrosial* Butter with the temper'd Cheese.
>
> (ll. 115–18)

Whereas traditional country house poems tend to obscure or minimize the labour that goes to produce them, Leapor's poem is all about the servants. She even risks a broadly comic treatment (influenced by Gay's *Shepherd's Week*) of the boorish Roger and Urs'la, generic rustics whose love-laments hinge on puddings, peas, and snoring.

Recent critical essays on Leapor have accentuated the near miraculous qualities of 'Mira' (her poetic name for herself): a gardener's daughter with limited education who by her early twenties could write sparkling, funny, stylistically accomplished verse without apparent traces of the class prejudice, frustration, and anger that drove the work of other labouring class women writers such as Collyer and later Yearsley.[32] Richard Greene's early study, drawing on a wider range of Leapor's verse than recent anthologies, reveals her frustration; a frustration directed less at institutionalized domestic labour than at an environment in which her poetic talents had no opportunity to flourish. 'To Lucinda', dated 1746, complains how she spent her childhood helping her gardener father:

> Whilst in laborious Toils I spent my Hours,
> Employ'd to cultivate the springing Flow'rs.
> Happy, I cry'd, are those who Leisure find,
> With Care, like this, to cultivate their Mind.
> [...]
> The Chains of Want forbid my Heart to rise,
> When she would soar to reach her Kindred Skies.[33]

Leapor's subversion of the pastoral lies not (as with Lady Mary) in the application of the eclogue form to urban content, but in the ironic disjunction between her own sophisticated intelligence and pastoral's intellectual vacuity. In 'Mira's Picture: A Pastoral', Leapor comically re-enacts her own experience of being seen as a freak and an oddity by her male and female neighbours. Phillario and Corydon struggle to accommodate 'Mira' within their poetical lexicon.

> PHILLARIO
> But who is she that walks from yonder Hill,
> With studious Brows, and Night-cap Dishabille?
> That looks a Stranger to the Beams of Day,
> And counts her Steps, and mutters all the Way?
>
> CORYDON
> 'Tis *Mira*, Daughter to a Friend of mine;
> 'Tis she that makes your what-d'ye call – your Rhyme.[34]

Phillario's tart response – '*She* read! – She'd better milk her brindled Cows' (l. 53) – is echoed in the chorus of rural female disapproval directed at Mira's poetic activities in ' An Epistle to Artemisia'. Parthenia's snidely bathetic collocation of Muse and shoes – in courting one Mira neglects to polish the other – descends into Sophronia's brutal emphasis on the harsh economic realities facing the aspiring female labourer.

> 'You thoughtless Baggage, when d'ye mind your Work?
> Still o'er a Table leans your bending Neck:
> Your Head will grow prepos'trous, like a Peck.
> Go, ply your Needle: You might earn your Bread;
> Or who must feed you when your Father's dead?'[35]

Mira's resistance to such 'Lectures' stems from her own 'stubborn Will' (l. 148). The line strikingly anticipates Yearsley's later assertion that 'Mine's a stubborn and a savage will'.[36] The 'stubborn will' may be seen as the particular prerogative of the labouring class woman poet, hemmed in on all sides by lack of education, financial pressure to engage in manual labour, patronage by her intellectual and social superiors, and by the demands of female propriety which prioritized domestic duty over writing. The stubborn will of the washerwoman Mary Collyer, writing at almost the same time as Leapor (though published more than a decade earlier) confronted all these obstacles. Indignation at what she considered to be Duck's patronizing treatment of women in his *Thresher's Labour* (1730) spurred Collyer into print with *The Woman's Labour*. Collyer rises above her personal experience of limited educational opportunity and poverty to speak as advocate for women en masse:

> Alas! What can you have
> From her, who ever was, and's still a Slave?
> No Learning ever was bestow'd on me;
> My Life was always spent in Drudgery:
> And not alone; alas! with Grief I find,
> It is the Portion of poor Woman-kind.[37]

The poem's lexis – 'Slavery', 'Custom', 'Tyranny' – recalls the feminist advocacy poems of the turn of the century such as Sarah Fyge Egerton's 'The Liberty' and 'The Emulation' (see Chapter 1 'Woman's Place').[38] Collyer's strong desire to pick a fight with Duck emerges in half-vocalized questions: 'I hope, that since we freely toil and sweat / To earn our Bread, you'll give us Time to eat' (ll. 57–8). Collyer responds in particular to Duck's dilatory treatment of women gleaners in the field, compressed by a georgic simile into flocks of chattering birds irrelevant to the real sweaty man's business of harvesting and threshing, business which Duck heroizes through masculine images of the Cyclops' workshop and Vulcan's forge. Collyer in her turn heroizes the female behind-scenes world of *The Thresher's Labour* – what most women nowadays recognizing as 'juggling' or 'multitasking' – out in the fields cleaning all day, up all night with teething children, yet still greeting their husbands with a clean house and a pot of food on the table when they return home from their own 'work' in the fields. Collyer's world of work has none of the redemptive pleasures of that of either Duck or Leapor. Whereas Crumble Hall's domestic tasks still seem part of the organic domestic economy of the 'big house', here they are paid for at an hourly rate by a 'Mistress' for whom the labouring women have no affection or respect. While Leapor's Sophronia scours her pewter with pride, Collyer's working women do so grudgingly. In this poem there is real class resentment. The demand for washerwomen is driven by the high-end market for luxury goods which need careful cleaning. The consequence of 'Cambricks and Muslins, which our Ladies wear, / Laces and Edgings, costly, fine and rare, / With Holland Shirts, Ruffles and Fringes too' is cracked hands from which the 'Blood runs trickling down' (ll. 159–61, 185).

And after all our Toil and Labour past,
Six-pence or Eight-Pence pays us off at last;
For all our Pains, no Prospect can we see
Attend us, but *Old Age*, and *Poverty.*

(ll. 198–201)

Collyer's depiction of the worker as wage-slave seems prescient of the kind of social indignation that came to be associated far more with the urban than with the rural. Her concluding simile is a half-hearted gesture towards the Virgilian georgic with an ironic twist:

So the industrious Bees do hourly strive
To bring their Loads of Honey to the Hive;
Their sordid Owners always reap the Gains,
And poorly recompense their Toil and Pains.

(ll. 243–6)

The georgic was 'the' dynamic genre of the eighteenth-century, encouraging poets to act productively with the contemporary British landscape, to combine work, trade, patriotism, national concern, continuity, and innovation.[39] But whereas a poet such as John Dyer in *The Fleece* might see economic exchange between workers and masters as part of a greater system of national good, Collyer can only see exploitation. Despite the fact that women poets of this period, as this chapter has shown, wrote extensively about both country and city, none of them before the end of the eighteenth century successfully attempted the one form – the georgic – which blended commercial enterprise, labour, and landscape. That they did not do so hints less at a lack of concern for such themes than a lack of confidence in handling them.[40]

Notes

1. *The Anne Finch Wellesley Manuscript Poems*, ed. by Barbara McGovern and Charles H. Hinnant (Athens and London: University of Georgia Press, 1998), pp. 56–9.
2. 'On my being charged with writing a lampoon at Tunbridge', l. 49, *Wellesley Manuscript Poems*, p. 76.
3. Paula Backscheider, *Eighteenth-Century Women Poets and their Poetry: Inventing Agency, Inventing Genre* (Baltimore: Johns Hopkins University Press, 2005), p. 388. A notable exception is Lady Mary Wortley Montagu, discussed below.

4. Ann Yearsley, *Clifton Hill*, in *Poems on Several Occasions* (London, 1785), pp. 127–47; James Thomson, *The Seasons* (London, 1730); John Philips, *Cyder* (London, 1708); Richard Dyer, *The Fleece* (London, 1757); William Cowper, *The Task* (1785).

5. Carol Barash, *English Women's Poetry, 1649–1714: Politics, Community, and Linguistic Authority* (Oxford: Clarendon Press, 1997); Kathryn R. King, *Jane Barker, Exile: A Literary Career, 1675–1725* (Oxford: Oxford University Press, 2000).

6. Magdalen College MS 343, II, 25–27v.

7. Barash, *English Women's Poetry*, p. 208.

8. Anne Finch, Countess of Winchilsea, 'Petition for an Absolute Retreat', in *Miscellany Poems, on Several Occasions* (London, 1713), p. 35; John Pomfret, *The Choice* (Edinburgh, 1701). All cited poems are referenced in full at first mention and thereafter referenced parenthetically in the text.

9. Andrew Marvell, 'The Garden', in *The Poems of Andrew Marvell*, ed. by Nigel Smith, Longman Annotated English Poets (Harlow: Pearson Education, 2003), pp. 152–9.

10. Andrew Marvell, *Upon Appleton House*, in *Poems*, ed. by Smith, p. 235 (ll. 605–6).

11. 'A Nocturnal Reverie', in *Eighteenth-Century Poetry: An Annotated Anthology*, ed. by David Fairer and Christine Gerrard, 2nd edn (Oxford: Blackwell, 2004), pp. 34–5.

12. Wordsworth included seventeen of Finch's poems in a private manuscript anthology he compiled for Lady Mary Lowther in 1819. *Poems and Extracts Chosen by William Wordsworth for an Album presented to Lady Mary Lowther, Christmas 1819*, ed. by Harold Littledale (London: H. Frowde, 1905).

13. *Wellesley Manuscript Poems*, pp. 45–6.

14. John Denham, *Coopers-Hill* (London, 1642); Edmund Waller, *St. James Park* (London, 1666); Alexander Pope, *Windsor-Forest* (1713) in vol. I of *The Twickenham Edition of the Poems of Alexander Pope*, ed. by E. Audra and Aubrey Williams (London: Methuen, 1961).

15. 'Upon the Hurricane', in *Eighteenth-Century Poetry*, ed. by Fairer and Gerrard, pp. 27–33 (ll. 25–6).

16. Jonathan Swift, 'Description of a City Shower', in *Eighteenth-Century Poetry*, ed. by Fairer and Gerrard, p. 76.

17. Martha Fowke, 'Invitation to a Country Cottage', in *Eighteenth-Century Poetry*, ed. by Fairer and Gerrard, pp. 206–7.

18. Martha Fowke [Sansom], *Clio: the Autobiography of Martha Fowke Sansom, 1687–1736*, ed. by Phyllis J. Guskin (London: Associated University Presses, 1997).

19. See especially David Fairer, *English Poetry of the Eighteenth-Century 1700–1789* (London: Longman, 2003), pp. 12–14.

20. Lady Mary Wortley Montagu, *Essays and Poems and 'Simplicity', a Comedy*, ed. by Robert Halsband and Isobel Grundy (Oxford: Clarendon Press, 1977), p. 197 (ll. 90–3).

21. *The Spectator*, ed. by Donald F. Bond, 5 vols (Oxford: Clarendon Press, 1965), I, 14–17 (p. 15). James Milner, *Three Letters, Relating to the South Sea Company and the Bank* (London, 1720), pp. 5–6. See also Catherine Ingrassia, *Authorship, Commerce, and Gender in Early Eighteenth-Century*

England: A Culture of Paper Credit (Cambridge: Cambridge University Press), pp. 22–39.

22. Anne Finch 'A Song on the South Sea' (composed 1720, pub.1724), in *Eighteenth-Century Women Poets: An Oxford Anthology*, ed. by Roger Lonsdale (Oxford: Oxford University Press, 1989), p. 26.

23. See Isobel Grundy, *Lady Mary Wortley Montagu: Comet of the Enlightenment* (Oxford: Oxford University Press, 1997) pp. 203–8 (p. 206).

24. Montagu, 'Epitaph', *Essays and Poems*, p. 216.

25. Montagu, 'Constantinople, To—', *Essays and Poems*, p. 206 (ll. 1–2).

26. Montagu, 'Epistle to Lord Bathurst', *Essays and Poems*, pp. 242–4.

27. John Barrell, *The Idea of Landscape and the Sense of Place 1730–1840* (Cambridge: Cambridge University Press, 1972), p. 21.

28. *Spectator*, I, 538.

29. Richard Savage, 'Grongar Hill', in *Miscellaneous Poems and Translations* (London, 1726), pp. 60–6 (ll. 91–2).

30. Mary Leapor, *Crumble Hall*, in *Eighteenth-Century Poetry*, ed. by Fairer and Gerrard, pp.322–6 (ll. 94–7, 102–8).

31. Fairer, *English Poetry*, p. 196; and see, for example, Donna Landry, *The Muses of Resistance: Laboring-Class Women's Poetry in Britain, 1739–1796* (Cambridge: Cambridge University Press, 1990), p. 190.

32. See David Fairer, 'Mary Leapor: *Crumble Hall*', in *A Companion to Eighteenth-Century Poetry*, ed. by Christine Gerrard (Oxford: Blackwell, 2006), pp. 223–36.

33. *The Works of Mary Leapor*, ed. Richard Greene and Ann Messenger (Oxford: Clarendon Press, 2003), p. 182.

34. Mary Leapor, 'Mira's Picture: A Pastoral', in *Eighteenth-Century Poetry*, ed. by Fairer and Gerrard, pp. 327–8 (ll. 29–34).

35. Mary Leapor, 'An Epistle to Artemisia', in *Eighteenth-Century Poetry*, ed. by Fairer and Gerrard, pp. 317–22 (ll. 154–8).

36. Anne Yearsley, *Poems on Several Occasions* (London, 1785), p. 72.

37. Mary Collyer, *The Woman's Labour*, in *Eighteenth-Century Poetry*, ed. by Fairer and Gerrard, pp. 268–73 (ll. 5–10).

38. Sarah Fyge Egerton, *Poems on Several Occasions, together with a pastoral. By Mrs. S. F.* (London, 1703), pp. 19–21 (pp. 108–9).

39. See Karen O'Brien, 'Imperial Georgic, 1660–1789', in *The Country and the City Revisited*, ed. by Gerald McLean, Donna Landry, and Joseph Ward (Cambridge: Cambridge University Press, 1999), pp. 160–79.

40. See Backscheider, *Eighteenth-Century Women Poets*, pp. 257–8, for georgic elements in Tollet's 'To My Brother at St John's College'.

Part II
Transformations

4
The Politics and Aesthetics of Dissent

Sharon Achinstein

In a letter from 1697 or 1698, when Elizabeth Singer reported that a friend of hers was borrowing her copy of the sermons of Stephen Charnock, she lamented, "'Tis pity, when there's so much divinity in the world, people should be forc'd to read *Ludlow's Memoirs* on Sundays."[1] To contrast the writings of Charnock, a Presbyterian nonconformist minister, with the *Memoirs of Edmund Ludlow* (1698), the radical republican, is to struggle with the two-faced legacy of revolutionary Puritanism.

Quietist or rebel? This double inheritance of the radical Civil War and Restoration dissenting past divided Whigs after the deposition of a Catholic monarch, James II, in favour of his Protestant son-in-law William of Orange in 1688, and it was a contest in which dissenting women poets also played a part. Rowe's preference for Charnock over Ludlow represents an ambivalent response to political action in the name of the divine: squarely supportive of a fully-armed William, with a Providential vision of the revolution of 1688, Rowe attempted a balance between conflicting forces: political accommodation, a powerful oppositional tradition, and a spiritual quest. In fact, many dissenting women writers took up an adversarial relationship to worldly politics, preferring to separate public from private and to direct their energies, passion, and literary effort, towards the intimate matters of family and friends, and, most of all, to explore the secret corridors of their spiritual lives. Rowe's writing in the 1690s exemplifies the dilemmas of Dissent; heretofore participants in a minority culture whose main representational mode was as persecuted victims, Rowe now finds herself victorious after 1688.

If the reign of William and Mary gave rise to women writers who engaged in public controversy in matters philosophical and scientific, it was also the era of consolidation of a robust private sphere of religious writing and withdrawal from oppositional activism in poetry, the flowering of religious love in poetry (see Chapter 11). Despite the new denominational divides, in the early eighteenth century women poets of all stripes shared a more general, cross-denominational interest in moral reform and in defending fideism against sceptics and atheists.[2] Indeed, the lines between Dissenters and orthodox were often malleable. The life story of Susanna Annesley Wesley (1669–1742) is a case in point. She came from sterling dissenting stock: her grandfather had sat in the Long Parliament; her father served the Parliamentary army and was Richard Cromwell's chaplain, suffering ejection come the Restoration; and her sister married John Dunton the printer. Susanna broke with her family early on to convert to the Church of England; later, she reverted to nonconformity when she took over the ministry of her local church; there she preached to audiences of near two hundred. Her many children, including John and Charles Wesley, went on to become scions of a new breed of Dissent in their Methodism. After her death, the Dissenters' burial ground, Bunhill Fields, claimed her body.

Who were the Dissenters? This term encompasses low and high, and includes a number of denominations that refused to come into the state church with the Act of Uniformity in 1662, including Baptists, Quakers, Independents, Congregationalists, Presbyterians, what Isabel Rivers has helpfully called a 'Nonconformist spectrum'. The experience of nonconformity also yielded new developments in Protestant theology, particularly in a theology of grace.[3] For many, the experience of persecution had a de-radicalizing effect – this was true in particular of the Quakers; but for others, it helped to consolidate a powerful memory and rallying point for resistance. Nonconformists often retained Calvinist beliefs that encouraged habits of self-scrutiny. That is lucky for us, because self-scrutiny also meant writing, composing spiritual autobiographies, keeping diaries, and writing devotional verse.[4] As Quaker Mary Mollineux (1651–96) has it:

> My Heart is full, and fluent to indite
> My Hand is therefore thus engag'd to write
> Much more than at the first I did intend,
> And yet I scarce can freely make an end.[5]

With a social radicalism that encouraged direct reading of the Bible, Dissenters promoted literacy down the social ladder, and they were at the forefront of the printing revolution.[6]

The coming of the Act of Toleration in 1689 gave Dissenters the right to worship as they pleased, but the social radicalism of their earlier struggles left a powerful legacy. In the early part of the eighteenth century, while they still suffered civil exclusions, Dissenters nonetheless continued to develop theologically, with a large split between those who emphasized rationality – freedom of thought and conscience above all – and those who brought about an evangelical revival and a religion of the heart, what Rivers calls 'affectionate religion',[7] under the leadership of Isaac Watts and Philip Doddridge. Over the course of the eighteenth century, while theologians and ministers may have struggled with the identity of their denominations once the experience of persecution no longer bound them together, numbers of women in dissenting churches were outstripping men. Women dissenting poets reveal these cracks in ecclesiology and politics, social reform, and personal introspection, displaying a heterogeneity of purpose that is truly remarkable. In the early eighteenth century, poets of religious dissent gave voice less to suffering souls than to the expression of personal relationships of friendship, affiliation, and affection.

1 Feminism?

Was Puritanism, and its dissenting legacy, bad for women? After all, it had been a nonconformist minister's admonitory sermon about women's proper role in the home that had sparked the Anglican Mary Lady Chudleigh to produce her feminist tract, *The Ladies Defence: Or, The Bride-Woman's Counsellor Answer'd* (1701). The marriage sermon preached by John Sprint in 1699 may not have been typical of nonconformist attitudes towards women, but it demands explanation why the early defences of women's competence, their rights to education and liberty, all came from Anglican feminist pens (see Chapter 1, 'Woman's Place'). Sprint had lashed out against Eve as the tempter of man. Were dissenting women interested in defending themselves from this charge?

It may, at first, appear they were not. Despite gender equality in salvational matters, the sociology of Dissent tells another story: in their domestic ideology, women and men Dissenters were eager to produce godliness inside the household, and that was seen primarily as a job for women. As Patricia Crawford has explored in detailed analysis of the leading dissenting family of Katharine Henry and her minister husband, Philip, the role of the family increased under the great period of persecution after 1660, when public modes of religion were outlawed.[8] Enlightenment ideals of maternity drew upon the Protestant ideology of women's role within the household as a help-meet to her husband and teacher to her children. This also accompanied the general trend towards the 'feminization of religion'.[9] Further, as Phyllis Mack and others have argued, there was in eighteenth-century British Protestantism the powerful 'figure of the spiritual mother', bound up with a 'general social preoccupation with motherhood and childrearing', as well as the Lockean psychology that emphasized the malleability of children.[10] Cultural and sociological norms among Dissenters tended to privatize women's roles.

This absence of feminist theorizing may make it hard to appreciate the important feminist practices undertaken by dissenting women. In literary circles, there were Dissenters, who both in manuscript and in print circulated their writings among nonconformist coteries and beyond: Elizabeth Singer Rowe (1674–1737), Mary Mollineux (1651–96), Jane Lead (1624–1704), Anne Steele (1717–78), and Mary Chandler (1687–1745) all achieved real eminence, though they are still relatively neglected and await scholarly modern editions; their writing was situated in a social context, neither completely public nor personal.[11]

In matters of worship, the case of women's agency is more equivocal. Women did achieve leadership roles in their congregations, particularly among the Quakers, who held separate women's meetings.[12] There were also women who took up leadership roles in Anglican congregations who made themselves into de facto nonconformists: Susanna Wesley's preaching was in her Anglican church, but preaching there made her nonconforming; Jane Lead's Philadelphian Society maintained strong ties with Anglican orthodoxy, though she too was buried in Bunhill Fields. Among nonconformist groups, although women outnumbered men in adherence to Dissent, there was, nonetheless, a diminishment in women's leadership roles in the eighteenth century.[13]

Further, for Dissenters, feminist ideology can be said to clash with theology, where ideologies of (an ungendered) human abasement formed the core of many nonconformist religious commitments. Dissenters' theology often laid great emphasis on the ungendered nature of the soul, and insisted on the spiritual worth of men and women alike, so to argue for women in particular would be antithetical to the otherworldly and immaterial claims of these discourses.[14] As the Quaker writer Anne Docwra (1624–1710) put it, 'This Light, Power and Spirit of the Lord God is tendred to all mankind, as well Women as Men, if they do wait in Faith and Patience to receive it.'[15] Or, according to the Quaker Mary Mollineux's 'Of Vanity':

> Reason, that honours Mankind more than Beast,
> Gives forth its Laws and Dictates in each Breast
> Virtue should therefore in both Sexes dwell.
>
> (p. 79)

Station and marital status may have conferred agency to dissenting women as much as their choice of religion: Mary Chandler was an unmarried, independent businesswoman who ran a milliner's shop in Bath. It was said that a deformity precluded her marriage, but she did receive at least one proposal. Her response was that she had outlived the need for romantic love ('But now quite other things my wish employs / Peace, liberty, and sun, to gild my days'). More to the point, she valued her freedom ('Your great estate would nothing add to me, / But care, and toil, and loss of liberty'):

> Sir, you may hold the string,
> I'd rather walk alone my own slow pace,
> Than drive with six, unless I choose the place.
> Imprisoned in a coach, I should repine:
> The chaise I hire, I drive and call it mine.
> And, when I will, I ramble, or retire
> To my own room, own bed, my garden, fire;
> Take up my book, or trifle with my pen.[16]

The daughter of a dissenting minister, Chandler achieved runaway success with *A Description of Bath* (1733), a long poem in heroic couplets describing the town and its environs. She added her *Poems* for the third edition (1736), and the work reached eight editions by 1767. *A Description of Bath* offers a typically derogatory and self-deprecating comparison of the poet to Pindar, Homer, Virgil, and Horace: 'My feeble Pen but faintly paints my Mind: / Myself unequal to the great Design'.[17] Yet this is an ambitious poem, as her friends recognized, and it sings praises to the architecture and pastimes of Bath, moralizing the health of the waters taken there: 'O! may returning HEALTH more *Wisdom* give, / Let *Death's* Approaches teach us how to *live*' (p. 5). Chandler was a Dissenter, and left unfinished at her death a poem on the 'Being and Attributes of God'.[18] Her published poetry, however, was worldly: neoclassical, written in beating tetrameter couplets, and bearing the influences of Virgil, Horace, and Pope, with allusions to Milton, Denham, Dryden, and Newton. Friendships with Rowe and the Countess of Hertford put her in the Bath circles of dissenting writers.[19] The simple, pure pleasures of countryside retreat are vaunted, and there is a sense of warm friendships and the valuing of small domestic details. Praise for a friend's garden is praise too for 'Hands divine' ('On Mr. B—'s Garden. To Mrs. S—', p. 71). A poem to her friend is appreciative even as it sets out a kind of *ars poetica* for a domestic, feminine art. 'To Miss Moor, On her Fire-Screen' praises her friend's needlework: 'You, my young Fair one, of your own / A new Creation can provide' (p. 68). Self-sufficiency and a robust sense of accomplishment fill her writing, as is seen in Chandler's 'My Own Epitaph': 'Here lies a true Maid, deformed and old; / That she never was handsome, ne'er needed be told', and goes on to express what meant most to her: 'She liv'd in much Peace, but ne'er courted Pleasure; / Her Book, and her Pen, had her Moments of Leisure' (p. 41). Although they did not engage directly in polemic about feminism, dissenting women's writing, then, could argue pretty well for the needs and worth of women.

2 Politics?

The Quaker Mary Southworth Mollineux, who had been given grounding in a classical education by her enlightened father, wrote poetry revolving around the biblical tradition, with adaptations of the stories of notable Israelites, including Elijah and Daniel, and rewritings of Genesis. She took an active role during the period of intense persecution of Dissent, petitioning for her husband's release from prison in 1690. Her *Fruits of Retirement* (1702) went into six editions across the eighteenth century, and the first poem of that collection, 'Of the Fall of Man' (1663), reveals her ambition to tell anew the ancient truths. The posthumous publication of her volume of poetry appeared during the flurry of polemic surrounding the accession of Queen Anne, when the question of toleration for Catholics and Dissenters once again emerged. This was the context for Defoe's pro-Dissenter *The Shortest Way with the Dissenters* (1702) and *More Short-Ways with the Dissenters* (1704), and Astell's anti-Dissenter reply, *A Fair Way with the Dissenters and their Patrons* (1704).[20] Mollineux's fiery voice harkened back to the prophetic tradition of English revolutionary Quakerism, recounting heroic power in 'On Daniel':

> Tho' Great *Goliah* glory in his Spear,
> And monstrous Stature, Little *David* shall,

Without *Saul*'s Armour, make the Giant fall;
And bring Deliverance to *Israel*'s Host,
Tho' the *Philistines* long against them boast:
And tho' worm *Jacob*'s Seed be often prov'd
With Tribulations, he is still belov'd,
And for his sake great Kings shall be reprov'd.
The Lord of Lords will get himself a Name,
He'll overturn, and overturn again,
Until he come, whose right it is, to reign.

(pp.122–3)

Dissenting women redeployed biblical stories in the service of their radical politics, what Paula Backscheider has called 'subversive narrative'.[21] But it was also the case that their poetry could express the voice of political triumph, not of opposition, as found in Elizabeth Singer Rowe's early poetry. Her first publication in *The Athenian Mercury* was an ode to William, 'Upon King William's Passing the Boyne', published in 1691. With praise for the quashing of Tyrconnell and the Jacobites in Ireland, the poem urges further military campaigns, 'On, on, Great William; for no Breast but Thine, / Was ever urg'd with such a Bold Design'.[22] Here, as in many places in Rowe, the language of John Milton's Satan – 'bold design' – is adopted; but here, it is not the voice of the losers. Another early poem, 'A Pindarick Poem on Habbakuk', also vaunts military action:

The *Mountains shook* as our dread Lord advanc'd,
And all the little *Hills* around 'em *danc'd*:
The neighb'ring *Streams* their verdant *Banks* o'reflow,
The *Waters* saw and trembled at the *sight*,
        Back to their *old Abyss* they go,
And bear the News to *everlasting Night*:
The *Mother Deep* within its hollow *Cavern* roars,
        And beats the *silent shores*.

(p. 20)

The poem ends with a cheer to William: 'So now, great God, wrapt in avenging *Thunder*, / Meet Thine and *William's Foes*, and tread them *grov'ling* under' (p. 21). Rather than the abject and melancholy Dissenter, victimized and persecuted, Rowe's biblical catalogues are studded with success stories. The 1696 volume of poetry published under the name *Philomela* is full-throttle anti-Jacobite rhetoric, with a long poem retelling the fall of Phaeton as a thinly-veiled allegory for the fate sure to meet the ambitious Pretender. In 1696 Rowe could be hailed as the Laureate to William by the Athenians, and her anti-Jacobite and militaristic writing was central to that political identity. The dissenting legacy here is the politics of holy war.

Rowe's *History of Joseph* is another rewriting of the Bible for political and personal reform, a major narrative poem, in which she distinguishes her work from those epic predecessors whose theme was war: 'A virgin Muse, a virgin theme requires'.[23] The political meanings of this story are hard to determine, since the actual date of composition of the poem has been debated; it may derive from the 1690s; or it might have been intended as a political allegory of the conflicts between Prince Frederick and his father George, part of a Whig opposition campaign in the 1730s. The work was a publishing success, running to seven editions, including a German translation.[24] Like Milton's *Paradise Lost*, the biblical narrative begins with the Satanic geography. Here the Temple of Molock is a place of 'uninterrupted night' (p. 4):

> In solemn council, and mature debate,
> T'avert the storm impending o'er their state.
> Th'apostate princes with resentment fir'd,
> Anxious, and bent on black designs, conspir'd
> To find out schemes successful to efface
> Great *Heber's* name, and crush the sacred race.
>
> (p. 5)

Rowe has turned the hellish council of the first book of Milton's *Paradise Lost* into an international, and very earthly, plot to overthrow the Israelites/English Protestants; her hero Joseph redeems his nation from destruction. Along the way, there are spicy love intrigues, a retelling of Israelite history from Abrahamic covenant, inset captivity tales, a critique of pagan mythology, and an attack on priestcraft. Her fine poetry captures the grand spaces of heaven, of spiritual longing as well as the sweetness of family reunion. Here is Joseph in the pit, a pastoralizing of a rather uncongenial landscape:

> The night prevails, and draws her sable train,
> With silent pace, along th'etherial plain.
> By fits the dancing stars exert their beams;
> The silver crescent glimmers on the streams;

> The sluggish waters, with a drowzy roar,
> And ling'ring motion, roll along the shore;
> Their murmur answers to the rustling breeze,
> That faintly whispers thro' the nodding trees;
> The peaceful echoes undisturb'd with sound,
> Lay slumbring in the cavern'd hills around;
> Frenzy and faction, love and envy slept;
> A still solemnity all nature kept;
> Devotion only wak'd, and to the skies,
> Directs the pris'ner's pious vows and eyes.
>
> (p. 25)

Set apart, imprisoned, but spiritually awake, Joseph offers the prayer of the devout. This passage carries the legacy of persecuted Dissent, and opens into the pietistic sense of religion as an antidote to faction.

3 Miltonic inheritances

One way of judging the question of dissenting women's gender politics is to explore their responses to Milton's Eve in *Paradise Lost*. Although many late eighteenth-century women writers considered Milton their poetic forebear,[25] attacks or defences of Milton's Eve became stock gestures in early feminism. The Anglican Tory writer Astell had charged Milton with hypocrisy: he had granted freedom to all except to women, who 'himself wou'd cry up Liberty to poor *Female Slaves*'.[26] For women writers, Milton has been called a 'Bogey', that is, an inhibition on women's creativity.[27] However, those attacking his portrayal of Eve in the period between 1688 and 1750 were not, as far as I can see, dissenting women.[28] On the contrary, for dissenting women poets, Milton was a model to emulate, a strong literary forebear, the national poet ranking the moderns equal to the classics.[29] Milton, to be sure, bore heavy ideological weight after the Glorious Revolution. Tonson's 1688 folio edition gave John Milton to a new period in English history, breathing life into the poet's reputation at a moment when the history of radical religion and antimonarchical politics could be braided together for a newly anointed king.[30] *Paradise Lost* set the standard for British poetry, and its visions of the garden as paradise echo throughout eighteenth-century dissenting women's writing.

Jane Lead, the founder of the Philadelphian Society, wrote directly against Milton's *Paradise Lost* in her *Fountain of Gardens* (1696) but she reversed his ending; paradise *can* be regained.[31] Her poem, 'Solomon's Porch', swells with the sense of paradise *now*:

> Ah dear Divine *Urania* now be kind;
> Speak thou, and leave the wretched Man behind.
> THE Glorious Aera *Now, Now, Now* begins.
> *Now, Now* the Great Angelick Trumpet sings:
> And Now in ev'ry Blast,
> Loves *Everlasting Gospel* Rings.[32]

This is true inspiration, not merely the literary kind, but a direct expression of the divine. Lead's kind of writing was that called 'enthusiasm', ever seen as a threat to state order and the unconscious underbelly of rationalist enlightenment.[33] Milton seems Lead's constant companion. She quotes Milton's *Ode on the Morning of Christ's Nativity*, in 'Solomon's Porch', as she transposes its historical past and eschatological future into an immediate present of salvation and mystical communion:

> Now Mighty Bard sing out thy Sonnet free,
> Nor doubt, it true shall be.
> Come Thou and joyn
> Thy loud Prophetick Voice with mine.
> 'Ring out ye Chrystal Sphears,
> 'Now bless our Humane Ears:
> '*For ye have* Power to touch our Senses so:
> 'Now *shall* your Silver Chime
> 'Move in Melodious time;
> 'And the *deep* Base of Heav'ns great *Orb* shall Blow.

Lead takes mastery over Milton, directing him to join *his* voice with *hers*.

Milton's muse, Urania, may have inspired Jane Lead to rewrite his cosmic tragedy, but his Urania served other dissenting women as a figure to approach more tentatively. It was against Milton's epic ambition that the Baptist Anne Steele (1716–78) positioned herself in her 'Ode on a Rural Prospect in June', when she invokes Urania. Her long poem, set out in eleven sections, retreats from Milton's cosmic scope but not from his spiritual investment in the natural world:

> But aim not, my ambitious song,
> To rise with Milton, or with Young,
> To whom Urania brought celestial fire;

A living ray from heavn's immortal choir,
That darted through the solid veil of night:
    Inspiring ray, that bade them soar
    Where morals never rose before,
While nature wonder'd at the daring flight.

    Unequal to so bold a choice,
    A humbler, safer lot be mine!
    Urania, tune my trembling voice
To subjects less exalted, yet divine![34]

Steele, like Lead, seems to have had Milton in her head, his literary style
her model in many poems published in her Bristol 1760 collection,
Miscellaneous Pieces, in Verse and Prose, by Theodosia. Often choosing
unrhymed iambics, in distinction to many women writers of the period,
and in challenge to the smooth couplets of Pope and his literary circle,
Steele experimented with forms ranging from Miltonic blank verse to
ode to other forms of rhyme to hymn meter. She paraphrased psalms;
reflected passionately on faith; commemorated the Fifth of November;
expressed gratitude after recovery from illness; mourned friends and
family; and above all, she longed for God. Her 'Ode to Melancholy'
is followed by an 'Ode to Hope', and there are echoes of Milton's
L'Allegro and *Il Penseroso*, companion poems depicting opposing states
of mind. Steele's hymns are still reprinted in Baptist hymn books, on
both sides of the Atlantic.[35] Her poem on friendship, 'To Amira', opens:
'Friendship disdains the studied forms of speech / She speaks a language forms can never teach' (p. 91), translating the dissenting protest
against set forms of worship into the register of poetry and human
bonds. It is all the more surprising, then, to have her poem, titled 'Filial
Submission' record without irony the contradictory impulses to rise and
to be abased. The poem opens:

    And can my heart aspire so high
        To say, 'My Father God!'
    Lord at my feet I fain would lie,
        And learn to kiss the rod.

(p. 132)

However this kind of submission offers another kind of liberty, that
is, the freedom to resist the claims of familial patriarchy, marriage, or

other embodied relationships. After her fiancé died by drowning, Steele remained unmarried. Her close circle was mostly nonconformist divines, focused on the Bristol Baptist College, and her brother remained central to her writing life. Instead of disappearing into a companionate-or-worse marriage, she was bolstered by the support she solicited from this community, from her female friends who appear in pseudonyms in her writings, and from her God.[36] Her poetry is filled with urgent questioning and daring assertion, protesting against limitations of form, as in her poem, 'The Fetter'd Mind', its four-beat couplets showing an urgency and energy:

> Active, busy, restless mind
> That canst never be confin'd;
> Whither, whither dost thou stray?

> (p. 35)

Elizabeth Singer Rowe was also an avid reader of Milton. In letters to her friends, in her poetic allusions and in her poetic form, Rowe looked to Milton as a model; he was enough of an everyday companion that she cited him to greet the morning, quoted him while moralizing to her sister-in-law, and noted her eagerness for the arrival of Signor Rolli's Italian translation.[37] Rowe's very literary identity was founded upon Milton's; her pen-name, 'Philomela', was chosen after Milton's figure in *Il Penseroso*, and she used it in publications in John Dunton's *Athenian Mercury* in the 1690s as well as in her romantic correspondence with her husband.[38]

For Rowe, however, Milton became the sign of loss, the poet of darkness and of internal states, Milton's Satan rather like the persecuted Dissenter or abject soul. Rowe rewrote Satan's view from hell several times over the course of her long writing life. In her *Select Translations from Tasso*, first published in Tonson's *Miscellanies* in 1704, and then published separately in 1738, Rowe begins at the start of Book 4, another hellish council scene, full of Miltonisms.[39] The sympathy for loss represents Rowe's legacy of melancholic and victimized Dissent. Despite her heroic triumphalism, Rowe's poetic output also reveals the strains in Providential violence. Rowe's 'A Description of Hell. In Imitation of Milton', first published in 1704, begins with strong emotional affect, summoning something of the despair of the poetics of violence:

> Deep, to unfathomable spaces deep,
> Descend the dark, detested paths of hell,

The gulphs of execration and despair,
Of pain, and rage, and pure unmingled woe;
The realms of endless death, and seats of night,
Uninterrupted night, which sees no dawn.

(ll. 1–6)

When women Dissenters turned to biblical history or to Milton, it was to seek a place in a cosmic struggle between good and evil; theirs might evoke the poetics of holy war, but their writing was a quest for conversation – with God, with friends, with themselves. Milton's muse is the inspiring model and his garden the prototype of heaven. The contradictions of living the myth of triumphant Protestantism despite the legacy of persecution are evident in the bounty of loss and yearning that fills this writing, the absences through which Dissenters so clearly mark their desires for union with their God, their difficulties in maintaining a heroic voice.

Notes

1. Elizabeth Singer Rowe, 'Letter IV', n.d. (1697?), *The Miscellaneous Works in Prose and Verse of Mrs. Elizabeth Rowe*, 2 vols (London, 1739), II, 26.
2. See Paula R. Backscheider, *Eighteenth-Century Women Poets and their Poetry* (Baltimore: Johns Hopkins University Press, 2005), chapter 4; and Susan Staves, *A Literary History of Women's Writing in Britain, 1660–1789* (Cambridge: Cambridge University Press, 2006), chapter 2.
3. Isabel Rivers, *Reason, Grace, and Sentiment: A Study of the Language of Religion and Ethics in England, 1660–1780*, 2 vols (Cambridge: Cambridge University Press, 1991), I, 90–5. See also Neil H. Keeble, *The Literary Culture of Nonconformity in Later Seventeenth-Century England* (Athens, GA: University of Georgia Press, 1987); Michael Watts, *The Dissenters: From the Reformation to the French Revolution* (Oxford: Clarendon Press, 1999); and Sharon Achinstein, *Literature and Dissent in Milton's England* (Cambridge: Cambridge University Press, 2003).
4. On women's spiritual autobiography, see Felicity A. Nussbaum, *The Autobiographical Subject: Gender and Ideology in Eighteenth-Century England* (Baltimore: Johns Hopkins University Press, 1989), chapter 4; and for Quaker women in particular, see Margaret Ezell, *Writing Women's Literary History* (Baltimore: Johns Hopkins University Press, 1996), pp. 132–60.
5. Mary Mollineux, 'The First Epistle to Cousin, F. R.', in *Fruits of Retirement* (London, 1702), p. 48. All Mollineux's poems cited below are from this volume and are referenced parenthetically in the text. On Mollineux, see Sharon Achinstein, 'Romance of the Spirit: Female Sexuality and Religious Desire in Early Modern England', *English Literary History*, 69 (2002), 413–38.
6. See Paula McDowell, *The Women of Grub Street: Press, Politics, and Gender in the London Literary Marketplace, 1678–1730* (Oxford: Clarendon Press, 1998), pp. 145–59.

7. Rivers, *Reason, Grace, and Sentiment*, p. 168.
8. See Patricia Crawford, 'Katharine and Philip Henry and their Children: A Case Study in Family Ideology', *Blood, Bodies and Families in Early Modern England* (London: Pearson, 2004), pp. 175–208.
9. Patricia Crawford, 'Anglicans, Catholics and Nonconformists after the Restoration, 1660–1720', in *Women and Religion in Old and New Worlds*, ed. by Susan E. Dinan and Debra Meyers (London: Routledge, 2001), pp. 157–86 (pp. 157, 175).
10. Phyllis Mack, 'Methodism and Motherhood', in *Culture and the Nonconformist Tradition*, ed. by Jane Shaw and Alan Krieder (Cardiff: University of Wales Press, 1999), pp. 26–42 (p. 28). For implications for female authorship, see Sarah Prescott, *Women, Authorship and Literary Culture, 1690–1740* (New York: Palgrave Macmillan, 2003), p. 101.
11. Margaret J.M. Ezell, *Social Authorship and the Advent of Print* (Baltimore: Johns Hopkins University Press, 1999), p. 38.
12. On developments in eighteenth-century Quakerism, see Phyllis Mack, *Visionary Women: Ecstatic Prophecy in Seventeenth-Century England* (Berkeley: University of California Press, 1992), chapter 10.
13. Patricia Crawford, *Women and Religion in England, 1500–1720* (London: Routledge, 1996), p. 189.
14. See Achinstein, 'Romance of the Spirit'.
15. Ann Docwra, *An Epistle of Love and Good Advice* (London, 1683), p. 4.
16. Mary Chandler, 'A True Tale. To Mrs J—s. Written at her Request', in *Eighteenth-Century Women Poets*, ed. by Roger Lonsdale (Oxford: Oxford University Press, 1989), pp. 153–5.
17. Mary Chandler, 'A Description of Bath', in *The Description of Bath. A Poem ... To which are added, Several Poems by the same Author*, 3rd edn (London, 1736), p. 20. All Chandler's poems cited below are from this volume and are referenced parenthetically in the text.
18. Janine Barchas, 'Chandler, Mary (1687–1745)', *Oxford Dictionary of National Biography*, Oxford University Press, 2004 <http://www.oxforddnb.com/view/article/5106> [accessed 16 Sept 2009].
19. The second to seventh editions of Chandler's *Description of Bath* were printed by Samuel Richardson for his brother-in-law, James Leake of Bath. See Oswald Doughty, 'A Bath Poetess of the Eighteenth Century [Mary Chandler]', *Review of English Studies*, 1 (1925), 404–21.
20. Daniel Defoe, *The Shortest Way with the Dissenters* (London, 1704); *More Short-Ways with the Dissenters* (1704); Mary Astell, *A Fair Way with the Dissenters and their Patrons* (1704).
21. Backscheider, *Eighteenth-Century Women Poets*, p. 152.
22. Elizabeth Singer Rowe, *Poems on Several Occasions* (London, 1696), p. 31. Unless otherwise indicated, all Rowe's poems cited below are from this volume and are referenced parenthetically in the text. On Rowe, see *The Early Modern Englishwoman: A Facsimile Library of Essential Works: Vol. 7: Elizabeth Singer [Rowe]*, ed. by Jennifer Richards (Aldershot: Ashgate, 2003); Henry F. Stecher, *Elizabeth Singer Rowe, the Poetess of Frome: A Study in Eighteenth-Century English Pietism* (Bern: Herbert Lang, 1973); and Madeleine Forell Marshall, *The Poetry of Elizabeth Singer Rowe, 1674–1737* (Lewiston, ME: Edwin Mellen Press, 1989).

23. Elizabeth Singer Rowe, *The History of Joseph. A Poem. In Eight Books* (London, 1736), p. 3. In 1737 this was reprinted in ten books.
24. Lori A. Davis Perry, 'The Literary Model for Elizabeth Singer Rowe's *History of Joseph*', *Notes and Queries*, 52.3 (2005), 349–51, sets it in the 1690s; Backscheider, *Eighteenth-Century Women Poets*, p. 152, places it among her 'mature' works.
25. Beth Kowaleski-Wallace, 'Milton's Daughters: The Education of Eighteenth-Century Women Writers', *Feminist Studies*, 12.2 (1986), 275–93 considers the influence of Milton on Elizabeth Carter, Hannah More, Maria Edgworth, and Fanny Burney.
26. Mary Astell, *Reflections upon Marriage*, in *Astell: Political Writings*, ed. by Patricia Springborg (Cambridge: Cambridge University Press, 1996), pp. 46–7.
27. Joseph Wittreich, *Feminist Milton* (Ithaca: Cornell University Press, 1987). The seminal piece is Sandra Gilbert, 'Patriarchal Poetry and Women Readers: Reflections on Milton's Bogey', *PMLA*, 93 (1978), 368–82.
28. On feminist responses to Milton by Chudleigh, Behn, and Astell see Shannon Miller, *Engendering the Fall: John Milton and Seventeenth-Century Writers* (Philadelphia: University of Pennsylvania Press, 2008).
29. In this sense, their responses to Milton were rather like those of men, chronicled by Dustin Griffin, *Regaining Paradise: Milton and the Eighteenth Century* (Cambridge: Cambridge University Press, 1986).
30. Nicholas von Maltzahn, 'The Whig Milton, 1667–1700', in *Milton and Republicanism*, ed. by David Armitage, Armand Himy, and Quentin Skinner (Cambridge: Cambridge University Press, 1995), pp. 229–53.
31. Joseph Wittreich, '"John, John, I blush for thee": Mapping Gender Discourse in *Paradise Lost*', in *Out of Bounds: Male Writers and Gender(ed) Criticism*, ed. by Laura Claridge and Elizabeth Langford (Amherst: University of Massachusetts Press, 1991), pp. 42–3.
32. Jane Lead, 'Solomon's Porch', in *Fountain of Gardens* (London, 1696), n.p.
33. Paula McDowell. 'Enlightenment Enthusiasms and the Spectacular Failure of the Philadelphian Society', *Eighteenth-Century Studies*, 35.4 (2002), 515–33. On 'Enthusiasm' and the traditions of inspired prophecy, see Sharon Achinstein, *Literature and Dissent in Milton's England*, pp. 154–66.
34. Anne Steele, 'Ode on a Rural Prospect in June', in *Miscellaneous Pieces in Verse and Prose, by Theodosia* (Bristol, 1780), pp. 43–4. All Steele's poems cited below are from this volume and are referenced parenthetically in the text.
35. J.R. Watson, *The English Hymn: A Critical and Historical Study* (Oxford: Clarendon, 1997), pp. 190–8.
36. On Steele, see Marjorie Reeves, 'Literary Women in Eighteenth-Century Nonconformist Circles', in *Culture and the Nonconformist Tradition*, ed. by Jane Shaw and Alan Krieder (Cardiff: University of Wales Press, 1999), pp. 7–25.
37. There are no dates for most of her printed letters. Elizabeth Rowe, *The Miscellaneous Works in Prose and Verse*, ed. by Mr. Theophilus Rowe, 2 vols (London, 1739), II (pp. 97, 58, 82, 111, 198). Rolli's translation appeared in 1729.
38. Rowe, *Works*, I, xvi: citing Milton's *Il Penseroso*, 62, 'most musical, most melancholy'.
39. On Rowe, see Sharon Achinstein, '"Pleasure by Description": Elizabeth Singer Rowe's Enlightened Milton', in *Milton and the Grounds of Contention*, ed. by Mark R. Kelley, Michael Lieb, and John T. Shawcross (Pittsburgh: Duquesne University Press, 2003), pp. 64–87.

5
The Scriblerian Project

Jill Campbell

In 'Satturday', the last of a set of *Town Eclogues* that the young Lady Mary Wortley Montagu (1689–1762) composed in 1715–16, the treatment of the poem's central character seems more satirical than sympathetic. Flavia has recently lost her beauty to a bout with smallpox; although the disease nearly took Flavia's life as well as scarring her severely, the woman poet who depicts her seems to concentrate on Flavia's vanity and the triviality of her concerns rather than on her suffering. After quickly sketching her subject in a posture of histrionic mourning, Montagu gives Flavia a monologue that burlesques her narrow views by adapting the high rhetorical conventions of pastoral elegy to the more mundane loss of beauty and female social power.[1] Like Montagu's other *Town Eclogues* and like the many 'mock' adaptations of classical forms by her male contemporaries, 'Satturday' thus plays satirically on an incongruity between time-honoured literary forms and the banal, trivial, or merely materialistic subject matter of contemporary life.

The world of these mock-forms is most often urban, and implicitly therefore debased: hence the connotations of Montagu's oxymoronic creation of *Town Eclogues*.[2] As the example of 'Satturday' suggests, the world of these mock-forms is also often distinctively feminine, a deflation following, as if inevitably, from the substitution of female concerns for heroic male ones. Pope relies on this effect throughout his mock-epic, *The Rape of the Lock* (1714); it appears in condensed form, for instance, in the comic levelling of significant and insignificant events (alternately male and female) in the catalogue that opens Canto IV:

> Not youthful Kings in Battel seiz'd alive,
> Not scornful Virgins who their Charms survive [...]
> Not Tyrants fierce that unrepenting die,

> Not *Cynthia* when her *Manteau's* pinn'd awry,
> E'er felt such Rage, Resentment and Despair,
> As Thou, sad Virgin! for thy ravish'd Hair.[3]

In the case of 'Satturday', however, the poet who manipulates this familiar play on effects of gender and scale is herself a woman, a potential satiric object in this literary game as well as an accomplished writing subject. Furthermore, what Montagu shares with Flavia goes beyond their sex and social class. Just a few months before her composition of 'Satturday', Montagu herself had fallen severely ill with smallpox. Her survival was for a time in question; and, although she did recover, she was left without eyelashes and with deeply pitted skin. Montagu later referred to 'Satturday' as 'express[ing] [...] her own sensations' after her illness.[4] The poem thus provides a particularly striking and confounding example of a frequent phenomenon in eighteenth-century writing: works that combine a woman's account of her distinctively female experience with the distanced, debunking perspective on women commonly found in the work of male contemporaries. In the case of 'Satturday', the circumstances of the poem's composition help explain this combination. They also offer an introduction to the complexity of relations between the members of the predominantly male literary culture of early eighteenth-century England; to women as favourite satiric objects in that culture; and to women as aspiring writers and active participants in both private and public literary scenes.

The work of Anne Finch, Countess of Winchilsea, as well as that of Lady Mary Wortley Montagu, cannot be considered in isolation from their male peers. While yearning for a lineage of female poetic forebears, both Finch and Montagu sometimes pursued their writing within social and literary circles dominated by men. Indeed, as we shall see, individual works by Finch and Montagu were written in direct response to, or in sustained dialogue with, congenial or antagonizing works by men.

1 The Scriblerus Club, Lady Mary Wortley Montagu, and mock forms

The actual composition of 'Satturday' seems clearly to be Montagu's, but the 'scheme' of which it formed a part, Montagu later reported, was 'first thought of in company with Pope and Gay'[5] – two of Montagu's male contemporaries most brilliantly active in the creation of the period's popular 'mock' forms: mock-pastoral, mock-georgic, mock-learned-scholarship, mock-epic, and ultimately nihilistic anti-epic as well. In roughly the period of Montagu's composition of her *Town Eclogues*, Pope and John Gay, along with their friends Jonathan Swift, Dr Arbuthnot, Thomas Parnell, and the Earl of Oxford, were meeting in a group that they playfully dubbed the 'Scriblerus Club'. Largely social in nature, this club also provided a creative meeting ground for its variously-talented but like-minded participants: its members shared a conservative Tory politics, and an energetically sceptical and debunking view of recent developments in science, medicine, philosophy, and literary culture. After entertaining various possible vehicles for their satire of these developments, the group settled on a mock biography of a learned fool they named Martinus Scriblerus, whose injudicious pursuit of pedantic learning of every sort allowed the Scriblerians to send up a great range of modern discourses. By the time Pope oversaw the publication of the Scriblerus Club's collaboratively-composed *Memoirs of Martinus Scriblerus* in 1741, the club itself was long disbanded; in fact, it had met regularly only in 1714. Yet its meetings had provided a collective breeding-ground for works by individual members that would appear over the course of ensuing decades: Jonathan Swift's *Gulliver's Travels* (1726), John Gay's *Beggar's Opera* ('a Newgate pastoral'; 1728), Alexander Pope's *Peri Bathous, or the Art of Sinking in Poetry* (1728), and his *Dunciads* (1728–29; 1742–43). These works of lasting repute have assured a place in literary history for the all-male Scriblerus Club as a highly-generative convergence of creative and iconoclastic minds, however brief the life of the club itself and however fragmentary its records.

It is less often remembered that a female friend of several Scriblerians, Lady Mary Wortley Montagu, also collaborated with them on conceiving and executing a closely-related project, the six mock-pastoral poems of her *Town Eclogues*. If Montagu's writing about Flavia initially strikes the reader as more like the satiric writings of eighteenth-century men on the vanity and triviality of women than like a rendering of female experience from the inside, perhaps it is because, working on the series in playful collaboration with Pope and Gay, Montagu had become for a time, in Valerie Rumbold's words, 'almost a Scriblerian'.[6]

Montagu was distinguished from her Scriblerian friends and collaborators not only by her sex, but also by her social class and political sympathies. Born Lady Mary Pierrepont, she was the daughter of Evelyn Pierrepont, a member of parliament, an earl, marquess, and ultimately a duke; the name by which her contemporaries addressed her, 'Lady Mary', was bestowed upon her at birth as the courtesy title due the daughter of an earl. In eloping with Edward Wortley Montagu in 1712, Lady Mary defied her father's wishes for her marriage but redoubled her family ties to the Whig party that Pope, Gay, and other Scriblerians so strongly associated with modern political corruption and the decay of culture: Edward was a close friend and sometime collaborator with the Whiggish Joseph Addison and Richard Steele and a promising young Whig politician in his own right. Both in the retrospective view of many historical narratives and in the fiercely partisan accounts of the time, Tory and Whig affiliations seem starkly opposed; and they indeed entailed contrasting cultural sympathies and inclinations as well as distinct political views. Yet Pope's multiple literary and social affiliations in the 1710s exemplify a surprising permeability of the boundaries between these party identifications: for a period, Pope moved fluidly between the Tory coterie identified with the Scriblerus Club and the circle of Whig wits and socialites, including Lady Mary, associated with Hampton Court. He also sustained a literary friendship in this period with Anne Finch, who, as a former maid of honour to the deposed Stuart family, represented yet another set of political attachments and views.

Pope encouraged both women's writing, sometimes praising it, even extravagantly. His admiration was mixed, however, with scepticism and subtle diminishment, and both women responded vigorously to his implicit or explicit disparagement. In the case of Montagu, her early friendship and collaborative ties with Pope would be succeeded in the 1730s by the public rancour of their exchange of unforgettable satiric attacks in verse. Even during the period of her friendships with Pope and Gay, Montagu's role as a fellow wit and respected collaborator coexisted with a strong pattern of associations with femaleness in Scriblerian writings – from feminine insubstantiality to grotesquely material sexuality and reproductive powers – which makes a woman's ultimate reduction to satiric object in the Scriblerian milieu seem almost inescapable.

Not only were the official members of the Scriblerus Club all male, but their declared targets of satire, as described above, were predominantly masculine as well. The scientific virtuosi, pedantic fools, philosophers driven mad by abstract and fantastic systems, relentlessly prolific producers of worthless cultural products, and shamelessly corrupt politicians that populate Scriblerian writings are overwhelmingly male. And yet female figures provide key centres of meaning and affect within many of their works. Both individual women and female personifications such as Mother Dullness in Pope's *Dunciad* or Criticism in Swift's *Battle of the Books* are invested with powerful and even visceral significance in the imaginative realization of some of the Scriblerians' most fundamental concerns.

In particular, despite their general readiness to dismiss and to parody the heated learned controversies of their time, the Scriblerians were deeply and ultimately ambivalently engaged in the great debates of the late seventeenth and eighteenth centuries on the nature of 'personal identity'.[7] Famously, John Locke had undertaken an examination of the basis for identity in the second edition of *An Essay Concerning Human Understanding* (1694); there, he offered 'consciousness', 'the sameness of a rational Being', as the criterion of 'personal identity',[8] thus challenging the old premise that the soul or self adheres in an essential, unchanging, and indivisible 'substance'. In *The Memoirs of Martinus Scriblerus* and elsewhere, the writers of the Scriblerus group vividly dramatize the potential absurdities entailed *both* by the older model of self-as-substance and by the new Lockean idea. Pursuing some of Locke's own doubts, they explore, in particular, the complementary possibilities that a single 'identity' might be shared by more than one person, or that more than one identity might adhere within a single 'person'. Often in their writings, individual women, claims about women in general, or female personifications of abstractions serve as figures of failures of identity, whether those failures are treated as nightmarishly threatening or comically absurd. Within *The Memoirs*, such failures appear most notably in the character(s) of Martin's 'Double Mistress', Lindamira-Indamora, a pair of conjoined twins: exhibited among other monsters in a freak show, the twins are comically grotesque, and yet they also prove the one object of Martin's fascinated erotic longing. When Martin's marriage to Lindamira is challenged legally on the grounds of both bigamy and incest, his lawyer insists upon his own criterion of 'individual' identity – it is located bodily in the 'member of Generation' – to argue that the twins, who share a single set of sexual organs, are one.[9] Ironically, the text that contains this literalizing 'thought experiment' in the splitting and merging of individual identity was created by a group of authors whose individual roles in its composition cannot be disjoined.

The fragmentation, incoherence, or temporal inconsistency of female identity is one of the most notable shared elements in the work of Pope, Swift, and Gay, with a heightened sense of women's physical being, and particularly of her sexual body, often accounting for her divisibility and subjection to change. Swift's group of 'Dressing Room' poems presents several graphically grotesque scenarios of women's failures to cohere: in 'The Lady's Dressing Room' (1732), Strephon is appalled to discover that his lover's splendid public self-presentation is contradicted by the evidence in her dressing room of her gross, effluvial, and excremental, physicality; in 'A Beautiful Young Nymph Going to Bed' (1731), Corinna dis-assembles her fine figure upon retiring to her room – taking off her artificial hair, picking out her crystal eye, removing her eyebrows and teeth, and so on – decomposing before the reader's eyes, only to 're-collect the scatter'd parts' the next morning to create again the illusion of a unified, organic form.[10] Montagu responded with a powerful satiric riposte to the former of these poems. In 'The Reasons that Induced Dr S[wift] to write a Poem call'd the Lady's Dressing room' (1732–34), she provides a 'back-story' to Swift's attack on women, explaining its genesis in Swift's own egregiously divided identity (the dignified 'Dean' of the Church seeks to purchase a prostitute's favours) and in his own fallible physicality (he becomes outraged when he 'trys – and trys' but finds himself unable to perform the acts that he has paid for) (l. 85, l. 65; pp. 273–6).

While Pope's poetry encompasses more winning portraits of women's aesthetic appeal and erotic charm, such as that of Belinda in *The Rape of the Lock*, the goddess Dullness who presides over the descent of England into chaos in *The Dunciad* is vested with a gross Swiftian physicality and incoherence. On a less allegorical plane, in *Epistle to a Lady* (1735), the general thesis that ties together the many portraits of individual women, some of them based on living originals, is that 'Woman's at best a Contradiction still'. Pope's one-time friend and collaborator, Lady Mary Wortley Montagu, appears within this poem's unflattering portrait gallery under the satiric epithet of Sappho; her character is exposed in Pope's portrayal as inconsistent both over time (first seen 'at her toilet's greasy task' and then 'fragrant at an ev'ning Mask') and at any one time (she wears 'diamonds with her dirty smock').[11] Although the content of this portrait focuses primarily on Montagu's supposed slovenliness, the name chosen by Pope for his treatment of Montagu in this and other poems foregrounds her aspirations as a writer, which Pope had celebrated and encouraged in their years of friendship, and which he again and again in their years of enmity implicitly or explicitly treats as matter for satiric attack.

In Pope's satires of Montagu and in other highly charged representations of individual women or symbolic female figures, the Scriblerians work through complex questions and conflicted, ambivalent positions not only on 'personal identity' in general but also, more particularly and perhaps even more urgently, on *authorship* – on the sources of creativity, and on the bounds of 'identity' for a writer. Their talented female contemporaries, Lady Mary Wortley Montagu and Anne Finch, countered the Scriblerians' use of misogynist satire as a vehicle for arguments about authorship both with vigorous, incisive objections to their portrayal of women and with complex, alternative accounts of writerly identity of their own.

2 Pope, Finch, and the figure of the woman writer

In various moods and tones, from scathing satiric condemnation to playful teasing or even witty compliment, Pope grounds women's poetic urges and aspirations in their bodies, treating women's acts of literary creation as functions, symptoms, or analogues of their bodily states. Women participants in public literary culture are almost entirely absent from the voluminous roll-call of individual dunces and hacks that makes up *The Dunciad*, where he preserves in both verse and its attendant footnotes the names of those whose reputations, he assures us, will vanish otherwise without a trace. As Valerie Rumbold observes, the women writers of Pope's time are dismissed yet more absolutely by their exclusion even from the apocalyptic cultural landscape of the poem; for the most part, they do not merit a mention.[12] A notable exception occurs within Book II, Pope's mock-epic rendering of heroic games in the modern, urban setting of the London streets. There Eliza Haywood, the prolific and highly successful novelist, figures not as a contender in one of the games, but as the top prize offered in a pissing contest between two booksellers. Pope intimates the nature of Haywood's value to the booksellers by offering a description of her enticing appearance rather than any account of her creative exertions, however debased. Modelling his description on the circular engraved frontispiece to her collected works that advertised her wares to the book-buying public, Pope equates Haywood's profitable writing career with the prostitution of her body. When he adds an element that does not appear in the engraved frontispiece – 'two babes of love close clinging to her waste' – he also identifies Haywood's literary productions with her biological, and illegitimate, children.[13]

Yet women who sell their literary productions in the public market are not the only ones whose writing Pope accounts for as a bodily product or condition. Indeed, Pope employs the terms of physical syndrome and symptomology particularly to explain the writing of leisured, aristocratic women, whose urge to write, he suggests, may be even more egregious and irrational than that of commercial hacks. Pope debunkingly somatizes female literary aspiration both in his generalized depictions of genteel women 'scribblers' and in specific attacks on his sometime-friends Lady Mary Wortley Montagu and Anne Finch, Countess of Winchilsea. In his devastatingly economical satiric attack on Montagu in the *The First Satire of the Second Book of Horace Imitated* (1733), Pope employs antithesis and grammatical parallelism within the tight space of a single couplet to liken the threat posed by Montagu's writings to her transmission of a venereal disease. Referring to Montagu there, too, as 'Sappho' – the great woman poet of the classical era, but one whose reputation was marred by an association with licentious desire – Pope compares the dangers Montagu presents to those of 'Slander or Poyson' from Delia (Delarivier Manley) or of 'Hard Words or Hanging' from the notoriously severe Judge Page:

> From furious *Sappho* scarce a milder Fate,
> P—x'd by her Love, or libell'd by her Hate [...][14]

When Pope ambiguously plays on the term 'pox', he conflates an unkind reference to one factual and indeed visible bodily condition (Montagu's severe scarring by small-pox) and the imputation of another unseen and merely posited, but scandalous one (syphilis or the 'great-pox'). Indeed, this latter possibility is only reinforced by Pope's pseudo-discreet omission of the letter 'o' from the middle of the word, which at once signals its unprintability and typographically 'poxes' the word itself. It is the other half of this same line, however, that extends the sense of contagious infection from Montagu's body to her use of words: seesawing between the double hazards of Montagu's 'Love' and of her 'Hate', the line carries forward the pairing of verbal and physical dangers posed by Delia ('Slander or Poyson') and Judge Page ('Hard Words or Hanging') to Montagu, whose verbal libelling of her enemies is equated with her sexual infection of her friends.

Pope's generalized treatment of amateur women writers in *The Rape of the Lock* (1714), embedded in the Cave of Spleen episode of Canto IV, seems gentler and more playful than this vitriolic attack; and yet his writer-friend Anne Finch apparently took umbrage at it, objecting in person or in a written text that does not survive. When the Gnome Umbriel descends to Spleen's cave, seeking the means to 'touch *Belinda* with Chagrin', he salutes Spleen's versatile powers to derange the physiological balance of women in the (roughly-demarcated) age of menstruation, hailing the 'wayward Queen' who 'rule[s] the Sex to Fifty from Fifteen':

> Parent of Vapours and of Female Wit,
> Who give th' *Hysteric* or *Poetic* Fit,
> On various Tempers act by various ways,
> Make some take Physick, others scribble Plays [...]

(IV.59–62; p. 189)

Again, the formal features of Pope's heroic couplet art swiftly establish a geometry within which 'Female Wit' rhymes with 'Fit' and the criss-cross of antitheses, pulled taut by rhythmic effects or the bipartite structuring of lines, equates poetic energy with hysteria and the composition of plays with the consumption of medicine for bodily ills. While we do not have evidence of Finch's specific response to these lines, we know of its existence from Pope's short, extravagantly chivalrous reply to it in 'Impromptu, To Lady Winchelsea, Occasion'd by Four Satyrical Verses on Women-Wits, in The Rape of the Lock' (composed c. 1714; published 1741). We can guess something of the nature of Finch's objections both from the content of Pope's reply and from the complaints Finch voices elsewhere, in extant writings, about men's damaging prejudices against women writers.

Having served as an attendant of Mary of Modena, wife of the future James II, Anne Finch (née Kingsmill) retired with her husband to his ancestral estate in Kent when James II resigned the throne. In 1712, Heneage Finch unexpectedly inherited both the estate and the family title, making his wife the Countess of Winchilsea. A year later, the Countess published a pamphlet containing a single poem – a Pindaric ode called 'The Spleen', offering a serious rather than mock-heroic treatment of that condition – and a slim volume of poems, *Miscellany Poems on Several Occasions*. A more substantial and varied body of Finch's work, however, was recorded and circulated in her lifetime only in manuscript form, in an octavo and an especially lavishly-prepared folio volume. Positioned within a manuscript volume, Finch's 'The Introduction' begins by explaining its own appearance in manuscript and not in print form:

> Did I, my lines intend for publick view,
> How many censures, wou'd their faults persue [...]
> True judges, might condemn their want of witt,
> And all might say, they're by a Woman writt.[15]

In the course of the poem that follows, Finch first laments women's consignment by men to the trivial pursuits of beauty and fashion or to 'the dull manage of a servile house'; then challenges the inevitability of women's limited capacities, declaring that "twas not ever thus'; assembles from scriptural history the evidence of a lineage of women leaders and female poetic forebears; and yet ultimately resigns herself to the constraints determined by her own time's 'mistaken rules'. Anticipating that an 'opposing faction' would mock and impede the aspiration of any woman who might strive to 'soar above the rest', Finch cautions her Muse to remain 'retired':

> Conscious of wants, still with contracted wing,
> To some few freinds, and to thy sorrows sing;
> For groves of Lawrell, thou wert never meant;
> Be dark enough thy shades, and be thou there content.
>
> (ll. 61–4; p. 6)

Thus, at the close of this strongly felt and cogently argued complaint, Finch seems to resign herself not only to the inexorable power of social forces but also to the limits of her own poetic powers. Even as her poetic wing 'contracts', however, her poem indeed confined to manuscript form and to the select readership of friends with access to that volume (it did not appear in print until 1903), the final line of Finch's poem notably exceeds its metrical bounds, straining against the dominant Augustan form of the iambic pentameter rhymed couplet. Ambiguously, the achievement of a claimed state of 'content' within obscurity and confinement is reached by Finch only in an extra-metrical foot, the word itself lying outside the formal confines of the poem's line length, even as its sounds echo those of the bitter alliterative concessions – 'conscious of wants', 'contracted wing' – of the preceding lines.

In fact, Finch's poetry is characterized in general by the bending or stretching of Augustan forms, often at crucial, expressive moments. Finch composed poems in an impressive variety of forms, including the Pindaric ode as interpreted by seventeenth- and eighteenth-century English poets, following Abraham Cowley's example. This loose version of the Pindaric ode allowed both for sudden shifts of emotion and for irregularities of form, such as variable line lengths, stanza lengths, and rhyme schemes. Even when writing in rhymed couplets, however, Finch's poetry is more flexible formally than Pope's: her couplets not infrequently extend into triplets and individual lines pass beyond the metrical limit of iambic pentameter into a sixth foot, forming Alexandrines – most often at significant moments of psychic stretching, struggle with excess, or some affirmation of plenitude (for example, lines 27–32 of 'The Introduction', as well as its closing lines).[16] While her Scriblerian contemporary Jonathan Swift famously went on record in this period with his scornful disapproval of poets' divergence from the demands of strict form (through the parodic excesses of the closing lines of his mock-pastoral 'Description of a City Shower', 1710 and

1735), Finch herself expressed yearning in 'The Nightingale' for a poetic 'Musick' that might be as 'free' and 'wild' as the bird's song, perhaps even transcending the use of words (ll. 1–9, 18–21; pp. 267–8). 'Scribbling' might be one less idealizing description of a free and wild writing that forgoes human 'sense'. Pope's 'Impromptu, to the Countess of Winchelsea' suggests that, in countering Pope's dismissal of women's 'scribbling' as one more effect of Spleen, Finch probably returned to invoking the accomplishments of earlier women writers, rather than advancing birdsong as a poetic model. Pope begins his 'Impromptu' by waving aside as fruitless the citation of such evidence from history: 'In vain you boast Poetic Names of yore, / And cite those *Sapho*'s we admire no more ...'.[17] While he thus abruptly, even rudely, denies the efficacy of Finch's argument, the very denial is explained as a form of extravagant politeness – as a tribute to Finch's own poetic achievements. It is by outshining all her predecessors, Pope gallantly asserts, that Finch dooms 'the Fall of ev'ry Female Wit' even as she writes in their praise. He concludes the poem with a metaphor: Finch's achievements efface those of her female predecessors in the same way that the (masculine) Sun 'shines himself till [the stars] are seen no more' (l. 3, ll. 11–12). The praise of Finch's 'Wit' and poetic powers thus comes at a cost: she is offered it at the expense of any lineage of female writers. Pope's flattery in the poem depends on the assumed impossibility of a community of women writers across time, on a necessary rivalry and mutual exclusivity of female achievement.

Finch herself at times seems to fear such an adversarial relation between women writers, as if their aspirations were inevitably structured as rivalries for male attention. In 'The Circuit of Appollo' (written c. 1702), she imagines Apollo's conundrum when, poised to adjudicate between the claims of the women poets of Kent, he recalls the fate of Paris, 'Since in Witt, or in Beauty, itt never was heard / One female cou'd yield t' have another preferr'd' (ll. 60–1; p. 94). The tone of these lines is light, set by the poem's rollicking anapaests. Faced, however, with Pope's implication in 'Impromptu' that an accomplished woman poet necessarily stands alone, Finch closed their four-stage debate with 'The Answer', which invokes the potential force of a group of women united in their rejection of both the strictures and the rewards of social courtesy. She acknowledges Pope's 'genteel [...] air' in his 'Impromptu', but warns him that women in fact 'rule the world our life's whole race'. Finch then conjures the threat of female vengeance for Pope's patronizing attitude by reminding him of Orpheus's fate once he had 'incense[d]' women with his 'scoffing rhimes': it is a group of Maeneds (female followers of Dionysius) who dismembered Orpheus and sent his head down the Hebrus, their wildly disinhibited, unruly noises drowning out the sound and overpowering the force even of his enchanting voice (ll.1–5, ll. 9–24; pp. 102–3).

The tables were turned in the struggle between a combined, if multi-vocal and possibly cacophonous, plurality and a singular lyric voice when three members of the Scriblerus Club – Pope, Gay, and Arbuthnot – joined forces in the 1717 play *Three Hours After Marriage* to attack Anne Finch in the person of the aristocratic poet and playwright, Phoebe Clinket. In this strange and entertaining hodge-podge of a play, the three male collaborators satirize Clinket's self-absorption and absurd poetic aspirations alongside other favourite Scriblerian targets, such as pedantic learning and modern science. Like the 'Double Mistress' episode in *The Memoirs of Martinus Scriblerus*, *Three Hours After Marriage* concerns itself with monsters and scientific curiosities, prominently featuring women among them. In the opening scene, Fossile, an aged doctor and collector of scientific curiosities, addresses his new wife as 'thou best of my Curiosities'. His wife is in fact more ordinary than Fossile thinks (she is a woman of the town, 'Mrs. Townley', whom he mistakes for that rarity, a trembling virgin); but shortly after Fossile and Townley's opening exchange, Fossile's niece, the real female freak of the play, appears on stage: '*Enter Clinket, and her Maid bearing a Writing-Desk on her Back. Clinket Writing, her Head-dress stain'd with ink, and Pens stuck in her Hair.*'[18]

Although modern editors of the play have defended the Scriblerians' treatment of Clinket as general rather than particular satire, downplaying its specific reference to Finch, contemporary readers understood the character to be an unkind portrayal by Pope of his sometime friend and literary associate.[19] A number of details in the play support this identification, although some of them might be recognized only by those, like Pope, who knew Finch well and had been privy to her manuscript volumes. The play even echoes at two points one of Finch's most memorable – repeatedly imitated and cited – passages of verse. Early in 'The Spleen' (a Pindaric ode, like some of Clinket's imagined productions), Finch contrasts mankind's bodily and psychic equilibrium before the Fall with a decayed state in which even sweet sensations may flood and disturb a body so overcharged by sensation that sweets must be countered by offensive scents:

> Now the *Jonquille* o'ercomes the feeble Brain;
> We faint beneath the Aromatick Pain,
> Till some offensive Scent thy Pow'rs appease,
> And Pleasure we resign for short, and nauseous Ease.

(ll. 39–42; p. 249)

Swift and the mature Pope might disdain the irregularities of form that characterize the Pindaric ode, apparent here in the metrical extension of the last of the four lines quoted. Yet Pope in fact honoured these lines by appropriation in the last section of Epistle I of 'Essay on Man' (1733), incorporating the phrase 'aromatic pain' to describe the ill effects of the heightened sensory powers we might wish for, as he builds to his poem's magisterial thesis that 'Whatever IS, is RIGHT.' 'Who finds not Providence', Pope declares, 'all good and wise, / Alike in what it gives, and what denies?'[20]

Despite Pope's repeated use of the collective male pronoun, Man, in these lines, they have a specific and pointed application to the aspirations of a woman such as Finch, who in 'The Introduction' and elsewhere complains bitterly of what 'Providence' – or the social dispensation – denies her sex. In the portrait of Clinket in *Three Hours After Marriage*, the Scriblerians reprove such female aspirations not with philosophizing but with involuted, treacherous ridicule. Finch's memorable lines about 'aromatic pain' are echoed and adapted in the play as well, in two particularly significant contexts: first in a discussion of Clinket's aspiration to have her plays staged (Act I; p. 14) and then again in Fossile's lament about his wife's sexual infidelity (Act II; p. 27). Paired, the two echoes of Finch's lines from 'The Spleen' create an associational link between the Scriblerians' distinct satiric targets of women's literary pretensions and women's false pretensions to sexual virtue: the two matters joined at an allusive root through a shared echo of the words of a real woman, one who *suffered*, indeed, from literary aspiration but whose sexual virtue was not in question.

The play reinforces this associational, non-logical link through its many metaphors that identify literary production with biological reproduction, thus colouring Clinket's poetic and dramatic aspirations with the potential for sexual scandal – as when Clinket asks Plotwell to pretend authorship to her play at its public reading, 'by fathering the unworthy Issue of my Muse' (Act I; p.14). This rhetorical pattern of metaphors leads into the actual confusions of reference at the plot's farcical close. The arrival onstage of Mrs Townley's baby, born before her wedding, coincides with the return of a letter from Clinket to Plotwell in which she refers to her play as 'the Child which you father'd' and as her unfortunate 'Offspring'. Taking his niece's language literally, Fossile laments that her poetry has 'reduc'd' her to sexual profligacy. When the confusion is cleared up, however, Fossile decides that he will adopt the real child onstage as his son and heir, despite its parentage. In the end, simply shrugging off the stock cuckold character's usual worries,

Fossile exclaims, 'What signifies whether a Man beget his Child or not?' Implicitly, the precise paternity of this collaboratively-written play may also fail to signify. Indeed, in Clinket's final lines the authors advance the suggestion that she, the play's satiric literary butt, may also be its self-reflexive author: affirming that 'every one has got something' from 'this Day's Adventure', Clinket congratulates her uncle that he has got 'a fine Child' from it; 'and I a Plot for a Comedy; and I'll this Moment set about it' (Act III; pp. 56–8). That comedy would presumably be none other than the one we have just read or watched. At the play's close, the Scriblerians imagine the moment of its inception and laughingly deliver the work of its composition into Clinket's ink-stained hands.

3 Pope, Montagu, and collaborative authorship

In Pope's relations with his more contentious and forcefully ambitious female contemporary, Lady Mary Wortley Montagu, the struggle over questions of authorship was fiercer and more conclusively damaging. Montagu, unlike Finch, was vulnerable to charges of transgressive sexual behaviour as well as of literary aspiration, and Pope's satiric attacks on her, as we have seen, frequently associate those two charges. In Montagu's own writing, including the *Town Eclogues* from the period of her friendship with Pope, she offers a complex but distinctively female perspective on the naturalness of women's sexual passion and the unjust constraints imposed on women by social custom and marriage law. The causes of Pope and Montagu's falling-out in the period between their friendship and their fierce public enmity remain obscure; but, as Isobel Grundy concludes, most probably 'sexual issues inflamed a quarrel based in authorship issues'. In their own terse, partial, or indirect explanations, Montagu and Pope both point to tensions about forms of shared authorship, disputed authorship, or authorship that eludes named, proprietary attribution. An enthusiastic and admiring collaborator with Montagu in the years of their friendship, Pope later objected bitterly to Montagu's blurring of the bounds of authorial identity and responsibility in the circulation of some of her manuscript writings.[21] While his participation in the Scriblerus Club and in other cooperative writing projects with men attest to Pope's own deep and indeed lingering investment in forms of shared, social authorship, his attacks on Montagu and on her courtier friend Lord Hervey (the 'Sporus' of *Epistle to Arbuthnot*) call for revulsion not only at the supposed incoherence of their identities but also, more specifically, at their characteristic blurring of individual voice and voice.[22]

The horror of authorial contamination or blending appears in Pope's satiric portraits of both Hervey and Montagu in his *First Satire of the Second Book of Horace*. Fittingly, the two of them responded to his attack with a collaboratively-written piece, their *Verses Address'd to an Imitator of the First Satire of the Second Book of Horace* (1733). One of the most effective features of this riposte is Hervey and Montagu's use of the first-person plural, 'we' and 'our'. Through these pronouns the co-authors not only acknowledge their poem's collaborative composition but also invoke a common humanity from which Pope is excluded. Indeed, his isolation and ultimate exile from the human community (he is last seen 'wandering like Cain') are implicitly linked by Montagu and Hervey to his investment in sole, proprietary authorship and to his marketing of his works in print.[23]

While Pope might seem devastatingly to dismiss Anne Finch in his debunking of female creative community in 'Impromptu' and in his treatment of one of her manuscript poems as mere waste-paper for the composition of his published *Iliad*, both Finch and Montagu offer rich counter-models of authorship to his own, ones grounded in social relations and shared creativity, rather than in a closely guarded delineation of the individual writing self. In fact, the Scriblerus Club had offered Pope, Swift, and their collaborators, male and female, a centre of such creativity in its time. The male Scriblerians consistently refused, however, to recognize this affinity in the collaborative practices of contemporary women.

Notes

1. 'Satturday' [sic], *Lady Mary Wortley Montagu: Essays and Poems and 'Simplicity, a Comedy'*, ed. by Robert Halsband and Isobel Grundy (Oxford: Oxford University Press, 1993), pp. 201–4. Subsequent references to works from Montagu's *Essays and Poems* are given parenthetically in the text.
2. As Isobel Grundy notes, Montagu herself called this set of poems simply 'Eclogs', and it was Horace Walpole who headlined the basic tension between the poems' genre and their content by titling them *Six Town Eclogues* when he published them in 1747 ('Lady Mary Wortley Montagu, *Six Town Eclogues* and Other Poems', in *A Companion to Eighteenth-Century Poetry*, ed. by Christine Gerrard (Oxford: Blackwell, 2006), pp. 184–96, (p. 185).
3. Alexander Pope, Canto IV, *The Rape of the Lock* (1714), in *The Rape of the Lock and Other Poems*, ed. by Geoffrey Tillotson, vol. II of the Twickenham Edition of the Poems of Alexander Pope, 3rd edn (London: Methuen, 1962), ll. 3–4, 7–10. Further references are given parenthetically in the text.
4. As reported by her grand-daughter, Lady Louisa Stuart, 'Biographical Anecdotes of Lady M W Montagu', *Essays and Poems*, p. 35.
5. See Isobel Grundy, *Lady Mary Wortley Montagu: Comet of the Enlightenment* (Oxford: Oxford University Press, 1999), p. 104.

6. Valerie Rumbold, *Women's Place in Pope's World* (Cambridge: Cambridge University Press, 1989), p. 134. For other important discussions of Montagu's *Town Eclogues* and of her relations with the Scriblerians, see Ann Messenger, *His and Hers: Essays in Restoration and Eighteenth-Century Literature* (Lexington: University of Kentucky, 1986); Grundy, *Comet of the Enlightenment*, pp. 90–4, 104–12; and Grundy, 'Lady Mary Wortley Montagu', pp. 184–8. Note especially Grundy's declaration that the old presumption of Pope's and Gay's 'part-authorship' of the *Eclogues* 'is a myth' (p. 186).

7. See especially Christopher Fox, *Locke and the Scriblerians: Identity and Consciousness in Early Eighteenth-Century Britain* (Berkeley: University of California Press, 1988).

8. John Locke, *An Essay Concerning Human Understanding*, Book 2: 9, ed. by Roger Woolhouse, Penguin Classics (Harmondsworth: Penguin, 1997), p. 302.

9. *Memoirs of the Extraordinary Life, Works, and Discoveries of Martinus Scriblerus*, ed. by Charles Kerby-Miller (New York: Russell and Russell, 1966), p. 157. See Appendix IV for Kerby-Miller's discussion and transcription of a manuscript fragment of the Double Mistress episode, which provides an instance of the collaborative composition of the *Memoirs*, as it is in Arbuthnot's handwriting with drastic alterations in the hand of Pope.

10. Jonathan Swift, 'A Beautiful Young Nymph Going to Bed. Written for the Honour of the *Fair Sex*', in *Jonathan Swift: Major Works*, ed. by Angus Ross and David Woolley (Oxford: Oxford University Press, 2003), l. 68, pp. 533–4.

11. Alexander Pope, *Epistle to a Lady*, in *Epistles to Several Persons (Moral Essays)*, ed. by F. W. Bateson, vol. III.ii of the Twickenham Edition of the Poems of Alexander Pope, 2nd edn (London: Methuen, 1961), l. 270, p. 72 and ll. 25–6, p. 52 and l. 24, p. 51.

12. Valerie Rumbold, 'Cut the Caterwauling: Women Writers (Not) in Pope's Dunciads', *The Review of English Studies*, 52 (2001), 524–39 (p. 525).

13. Alexander Pope, *The Dunciad* (1728), in *The Dunciad*, ed. by James Sutherland, vol. V of the Twickenham Edition of the Poems of Alexander Pope, 2nd edn revised (London: Methuen, 1963), Book II, ll. 150, p. 120.

14. Alexander Pope, *The First Satire of the Second Book of Horace, Imitated* (1733), in *Imitations of Horace*, ed. by John Butt, vol. IV of the Twickenham Edition of the Poems of Alexander Pope, 2nd edn (London: Methuen, 1953), ll. 81–4, p. 13.

15. Anne Finch, 'The Introduction', in *The Poems of Anne Countess of Winchilsea*, ed. by Myra Reynolds (Chicago: University of Chicago Press, 1903), ll.1–2, ll. 7–8, p. 4. All subsequent references to Anne Finch's poems are taken from this edition and are given parenthetically in the text.

16. For an excellent discussion of Finch's 'shrewd and ingenious' use of enjambed lines in a period that generally scorned enjambment within rhymed couplets, see Richard Bradford, 'Rhyming Couplets and Blank Verse', in *A Companion to Eighteenth-Century Poetry*, ed. by Christine Gerrard (Oxford: Blackwell, 2006), pp. 341–55, (pp. 346–7).

17. Alexander Pope, 'Impromptu, to Lady Winchelsea', in *Minor Poems*, ed. by Norman Ault and John Butt, vol. VI of the Twickenham Edition of the Poems of Alexander Pope (London: Methuen, 1954), ll. 1–2, p. 120. Subsequent references are given parenthetically in the text.

18. *Three Hours after Marriage*, ed. by Richard Morton and William M. Peterson (Painesville, OH: Lake Erie College Press, 1961), Act I, pp. 6–7. Subsequent references are given parenthetically in the text.

19. See Morton and Peterson's introduction, which downplays the specific reference; and the Appendix to their edition, which reproduces two eighteenth-century 'keys' to the play, both of which insist on the identification of Clinket as Finch.

20. Pope, *Essay on Man*, in *An Essay on Man*, ed. by Maynard Mack, vol. III.i of the Twickenham Edition of the Poems of Alexander Pope (London: Methuen, 1956), Epistle I, l. 200, p. 40, and l. 294, p. 51, and ll. 205–6. p. 40.

21. Grundy, *Comet of the Enlightenment*, pp. 270–4.

22. Grundy cannily notes 'Montagu's penchant for collaboration, even in intimate personal poetry', as well as her 'penchant for ventriloquizing' ('Lady Mary Wortley Montagu', pp. 186, 194).

23. Lady Mary Wortley Montague and Lord Hervey, *Verses Address'd to an Imitator of the First Satire of the Second Book of Horace* (1733), ll. 1–15, ll. 89–112; pp. 265–70.

6
Women Writers and the Rise of the Novel

Kate Williams

The traditional narrative of the English novel in the eighteenth century holds that its origins were male, however much writers such as Jane Austen, Frances Burney, and Charlotte Smith came to dominate the genre. More specifically, Daniel Defoe, Henry Fielding, and Samuel Richardson, the triumvirate proposed in Ian Watt's *The Rise of the Novel* (1957), created the works that founded the realist English novel. And yet such a paradigm occludes the rich tradition of early fiction by women, not only the works of Aphra Behn and Delarivier Manley, but also those by novelists active in the 1720s: Eliza Haywood, Penelope Aubin, Mary Davys, and Elizabeth Rowe. The latter pared the seduction plot away from the political focus of Behn and Manley to focus their texts on a woman's response to sexual experience and betrayal – and were thus particularly relevant to the work of Richardson. He may have claimed to his friend Aaron Hill in 1741 that he offered a 'new species of writing', and avowed himself ignorant of previous fictional trends, but the work of 1720s female authors reverberated vividly in his novels.[1]

Scholarship by Ros Ballaster, Paula Backscheider, Christine Blouch, Sarah Prescott, and others, has shown the richness and complexity of fiction by Haywood and her contemporaries.[2] However, although Margaret Doody noted in 1974 that both Richardson and Haywood attempted to create a 'language of love, not just a language about love', research aiming to combat assertions of originality by Richardson (and Watt) by exploring textual precedents has surveyed every other possible form, from sermons to plays to folk tales.[3] If fiction by women is incorporated, it is presented as a disreputable tradition that required reformation. As William Warner argued, women produced semi-pornographic 'formula fiction', and Richardson aimed to 'purif[y] writing', 'elevating and sublimating' themes, and redirecting their indulgent fantasies for moral ends.[4]

Although Richardson's work as a printer exposed him to contemporary fiction, his sole mention of Haywood occurred in a 1751 letter to his friend Sarah Chapone, in which he avowed that writers such as Laetitia Pilkington made 'the Behn's, the Manley's, the Haywood's, look white'.[5] Earlier, however, he had professed to his friend, George Cheyne, that his aim was to 'catch young and airy minds' with 'Love-scenes', but by adding a moral he would show how such scenes 'may be directed to laudable Meanings and Purposes, in order to decry such Novels and Romances, as have a Tendency to inflame and corrupt'.[6] But his plan was impossible to execute: rather than suppressing its power, his texts recuperated, prolonged, and complicated the appeal of the love scene, and inspired a host of readings that were more engrossed by 'Love-scenes' than 'laudable Meanings'.

1 Women writers

In contrast to predecessors such as Behn and Manley, Haywood, Aubin, Davys, and Rowe wrote short, third-person fictions.[7] Their tales of seduction were not directed towards a specific wider political point, but created as textual experiences in their own right, with detailed representations of the heroine's sexual feeling and her misery at her betrayal. In many of the novels, the heroine resists her father's choice of a suitor, only to fall into the clutches of a rake. After charming her in a verdant grove, he imprisons her and seduces or attacks her in the pivotal scene of the novel: the 'fatal Point of Time, when [...] only raging influences govern'd, to ruin her, at once, for ever'.[8] Soon after, he deserts her, leaving her to bemoan her fate. In such a plot, sexual attempts by men functioned as revelatory of a woman's character and strength, the cynicism of men and their refusal to feel sentiments of love, and a fundamental sexual inequality in which women were the possessions of either husbands or fathers.

Readers in the 1720s embraced these short seduction texts with enthusiasm. Haywood's four-volume works, *Secret Histories, Novels and Poems* appeared in 1725 and she published over forty new fictions between 1721 and 1730. Aubin's seven novels appeared between 1721 and 1728, as well as four sensationalized translations. Davys's two volume *Works* appeared in 1725, and Rowe's *Friendship in Death* in 1728 and the first volume of *Letters Moral and Entertaining* in the following year. Public interest in new seduction novels waned in the following decade, and Haywood turned to dramatic and political works, but the texts continued to be reprinted and Richardson's business was involved in their reissue. In 1732, his house printed two volumes of the third edition of Haywood's *Secret Histories, Novels and Poems*, which included *Love in Excess* (1719–20), *Lasselia* (1723), *The Rash Resolve* (1724), and *The Masqueraders* (1724–25).[9]

Richardson claimed to his Dutch translator, Johannes Stinstra, that he happened to ponder the plight of exploited maidservants while writing some sample piece for his guide to letter writing, *Familiar Letters* (1741), and 'hence sprung *Pamela'*.[10] And yet he was exposed to 1720s fiction: his house printed Haywood's volumes, and at the same time as he was writing his first novel, his house was preparing to print editions of Rowe's *Friendship in Death* and *Letters Moral and Entertaining*, which feature tales of maids abandoned and also marrying their masters. He was also, it would appear, authoring the preface to a complete edition of Aubin's fiction, *A Collection of Entertaining Histories and Novels* (1739).[11] The six-page preface praised Aubin's desire to inculcate virtue, judging her contemporaries 'fallen angels' who aimed to turn their readers 'depraved' by attempting to 'paint the guilty Scenes of Folly and Vanity in such Colours' to render the most 'pernicious Vices amiable'. Aubin, by contrast, used sexual content in order to lend her virtuous argument 'Force' in readers' minds.[12] The notion that sexualized content could be bent to encourage moral purpose and devote readers to abstinence and sexual respect was a paradigm that Richardson deployed repeatedly. Aubin's novels revel in plots of abduction and seduction and show few instances of vitiated men repenting their rapacity, and Richardson imputed to her a moral purpose that had more to do with his practice than her own.

Haywood's novels, as Doody noted, produced a language that founded 'the erotic as constantly significant', an endeavour she shared with Richardson.[13] Haywood, and to a lesser extent Rowe, deployed an intense language that encapsulated the physical and psychological sensations of sexual desire. Within this, Haywood distinguished between masculine and feminine ardour: her virtuous heroines dream, sigh, faint, and totter while men are intent on sexual content. A woman's passion functions in the absence of the male, whom she imagines worshipping her, just as Lasselia enjoys her 'Dreams' of her beloved Monsieur de l'Amye 'dissolving, melting in amorous Languishments'.[14] Male desire, by contrast, is prompted by the presence of the woman and it is an acquisitive, extroverted gaze that itemizes her into a series of body parts. In *Love in Excess*, D'Elmont stares at Melliora, slumbering over a volume of Ovid, and relishes how her nightgown 'discovered a thousand beauties'.[15] In *The Masqueraders*, Dorinda faints and Philectus savours her 'Neck, her Breasts, her fine proportion'd Hands and Arms', declaring that 'there was no part of her expos'd to view that did not discover a Beauty'.[16] Men and women imagine dominance over each other, but men, with their desire for feeling the sensation of control and pleasure in the woman's subjugation, tend to win. Thus when de l'Amye finds Lasselia, he neither melts nor dissolves but actively reduces her to 'trembling 'twixt Desire and Fear'.[17]

The essential plot of a young girl seduced by a rake became crucial to fiction. Aubin's *Collection of Entertaining Novels* featured over forty separate tales of a rake who abducts a young middle-class girl from her garden into a coach and carries her to a clandestine house where he courts, drugs, rapes, and imprisons her. Unlike Haywood's novels, which focused on one or two stories of seduction, Aubin's narratives encased various tale-tellings – including one in *Charlotta du Pont* (1723) that closely foreshadowed *Clarissa*: Dorinda is seduced from her father's garden by Leander, lodged in London with a bawd in disguise, and then her lover arranges for her to be imprisoned for debt. Unlike Clarissa, however, she returns to the bawd to learn her arts and becomes a hardened prostitute – the sole way, it seems to her, to take control of her exploitation.[18]

Davys combined the abduction-seduction plot with conduct-book language of reformation and rakes who stage complicated scenarios to punish women for their presumption. In *The Reform'd Coquet* (1724), Alanthus allows the near-rape of his flirtatious ward, Amoranda so that he can inform her that he will not rescue her, for he knows that she will have more fear if she experiences the prospect of being saved, which is then removed. Likewise, affronted by Nancy Friendly's teasing, Sir John Gaillard, in *The Accomplish'd Rake* (1727), resolves to 'have her' in the way he judges cruellest, 'unknown to herself', by drugging and raping her in an inn.[19]

Rowe infused the seduction plot with religious themes and posited a solution to the conundrum that a woman's sensitivity to passion, as in cases such as Haywood's Melliora, revealed moral worth but rendered her vulnerable to seduction. In her fiction, a seduced heroine can admit her passions after death as what was once her 'crime' becomes her 'glory' as she dies and meets Christ in 'an enchanting land of Love'.[20] The sight of women experiencing a pleasurable union with Christ proves erotically appealing for men. Rowe's Leander watches a lovely girl die and enjoys how a 'languishing beauty adorned her face, charming beyond all the vivacity of health' as she expires 'perfectly graceful in the height of her disorder'.[21] On earth, in contrast, sexual love is neither redemptive nor a conduit to concord but a field for the battle between the sexes.

2 The mid-century novel

Despite professing a wish to decry novels and romances, Richardson packaged his texts with assurances that readers would experience physical responses, just as 1720s texts were advertised as offering lachrymose or erotic encounters. In a prefatory poem to the 1732 edition of *Secret Histories*, James Sterling wrote that Haywood could 'Command the throbbing breast, and wart'ry eye' until 'our captive spirits ebb and flow', and readers 'melt in soft desires'.[22] In his preface to *Pamela*, Richardson's friend, Aaron Hill, who knew Haywood well, declared that 'Smiles and Tears obey thy moving Skill / and Passion's ruffled Empire waits thy Will' (*Pamela*, p. 519), and later pleased his friend by declaring that *Clarissa* had a 'force that can tear the heartstrings'.[23] And yet, contrary to such agreeable promises, Richardson's multi-epistolary form encouraged sceptical interrogation rather than the pleasing certainty of physical response. His texts revealed seduction itself as an act of interpretation. In his hands, the lexicons of 1720s fiction became an exaggerated, extravagant discourse, wielded by the characters in an attempt to make others tearfully or throbbingly submissive to their narrative.

Richardson set both novels at the time when readers were eagerly consuming fiction by Haywood and others: *Pamela* (1740) between 1721 and 1730, and *Clarissa* (1747–48) in 1721, 1727, or, most likely, in 1732 – the same year as he printed volumes of Haywood's *Secret Histories*.[24] Pamela and B. delight in styling themselves as amatory characters. B., a rather weak young man, vaunts that 'we should make a very pretty Story in Romance' and compares himself to a 'wicked Ravisher' (*Pamela*, p. 32). When he tries to pull her onto his knee, she responds in similarly vivid fashion:

> like as I had read in a Book a Night or two before, Angels, and Saints, and all the Host of Heaven, defend me! And may I never survive one Moment, that fatal one in which I shall forfeit my Innocence.
>
> (*Pamela*, p. 31)

Pamela, we are told, 'lov'd reading', and amatory fiction abounded with threatened women invoking angels and pledging to die rather than suffer the fatal moment. When D'Elmont breaks into her bedroom, Haywood's Melliora begs 'ye saints! [...] ye ministring angels! whose business 'tis to guard the innocent! protect and shield my virtue!' and cried, 'I'll resign my life!' and die 'a victim to your cruel, fatal passion' (*Love in Excess*, p. 117).[25] B. embraces his role as a ravisher, booming that Pamela cannot lose her 'Innocence' if 'oblig'd to yield to a Force' that she 'cannot withstand' (*Pamela*, p. 32 – they are debating whether she will sit on his knee). As he declares, after reading her letters to her parents about him, 'You have given me a Character, *Pamela*, and blame me not that I act up to it' (*Pamela*, p. 210).

Fiction of the 1720s tended to feature vulpine maids. The heroine of Haywood's *Fantomina* (1725), dresses as a country maid to trick Beauplaisir into her arms, Rowe's maids trap men by reminding them of their virtue, and lady's maid Gigantilla, heroine of Haywood's *The Perplex'd Dutchess; or, Treachery Rewarded* (1727) pretends virtue to ensnare the Duke of Malfi into marriage. Richardson pointedly subtitled his novel *Virtue Rewarded*, and attempted to resist such plots by showing B. as repentant, Pamela as virtuous, and closing with their marriage.[26]

Much to Richardson's disappointment, however, many readers approached the story with the interpretative tools suited to a 1720s text about a manipulative maid. Hosts of texts exploited the success of *Pamela* by satirizing, continuing, or revising the story, and nearly all focused on the sexual dramatics early in the novel that recalled scenes from 1720s novels – and presented Pamela as pretending virtue to win B. Henry Fielding's *Shamela* (1741) featured a second Gigantilla, boasting her 'Vartue' to tempt Squire Booby. In a satire on the scene when Pamela's faint prompts B.'s repentance, Shamela plots to allow Booby to fondle her in bed and pretends to swoon.[27] In Fielding's novel, virtuous girls cannot pretend sexual feeling, and the text thus propagates the conventions of 1720s texts: honest virgins like Haywood's Melliora glow, blush, throb, and faint with a passion they do not understand; only those, like Fantomina, who have lost their innocence, can pretend, and true passion is alien to them.

Similarly, in Haywood's *Anti-Pamela* (1741), Syrena Tricksy is as skilled as 'the most experienc'd Actresses' at feigning sexual 'Agitations' in order to manipulate men. She even pretends frenzy, nearly capturing Mr L by begging to be taken from this 'fatal House', and vowing to stab herself with a penknife.[28] In *Anti-Pamela*, Haywood recognized and satirized Richardson's borrowings from her work and mocked the way in which he had imported into his Lincolnshire setting forms of male aggression that she had identified with Catholic Italy and Southern Spain. Haywood's most violent narratives took place in Castile or Andalucia, such as in *The Lucky Rape* (1727), or Rome and Venice, such as in *Idalia* or *The Fruitless Enquiry* (1727). In contrast, those set in England often featured men who were easily fooled and women who toyed with their desires, such as in *The Fair Hebrew* (1729) and *Irish Artifice* (1728). *Anti-Pamela* recalled such London texts and the notion that the English were more concerned with financial gain than sexual conquest. And yet both *Shamela* and *Anti-Pamela* were closer to *Pamela* than they appeared: in all three, the 1720s novel's lexicon of love, of throbbing, crying out, and fainting was not a signifier of true feeling but a discourse to be wielded for purposes of self-aggrandisement.

In *Pamela*, 1720s discourses of throbbing and fainting were a linguistic tool that worked to further the courtship and enable a marriage. But readers interpreted things differently, and in his second novel, Richardson was less optimistic about the powers of reclaiming sexualized language, and using love scenes to encourage adherence to 'laudable Meanings'. In *Clarissa*, the 1720s lexicon of desire becomes Lovelace's weapon to justify his attacks on Clarissa and recast her resistance as tremulous quiescence to his erotic authority. She explains to Anna Howe that she fled from her home because she panicked, confused by Lovelace's cries that armed servants pursued her, and was 'hurried to the chariot' where he 'in my fright, lifted me in'.[29] Lovelace writes to his friend, Belford, that she came because she was overwhelmed with desire. As Haywood's Melliora 'sunk wholly' into D'Elmont's arms in a grove at night, crying of her 'susceptible and tender heart' that 'you may feel it throb, it beats against my breast' (*Love in Excess*, p. 124) so Lovelace declares the 'fire' of Clarissa's eyes 'began to sink into a less dazzling languor' as she 'trembled: nor knew she how to support the agitations of a heart she had never found so ungovernable' (*Clarissa*, L. 99, p. 400). He presses her swelling chest to his bosom, relishing '[h]ow near, how sweetly near the throbbing partners' (*Clarissa*, L. 99, p. 400).

Richardson showed Lovelace converting and exaggerating amatory language to excuse his attempt to kidnap, abuse, and finally rape Clarissa. When D'Elmont invades Melliora's room, he grasps her, shouting, 'I have thee thus! thus, naked in my arms, trembling, defenceless, yielding, panting with equal wishes' (*Love in Excess*, p. 117). Likewise, Lovelace breaks in upon Clarissa at night and relishes how her 'sweet bosom, as I clasped her to mine, heaved and panted' pronouncing erotic communion as he feels her 'dear heart flutter, flutter, flutter, against mine'. Declaring 'equal wishes' in her fear and distress, he itemizes her body like an amatory rake, proclaiming how it invites his attempt: it is 'charming', bares itself to him and glows (*Clarissa*, L. 225, p. 723):

> Her bared shoulders and arms, so inimitably fair and lovely: her spread hands crossed over her charming neck; yet not half concealing its glossy beauties [...] ; and at last her lips uttering what every indignant look and glowing feature portended.
>
> > (*Clarissa*, L. 225, p. 724)

A lexicon of fluttering, throbbing, fainting, and glowing, created to represent female desire, becomes the tool of Lovelace's diabolical plan.

Richardson's effort to suggest 1720s fiction as a nefarious discourse that enabled oppression by associating it with Lovelace's malevolent acts was problematized by the structure of his text. The plot of abduction and seduction, followed by regret, recuperated the textual principle of the earlier fictions that women live most intensely when under sexual threat and a female can only achieve dynamic growth through an experience of sexual aggression imposed by a man. Although Clarissa resists male power, the plot acts to recognize that power, for there is little she can do but die. Moreover, by showing her attaining liberation through envisioning herself in rapturous union with Christ, the text evokes Rowe's suggestion that passionate women could only find fulfilment in heaven. Just as Rowe showed characters finding dying women erotic, so Belford expresses his admiration for Clarissa as she dies by itemizing her charms, like a rake pondering seduction. He admires the 'charming serenity overspreading her sweet face' (L. 482, p. 1362), describes her as a 'lovely skeleton' (L. 419, p. 1231), 'her charming hair in natural ringlets [...] shading [...] the loveliest neck in the world' (p. 1065), as she is '[e]ver elegant' (L. 471, p. 1345) in her nightgown, just as Lovelace thinks Clarissa 'sweetly elegant' (L. 225, p. 726) in her nightdress when she struggles against him and he praises her 'wavy ringlets [...] wantoning in and about a neck that is beautiful beyond description'(L. 99, p. 399). Clarissa may attempt to control representations of herself, but she is finally judged and appraised, like a 1720s heroine, by the itemizing gaze.

Richardson's friend, Lady Bradshaigh, described to him how she read *Clarissa* in amatory fashion, suffering 'Agonies' as she dropped the book and 'let fall a Flood of Tears', unable to read further.[30] He encouraged such confessions, telling her that she should define her 'Susceptibility' as not 'Weakness' but 'Humanity, and see how your Sentences will run'.[31] Richardson was delighted to imagine readers overwhelmed by sensations very like those offered to the consumers of Haywood. Less gratifying to him, however, was their habit of reading it in other ways commensurate with amatory expectations: aroused by Clarissa's seduction and critical of her for wilfully putting herself into Lovelace's power.[32] He revised his text to render Clarissa more saintly and Lovelace more degenerate, eventually publishing five versions. In the third, most altered text of 1751, he included a passage where Lovelace imagined raping Anna Howe and her mother. Still, readers found enthusiastically for Lovelace and declared, in the words of one critic, that the 'natural catastrophe' of the novel was to provoke the reader's desire to 'enjoy Clarissa'.[33] As Richardson found, 'love scenes' attracted an eager public, but came with their own coordinates of expectations, and readers came to distrust his declaration that his text was directed to laudable meanings.

Richardson avowed to Lady Bradshaigh that *Pamela* had taught Fielding 'how to write to please', for before *Joseph Andrews* ('a lewd and ungenerous engraftment') the 'poor man wrote without being read'.[34] Fielding knew Haywood and had satirized her as the bustling 'Mrs Novel' in his play, 'The Author's Farce' (1730). He poked fun in *Tom Jones* (1749) at excessive romance and melodramatic seduction plots, but he also reworked the notion that amatory passion, the throbs and glows, signified true feeling and gentility of character. *Pamela*, *Clarissa*, and *Anti-Pamela* might have presented throbs of passion as a discourse that characters wielded for their own ends, but Fielding showed the virtue of his heroes by attributing to them a physically manifest ardour that 1720s novelists associated with young virgins. Just as 'a thousand Sighs heave the Bosom of Joseph' in *Joseph Andrews* (1741) so Tom blushes, stammers, grows pale, and sighs at the sight or thought of Sophia Western.[35] When he encounters her in a grove, he does not attack her but 'fell a-trembling as if he had been shaken with the fit of an ague' (*Tom Jones*, p. 207). By streams, with 'gentle breezes fanning the leaves', he dreams of his beloved, like any 1720s heroine. There, he is animated by the dissolving worship that virgins such as Lasselia believe men feel, as his 'warm heart melt[s] with tenderness' and he cries that even if he never experienced her body 'still shalt thou alone have possession of my thoughts, my love, my soul' (*Tom Jones*, p. 222).

Tom's throbbing emotion contrasts with the pragmatism of Mr Blifil, who cares nothing for the 'absolute possession of the heart of his mistress, which romantic lovers require' and it engenders the narrative's comic end (*Tom Jones*, p. 255). Like any Haywoodian heroine, Sophia is banished by her father and nearly seduced in 'a Fatal Hour' by the vitiated Lord Fellamar (*Tom Jones*, p. 698). Her story ends happily, thanks not only to her father's drunken arrival at Fellamar's but also to the restrained, even feminine, quality of Tom's passion. But his self-control reflects their relative positions: she is too much his social superior for him to treat her as a sexual resource. Fielding addressed the problem that male passion was proved by a language of rapacity, which made marriage impossible, by creating a male hero whose situation is initially much inferior to that of his beloved.

Haywood's *The History of Miss Betsy Thoughtless* (1751) is longer than her 1720s texts and reflects a desire for more detailed, sentimental narratives, rather than the short seduction plot. In her tale of Betsy's attempts to keep her virtue and her love for Truelove intact in contemporary London, excessive romance is satirized. Love language, as in *Clarissa*, is associated with rakes, and the text satirizes the contrast between Gaylove's vow that 'I cannot live, if longer denied the sight of you!' and his suggestion of a rendezvous at a 'habit-shop in Covent-Garden'. As one alderman complains, 'romantic idle notions' will not 'buy a joint of mutton'.[36] And yet the only way in which her friend, Miss Forward, can explain her seduction is by evoking the amatory grove. Just as Amena in *Love in Excess* is ruined in a grassy enclave where 'not a breath but flew winged with desire and sent soft thrilling wishes to the soul' (*Love in Excess*, p. 58), so Miss Forward describes an arbour where 'only gentle zephyrs, with their fanning wings, wafted a thousand odours from the neighbouring plants', an 'enchanting scene' where 'nature herself seemed to conspire my ruin'.[37] There is no way for a woman to discuss illicit passion other than, as in the 1720s novel, projecting the sexual emotion onto the grove in which she is ruined. As Richardson and Fielding found, amatory language could be mocked and maligned, but there were few other ways of describing female passion.

Haywood, Aubin, Davys, and Rowe had a crucial influence on the mid-century novel but received little credit for their contribution. Readers in the 1740s and 1750s recognized and satirized the 1720s content, but successive readers and scholars came to believe Richardson and Fielding's claims of originality. As their books became canonical, so the development of representations of sexual feeling by the novelists of the 1720s as vital to fiction work lived on, but often through Richardson's conflicted readings and his association of erotic language with exploitative male desire. Although the variety and complexity of the 1720s texts was elided, the plot of abduction and seduction was enshrined as crucial to the feminocentric novel. The convention that the driving force of a narrative should be male passion and the plot that a woman lives most intensely when not choosing for herself, but resisting sexual threat, proved fertile ground for future novelists such as Jane Austen, Frances Burney, and Charlotte Smith to recall, satirize, and undermine.

Notes

1. Samuel Richardson to Aaron Hill, 1741, *The Selected Letters of Samuel Richardson*, ed. by John Carroll (Oxford: Clarendon Press, 1964), p. 41. For Richardson as founder of the novel with Defoe and Fielding, see Ian Watt, *The Rise of the Novel: Studies in Defoe, Richardson and Fielding* (1957; Harmondsworth: Pelican, 1976).
2. See Ros Ballaster, *Seductive Forms: Women's Amatory Fiction from 1684 to 1740* (Oxford: Clarendon Press, 1992), pp. 7–30, 153–95; Paula Backscheider, 'The Shadow of an Author: Eliza Haywood', *Eighteenth-Century Fiction*, 11 (1998), 79–100; Christine Blouch, '"What Ann Lang Read": Eliza Haywood and her Readers', in *The Passionate Fictions of Eliza Haywood: Essays on her Life and Work*, ed. by Kirsten T. Saxton and Rebecca P. Bocchicchio (Lexington: University Press of Kentucky, 2000), pp. 300–26; Sarah Prescott, *Women, Authorship and Literary Culture, 1690–1740* (Basingstoke: Palgrave, 2003).
3. Margaret Doody, *A Natural Passion: A Study of the Novels of Samuel Richardson* (Oxford: Clarendon Press, 1974), p. 149.
4. William B. Warner, *Licensing Entertainment: The Elevation of Novel Reading in Britain, 1684–1750* (Berkeley: University of California Press, 1998), pp. 147, 197.
5. Richardson to Sarah Chapone, 11 January 1751, Victoria and Albert Museum Forster Manuscripts XII, II, fol. 7. Carroll reads 'Heywoods' but it seems to me to be correctly spelt (Richardson, *Selected Letters*, ed. by Carroll, p. 173, n. 68).
6. Richardson, 31 August 1741, *Selected Letters*, ed. by Carroll, pp. 46–8.
7. The texts were third person, with the exception of the two epistolary novels, Davys's *Familiar Letters* (London, 1725) and Rowe's collection of letters from the dead in heaven to the living, *Friendship in Death* (London, 1728).
8. Eliza Haywood, *Idalia* (London, 1723), p. 11.
9. Keith Maslen, *Samuel Richardson of London, Printer: A Study of his Printing* (Dunedin: University of Otago Press, 2001), p. 90.
10. Richardson, 2 June 1753, *Selected Letters*, ed. by Carroll, p. 232.
11. For evidence of Richardson's authorship, see Wolfgang Zach, 'Mrs. Aubin and Richardson's Earliest Literary Manifesto (1739)', *English Studies*, 62 (1981), 271–85. See also Thomas Keymer, 'Introduction', to *Pamela; or, Virtue Rewarded*, ed. by Thomas Keymer and Alice Wakely (Oxford: Oxford University Press, 2001) p. xxi, n. 31. Hereinafter cited as *Pamela* and included in the main body of the text.
12. Samuel Richardson, 'Preface' to Penelope Aubin, *A Collection of Entertaining Histories and Novels* (London, 1739), pp. 2, 3.
13. Doody, *A Natural Passion*, p.143.
14. Eliza Haywood, *Lasselia; or, The Self-Abandon'd*, ed. by Jerry C. Beasley (Lexington: University Press of Kentucky, 1999), pp. 116–17.
15. Eliza Haywood, *Love in Excess*, ed. by David Oakleaf (Peterborough, Ontario: Broadview, 1993), p. 108. Hereinafter cited as *Love in Excess* and included in the main body of the text.
16. Eliza Haywood, *The Masqueraders* (London, 1724), p. 7.
17. Haywood, *Lasselia*, p.119.
18. Penelope Aubin, *Charlotta du Pont* (London, 1723), pp. 8–10.

19. Mary Davys, *The Reform'd Coquet* and *The Accomplish'd Rake*, in *The Reform'd Coquet, Familiar Letters betwixt a Gentleman and a Lady, and The Accomplish'd Rake*, ed. by Martha Bowden (Lexington: University Press of Kentucky, 1999), p. 165.
20. Elizabeth Rowe, *Friendship in Death* (London, 1728), pp. 15, 7–8.
21. Elizabeth Rowe, *Letters Moral and Entertaining*, 3 vols, 2nd edn (London, 1733–34), I, 148.
22. James Sterling, 'To Mrs Eliza Haywood on Her Writings', in Haywood, *Secret Histories, Novels and Poems*, 4 vols (London, 1725), I, ll. 32–2 and l. 26.
23. Aaron Hill to Samuel Richardson, 8 March 1749, in *The Correspondence of Samuel Richardson*, ed. Anna Laetitia Barbauld, 6 vols (1804), IV, 56.
24. Richardson wrote in the preface to the sequel, *Pamela in her Exalted Condition* (London, 1741) that the events of the original story occurred between 1717 and 1730 and political references square the action with the period of Robert Walpole's ministry from 1721 to 1742. See Richardson, *Pamela; In her Exalted Condition* (London, 1741), pp. iii, iv. On references to Walpole, see Morris Golden, 'Public Context and Imagining Self in *Pamela* and *Shamela*', *ELH*, 53 (1986), 311–29.
25. For similar scenes of protesting heroines, see Eliza Haywood, *The Rash Resolve* (London: 1724), pp. 20–4; *Lasselia*, p. 120; Rowe, *Friendship in Death*, pp. 48–9, Mary Davys, *The Reform'd Coquet*, ed. by Bowden, p. 59.
26. See Eliza Haywood, *Fantomina*, in *Popular Fiction by Women, 1660–1730: An Anthology*, ed. by Paula R. Backscheider and John J. Richetti (Oxford: Oxford University Press, 1996), p. 235; Elizabeth Rowe, *Friendship in Death*, pp. 66–9; *Letters Moral and Entertaining*, II, 219–30; I, 386–94.
27. Henry Fielding, *Shamela* in *Joseph Andrews and Shamela*, ed. by Douglas Brooks-Davies and Martin Battestin, revised and introduced by Thomas Keymer (Oxford: Oxford University Press 1999), p. 22.
28. Eliza Haywood, *Anti-Pamela*, in *Anti-Pamela and Shamela*, ed. by Catherine Ingrassia (Peterborough, Ontario: Broadview, 2004), pp. 54, 114–15.
29. Samuel Richardson, *Clarissa or The History of a Young Lady*, ed. by Angus Ross (Harmondsworth: Penguin, 1985) , L. 98 , p. 387. Hereinafter cited as *Clarissa* and included in the main body of the text.
30. Lady Bradshaigh to Richardson, 6 January 1749, Victoria and Albert Museum Forster Manuscripts, FM XI, fols 13.
31. Richardson to Lady Bradshaigh, no date [1749?], Forster Manuscripts, XI, fol. 7.
32. Critics declared her a 'Coquet' a 'Prude' and 'undutiful Daughter' and 'too fond of a Rake'. See Sarah Fielding, *Remarks on Clarissa* (London, 1749), pp. 10–11.
33. Anon., *Critical Remarks on Sir Charles Grandison, Clarissa, and Pamela*, ed. by A.D. McKillop, Augustan Reprint Society No. 21 (Los Angeles: Williams Andrews Clark Memorial Library, 1950), p. 46.
34. Richardson, 1749, in *Selected Letters*, ed. by Carroll, p. 133.
35. Henry Fielding, *Joseph Andrews* in *Joseph Andrews and Shamela*, ed. by Douglas Brooks-Davies and Martin Battestin, p. 42.
36. Eliza Haywood, *The History of Miss Betsy Thoughtless*, ed. by Christine Blouch (Peterborough, Ontario: Broadview, 1998), pp. 32, 37.
37. Haywood, *Betsy Thoughtless*, p. 75. For another example of the woman projecting her sexual feelings onto the grove in which she succumbed, see Rowe, *Letters Moral and Entertaining*, I, 108.

Part III
Writing Modes

7
Scribal and Print Publication

Kathryn R. King

'Well, but the joy to see my works in print!' wrote Mary Jones to her friend, Lady Bowyer, 'Myself too pictured in a mezzotint', droll self-imaginings that are countered elsewhere in the 'Epistle to Lady Bowyer' by the poet's Horatian preference to 'live unknown, unenvied too'.[1] Her proud indifference to public notice notwithstanding, the 'Epistle' would appear in print some fifteen years later as the lead poem in a handsomely mounted *Miscellanies in Prose and Verse* (1750) that sported the names of some 1400 subscribers. Jones makes the usual apologies: she had been prevailed upon by 'friends' and agreed to publication ('so disagreeable a task') only with a view toward assisting an aged and helpless relation, and as for the poems, they are nothing, 'it being quite accidental' that her 'thoughts ever rambled into rhyme'.[2] Yet, critics then and now agree that her witty verse is in fact unusually accomplished. The ironies are many, and they dramatize the uncertain meaning of print at this time. The volume is obviously a product of the book trade, the 1400 printed copies to be 'delivered' to its paid subscribers well in excess of expected print runs for a volume of this sort, and the imprint bears the name of London bookseller Robert Dodsley, publisher of Pope, Johnson, and others. *Miscellanies* is no less obviously the product of an amateur literary culture as attested by the coterie verse, much of it addressed to friends, and even more strikingly by the inclusion of the poet's 'private' letters to women friends. Is Jones a gentlewoman amateur or a writer for pay? Is the volume a typographical replication of a manuscript-based sociable interaction or the artifact of a print culture well aware of the commercial value of just such glimpses into private, largely feminine, aristocratically inflected worlds? Such questions are unanswerable, at least in any simple form, for the Jones volume is a near perfect example of that paradoxical 'publishing of the private' that in recent analysis fosters the modern separation of 'the public' and 'the private': a separation at once emergent and highly unstable throughout our period.[3]

This chapter considers the uses women made of print and script at a time when these media carried shifting cultural meanings and could therefore be exploited to serve a variety of authorial purposes. Consider the phenomenon of coterie circulation. At its most 'private' coterie writing was a sociable exchange of handwritten texts for the amusement of oneself and the inevitable 'few friends'. But as the Jones subscription volume illustrates, by mid-century coterie exchange could blend almost indistinguishably with the now dominant culture of print and coexist in mutually useful ways with the London-centred book trades. Even in the previous century coteries had occupied equivocal positions along the public-private continuum. Friends might copy and distribute a particularly pleasing poem until there were 'More copies of it abroad than I could have imagin'd', as Katherine Philips ('Orinda'), foremost manuscript poet of the Restoration period, discovered with genuine dismay.[4] Jane Barker, one of many women in our period who took Orinda as a model, found a handwritten autobiographical 'treatise' intended for private circulation marketed in 1713 as *Love Intrigues*, a novel, its mildly racy commercial title slapped upon it by the rogue bookseller Edmund Curll who attributed it to 'a Young Lady' (Barker was in her sixties at the time).[5] There is no reason to think Mary Astell sought print publication when she began a philosophical correspondence with John Norris but she could hardly have been too surprised when after only ten months this well-published clergyman shepherded their letters into print.[6] Elizabeth Carter's 'Ode to Wisdom' first appeared, to her surprise, in *Clarissa* (1747). Richardson did not know the author and later apologized.[7] The boundaries between 'private' and 'public' were porous throughout the period 1690–1750, and if the interpenetration of print and manuscript cultures presented women writers with well-documented hazards, it also offered them new ways to reach larger, more extended, and diversified readerships via new modes of print-based public-sphere circulation.

An earlier stage of feminist literary history had a tidier storyline, which, over-simplified further still, goes something this. Over the course of the century men and women came increasingly to occupy separate spheres, and at first the field of female authorship was itself divisible into two camps: the retiring, well-bred daughters of Orinda (Anne Finch, Countess of Winchilsea, and Elizabeth Singer Rowe are the oft-named) discreetly circulated verse in manuscript while out on the streets Aphra Behn and her noisier marketplace-oriented daughters Delarivier Manley and Eliza Haywood, the triumvirate of wit, pioneered such modern forms as the novel and journalism while engaging as well in commercial playwriting and other kinds of writing for pay. The emergence of the female author and the 'entry into print' seemed, then, much the same thing. This progressive narrative has been challenged from several directions, however. First, the case for print as the engine of modernity made by Elizabeth Eisenstein in her landmark study *The Printing Press as an Agent of Change* (1979) has been criticized for its failure to take into account synchronic variation within the field of print, to say nothing of the range of opportunities represented by an ongoing manuscript culture.[8] Second, assumptions about the superior authority of print have been challenged by findings from the counter-field of manuscript studies, most importantly for our period the work of Harold Love, much of it distilled in *Scribal Publication in Seventeenth-Century England* (1993), and that of Peter Beal in his *Index of English Literary Manuscripts* (1980–93) and in his Lyell Lectures published as *In Praise of Scribes: Manuscripts and their Makers in Seventeenth-Century England* (1998).[9] This work, along with case studies published yearly in *English Manuscript Studies, 1100–1700*, has made it impossible to ignore the role played by scribal transmission into the eighteenth century. Third, shifts in emphasis within feminist studies have resulted in large-scale revisions in the way we think about women vis-à-vis both print and manuscript cultures. Earlier interpretative models tended to associate script with privation – 'silencing' – and print-averse poets, Philips and Finch for example, were said to fear 'publication as a kind of sexual self-display',[10] but the focus upon absence and exclusion that characterized an earlier phase of feminist recovery has been replaced in the last decade by interest in female creative agency in all its forms.

These developments converge in the work of Margaret Ezell. In three compelling monographs – *The Patriarch's Wife: Literary Evidence and the History of the Family* (1987), *Writing Women's Literary History* (1993), and *Social Authorship and the Advent of Print* (1999) – Ezell argues that the rise of print and the commerce of letters did not mean the demise of coterie writing: scribal practices continued to flourish alongside the newer print forms. Her insistence that the creative agency of women found expression through a much wider range of media, technologies, and publication practices than had been thought and that handwritten texts 'count' has inspired archival investigations that are already bearing fruit: in electronic form, the database of women's manuscripts compiled by the Perdita Project and, in print, the essays in *Women's Writing and the Circulation of Ideas: Manuscript Publication in England,*

1550–1800 (2002) that together point toward a 'broader conception of the practice of authorship, including various modes of collaborative writing and methods of publication that operate outside of the publishing industry centered in London'.[11] Emphasis on female agency is evident in innovative approaches to women in print culture as well. Paula McDowell, to take just one example, looked into previously unexamined sites for evidence of women's participation in the emerging public sphere. *The Women of Grub Street: Press, Politics, and Gender in the London Literary Marketplace 1678–1730* (1998)[12] re-envisioned the print marketplace as a 'newly pluralist' site for unsuspected new 'democratic possibilities', specifically the political writings of women of middling and lower ranks. The once accepted narrative of linked 'rises' – of print, the bourgeois public sphere, the literary marketplace, the novel, and professional female authorship – is now judged to be misleading in both its details and storyline. Clear-cut oppositions between print (vigorous, demotic, progressive) and manuscript (attenuated, elitist, nostalgic), along with the broader ones in which they are usually nested (print/ public/masculine v. manuscript/private/feminine), are now regarded as too sharply drawn, too dismissive of the vitality and continuing force of manuscript culture and women's important role within it, and too liable to filter out information about women's actual writing practices. Increasingly, we have come to understand manuscript and print cultures in our period in terms of coexistence and complex interplay, offering women of various class positions and regional locations a diversity of publication possibilities to suit a host of different purposes.[13]

1 Coterie writing and the ambiguities of manuscript

Although print acquired new kinds of cultural authority in our period, manuscript continued to be the prestige medium. Attitudes toward manuscript circulation varied according to a complex range of factors. Among elite writers preference for the handwritten text was tied to class prejudice: scribal transmission kept one's compositions out of the sullying hands of lesser creatures and avoided the commercial associations of print. Harold Love's observation that the 'stigma of print bore particularly hard on women writers'[14] may overstate the situation generally but is true enough for women in the upper social strata. Lady Mary Wortley Montagu offers a well-known case in point. With wealth and rank she inherited an aristocrat's disdain for print as demeaning. She kept a private album of verses to show friends and permitted them to make copies (one form of scribal publication) but when she wanted to comment on public issues (or persons) she turned, inevitably, to print. Her first print appearance was a contribution to *The Spectator* (number 573, 28 July 1714) and she would later deliver, again anonymously, a splendidly scabrous riposte to Swift in the form of a handsomely printed folio entitled *The Dean's Provocation for Writing the Lady's Dressing-Room* (1734) that used the name of a trade publisher in its imprint to launder its origins. Montagu's experience of print was 'painfully conflicted': she was 'now secretly wangling herself into print, now actively self-censoring'.[15] A similar history of conflict was played out in the writing life of the poet Anne Finch, Countess of Winchilsea. Bowing to the pressure of the ubiquitous 'friends' she agreed to a volume-length transcription of her verses (her husband acted as her amanuensis) but insisted she would 'ever resist' the 'more daring manefestation [sic]' of print.[16] Not too much later, however, *Miscellany Poems* (1713) daringly manifested: 'Permission is at last obtained for the Printing' the bookseller was pleased to announce (wrongly, as it turns out).[17] The greater part of Finch's verse did not see print until the twentieth century. For women of rank print was unsuitable 'except in circumstances of the most careful decorum and discretion',[18] and yet, for all their class-based misgivings, women such as Montagu and Finch were drawn to the potentialities of the medium. Their willingness to forgo the control offered by traditional scribal methods in order to reach the impersonal public-sphere reader testifies to the fact that, for all its liabilities, print had become the acknowledged lingua franca of cultural exchange.

Women of the middling ranks were drawn to manuscript exchange for a variety of reasons. One, certainly, was sociability. In a verse epistle, a form favoured in coterie circles, Jane Brereton claimed the privilege of showing her 'dullness to a private friend or two', adding a mischievous parentheses: '(As to the world male writers often do)'.[19] In addition to literary friendships, social authorship offered women possibilities for patronage and social protection and, to the ambitious, access to more extensive or prestigious script-based literary networks. The provincial poets Elizabeth Singer (Somerset) and Jane Barker (Lincolnshire) are well-documented examples of women who attracted the notice of titled women and circulated their writings in aristocratic female-friendship circles. But coteries could also offer access to print. Many women participated in mixed-sex groups that included men with book-trade connections. The Dublin poets Mary Barber, Laetitia Pilkington, and Constantia Grierson (an accomplished printer herself) belonged to a self-styled *Senatus Consultum*, an exchange-and-critique circle whose female participants looked quite naturally to the group's best-known member for career advancement, although the danger of relying upon Jonathan Swift as an ally would be brought home to them only too clearly. Before her remarkable achievements as a marketplace novelist Eliza Haywood exchanged handwritten verses with fellow 'Hillarians', a group of artists and writers who orbited around Aaron Hill, the sexually charismatic man-of-letters with extensive book-trade and playhouse connections. Hill materially supported some of her earliest ventures into print.[20] Barker traded poems with Cambridge students and a young London bookseller, Benjamin Crayle, who printed some of them in *Poetical Recreations* (1688).[21] She later transcribed them into a manuscript volume now preserved at Magdalen College, Oxford, 'corrected by her own hand', with a note that they had been printed without her consent. And that may be. But judging from manuscript lines praising her 'copartner[s]', the Cambridge friends (the 'gayest, sweetest, gentlest, youths on earth') who helped put together 'the little printed book', she was anything but resentful. Besides, a woman who exchanges verses with an aspiring London bookseller is probably not greatly averse to seeing her poetry in print.[22]

An instructive figure in the annals of female engagement with male 'co-partners' is the immensely popular devotional writer and poet known to her contemporaries as the pious Mrs Rowe, discussed earlier as Elizabeth Singer (her maiden name). A model and inspiration to the self-consciously virtuous Bluestocking writers of the next generation, she was possibly the most beloved female author of the eighteenth century (the posthumous publication of her titles is staggering). Recent scholarship regards her as a key figure for study of 'respectable' female authorship in the second half of the eighteenth century. Study of the earliest phase of her career tells us that she was also one of the seventeenth century's most inventively self-fashioning authors. All the while she was cultivating elite connections with the nobility and gentry at Longleat, the nearby country seat of the Weymouth family, she was orchestrating her entry into print by way of multi-layered exchange with John Dunton, the ebullient London bookseller who in 1691 founded the popular periodical *The Athenian Mercury*, the interactive format of which offered an avenue into print for aspiring provincial talents that Singer, still in her teens, was quick to exploit. Employing the public gallantry he helped bring into fashion, Dunton hailed Singer in print as the bright unknown and, after filling the pages of the *Mercury* with verses by the 'Pindarick Lady', as he called her, invited her to join him in a private 'Platonick' correspondence. They exchanged letters as Cloris and Philaret that he would later threaten to publish. To her lasting consternation Singer found herself entangled in print and out of it with a man unable or perhaps unwilling to distinguish between print and 'real life', a print-world impresario for whom the endlessly permeable membrane between private self and public self-representation was vanishingly thin. Eventually, he fell in love with the still unseen Cloris and proposed marriage. He narrates the collapse of his platonic pretensions in the hilarious 'The Double Courtship' in which he depicts himself 'sighing and whining *and all but hanging* to enjoy her Person'.[23] He seems never to have left off pursuing her in print. This *buffo* episode might be said to offer a fairly straightforward instance of the vulnerability of women to unwanted male attentions in a book trade under male control except for the fact of Singer's own performative ingenuity in the affair: the whole time she was playing a double game in relation to the *Mercury* – gracing its pages as 'the Pindarick Lady of the West' while as 'Cloris' exchanging platonic letters with its proprietor – she was engaged behind the cover of still another pseudonym, 'Philomela', in manuscript exchanges with the great folk at Longleat who encouraged her love for Tasso. To complicate matters further, in 1696 she would publish verses in print as 'Philomela' under Dunton's auspices. The point is not that the pious Mrs Rowe began her writing life steeped in duplicity but rather that she shared the period fascination with theatricality, masks, performance, and disguise. This love of role-playing combined with a literary culture that favoured concealment (anonymous and pseudonymous publication would be the rule throughout the century) to create a kind of conceptual stage on which the young Singer was able to experiment with different identities as she crafted poetic personae for different audiences.[24]

The confusion of 'public' and 'private' that is a striking feature of the pas de deux performed by Singer and Dunton in the *Athenian Mercury* in the 1690s reappears in the 1730s on the pages of the *Gentleman's Magazine*, a monthly that became for its generation the leading venue for provincial poetic amateurs. In the heyday of the amateur poetry craze the magazine devoted as many as eight double-column pages to poetry each month, offering opportunities for men and women to appear in print cloaked by pseudonyms. The Welsh poet Jane Brereton, writing as 'Melissa', regularly sent verses and became one of a mixed-sex virtual coterie whose members interacted on the pages of the magazine. Brereton entered into playful on-page debate with 'Fido' unaware that in real life he was a vintner in her neighbourhood until he created a local sensation by slitting his throat.[25] For a less lurid example of the blurred line between the print world and real life we might consider a print format that came into its own during this period, the poetic miscellany. The miscellany provided verse with a social setting, important for women because the sociability thus projected mitigated the appearance of unseemly ambition or unladylike self-interest while evoking, nostalgically perhaps, the collaborative nature of amateur coterie writing. Miscellanies were products of the press, their printed pages offering themselves to unknown eyes, but – and here was part of the fascination – the verse they contained could easily be read as private exchanges, typographical replications of the very poems that celebrity authors copied and shared amongst themselves. This sense of the private made public is played up on the title page of Anthony Hammond's *A New Miscellany of Original Poems* (1720), which declares the verses to be 'Now first Published from their Respective MANUSCRIPTS'. (The 'most eminent hands' represented in the *Miscellany* included Lady Mary Wortley Montagu, Martha Fowke, Susanna Centlivre, and Delarivier Manley: as intriguing a mix of women writers as one is likely to find.) Many of the poems capture the easy impromptu informality of the handwritten text, some with titles that teasingly evoke the interplay of manuscript and print – 'Written in the Blank Leaf of Mrs. Manley's Tragedy', for example – or that reproduce something of their London scribal provenance, such as 'Verses, said to be set up near the House of Commons'. Miscellanies could seem to point off-page to enigmatic relationships, giving them the whiff of a titillating 'secret history'. One of the most intriguing in this respect, the *Miscellaneous Poems and Translations* (1726) compiled by Richard Savage, may look today like a 'rather anodyne benefit volume', as Christine Gerrard has said, but its 'urbane surface conceals stronger emotions'.[26] Verses by, to, and about women – such as 'Miranda' (Hill's wife) and others still unidentified, 'Evandra', 'Aurelia', and 'Daphne' – testify to the inner turmoil of a sexually charged literary circle that nurtured, in addition to a number of male poetic talents, two important and famously inimical women from the 1720s, Haywood and Mrs Sansom ('Clio'), the former Martha Fowke. Taken together the miscellany offers the *frisson* of an implied but never quite fulfilled disclosure of the sexual tensions that rocked the Hillarian circle at this time.

The tendency of texts to be 'neither private nor public in the conventional sense of the terms'[27] is one crucial aspect of literary culture in this period. The thrill of the private made public vibrates through many of the most popular forms, the miscellanies and magazine verse-exchanges just discussed but also important forms such as verse epistles, epistolary novels, collections of letters ('real' and concocted), satires and other prose fictions turning on the conceit of the discovered manuscript, the scandalous *romans à clef* that created such agreeable noise: all to some degree tantalize with the pleasure of a glimpse through the keyhole into the supposed private lives of their creators or contributors (or satiric victims). We know that, in a different register, manuscript circulation could be a medium of intellectual or learned exchange by which 'women could and did comment on public issues concerning social and political matters'.[28] But that intermediate quality, 'neither private nor public', can apply to many *printed* texts as well. A printed text, David Fairer reminds us, 'most obviously represents an expansion of readership', and once in print, privacy becomes a public property, available to thousands of unknown readers. Poets in our period were aware that a 'poem's *notional* reader and *actual* reader' might not be the same so they 'had to be more alert to matters of taste and tone, and perhaps work harder to create a responsive readership'.[29] Fairer is not making a claim about women specifically here, but his insistence that critics attend to the importance of voice, tone, and persona in the context of the teasing overlap of 'public' and 'private' has implications for ongoing work on women's writings. Gone are the days when a critic would confuse Mr Spectator with Joseph Addison, Gulliver with Jonathan Swift, or even 'Pope' with Pope: these speakers are understood to be personae, fictive masks. But it is common, still, to find Haywood identified with her 'Female Spectator', editor of a monthly periodical 1744–46, and downright uncommon for a critic to pause to consider what it means that her *Memoirs of a Certain Island* (1724–25)[30] is narrated by an increasingly fatuous Cupid or that the secret histories making up *A Spy upon the Conjurer* (1724)[31] come in a letter purportedly written by the hyperbolically love-lorn 'Justicia', her romance susceptibilities arguably a reflexive joke on the author herself; to complicate matters further, the persona of Justicia may also invoke earlier scandal narrators, the name recalling Astrea (goddess of Justice) of Manley's earlier scandal chronicle *New Atalantis* (1709) with possible reference to Aphra Behn's well-known *nom de plume* of the 1680s. Criticism of various sects and denominations would be richer for a deeper engagement with the personae crafted and deployed by women in our period.

2 Writing for pay and the ambiguities of print

The immediate result of the expiration of the Licensing Act in 1695 was a rapid expansion in the number of printers and presses in London and the provinces that created unprecedented opportunities for paid work in the book trades.[32] Women continued to work in areas that had traditionally drawn upon female labour – printing, publishing, retail sales, bookbinding, papermaking, and so on – but starting in the Restoration period with Aphra Behn and increasingly from the 1690s onwards they began to earn their bread, or part of it anyway, in a line of work that, although ill-paid and precarious, offered a distinctly modern kind of livelihood: paid authorship. For women with literary ambitions or, as was probably more often the case, suffering financial hardship, who possessed a certain fluency, a tolerance for risk, an unfussiness when it came to the stigma of trade, and the imagination to shape a public identity in the absence of useful precedents, the literary marketplace represented an emerging and as yet ill-understood realm of possibilities.

The story of authorship for pay is encapsulated in the career of Eliza Haywood, a writer of prodigious output who stands as the premier example of the female 'dependent professional' in the period, that is, a writer obliged to live upon the proceeds of her pen; a 'hack' or 'low scribbler' in earlier parlance.[33] Between 1719 and 1756, the year of her death, she print-published many of the usual marketplace forms: verse encomia, plays (tragedies and comedies, including one musical), amatory novels (her first venture in the field, *Love in Excess* (1719–20), launched a vogue for amatory fiction that lasted more than a decade), 'spies', secret histories and scandal chronicles, periodical journalism, domestic novels, 'oriental' political satire, dramatic historiography, epistles 'from the ladies', conduct manuals, translations from the French ranging from 'polite' entertainments to obscene erotic tales, and more – some seventy-odd titles over nearly four decades. She was now and then an actress. She repaired a play for John Rich at Lincoln's Inn Fields and collaborated in creating a successful ballad-opera version of Henry Fielding's *Tom Thumb* (it became *The Opera of Operas*).[34] In the early 1740s she would branch out into the retail side of the print trade, opening a pamphlet shop in Covent Garden at the sign of Fame, and would go on to publish on a small scale (mostly pamphlets and broadsides), although she seems never to have financed the printing of the considerably more substantial products of her own pen. She may have set up the retail shop in order to help out her longtime friend and sometime literary collaborator, the financially feckless William Hatchett.[35] Haywood's detractors see her as a low scribbler, 'desperate for money', but I see a thorough-going professional whose tireless energies, astonishing productivity, and rock-solid work ethic qualify her for consideration as the century's foremost female literary entrepreneur and place her alongside Defoe and Pope as exemplifying the commercial orientation of literature in the first half of the century.[36]

There is no reason to think that Haywood herself would take pleasure in the terms of my praise: certainly she commenced authoring with a nobler set of aspirations. Her affair with Savage, if it ever occurred, has overshadowed her brief, intensely literary friendship with Hill, partly traceable in the manuscript verse they exchanged between *c.* 1718–21, some of it printed in *Poems on Several Occasions* (1724).[37] These verses reveal that while still in her twenties, before harnessing herself to the demands of the subsistence writing that consumed the better part of her writing life, Haywood yearned for literary glory of a high-minded, old-fashioned sort.[38] It was during the period of her close association with Hill that she brought out her only subscription volume, a method of publication by advance payment often used to lend a note of aristocratic sanction to a print venture (subscriber lists usually boast a healthy sprinkling of titled and gentry names).[39] The desire for fame that pulses through her poems to Hill is strongly present in the front matter to *The Fair Captive* (1721), the play she was hired to amend for performance at Lincoln's Inns Fields, which was, significantly, her first known piece of hack work. She expresses distaste for marketplace venality, the 'meaner Views [that] cou'd wing the Poet's Flight' and seeks to set herself apart from Grub Street writers by emphasizing the contrast between the still uncorrupted purity of her aspirations and the 'thousand servile Practices' by which 'the Noblest *Art*' is debased into 'a *Trade*'.[40] Later in the decade when Haywood had put together a long string of commercial titles, her identity as a hack consolidated, Savage would taunt her with being a 'printer's drudge'. He knew how to hurt her.

It is fitting that when Haywood set up a retail shop in 1742 she would publish and sell under the sign of Fame. To her admirers today 'Fame' seems a deliberate play on the scandal of her name and writings. But those familiar with period political iconography will know that Fame was the winged woman of allegorical prints whose trumpet sounded the triumph of virtue over corruption: the figure of Fame on her sign may have hinted at the oppositional tendency of the materials on offer. Perhaps she was remembering earlier hankerings after literary fame. From newspaper advertisements and trade lists we know that from 1742 Haywood sold books, sixpenny political pamphlets, broadsides, unperformed plays, erotica, and other ephemera at Fame and would do so for the next two years at least. She may have published on a small scale for the rest of the decade. In December 1749 the prosperous bookseller Charles Corbett deposed to having 'sold several things Wrote & Published by the s^d Mrs Haywood',[41] suggesting that, operating well below the radar, she had been publishing pamphlets (topical and cheap by definition) out of her lodgings and leaving no trace in surviving imprints. There were doubtless many other women working like this at the lower levels of the trade.

Haywood's involvement in the retail and publishing end of the trade points to a feature of professional female authorship in the first half of the century that is sometimes overlooked: its close ties with the printer's and stationer's trades. It seems symbolically apt that Tory journalist, playwright, autobiographer, and scandal chronicler Delarivier Manley, one of the first full-fledged professionals, should live above a print shop. Mary Davys, novelist and playwright, another of the first generation of professional writers, opened a coffee shop where, if contemporary practice elsewhere is any guide, she would have supplied customers with the latest papers and pamphlets. Laetitia Pilkington struggled unsuccessfully to live by her pen in London after a ruinous divorce in 1738 (she would be imprisoned for debt for nine weeks in 1742), in spite of a talent for sparkling impromptu verse and a willingness to put her wits to the service of dim gentlemen happy to trade guineas for songs they could pass off as their own. Her biographer writes 'All kinds of writing could be bought from Grub Street writers, some of whom were women. We know almost nothing about them, but there must have been others besides Mrs Pilkingon writing poems, petitions, and pretend billets-doux.' After her release from prison, with financial assistance from surprising quarters, Colley Cibber and Samuel Richardson among others, she opened a little pamphlet shop (with a speciality in prints) in St James's Street and continued to ghost letters and petitions for a flat fee of twelve pence.[42] Elizabeth Boyd proposed using proceeds from the subscription edition of *The Happy-Unfortunate* (1732) to set up a shop selling 'Papers, Pens, Ink, Wax, Wafers, Black Lead Pencils, Pocket Books, Almanacks, Plays, Pamphlets, and all Manner of Stationary [sic] Goods'.[43] Her imprints suggest an effort to set up a place of business where she might attract people of fashion. A pamphlet-poem from 1740 has Boyd selling self-published poems at 'a cook's-shop, the sign of the Leg of Pork and Sausages, in Leicester-street, by Swallow-street' but by that December she was able to announce the existence of 'the new pamphlet shop' located 'over-against the Crooked-Billet in Leicester-street' and later, in 1745, when she tried her hand at periodical publication with the intriguingly titled *The Snail; or, The Lady's Lucubrations*, she directed customers to Vine Street in the St James area. One wants to know more about this resourceful woman who vended poems in a cook's shop and distributed her snail-like lucubrations from a pamphlet shop in the vicinity of the court.

Awareness of all this para-authorial traffic in retail book sales, ghost-writing, the instruments and matter of the handwritten text ('Papers, Pens, Ink, Wax, Wafers, Black Lead Pencils'), to say nothing of the 'Proposals' and begging letters for support which seem to have gone with the job, gives us a fuller sense of authorship as work, an economic activity that unites the interior welling up of 'private' inspiration with the sheer materiality of writing as practised, as we see in the case of a Pilkington or a Boyd, at the commercial meeting place of the cultures of manuscript and print. It attests as well to the sheer difficulty of staying afloat at a time when the places and preferment received by men as remuneration for their labours with the pen were generally unavailable to women, who were thus obliged to look to booksellers (and grateful recipients of dedications) for payment; and we are reminded by one book trade historian that 'the most common form of payment between publisher and writer in the eighteenth century was no payment at all'.[44] Recent years have seen a proliferation of images of writing women, quills in hand, gracing covers and dust-jackets of anthologies and biographies. They are finely dressed, contemplative, and serene; they gaze inward or look mildly at the viewer. These ladies are to be preferred, perhaps, to the whorish slatterns of misogynist stereotype, the ink-spattered Phoebe Clinket (John Gay, *Three Hours after Marriage* in 1717) and nasty 'greasy' Sappho (Alexander Pope, 'Of the Characters of Women', Epistle II of *Moral Essays*, l. 25 in 1735), but their writerly composure is far removed, surely, from the workaday realities of an Elizabeth Boyd selling poems at the Leg of Pork and Sausages or one of the novelists for whom erstwhile poetic amateur Jane Barker spoke when she declared in 1723 that a 'smear'd Finger' does no great harm after all. We need to attend more closely to the 'smear'd' circumstances of writing and publishing in this early phase of professional female authorship. The print shops, pamphlet shops, sale of ink and paper, offer scope for a re-envisioning of female authorship somewhere in the commerce-inflected middle ground where images more rough-edged but honest might be substituted for those well-coiffed ladies with quills.

3 Conclusions

Generalizations about women's publication choices are tricky for a period when cultural meanings of both print and manuscript, and their relation to 'privacy' and 'publicity', were in flux; the result in no small part of changes in consciousness brought about by the technology and institution of printing. Print enabled the paradoxical 'publication of the private' while it seemed also 'to hold in suspension' that separation of public and private that 'it historically helped enforce' and thus created the conditions that render Michael McKeon's question a 'conundrum': 'Is printing a public or a private activity?'[45] Theoretical models that conceptualize the emergence of female authorship in relation to opposed spheres – the private domestic sphere constructed in ever-hardening opposition to the bourgeois public one, understood to be male – have come to seem inadequate, yet it does not follow that we need a new model. Instead of revamped theories I would argue for a higher order of attentiveness: first, to the nuanced spectrum of often overlapping publication possibilities available during the period, and, second, to the astonishing variety of actual writing and publishing choices exercised by actual women in the eighteenth century. The fact that the technologies and culture of print became dominant in our period should not permit us to forget that an amateur coterie-based literary manuscript culture continued to thrive, allowing authors to shuttle back and forth between scribal and printed media and modes of circulation. Coterie poets, provincial amateurs, lettered women, and women of high social rank continued to use the handwritten text for sociable purposes and resorted to scribal mechanisms when they wished to control the readership, circulation, and reception of their writings; but in a period increasingly attuned to the power of public opinion, when poets and men of wit conducted private feuds and exemplary friendships in public spaces, it was inevitable that some women would decline to limit their enmities and affections to coterie circles, even if their forays into print required subterfuge. Print also offered access to the expanding public sphere of national opinion; as well, obviously, it held out the possibility of personal income, however meagre. And then, of course, there is Mary Jones's 'joy to see my works in print!' For a complex range of reasons women writers of every stripe and persuasion found it expedient to turn now and then to technologies of print.

In the story as I have told it Eliza Haywood stands as laudatory symbol of female authorship to come, but that is emphatically not the way her female contemporaries or their immediate successors would have seen things. In the second half of the century Haywood and her brand of commercially driven scribbling had to be repudiated in order that the redeeming power of female virtue could gain full cultural play. In 1737, when she was just twenty, Elizabeth Carter, a leading figure in the group of the strenuously respectable Bluestocking women discussed by Betty Schellenberg in the next volume in this series, wrote an elegy on Mrs Rowe published in the *Gentleman's Magazine*. Rowe's 'chaste' and 'generous' writing corrects the 'lawless freedoms' of certain 'female wits' – Haywood is unnamed but clearly implied – and sets the pattern for a new, more uplifting, more broadly acceptable kind of female author who teaches her readers to 'relish pleasures of a nobler kind'. Haywood and others of her generation enlarged tremendously the public space available for women writers; the next generation would work to make that space respectable and for that they needed to banish Haywood and her 'low' ilk to the shadows of a disowned literary past. As literary historian Susan Staves notes, Carter's elegy 'constructed a history of women's writing as an earlier dark age of licentiousness and misogyny, of female wits enthralled by "Th'intriguing novel and the wanton tale", ended by the triumphant career of Rowe'.[46] The story of the re-fashioning of female authorship around images of piety, intellectual accomplishment, and moral rectitude in the next generation takes place, however, within the frame of a larger story of interlinking female creative agency that I would stress by way of conclusion. The Bluestockings relied upon non-print forms of expression, conversation and letter-writing in particular, to claim a nationally recognized cultural authority. In this they were, like their predecessors, determined to exploit to the full the media best suited to their purposes. Gender, class, region, religion, age, ethnicity, sexuality, generation: all were limiting factors but all represented a repertoire of possibilities as well. So too the available genres, poetic kinds, rhetorical modes, and formats extend possibilities for the woman who writes. As we chart the accomplishments of our female forebears we must learn to attend to their publication choices as well.

Notes

1. *Eighteenth-Century Women Poets*, ed. by Roger Lonsdale (Oxford: Oxford University Press, 1990), p. 157.
2. Mary Jones, 'Epistle to Lady Bowyer,' *Miscellanies in Prose and Verse* (Oxford, 1750), pp. 50, vi.
3. See Michael McKeon, *The Secret History of Domesticity: Public, Private, and the Division of Knowledge* (Baltimore: Johns Hopkins University Press, 2005), esp. chapter 2.
4. See Elizabeth H. Hageman and Andrea Sununu, '"More copies of it abroad than I could have imagin'd": Further Manuscript Texts of Katherine Philips, "the matchless Orinda"', *English Manuscript Studies*, 5 (1995), 127–69.
5. See 'The Passage into Print', in Kathryn R. King, *Jane Barker, Exile, A Literary Career 1675–1725* (Oxford: Clarendon Press, 2000), pp. 182–9.
6. See Ruth Perry, *The Celebrated Mary Astell: An Early English Feminist* (Chicago: University of Chicago Press, 1986), pp. 73–82.

7. Elizabeth Carter, 'Ode to Wisdom', in *Eighteenth-Century Women Poets*, ed. by Lonsdale, p. 166.
8. Elizabeth Eisenstein, ed., *The Printing Press as an Agent of Change: Communications and Cultural Transformations in Early Modern Europe*, 2 vols (Cambridge: Cambridge University Press. 1979). For a summary of these criticisms, see Leslie Howsam, *Old Books and New Histories: An Orientation to Studies in Book and Print Culture* (Toronto: University of Toronto Press, 2006).
9. Harold Love, *Scribal Publication in Seventeenth-Century England* (Oxford: Clarendon Press, 1993); *Index of English Literary Manuscripts. Vol. 2: 1625–1700*, compiled by Peter Beal, 2 vols (London: Mansel, 1987–93); Peter Beal, *In Praise of Scribes: Manuscripts and their Makers in Seventeenth-Century England* (Oxford: Oxford University Press, 1998).
10. Dorothy Mermin, 'Women Becoming Poets: Katherine Philips, Aphra Behn, Anne Finch', *ELH*, 57 (1990), 335–55 (p. 336).
11. Margaret Ezell, *The Patriarch's Wife: Literary Evidence and the History of the Family* (Chapel Hill, NC: University of North Carolina Press, 1987), *Writing Women's Literary History* (Baltimore and London: Johns Hopkins University Press, 1993), and *Social Authorship and the Advent of Print* (Baltimore and London: Johns Hopkins University Press, 1999); George L. Justice, 'Introduction', in *Women's Writing and the Circulation of Ideas: Manuscript Publication in England, 1550–1800*, ed. by George L. Justice and Nathan Tinker (Cambridge: Cambridge University Press, 2002), p. 1; *Perdita Manuscripts: Women Writers 1500–1700*, Adam Matthew Digital <http://www.amdigital.co.uk>.
12. Paula McDowell, *The Women of Grub Street: Press, Politics, and Gender in the London Literary Marketplace 1678–1730* (Oxford: Oxford University Press, 1998).
13. My language here and throughout is indebted to David Fairer's suggestive chapter 'Between Manuscript and Print' in his *English Poetry of the Eighteenth Century, 1700–1789* (London: Longman, 2003), pp. 1–20.
14. Love, *Scribal Publication*, p. 54.
15. Isobel Grundy, *Lady Mary Wortley Montagu: Comet of the Enlightenment* (Oxford: Oxford University Press, 1999), pp. 342–3, xviii, xix.
16. *The Poems of Anne Countess of Winchilsea*, ed. by Myra Reynolds (Chicago: University of Chicago Press, 1903; reissued New York: AMS Press, 1974), p. 7.
17. Anne Finch, Countess of Winchilsea, 'The Bookseller to the Reader', in *Miscellany Poems, On Several Occasions* (London, 1713), p. A2
18. Isobel Grundy, 'The Politics of Female Authorship: Lady Mary Wortley Montagu's Reaction to the Printing of Her Poems', *The Book Collector*, 31 (1982), 19–37 (p. 19).
19. Jane Brereton, 'Epistle to Mrs Anne Griffiths. Written from London, in 1718', in *Eighteenth-Century Women Poets*, ed. by Lonsdale, p. 80.
20. See Christine Gerrard, *Aaron Hill: The Muses' Projector 1685–1750* (Oxford: Oxford University Press, 2003), esp. pp. 66–71.
21. Jane Barker, *Poetical Recreations: Consisting of Original Poems, Songs, Odes &C. With Several New Translations* (London, 1688).
22. Magdalen College, Oxford (MS 343). See Kathryn R. King, *Jane Barker, Exile*, pp. 30–8, and *The Poems of Jane Barker: The Magdalen Manuscript*, ed. by Kathryn R. King (Oxford: Magdalen College, 1998).

23. John Dunton, 'The Double Courtship', in *Athenianism: or, the New Projects of John Dunton* (London, 1710), pp. 1–61 (p. 13).
24. See Kathryn R. King, 'Elizabeth Singer Rowe's Tactical Use of Print,' in *Women's Writing and the Circulation of Ideas*, ed. by Justice and Tinker, pp. 158–81; see also Sarah Prescott, 'Provincial Networks, Dissenting Connections, and Noble Friends: Elizabeth Singer Rowe and Female Authorship in Early Eighteenth-Century England', *Eighteenth-Century Life*, 25 (2001), 29–42, reprinted as chapter 6 in her *Women, Authorship and Literary Culture, 1690–1740* (Basingstoke: Palgrave Macmillan, 2003), pp. 167–86.
25. See Anthony D. Barker, 'Poetry from the Provinces: Amateur Poets in the *Gentleman's Magazine* in the 1730s and 1740s', in *Tradition in Transition: Women Writers, Marginal Texts, and the Eighteenth-Century Canon*, ed. by Alvaro Ribeiro and James G. Basker (Oxford: Clarendon Press, 1996), pp. 41–56 (p. 254).
26. Gerrard, *The Muses Projector*, p. 96. For a reconstruction of some of the relations hinted at in the Savage miscellany, see pp. 96–101.
27. Ezell, *Social Authorship*, p. 40.
28. Ibid.
29. Fairer, ed., *English Poetry*, p. 6.
30. Eliza Haywood, *Memoirs of a Certain Island Adjacent to the Kingdom of Utopia*, 2 vols (London, 1724–25).
31. Eliza Haywood, *A Spy Upon the Conjurer* (London, 1724).
32. For an overview of women's involvement in the London book trade during this period, see Paula McDowell, *The Women of Grub Street: Press, Politics, and Gender in the London Literary Marketplace 1678–1730* (Oxford: Clarendon Press, 1998), pp. 33–62.
33. For the dependent professional, see Prescott, *Women, Authorship and Literary Culture* , esp. pp. 15–24. The term was introduced by Cheryl Turner in *Living by the Pen: Women Writers in the Eighteenth Century* (London: Routledge, 1992), p. 60.
34. Eliza Haywood, *The Fair Captive* (London, 1721) was revised from a manuscript by Captain Robert Hurst at the request of John Rich, manager of the New Theatre. Eliza Haywood and William Hatchett, *The Opera of Operas; or, Tom Thumb the Great* (London, 1733).
35. For Hatchett and the Covent Garden shop, see the scattered references in Patrick Spedding, *A Bibliography of Eliza Haywood* (London: Pickering & Chatto, 2004), esp. pp. 687–9.
36. The quote is from Susan Staves, *A Literary History of Women's Writing in Britain, 1660–1789* (Cambridge: Cambridge University Press, 2006), p. 167.
37. Eliza Haywood, *Poems on Several Occasions*, vol. 4 of *The Works of Mrs Eliza Haywood*, 4 vols (London, 1724).
38. For relations between Haywood, Savage, and Hill, see Kathryn R. King, 'Eliza Haywood, Savage Love, and Biographical Uncertainty', *Review of English Studies*, 59 (2008), 722–39.
39. For the complex contemporary meanings of subscription publication, see Thomas Lockwood, 'Subscription-Hunters and their Prey', *Studies in the Literary Imagination*, 34 (2001), 121–35. The publication was the moderately high-end translation *Letters from a Lady of Quality* (London, 1721). The fact

that she never again published by subscription may reflect her marginal social and professional position; unable as a professional to garner philanthropic support as a worthy object of charity but lacking sufficient 'interest' with persons of influence to get together a substantial subscription list.

40. Eliza Haywood, *The Fair Captive* (London, 1721).
41. Quoted in Spedding, *A Bibliography of Eliza Haywood*, p. 750.
42. Norma Clarke, *Queen of the Wits: A Life of Laetitia Pilkington* (London: Faber and Faber, 2008), p. 208.
43. Elizabeth Boyd, 'Advertisement' after list of subscribers, *The Happy-Unfortunate; or, the Female Page. A Novel, In Three Parts*, (London, 1732), n.p.
44. Terry Belanger, 'Publishers and Writers in Eighteenth-Century England', in *Books and their Readers in Eighteenth-Century England*, ed. by Isabel Rivers (Leicester: Leicester University Press; New York: St Martin's Press, 1982), pp. 5–25 (p. 21).
45. McKeon, *Secret History*, p. 53.
46. Staves, *A Literary History of Women's Writing*, p. 227. 'On the Death of Mrs. Rowe' is reprinted in *Eighteenth-Century Women Poets*, ed. by Lonsdale, p. 167.

8
Drama

Jane Spencer

A story often told about Susanna Centlivre, one of the most popular and long-enduring British playwrights of the period 1690–1750, concerns the actor Robert Wilks's reaction to her play *The Busie Body* (1709). At a meeting to read through the script, he threw his part into the pit, exclaiming that 'no body would bear to hear such Stuff'.[1] Such an attack was a serious matter, even for an experienced playwright like Centlivre, who had been staging her plays in London since 1700. As a leading actor, Wilks had considerable control over the repertoire; a year after this encounter, he, Colley Cibber, and Thomas Doggett formed the triumvirate of actor-managers who brought a new government to Drury Lane theatre. Luckily, Drury Lane went ahead with Centlivre's play despite Wilks's disdain, and it was a hit, with a good run that season and a long popularity in the repertoire. But his attack was probably typical of many responses to female-authored work in the eighteenth-century theatre, and is one indication of the climate in which Centlivre wrote: a difficult one for playwrights in general, with added obstacles for women. Her success in the theatre was won against the odds.

Not that economic and social conditions were unfavourable to the theatre. Britain's growing commercial prosperity in these years fostered wide demand for all forms of public entertainment. Acting companies toured the country, and provincial towns began to build their own theatres. Over in Ireland, Dublin's Smock Alley Theatre had been running since 1662. London, however, remained the theatrical capital, and the place to bring out new plays; and this was not so easy as we might expect in a time when audiences were increasing. The patents granted by Charles II, restricting spoken drama to two companies, reduced the theatrical competition that would have discouraged managers from relying on the cheap, safe option of established plays. The patents' legal status was challenged, theatre managements changed amid a series of disputes, and alternative kinds of performance, notably opera, grew outside the patented theatres. In the complex and often volatile conditions of this period, some times were more encouraging than others for the playwright; but none were easy. Judith Milhous and Robert Hume find that in the late 1600s a few writers, including Aphra Behn, were able to make at least a proportion of their income over several years from plays, but conclude that from 1700 until the 1780s, nobody in Britain was making a living as a playwright. For women, the prospects were considerably worse than for men: on average, their plays had lower box-office returns than men's and brought their authors significantly less money.[2] Commercial writing – selling pleasure to the public – was often, in varying tones from jest to earnest, compared to prostitution, and the association was always stronger when the author was a woman, whose sexual body was understood to be implicated in the productions of her mind. But if women playwrights were selling themselves, they were not making much out of the deal.

Still, women wrote for the theatre in greater numbers than ever before. Like all dramatists they had to negotiate their way through the movement for stage reform which set in during the 1690s, when the theatre was under attack for immorality and profanity. Some, like Catharine Trotter, embraced the idea of reform and aimed to write moral plays; others, like Susanna Centlivre, were more equivocal, opposing the idea of a didactic theatre while pragmatically toning their work down in comparison to that of their predecessors. Comedy was undergoing a shift from the 'hard', cynical, and sexually explicit forms popular in the Restoration to a 'softer' drama in which wit and intrigue were made compatible with more positive (though often thoughtfully questioning) attitudes to marriage and a gentler treatment of the butts of humour. Some of the 'humane' comedies of the early eighteenth century, with their clever plotting, witty dialogue, high spirits, and occasional serious reflections, still work well on the stage today. The period's tragedies have not fared so well, tending as they do to the sensational or the sententious; but as a prestigious form for broaching political and philosophical concerns, they are worth attention. This chapter will combine an overview of women's main contributions to the drama with brief discussions of three sample plays: Mary Pix's intrigue comedy, *The Innocent Mistress* (1697), Catharine Trotter's politically and philosophically ambitious *The Revolution of Sweden* (1706), and Susanna Centlivre's extraordinarily popular comedy *The Busie Body* (1709). In an age in which England increasingly saw itself as the country of liberty, these plays examined the kinds of liberty that were available (or not) to women.

In the 1670s and 1680s, Aphra Behn had shown that a woman could have a successful career writing for the public theatre. Her example was an inspiration to a later generation of female playwrights, and her work, especially the intrigue comedy *The Rover* (1677), remained a presence in the London theatres throughout the period to 1750. After her death there was an interval of several years before any new plays by women were staged. Then, in the 1695–96 season, four new female playwrights appeared. They did not work closely together, and Catharine Trotter and Delarivier Manley were later to be opponents; but for this season, these women expressed a female solidarity as they stormed the theatre. Their prologues, epilogues, and the commendatory verses they wrote for each other made it clear that they were conscious of invading male territory. Women's sudden appearance was linked to the changing conditions of the theatre. In this season, after years of the United Company at Drury Lane, which had little interest in new plays, a group of actors led by Thomas Betterton, Elizabeth Barry, and Anne Bracegirdle rebelled against the management of the outside investor Christopher Rich, and were allowed a licence to set up a new company in Lincoln's Inn Fields. All at once there was renewed competition and demand for new plays: a climate that encouraged women as well as men to bring their work forward.

The fragile new company took risks, one of the earliest being the staging in September 1695 of *She Ventures, and He Wins*, a new comedy by an untried playwright known only by her pseudonym, Ariadne. Its plot, involving dominant female characters and passive men, also took risks, and the author did not have the dramatic skill of a Behn or Centlivre to make gender role reversal attractive to an audience. The play failed, Lincoln's Inn Fields had to close temporarily, and Ariadne seems not to have ventured again. Other women making their debut did better. Catharine Trotter's *Agnes de Castro*, a tragedy based on a Behn novel, was staged at Drury Lane late in 1695, and Trotter went on to produce three more tragedies and a comedy before retiring from the stage and concentrating on philosophy. Delarivier Manley's comedy, *The Lost Lover*, and her first tragedy, *The Royal Mischief*, were both staged in the spring of 1696: the comedy flopped but the tragedy had a six-nights' run and is still of interest for its unusually sympathetic treatment of a stock character type, the erotic and aggressive woman. Manley went on to produce two further plays in 1706 and 1717, but her greatest success and claim to fame was the politically motivated prose fiction of *The New Atalantis* (1709).

1 Mary Pix

Of the four women who first staged plays in the 1695–96 season, Mary Pix, whose tragedy *Ibrahim, the Thirteenth Emperor of the Turks* was performed at Drury Lane in 1696, went on to have the most sustained dramatic success. She seems to have been a well-liked figure. When the women playwrights of 1695–96 roused the predictably misogynist reaction of a satirical play, *The Female Wits*, its portrait of Pix was notably better humoured than its attacks on Trotter and Manley.[3] Pix produced six comedies and seven tragedies in the decade to 1706, her plays becoming a regular feature in the Lincoln's Inn Fields repertoire. Despite her consistent and modestly successful stage career, she has roused less critical interest than Manley and Trotter, who in their different ways made strong claims for women writers and challenged theatrical conventions for the representation of women. Jacqueline Pearson finds that Pix deals in conventional gender stereotypes, and that, like her male contemporaries, she gives women on average only about a third of the lines in her plays, while Trotter and Manley make women's speech more prominent.[4] Derek Hughes, pointing out that Pix provides socially conservative endings in which law and order are made compatible with desire, goes so far as to call her 'a slavish upholder of male authority'.[5] Indeed, Pix's smaller appetite for challenging the sexism of the contemporary theatre may well have contributed to her relatively easier acceptance within it; but her success should be attributed to her clever stagecraft, especially her handling of witty, swift-paced comedy of multiple plots.

The Innocent Mistress (1697) is a good example of Pix's clever weaving of complex intrigue plots. Influenced by Aphra Behn, whose heroine Hellena, like Pix's Mrs Beauclair, appears in male disguise to interrupt her lover's scene with a rival mistress, and by Congreve, whose famous couple Valentine and Angelica in *Love for Love* (1695) provide another model for her witty lovers, it presents a multitude of plots examining love-relationships across the spectrum of attitudes from idealism to cynicism. Bellinda, the innocent mistress of the title, has left home to avoid unwanted marriage and is now hopelessly in love with the married Sir Charles Beauclair, with whom she is pursuing a determinedly platonic relationship. This serious couple is balanced by the witty Mrs Beauclair and Sir Francis Wildair, whose relationship turns on her endeavours to reform a rake. Before reforming, Wildair has assignations with the kept mistress of Flywife, who, as his name implies, has a chequered marital history: when he turns out to be the first husband, long presumed dead, of Sir Charles's present wife, the virtuous couple are released from their agonized attempts to part. Meanwhile Arabella has escaped from Lady Beauclair's attempts to force her into marriage with her brother Cheatall, and has agreed to marry Beaumont; and Lady Beauclair's daughter Peggy is tricked into marrying Spendall, who turns out not to be rich after all. Even the servants Gentil and Eugenia, after playing their parts in the numerous plots of courtship and trickery, are themselves to marry. The various intrigues are held together by the relationship of all participants to the central triangle of Sir Charles, Lady Beauclair, and Bellinda. The two women represent conventional poles of feminine virtue and depravity. Bellinda, tender yet devoted to 'virgin modesty', receives in Sir Charles 'the reward of virtue and constant love'.[6] Lady Beauclair, defined in the cast-list as 'an ill-bred woman', is the source of everyone's problems, her worst action being to have Arabella locked up. Once defeated she leaves the stage, refusing the movement for comic reconciliation and turning her aggression inwards: 'I could find in my heart to lock myself up and never see your ugly faces again.'[7]

2 Catharine Trotter

If Pix tended to shape her plays according to the conventions that audiences would most readily accept, Trotter was more challenging. Her comedy *Love at a Loss* (1700) deliberately leaves the audience uneasy over an ending in which Lesbia has to accept the other characters' votes for her marriage with her seducer instead of to the man she loves. It was in tragedy, though, that Trotter was most ambitious, especially in her final play, *The Revolution of Sweden* (1706). This depicts the accession of Gustavus Vasa to the Swedish throne, as related in René-Aubert Vertot's *The History of the Revolutions in Sweden* (tr. 1696). Gustavus, who led the Swedes against Danish occupation, was the country's first Protestant ruler and founder of the Swedish nation: in eighteenth-century Britain he represented the successful struggle for political liberty, and Trotter's use of him has a clear political purpose. As Anne Kelley notes, Trotter's play, dedicated to the daughter of the Duke and Duchess of Marlborough, was produced while the Whigs were engaged in trying to secure the Protestant, Hanoverian succession promised in the 1701 Act of Settlement.[8] Trotter's Constantia, a new character not found in Vertot, defends Swedish rebellion in terms echoing those of Locke's contract theory, expounded in his *Two Treatises of Government*:

> When Kings who are in Trust
> The Guardians of the Laws, the publick Peace and Welfare,
> Confess no Law but Arbitrary Will,
> Or know no use of Pow'r but to Oppress,
> And Injure, with Impunity, themselves
> Disown their Office, tacitly acquit
> The People, of whose due Obedience, just
> Protection, is the Natural and Essential Condition.[9]

It is significant that Trotter makes a woman the main speaker for contract and limited government. Her play is the dramatic expression of a feminism developed from Lockean ideas, based on reason, the limitation of ruling powers in matrimonial as well as national government, and the questioning of received views about women's weak and too tender nature. A man torn between love and honour was the usual focus of seventeenth-century heroic tragedies, with women standing for love's claims either as the virtuous and passive objects of desire or its active and villainous subjects. Trotter revises this staple of heroic plot: Arwide risks his life and Swedish interests in an attempt to rescue his wife from the Danes, but two women, Constantia and Christina, are the play's twin centres, and both refuse the role of love-object, intervening in public affairs and taking national obligation to be more important than wifely duty or personal feeling. Trotter takes an element from Vertot's history – Christina, who acts to save Gustavus – doubles it by creating the similar actions of Constantia, and transforms its significance. Vertot speculates that Christina acted as she did out of tenderness for Gustavus: both Trotter's heroines are motivated by public duty untainted by sexual desire. Christina, having warned Gustavus of her husband's plot against him, spends the duration of the play in male disguise hiding from her husband's revenge; that he kills her in the end is the tragic element of the play. Constantia, tricked into believing that Arwide has betrayed the Swedes, also tells Gustavus of her husband's treachery. Christina, dying of her wounds, revives after a lengthy faint on stage (an awakening mocked by the audience) and convinces the senators of Arwide's innocence. While Christina dies and Beron is punished, Arwide and Constantia will live under the just rule of a king who gladly acknowledges his contract with his subjects. Beron's villainy and Arwide's essential goodness show in their respective attitudes to their wives' patriotism. To Beron, Christina's betrayal of him must have been motivated by lust, and he plans to punish her as a 'Strumpet', 'Fix'd on a Rack, exposed to publick view, / Till she expire' (ed. by Anne Kelley *ECWP* II, 234). Arwide, even when facing execution, praises Constantia for putting country above husband:

> With such Appearances against me, what thou didst
> Deserves the highest Honours – Come to my Heart,
> To which thou'rt now more Dear than ever.

(ed. by Anne Kelley, ECWP II, p. 272)

William Congreve, to whom Trotter sent the play in 1703, praised its design but wondered whether 'those of your own sex will approve as much of the heroic virtue of *Constantia* and *Christina*, as if they had been engaged in some *belle passion*' (ed. by Anne Kelley, *ECWP* II, p. xxx). It is as likely that the men in the audience failed to warm to female characters of such cool judgement and limited notions of wifely obligation. *The Revolution of Sweden* had a fair run of six nights at the Haymarket, but was not revived.

3 Susanna Centlivre

Of all the female dramatists who emerged in this period, Susanna Centlivre is the most significant. She began her career with a tragi-comedy, *The Perjur'd Husband* (1700), and wrote nineteen plays in all, most of them comedies. Particularly successful were *The Gamester* (1705); *The Busie Body* (1707), which led to a sequel, *Mar-Plot*, the following year; *The Wonder: A Woman Keeps a Secret* (1714); and *A Bold Stroke for a Wife* (1718). She specialized in swift moving, tightly plotted intrigue comedy with an inventive use of stage business. She was an actor's writer, and till the revival of critical interest in stage spectacle she was not much admired by literary critics, who were generally in search of a more poetic drama. Recently, however, she has been praised as a playwright of ideas who explores contract theory and female claims to authority.[10]

The Busie Body features two couples outwitting men of the older generation: Sir Jealous Traffick who, having imported to England the 'Spanish' custom of secluding young women, keeps his daughter Isabinda away from her lover, Charles; and Sir Francis Gripe, Miranda's guardian, who intends to marry his rich young ward. To foil their plans is to uphold English liberty against Spanish tyranny at a time when

England and Spain are at war, and to assert a young woman's right to control her person and fortune rather than to be the object of men's commerce. These themes are underlined by Isabinda's declaration that though she hates the Spanish nation, she is happy to make use of Spanish tricks such as ladders and secret meetings to gain her desires; by Miranda's allowing Sir Francis to sell Sir George Airy an interview with her for £100, then making use of the occasion to pursue her own designs on Sir George, as well as pocketing the fee; and by her tricking her guardian through promises of marriage into drawing up the legal documents of consent that she promptly turns into the basis for her marriage with Sir George. In a theatre keen to explore the implications of Lockean contract theory, Centlivre provides a patriotic, Whiggish plot with an optimistic feminist slant: Miranda, the freedom-loving English heroine, resists attempts to treat her as property and enters into her own contract.

But the contract, of course, is a marriage contract, bringing the heroine up against a contradiction that feminist thinkers have found at the heart of liberal theory: men and women are considered free agents able to enter into contracts, but a woman entering marriage loses that legal agency and control of her body and property. Anxieties surrounding marriage surface in comedy of this period in the examination of unhappy marriages by dramatists such as Southerne and Vanbrugh, and in the common 'proviso' scene in which young lovers stipulate to each other the terms for an acceptable relationship. In *The Busie Body*, these anxieties are evident in Miranda's adoption of a double identity in courtship: the masked lady who captivates Sir George by her wit, and the beautiful but silent heiress. Having 'try'd [him] in Conversation, inquir'd into his Character', and been convinced of his love, she is ready to reveal herself and marry, though anxiety remains evident in her remark that it was her money that won him (ed. by Jacqueline Pearson, *ECWP* III, p. 98). At this point, when she is giving up her courtship power, her designs are threatened by the busybody of the play's title, Marplot.

Marplot is the play's most novel character, and his popularity kept *The Busie Body* in the repertoire till the nineteenth century. Comic bunglers in love-intrigues had been created before, but Marplot engages in no loves of his own, rather interfering unintentionally in those of others. Though a gentleman, he is too cowardly to fight, and his friends treat him like a servant, giving him errands which usually go wrong. His ambiguous gender status – Centlivre refers to him as one of those 'Men Like Women' who want male protection – and his obsession with his male friends' affairs make him, as Nancy Copeland suggests, a figure for 'sublimated homosexual desire',[11] and tend to establish, by contrast, the effective and rational femininity of the heroine, and the proper masculinity of the hero. Yet when his blunders threaten to expose the plotting lovers to Sir Francis, it is the leading man whose status is undermined – not in masculinity but in humanity. To escape detection, Sir George hides behind the chimney-board. Desperate to stop Sir Francis opening the chimney-board up, Miranda claims that she has a pet monkey hidden there, which must not be let out till it is tamed. Marplot, eager to see the monkey himself, struggles with Miranda to gain access to the chimney. Sir Francis is luckily out of the room by the time Marplot discovers Sir George. Marplot as ever, is sorry to have caused trouble, but, he tells Miranda, 'when you talk'd of a Monkey, who the Devil dreamt of Sir *George?*' (ed. by Jacqueline Pearson, *ECWP* III, p. 101).

Centlivre taps in here to fears prevalent since the Renaissance concerning monkeys and apes, whose disturbing likeness to humans challenged 'man's' distinct and elevated position as the bearer of God's image. The sceptical poet Rochester, delighting in such challenge, made his Artemisia call a monkey the 'curious little miniature of man',[12] a phrase echoed by Marplot as he proclaims his desire for the animal in the chimney. Monkeys threatened to undermine human identity, a threat often parried by likening the monkey to the fop, a degraded and effeminate man. They were represented as ladies' pets, subject to their power, objects of their inordinate and misplaced affection.[13] In Colley Cibber's *The Double Gallant* (1707), Lady Dainty delights in her monkey, who would make an excellent fop in a periwig, and taunts her lover, Careless, that he'll need to be as good as her monkey if he wants her favour.[14] This feminine deployment of the monkey as a weapon in the sex war is punished when Careless tricks Lady Dainty into marriage. In *The Busie Body*, Centlivre reworks the monkey trope within the context of a less aggressive love contest, won by the woman. Miranda calls her lover a monkey only in order to save him and promote their wedding; but the ostensibly accidental slight to his human dignity, a slight usually offered to fops and fools, encodes her fear of handing over the power that belongs to her in courtship to a man who will not, like the monkey, remain a little pet, but may, like the monkey, be dangerous untamed. As she confides to her maid Patch in the following scene, 'there's no Remedy from a Husband, but the Grave' (ed. by Jacqueline Pearson, *ECWP* III, 103).

Once Centlivre stopped writing plays in 1722, no female playwright of comparable stature wrote for the English stage until the later eighteenth century, when Hannah Cowley and Elizabeth Inchbald appeared. Eliza Haywood produced some interesting drama, her *A Wife to be Lett* (1723) exploring the dilemma of a woman whose unlovable husband offers to prostitute her to a man she finds attractive; but the best of Haywood's enormously prolific writing was in other genres, especially the novel. Women writers, who at the turn of the century had been prominent in helping to establish the parameters for a lively and witty but 'reformed' comedy, played comparatively little part in the flowering of new forms of dramatic satire in the short, fertile period between John Gay's *Beggar's Opera* (1728) and the Licensing Act of 1737, which renewed lapsed theatrical censorship and severely curbed the expansion and creativity of the London theatres. Henry Fielding's dramas dominated the early 1730s, and one popular new play by a woman was an adaptation of his *Tom Thumb*: Eliza Haywood's *The Opera of Operas*, written with Thomas Hatchett. Very few new plays by women were performed in between the Licensing Act and the middle of the century, though one or two women with strong theatrical connections had work performed: Charlotte Charke's puppet-show *Tit for Tat* in 1743, the actress Catherine Clive's *The Rehearsal: or, Bays in Petticoats* in 1750. At this point the rapidly rising novel offered better opportunities than the stage for women writers, and it would not be until the different conditions of a more refined late-century theatre that new female playwrights would emerge. The period 1690–1750 was an uneven and challenging one for women playwrights: they had their most lasting impact in the form of Susanna Centlivre, whose comedies were to be a dominant force in the repertoire into the nineteenth century.

Notes

1. John Wilson Bowyer, *The Celebrated Mrs. Centlivre* (Durham, NC: Duke University Press, 1952), p. 96.
2. Judith Milhous and Robert D. Hume, 'Playwrights' Remuneration in Eighteenth-Century London', *Harvard Library Bulletin*, 47 (1999), 3–90.
3. *The Female Wits* (1696), in *The Female Wits: Women Dramatists on the London Stage, 1660–1720*, ed. by Fidelis Morgan, 2nd edn (London: Virago, 1988).
4. Jacqueline Pearson, *The Prostituted Muse: Images of Women and Women Dramatists 1642–1737* (London: Harvester, 1988), p. 172.
5. Derek Hughes, *English Drama 1660–1700* (Oxford: Clarendon Press, 1996), p. 419.
6. Mary Pix, *The Innocent Mistress*, 5.5, in *Eighteenth-Century Women Dramatists*, ed. by Melinda C. Finberg (Oxford: Oxford University Press, 2001), p. 72.
7. Ibid., 5.4, p. 70.

8. Anne Kelley, *Catharine Trotter: An Early Modern Writer in the Vanguard of Feminism* (Aldershot: Ashgate, 2002), p. 135.
9. Catharine Trotter, *The Revolution of Sweden,* ed. by Anne Kelley in *Eighteenth-Century Women Playwrights,* 6 vols, general editor Derek Hughes (London: Pickering and Chatto, 2001), II, 221–2. Hereinafter cited as *ECWP* with volume editor and number and included in the main body of the text.
10. Misty G. Anderson, *Female Playwrights and Eighteenth-Century Comedy: Negotiating Marriage on the London Stage* (Basingstoke: Palgrave, 2002), pp. 109–38; Nancy Copeland, *Staging Gender in Behn and Centlivre: Women's Comedy and the Theatre* (Aldershot: Ashgate, 2004).
11. Copeland, *Staging Gender,* p.107.
12. John Wilmot, Earl of Rochester, *A Letter from Artemisia in the Town to Chloe in the Country,* in *The Complete Poems of John Wilmot Earl of Rochester,* ed. by David M. Veith (New Haven: Yale University Press, 1968), pp. 104–12 (p. 108, l. 143).
13. Laura Brown, *Fables of Modernity: Literature and Culture in the English Eighteenth Century* (Ithaca and London: Cornell University Press, 2001), chapter 6; Susan Wiseman, 'Monstrous Perfectibility: Ape-Human Transformations in Hobbes, Bulwer, Tyson', in *At the Borders of the Human: Beasts, Bodies and Natural Philosophy in the Early Modern Period,* ed. by Erica Fudge, Ruth Gilbert, and Susan Wiseman (London: Macmillan, 1999), pp. 215–38.
14. Colley Cibber, *The Double Gallant* (London, 1707), p. 30.

9
The Periodical

Shawn Lisa Maurer

From the literary periodical's inception in the last decade of the seventeenth century, women readers – and attention to female behaviour, experiences, and concerns – formed an integral part of the development and considerable popular success of this new and increasingly influential genre. Indeed an address to women, conceived within the pages of periodicals as a 'definable "special interest group"' became, early on, a standard rhetorical manoeuvre on the part of periodical editors.[1] Through a variety of formats – including the question-and-answer periodical, the miscellany (an earlier term for magazine), the diary-almanac, and the single-essay periodical – these daily, weekly, or monthly publications constructed an appearance of direct and even intimate relationship with their readership; the genre simultaneously came to depend upon those readers' own submissions, thereby creating space in which women as well as men might see themselves in print.[2] Arguing for a '"pluralist" model of women's literary production', Sarah Prescott asserts that in the course of the eighteenth century, 'more and more women reached a wider audience through the pages of periodicals which, in turn, came to rely increasingly on the contributions of women'.[3]

Thus the genre's putative founder, the author-bookseller John Dunton, proposed to 'Resolv[e]', in anonymous format, 'All the Most Nice and Curious Questions Proposed by the Ingenious' in the title of his (for the time) long-lived *Athenian Gazette or Casuistical Mercury* (subsequently titled the *Athenian Mercury*), published twice weekly between 1691 and 1697; the phrase 'of Either Sex' was included in the title of the second volume, in recognition of the '*pressing* and *numerous*' contributions from 'the *Fair Sex*'.[4] Printed amidst readers' scientific, philosophical, and theological queries, questions about love, sex, and conjugal relations were soon collected into special 'Ladies Issues' to be answered on the first Tuesday of each month. Refusing to marginalize women and their concerns, the *Athenian Mercury* adopted instead a chivalric and at times instructive pose toward its female audience, asserting that women's letters, and their 'Questions of Courtship, Love and Marriage', demanded not only the 'considerable *Time* and *Thought*' of the periodical's male editors, but also contained serious implications for 'the good and welfare of larger Societies, and the whole Commonwealth'.[5]

Published from January 1692 to September 1694, Huguenot author and translator Pierre Motteux's innovative *Gentleman's Journal*, the first monthly English miscellany, paid similarly deferential attention to women, claiming in the first issue that 'The fair sex need never fear to be exposed to the Blush, when they honour this with a Reading'; indeed Motteux concludes his address by stating that 'this is no less the *Ladies Journal* than the *Gentleman's*'.[6] Like Dunton, Motteux cultivated an audience of female readers and writers, soliciting their correspondence and showcasing their literary contributions. Whereas Dunton exploited the seemingly private mode of epistolary discourse within the public forum of his 'Question Project', Motteux in turn made commercial use of coterie literary practices, drawing on an active community of amateur women writers to provide verse and prose for his miscellany.[7]

Perhaps most famously, the inaugural issue of Richard Steele's pioneering essay-periodical the *Tatler* (1709–11) announced the intention of its eidolon (or editorial persona) Isaac Bickerstaff '*to have something which may be of Entertainment to the Fair Sex, in Honour of whom I have invented the Title of this Paper*',[8] while the subsequent *Spectator* (1711–12, 1714), produced jointly by Steele and Joseph Addison, contributed to this seemingly feminized discourse by claiming that its eidolon, Mr. Spectator, 'shall dedicate a considerable Share of these my Speculations' to women, leading them 'through all the becoming Duties of Virginity, Marriage, and Widowhood'.[9] Yet in contrast to earlier efforts by Dunton and Motteux, in which a belief in 'The Equality of both Sexes' formed an integral part of each publication's attitude and agenda,[10] they asserted an inherent gender difference, 'a Sort of Sex in Souls', in which spirits, minds, and even virtues 'have respectively a Masculine and a Feminine Cast' (no. 172, 16 May 1710, *Tatler* III, p. 444). Thus, whereas Bickerstaff harnessed the debased associations of 'tattle' to a manners-and-morals agenda designed in part for women, so too did Mr. Spectator, in maintaining that 'there are none to whom this Paper will be more useful, than to the female World', construct a leisured woman reader desperately in need of the 'proper Employments and Diversions' provided by his publication (no. 10, 12 March 1711, I, p. 46).

As the *Tatler* influentially 'sought to instill a sentimental domestic ideal that redefined the qualities desired by one sex in another',[11] the *Spectator* further refined a belief in 'proper Spheres' for men and women (no. 57, 5 May 1711, I, p. 241), consolidating men's interests by excluding women not only from the all-male Spectator Club, but also from the ostensibly masculine realms of business and party politics.

Emerging with the publications of Addison and Steele as an entertaining and instructive literary phenomenon, the developing periodical genre used its foundational association with women as a way to distinguish itself from the seemingly ephemeral, dangerously partisan – as well as purportedly masculine – arena of party politics associated with newspapers. In this way, periodicals created a new discursive and ostensibly apolitical space in which to discuss social issues. Earlier scholars of these texts have understandably chosen to associate this realm primarily with women, focusing not only on the significant emergence of a female readership but also on the periodical's influential formation of bourgeois femininity.[12] In particular, Kathryn Shevelow's ground-breaking 1989 study, *Women and Print Culture: The Construction of Femininity in the Early Periodical*, detailed the ways in which women's representation 'as readers, as writers, as correspondents, and as illustrative figures' resulted in the creation of the 'domestic woman, constructed in a relation of difference to man'; most of all, Shevelow's book emphasized the genre's crucial contribution to an ideology of separate spheres: 'Defining the private and the public spheres of activity and experience as separated by gender, the periodical represented the private as the feminine, reproductive, apolitical arena of home and family in opposition to the masculine, productive, political realm of work and society.'[13]

Subsequently, critics have increasingly refined the terms of Shevelow's 'domestic thesis',[14] uncovering not only the significant presence of working and middling-class women in the printing and bookselling trades, but also postulating ways in which men, too, were shaped by participation in the so-called private domestic arena.[15] In addition, scholars have explored these texts' representations of women in the public sphere of polite discourse, as well as women's participation in party politics.[16] While periodical literature's efforts to replace polemic with petticoats – what Jonathan Swift, in a deprecating reference to the *Spectator*, called 'fair-sexing it'[17] – may have functioned in part to obscure women's economic and political role in the periodical enterprise, these recent critical studies have established more permeable and often overlapping boundaries between the ostensibly oppositional categories of public and private, political and domestic, professional and amateur, even male and female.

'Fair-sexing it', then, might comprise a lucrative strategy on the part of male authors, but we need to be wary of how fully to accept the ideological implications of this gendered divide. As Iona Italia writes, during the eighteenth century 'it is almost impossible to identify a separate tradition of periodical writing by or for women'.[18] In particular, critics' unquestioned use of the terms 'women's periodical' or 'women's magazine' to describe publications from this period that focused on women's concerns problematically elides a 'feminine' content with female readership, thereby not only limiting the breadth of women's representation and involvement in periodical texts, but also at times erasing men's own inscription within emerging ideologies of gender and class.[19] Helen Berry's statistical analysis of questions from the first five volumes (1691–92) of the *Athenian Mercury*'s 'Ladies Issues' in which the sex of the correspondent was mentioned identifies twice as many queries from men as from women; although the issue of authenticity remains unresolved, both male and female readers are represented in that work as offering questions on gender-related topics.[20] Conversely, women contributed both openly and anonymously to political discourse within periodicals, conceiving their work as providing intellectual fare for coffeehouses as well as tea-tables. Indeed, in much the same way that recent studies have revealed the eighteenth-century London coffeehouses to be less the rational public sphere envisioned by Jürgen Habermas and his followers and more a site of contention and sexual tension,[21] so too must we continually interrogate the ways in which influential periodicals like the *Tatler* and *Spectator* presented as already solidified the very gendered and class-based distinctions they were themselves instrumental in generating.

Thus, while religious, political, economic or status differences between women were being subsumed within the broader category of the genteel middle-class woman, as print 'made it easier for notions of appropriate female behaviour to be codified and dispersed across social and geographical boundaries',[22] emerging genres such as the periodical expanded possible outlets for women's own literary efforts. Furthering the pioneering work of Margaret Ezell,[23] recent studies by Sarah Prescott and E. J. Clery have explored the commercial and personal relationship between John Dunton and Elizabeth Singer (Rowe), dubbed the 'Pindarick Lady' for her poetical contributions to his periodical; in the following century, Edward Cave's popular *Gentleman's Magazine*, launched in 1731, would be 'instrumental in publishing and promoting women's poetry' by printing their work and functioning as a springboard for future collections of verse.[24]

Equally significantly, female figures emerged as editors in their own right. As Tedra Osell cautions, 'We should not allow Steele's and Addison's voices, however dominant, to drown out the babble and chitchat of the gatecrashers who surrounded their tête-à-tête, for it was the gatecrashers who pushed to make the party truly open to the public.'[25] Ironically, the first female editorial persona came from the pages of the *Tatler* itself in the form of Jenny Distaff, younger half-sister to the *Tatler*'s eidolon Isaac Bickerstaff. While the witty and independent Jenny must eventually succumb to Bickerstaff's reformist agenda through an arranged marriage with the 'Man of Business' Tranquillus,[26] her female successors, speaking in editorial registers ranging from the *Whisperer* to the *Tatling Harlot* to Mrs. Penelope Prattle's *Parrot*, explicitly challenged an emerging domestic ideology through editorial personae who were at times neither married nor chaste.[27]

The most successful and long-lived of the 'alternative-*Tatlers*' to follow in the wake of Steele's success,[28] the *Female Tatler* appeared in July 1709 as a purveyor of gossip, scandal, and occasional moralizing. Largely disregarded until recent years, this polyvocal publication, produced initially by a 'Mrs. Crackenthorpe, A Lady that knows everything' and subsequently by a 'Society of Ladies',[29] provides a rich source for investigating relations between authorship and authorial identity in this period.[30] As a text with multiple authors, at least two of whom may have been male, the periodical's editorial pose, what Osell has termed 'rhetorical femininity', served both to consolidate and to challenge female behavioural norms.[31] Through the first-person voices of Phoebe Crackenthorpe and her six female successors, the *Female Tatler* effectively associated both textual authority and a broad range of subject matter – including literature, history, politics, and philosophy – with educated writing women, regardless of whether those editorial figures were themselves composed by females.

Initially, Mrs. Crackenthorpe positions herself as complement rather than rival to the *Tatler*'s Isaac Bickerstaff, as she promises to publish on alternating days to prevent readers' confusing the two works. At the same time, gender difference becomes crucial to the *Female Tatler*'s undertaking, as its editor attempts to recoup periodical writing as a female enterprise since 'tatling was ever adjudg'd peculiar to our sex'.[32] Indeed the *Female Tatler*'s motto *Sum Canna Vocalis* or 'I am a talking Reed' associates the 'knowing' Mrs. Crackenthorpe with the irrepressible nature of speech itself by alluding to Ovid's tale of two men who could not keep their mouths shut. King Midas, cleansed of the dangerous golden touch, foolishly questions the musical superiority of Apollo over

Pan; Midas's barber, in turn, whispers the secret of the king's subsequent punishment – 'Midas has Ass's Ears' – into a hole in the riverbank, where the speaking reeds later grow. As the motto signals the transformation of nature, in the form of reeds played by the wind, into the culture of human discourse, so too does the publication's own ability to metamorphose private scandal into public intelligence necessarily broaden the definition of 'women's sphere'.

Thus whereas Bickerstaff's reports come from a variety of (predominantly male) London coffeehouses or his 'own Apartment' (no. 1), Mrs. Crackenthorpe subsumes the whole within her own domestic part – the drawing room which, by including 'half the Nation' on her twice-weekly visiting days, comprises 'a true history of the world'; and her numerous visitors represent a broad spectrum of polite and commercial society: 'grave statesmen, airy beaus, lawyers, cits, poets and parsons, and ladies of all degrees' (no. 1, FT, p. 2). While contemporary readers and rival publications avidly speculated about the identity of Mrs. Crackenthorpe,[33] the editor herself uses aspersions against her authenticity to assert women's equal intelligence, citing not just her own but the entire sex's 'finer thread of understanding' and superior 'natural parts' (no. 11, 29 July–1 August 1709, FT, p. 25). Yet despite the persistent claim of intellectual parity with men, the publication's female eidolons are unable to position themselves as literary professionals, as their 'civilizing influence' derives, at least in part, from their genteel, and thus ostensibly amateur, status.[34] Accordingly, in the first number Mrs. Crackenthorpe cites her 'estate of £300 per annum' and the fact that she has always kept 'two maids and a footman' as proof that she does not write 'merely for [...] profit' (FT, p. 3); near the end of the periodical's run, the scholarly Lucinda, although herself a gentlewoman, directly questions this restriction, asking 'why may not Women write Tatlers as well as Men' regardless of whether such writing is done 'for Money or for Diversion', since 'no Employment can be more Honourable or Commendable'.[35]

It quickly becomes apparent, however, that despite her refined pose Mrs. Crackenthorpe cannot sustain her inaugural pledge to avoid naming names and only 'gently to correct' her readers' 'vices and vanities' – indeed her publication, largely a scandal sheet, was brought before the Grand Jury of Middlesex in October 1709 for being 'a great nuisance' ('Introduction', FT, p. x). Although papers written by the Society of Ladies also contain provocative, if not explicitly libellous, content, their contributions come closer to being 'diverting, innocent, or instructive' (no. 51, 31 October–2 November 1709, FT, p. 118): particularly in relation to women. Sparked by the *Tatler's* patronizing omission of women from its 'Palace of Fame' (no. 84, 22 October 1709, *Tatler*, II, pp. 32–4), the sisters Lucinda and Artesia facilitate a heated discussion of qualifications for their own list of worthy women. Attempting to right the fact that 'the Writing of History has been all along engross'd by the Men', their project results in three full issues describing the significant accomplishments of females both ancient and modern.[36] While redressing past biases, Lucinda and Artesia also engage with pressing contemporary concerns through a lengthy exchange, initiated by letters from their uncle and aunt, over the correct course of action for their cousin 'Pompey'. While their patriotic uncle desires his youngest son to become a soldier like his brothers 'Cesar' and 'Alexander', killed in war, their grieving aunt wishes him to remain a merchant and inherit the estate forfeited by his brothers' early deaths. The numbers that follow, in which Lucinda takes the aunt's side, Artesia the uncle's, serve not only to humanize a controversial military issue – England's continued involvement in the War of the Spanish Succession – but also to make the sisters and their opinions central to an overtly political debate.[37]

A year and a half after the *Female Tatler's* abrupt end, such political discussion took new form when the recognized fiction writer Delarivier Manley took over from her friend and associate Jonathan Swift as editor of the *Examiner*, the government-subsidized Tory propaganda organ. Fostering party unity while attacking the Whig's own paper, the *Medley*, Manley's run of seven issues unquestionably demonstrates her place as a 'fully legitimised member of the Tory writing team',[38] yet it would be several decades before a woman was herself to found a political journal. Lady Mary Wortley Montagu, aristocratic wife to a Whig diplomat, had earlier dabbled in periodical journalism, anonymously authoring both an entertaining letter to the *Spectator* and a more serious missive for *The Flying-Post; or Post-Master*. Presenting a witty retort to male misogyny in the former through the persona of the much-married 'Mrs. President', Montagu chose in the latter to assume the character of a 'Turkey Merchant' to defend the smallpox inoculation she so strongly championed.[39] In *The Nonsense of Common Sense*, which ran weekly between 16 December 1737 and 14 March 1738,[40] Montagu again employed a masculine voice: this time to criticize the opposition paper *Common Sense* and 'to serve an unhappy worthy man', possibly the beleaguered Whig prime minister Sir Robert Walpole, whose mistress Maria Skerrett was Montagu's friend.[41]

In her short-lived publication, its title probably inspired by *Common Sense's* sardonic invocation of 'Nonsense', patron goddess of 'the Ladies, the Poetasters, and the M[inistry]',[42] Montagu creates a fictional male persona through which to address – and often dismiss as unworthy[43] – that paper's seemingly erroneous viewpoint, condemning not only its misguided political beliefs but also the woman-hating attitudes that Montagu perceived to be increasingly prevalent in male-authored periodicals.[44] Through a clever melding of social and political critique, the male narrator obscures (for Montagu kept her authorship a carefully guarded secret) yet simultaneously displays female capabilities, as the proposed arguments for women's reason become, if only to the knowing few, demonstrations of that very capacity. While Montagu's production of this wide-ranging periodical – which encompasses such diverse subjects as woollen manufacture, Italian castrati, and freedom of the press – functions implicitly to promote women's wit and intelligence, the narrator, in the sixth number, explicitly defends women's position by seeing female inferiority as a product of nurture rather than nature. Contending that women must be educated as well as treated as 'rational sensible Being[s]' in order to become 'not only the most aimable but the most Estimable Figures in Life' (no. VI, Tuesday 14 January 1738, *Essays and Poems*, p. 134), Montagu's narrator rebukes male authors, as well as their male readers, for promoting attitudes that have denigrated women while also shortchanging men.

While Montagu's editor, nostalgic for a time in which both sexes valued reason and politeness, cites Sir Richard Steele as the embodiment of 'Virtue and good sense' (no. VII, Tuesday 14 February 1738, *Essays and Poems*, p. 136), the author of the eighteenth century's most celebrated female-authored periodical, *The Female Spectator*, sees her own antecedent as the renowned Mr. Spectator. Despite being long touted as the first periodical written by a woman for women, Eliza Haywood's publication, published in twenty-four monthly 'books' between 1744 and 1746, has only now begun to receive sustained scholarly attention as a central part of Haywood's extensive oeuvre, which included amatory and didactic fiction, secret histories, drama, and conduct literature as well as periodicals.[45] Composed jointly by an unnamed eidolon – the Female Spectator herself – and an association comprised of a 'Wife', a 'Widow of Quality', and a young Lady,[46] the publication seems modelled upon that of their 'great predecessor' Mr. Spectator who, according to a laudatory poem printed in the *Gentleman's Magazine*, would be 'the first to speak your page's worth'.[47] At the same time, although the *Female Spectator*'s club members represent the female life stages – 'Virginity, Marriage, and Widowhood' – earlier claimed as part of the *Spectator*'s domain, Haywood's own 'coterie of female contributors'[48] cleverly redresses the earlier publication's glaring omission of women from the masculine realm of the Spectator Club.[49]

Yet as critics have been less quick to note, Haywood's text also displays significant continuities with another, less recognized periodical: *The Female Tatler*.[50] Indeed Haywood's publication might be said to combine the all-knowing Mrs. Crackenthorpe, embodied by the worldly Female Spectator herself, with the 'Society of Ladies' who share authorship of the earlier periodical's second half. Operating, like Mrs. Crackenthorpe, out of the domestic space of her 'own Lodgings', the Female Spectator cites past experience and wide-ranging observation, in tandem with 'an Education more liberal than is ordinarily allowed to Persons of my Sex', as qualifications for her desire to be 'both Useful and Entertaining to the Publick' (*Selected Works* Set 2, II, *FS* Book 1, p. 18). Herself a reformed coquet,[51] she aims to impart to readers her own recently-acquired capacity for self-knowledge and self-control by tapping into the 'reigning Humour' of readerly curiosity, so 'that the Gratification [...] from being made acquainted with other People's Affairs, should at the same Time teach every one to regulate their own' (*FS* Book 1, p. 18).

Although her subsequent claim to 'expose the Vice, not the Person' (*FS* Book 1, p. 20) represents an established periodical formula, *The Female Spectator*'s collective narrative structure offers, by contrast, a significant departure from the generic norm. Noting that her collaborators – the exemplary wife Mira, the fashionable unnamed widow, and the merchant's daughter Euphrosine –'are to be consider'd only as several Members of one Body, of which I am the Mouth' (*FS* Book 1, p. 19), the narrator positions herself as a facilitator and discussant rather than ultimate moral arbiter.[52] Speech plays a crucial role in *The Female Spectator*, whether depicted as part of the club's own twice-weekly planning sessions or incorporated into the actual text, as in a supposed male reader's lengthy transcription of a political dialogue between an English and a Hanoverian lady.[53] Indeed throughout the periodical, reading, writing, and speaking become 'inextricably linked': 'By recording a conversation between and among women about their daily challenges, Haywood creates a new and important space for observed (if not lived) experience.'[54]

Exemplifying the broader cultural shift in which 'manuscript culture' becomes 'transmitted into print culture',[55] Haywood's *The Female Spectator* reworks established literary modes to suit her own reforming and commercial purposes. Thus Haywood adapts the essay, traditionally used by male writers as a 'form of advancing knowledge', into a forum for female education by including within her publication discussions of social, religious, political, and scientific topics, thereby attempting 'to distribute that knowledge in ways that bridge the educational gap between men and women'.[56] Moreover, as Robert Jones argues, Haywood rewrites the discourse of taste 'as an educative discourse', presenting women's ability to recognize and cultivate 'refin'd Taste' as a way to authorize their discussion, in public, of topics that would otherwise be 'thought to lie beyond the province of women's experience as it had previously been defined'.[57] In addition, Haywood uses female correspondents' letters, whether authentic or fictional, as a means of creating 'epistolary networks' in which the sharing of information and experiences could function as an educational tool.[58] Thus in Book 10, a letter from 'Cleora' emphasizes that in order to 'improve the Minds and Manners of our unthinking Sex', the Female Spectator must first address 'the Fault of wrong Education', maintaining, *pace* Steele, that since 'There is, undoubtedly, no Sexes in Souls', women must, like men, cultivate minds as well as simply bodies (*Selected Works*, Set 2, II, *FS* Book 10, p. 355).

Yet while employing multiple textual strategies for empowering female readers, the Female Spectator also seeks 'to be as universally read as possible', announcing in the first issue that her publication is intended to instruct 'our Youth of both Sexes' (*FS* Book 1, p. 18, p. 20). Indeed much recent scholarship on *The Female Spectator* has sought to complicate earlier, often feminist, 'misprizings' of the publication's 'public-political involvement': readings in which both politics and men have played surprisingly little part.[59] In much of this previous criticism, *The Female Spectator* is seen to herald a turning point in Haywood's two-pronged career, representing the movement away from earlier, explicitly erotic and political writing toward the didactic work, like her most famous novel *The History of Miss Betsy Thoughtless* (1751).[60] Yet as critics have revealed the political contours of Haywood's earlier 'scandalous' fiction and unpacked the domestic underpinnings of her political satire,[61] so too have recent readings of *The Female Spectator* uncovered not a 'new and improved' Haywood but rather the authorial and narrative strategies of an author with a canny understanding of the intersections of print, publicity, gender, and moral reform.[62] In particular, scholarship on *The Female Spectator* has emphasized the connections between Haywood's 'literary professionalism' and her political writing, recovering the lost political valence of her response, both overt and implicit, to the heated and at times dangerous political climate at home and abroad.[63] In addition, critics have noted how the periodical's extensive inclusion of male correspondents writing from such locations as 'coffeehouses, taverns, the Inner Temple, Oxford, Westminster, [and] the City' functioned to establish 'a veritable community of male readers' willing to 'seek a woman's counsel on a wide range of issues' and entering 'happily into dialogue in terms of near parity with a small circle of thoughtful women'.[64] Although specific information on the publication's readership remains, like our knowledge of Haywood's biography, distressingly vague,[65] what Kathryn King calls the 'rhetorical effect' of including these male correspondents functions to break down rather than reinforce the idea of separate discursive spheres for men and women. Creating, in effect, a kind of 'virtual salon' in which the periodical acts as a model of polite and 'cross-gender dialogue', Haywood's *Female Spectator* breaks new ground while staying within familiar bounds of feminine propriety.[66]

Until the middle of the eighteenth century, therefore, the developing periodical genre provided women writers with a powerful imaginative, educative, and often politicized platform for their literary efforts. Indeed Haywood would herself go on to publish two additional weekly periodicals, the overtly political *Parrot* (1746) and the more conventional *Young Lady* (1756),[67] while novelists Frances Brooke and Charlotte Lennox produced, respectively, *The Old Maid*, authored by the witty 'Mary Singleton, Spinster' (1755–56) and the *Lady's Museum* (1760–61), which innovatively serialized Lennox's own novels. At the same time, the eighteenth-century periodical as defined by its single-essay structure and ingenious editorial persona would be gradually replaced by the magazine – a miscellaneous and generally anonymous format in which women's own participation would be largely circumscribed. In these women's magazines, which flourished in the later eighteenth century and continue to the present day,[68] women would be defined more and more as literary 'consumers rather than producers',[69] educated in the consuming practices that would increasingly come to validate their worth and desirability as women.

Notes

1. Ros Ballaster, Margaret Beetham, Elizabeth Fraser, and Sandra Hebron, *Women's Worlds: Ideology, Femininity and the Women's Magazine* (London: Macmillan, 1991), p. 48.
2. For the genealogy of the periodical and its relationship to readers, see Kathryn Shevelow, 'Early Periodicals and their Readers', in her *Women and Print Culture: The Construction of Femininity in the Early Periodical* (London: Routledge, 1989), pp. 22–57; Ballaster et al., *Women's Worlds*, chapter 2: 'Eighteenth-Century

Women's Magazines'; Shawn Lisa Maurer, *Proposing Men: Dialectics of Gender and Class in the Early English Periodical* (Stanford: Stanford University Press, 1998), pp. 6–17; and Iona Italia, *The Rise of Literary Journalism in the Eighteenth Century: Anxious Employment* (London: Routledge, 2005), pp. 1–22.

3. Sarah Prescott, *Women, Authorship and Literary Culture, 1690–1740* (Basingstoke: Palgrave Macmillan, 2003), pp. 2, 35.
4. *Athenian Mercury*, vol. I, no. 18, 23 May 1691.
5. *Athenian Mercury*, vol. III, no. 13, 8 September 1691. For a full-length study of gender relations as embodied in the *Athenian Mercury*, see Helen Berry, *Gender, Society and Print Culture in Late-Stuart England: The Cultural World of the 'Athenian Mercury'* (Aldershot: Ashgate, 2003). In addition to analysis of broader issues related to print culture and readership, Berry devotes individual chapters to examinations of the body, courtship, and sexual behaviour in Dunton's periodical.
6. Issue for January 1692, p. 1.
7. See Margaret J.M. Ezell, 'The *Gentleman's Journal* and the Commercialization of Restoration Coterie Literary Practices', *Modern Philology*, 89.3 (1992), 323–40.
8. *Tatler*, no. 1, 12 April 1702, in *The Tatler*, ed. by Donald F. Bond, 3 vols (Oxford: Clarendon Press, 1987), I, 15–23, (p. 15). Hereinafter cited as *Tatler* and included in the main body of the text.
9. *Spectator*, no. 4, 5 March 1711, in *The Spectator*, ed. by Donald F. Bond (Oxford: Clarendon Press, 1965), I, 18–22, (p. 21). Hereinafter cited as *Spectator* and included in the main body of the text.
10. The phrase comes from the title of an essay by Motteux, published in the May 1692 issue of the *Gentleman's Journal*. For Dunton's feminist agenda, see Berry, *Gender, Society and Print Culture*; E.J. Clery, in her study of *The Feminization Debate in Eighteenth-Century England: Literature, Commerce and Luxury* (Basingstoke: Palgrave Macmillan, 2004), terms Dunton the 'greatest early innovator of the discourse of feminization' (p. 26).
11. Shevelow, *Women and Print Culture*, pp. 94–5.
12. See work by Rae Blanchard, 'Richard Steele and the Status of Women', *Studies in Philology*, 26 (1929), 325–55; Bertha Monica Stearns, 'The First English Periodical for Women', *Modern Philology*, 28 (1930), 45–59 and 'Early English Periodicals for Ladies (1700–1760)', *PMLA*, 48 (1933), 38–60; Alison Adburgham, *Women in Print: Writing Women and Women's Magazines from the Restoration to the Accession of Victoria* (London: Allen and Unwin, 1971); Cynthia White, *Women's Magazines 1693–1968* (London: Michael Joseph, 1970); Shevelow, *Women and Print Culture*; and Ballaster et al., *Women's Worlds*.
13. Shevelow, *Women and Print Culture*, pp. 4, 5, 15.
14. The phrase comes from Lawrence Klein's influential essay, 'Gender and the Public/Private Distinction in the Eighteenth Century: Some Questions about Evidence and Analytic Procedure', *Eighteenth-Century Studies*, 29.1 (1996), 97–109 (p. 97). Klein had earlier questioned Shevelow's work in 'Gender, Conversation and the Public Sphere in Early Eighteenth-Century England', maintaining that 'Shevelow's account fails to explain the ideological grounds for women's greater participation in print culture' (in *Textuality and Sexuality: Reading Theories and Practices*, ed. by Judith Sill and Michael Worton

(Manchester: Manchester University Press, 1993), pp. 100–15 (p. 102)).
Several recent book-length studies can be seen as necessary efforts toward
such explanation; all three include significant accounts of women and periodical literature. See Paula McDowell's *The Women of Grub Street: Press, Politics,
and Gender in the London Literary Marketplace 1678–1730* (London: Clarendon,
1998); Sarah Prescott's *Women, Authorship and Literary Culture*; and E.J. Clery's
The Feminization Debate in Eighteenth-Century England.

15. For women in the printing trades, see McDowell, *Women of Grub Street*; for
    periodicals' construction of male readers, see Maurer, *Proposing Men*.
16. For the idea of 'sociable learning' with its concomitant 'legitimation of female
    publicity' as endorsed within Addison and Steele's periodicals, see Klein,
    'Gender, Conversation and the Public Sphere', p. 104. See also essays by Sarah
    Prescott and Jane Spencer, 'Prattling, Tattling, and Knowing Everything: Public
    Authority and the Female Editorial Persona in the Early Essay-Periodical',
    British Journal of Eighteenth-Century Studies, 23 (2000), 43–57 and Tedra Osell,
    'Tatling Women in the Public Sphere: Rhetorical Femininity and the English
    Essay Periodical', *Eighteenth-Century Studies*, 38.2 (2005), 283–300.
17. 'I will not meddle with the *Spectator* – let him fair-sex it to the world's end'
    (Letter 40, *Journal to Stella*, 8 February 1712, ed. by Harold Williams (Oxford:
    Clarendon Press, 1948), II, 482).
18. Italia, *The Rise of Literary Journalism*, p. 4.
19. For this critique, see Maurer, *Proposing Men*, chapter 9: 'A Women's
    Magazine?' It was not until the last quarter of the eighteenth century that
    the idea of a 'separate agenda' for women readers solidified into the form we
    know today. See Ballaster et al., *Women's Worlds*, pp. 61–74.
20. Berry, *Gender, Society and Print Culture*, table 3, p. 246 and chapter 3:
    'Authenticity and Women Readers'.
21. See McDowell, *Women of Grub Street*; and Brian Cowan, *The Social Life of
    Coffee: The Emergence of the British Coffeehouse* (New Haven: Yale University
    Press, 2005).
22. McDowell, *Women of Grub Street*, p. 291.
23. In addition to Ezell's article on the *Gentleman's Journal*, cited above, see her
    Writing Women's Literary History (Baltimore: Johns Hopkins University Press,
    1993) and *Social Authorship and the Advent of Print* (Baltimore: Johns Hopkins
    University Press, 1999).
24. Prescott, *Women, Authorship and Literary Culture*, p. 35. Both books contribute
    to the reassessment of Rowe's 'relatively marginal' place in women's literary
    history (ibid., p. 141). Prescott maintains that 'Rowe's poetry was to become
    central to the *Mercury*'s success' (ibid., p. 143), while Clery, *Feminization
    Debate*, chapter 2: 'The *Athenian Mercury* and the Pindarick Lady', reads
    Dunton's publication of Rowe's *Poems on Several Occasions* (1696) as
    'the culmination of the Athenian project' (p. 38). See Prescott, *Women,
    Authorship and Literary Culture*, chapters 5 and 6: 'Gender, Authorship, and
    Whig Poetics' and 'Provincial Networks, Dissenting Connections and Noble
    Friends'. Although Berry, by contrast, makes only passing mention of Rowe
    in her monograph *Gender, Society and Print Culture*, on the *Athenian Mercury*,
    her study emphasizes the radical nature of Dunton's inclusion of women's
    letters and poetry in his publication.
25. Osell, 'Tatling Women', p. 284.

26. Jenny Distaff appears in *Tatler* nos 10, 33, 75, 79, 85, 104, 143. While she authors the first two numbers, the following five are recounted by Bickerstaff, and concern his 'disposal' of Jenny in marriage. Although she reappears as editor in no. 247, it is to answer a woman's letter rather than discuss her own situation. For discussions of Jenny and her relation to Bickerstaff, see Shevelow, 'Fathers and Daughters: Women as Readers of the *Tatler*', in *Gender and Reading*, ed. by Elizabeth Flynn and Patrocino Schweickart (Baltimore: Johns Hopkins University Press, 1986), pp. 107–23 and *Women and Print Culture*, pp. 116–29; Maurer, *Proposing Men*, pp. 109–14; and Italia, *The Rise of Literary Journalism*, pp. 43–47. Tellingly, the well-written but short-lived *Whisperer* is narrated by a runaway Jenny Distaff: 'My Brother having design'd me a Husband, chosen altogether by his own Notions of the Convenient and the Happy, [...] I thought fit to avoid the Match, by Giving him the Slip, and Setting up for myself' (no. 1, 11 October 1709). The *Whisperer* is reprinted, along with *The Tatling Harlot*, in Richmond P. Bond, *Contemporaries of the 'Tatler' and 'Spectator'*, Augustan Reprint Society no. 47 (Los Angeles: Williams Andrew Clark Memorial Library, 1954).

27. All three publications were published anonymously and remain unattributed; few numbers of each survive. *The Parrot* of 1728, written by 'Mrs. Penelope Prattle', should not be confused with the later (1746) publication written by Eliza Haywood. Although some critics have claimed Haywood as the author of the earlier publication, this attribution has been rejected by Haywood's most recent bibliographer. See Patrick Spedding, *A Bibliography of Eliza Haywood* (London: Pickering and Chatto, 2000), pp. 650–2. For a useful reading of the *Whisperer* and *The Tatling Harlot* in relation to the *Tatler*, see Osell, 'Tatling Women'.

28. The phrase is from M.M. Goldsmith's introduction to Bernard Mandeville, *By a Society of Ladies: Essays in 'The Female Tatler'*, ed. by M.M. Goldsmith (Bristol: Thoemmes Press, 1999), p. 41.

29. Indeed the history is even more complicated, in that Mrs. Crackenthorpe, claiming in the eighteenth number to have been 'disengenuously treated by the first printer of this paper', left her first publisher, B. Bragge, and resumed publishing nos 19 through 51 under the imprint of A[bigail] Baldwin. At the same, a rival Mrs. Crackenthorpe emerged, publishing nos 19 through 44 simultaneously with those of A. Baldwin, but under the original imprint of B. Bragge. Scholars have established the Bragge/Baldwin Mrs. Crackenthorpe as the same person. Numbers written by the 'Society of Ladies' began with number 52 and continued through 111 (really 115, due to faulty numeration).

30. For a discussion of the tensions surrounding the supposed female authorship of this periodical, see Italia, *The Rise of Literary Journalism*, chapter 2: '"The Conversation of my Drawing-Room": The Female Editor and the Public Sphere in the *Female Tatler*'. For a useful discussion of issues related to authorial identity, see Manushag Powell, 'The Performance of Authorship in Eighteenth-Century English Periodicals', unpublished doctoral dissertation, University of California, Los Angeles, 2006.

31. Although *The Female Tatler* is still at times associated with Delarivier Manley, that attribution has been largely disproved, most recently by Ruth Herman,

The Business of A Woman: The Political Writings of Delarivier Manley (Newark: Delaware University Press, 2003), pp. 223–4, and confirmed by the publication's exclusion from the subsequent five volume edition of *The Selected Works of Delarivier Manley* (London: Pickering and Chatto, 2005). Most scholars follow Walter Graham in attributing the original 'Mrs. Crackenthorpe' persona to playwright Thomas Baker. Walter Graham, 'Thomas Baker, Mrs. Manley, and the "Female Tatler"', *Modern Philology*, 34.3 (1937), 267–72. For a useful overview of scholarship on this issue, see Italia, *The Rise of Literary Journalism*, pp. 49–51. Critical acceptance of Bernard Mandeville as the author of papers by two of the society's ladies, the sisters Lucinda and Artesia, has been less controversial. Goldsmith's *By a Society of Ladies* provides a critical introduction to and modern edition of the sisters' 33 numbers; in the introductory essay Goldsmith writes that 'Mandeville's authorship of the Lucinda-Artesia papers is now universally accepted by those who write on Mandeville' (p. 47, fn 82). Hereinafter cited as *By a Society of Ladies* and included in the main body of the text. It has also been suggested, although not definitely established, that playwright Susanna Centlivre wrote as one or more of the Society's other ladies.

32. No. 1, 8 July 1709, in *The Female Tatler*, ed. and intro. by Fidelis Morgan (London: Everyman, 1992), p. 1. Hereinafter cited as *FT* and included in the main body of the text.

33. Italia, *The Rise of Literary Journalism*, pp. 52–3.

34. Ibid., pp. 54–5.

35. No. 96, 17–20 February 1710, *By a Society of Ladies*, pp. 198–203 (p. 201). In terms of 'profit', Goldsmith estimates that the periodical's circulation of 'as many as four hundred copies' of each issue of *The Female Tatler*, although small in relation to the 2500 copies for each number put out by the extremely successful *Tatler*, was nevertheless commercially viable by the standards of the time (*By a Society of Ladies*, p. 48).

36. Quotation from no. 88, 25–27 January 1710, *By A Society of Ladies*, p. 171; subsequent numbers are 88*, 30 January–1 February 1710 [should be No. 90], pp. 175–80; 90, 3–6 February 1710, pp. 180–5; and 92, 8–10 February 1710, pp. 186–93.

37. See nos 77, 30 December 1709–2 January 1710, *By A Society of Ladies*, pp. 141–6; 78, 2–4 January 1710, pp. 146–50; 80, 6–9 January 1710, pp. 150–5; and 84, 16–18 January 1710, pp. 160–4.

38. *Selected Works of Delarivier Manley*, V, ed. by Ruth Herman (London: Pickering & Chatto, 2005), p. 1. This edition is the first to reprint Manley's *Examiner* texts. For further analysis, see Ruth Herman, *The Business of A Woman*, chapter 5: 'Mistress *Examiner*'. As Paula McDowell notes, Manley assumed authorship of the *Examiner* in the same week as Addison's Mr. Spectator was humorously censuring women's 'party rage' in *Spectator* no. 57, declaring that 'There is nothing so bad for the Face as Party Zeal' (quoted in McDowell, *Women of Grub Street*, p. 277).

39. *Spectator* no. 573 (28 July 1714) and the *Flying-Post* for 11–13 September 1722. Both are reprinted in Lady Mary Wortley Montagu, *Essays and Poems and 'Simplicity', A Comedy*, ed. by Robert Halsband and Isobel Grundy (Oxford: Clarendon Press, 1993), pp. 69–74, 95–7. Hereinafter cited as *Essays and Poems* and included in the main body of the text.

40. Nine numbers are known to have survived. Robert Halsband was the first to identify and reprint them as Montagu's in 1974. A critical edition of the periodical appears in *Essays and Poems*, pp. 105–49.
41. Isobel Grundy, *Lady Mary Wortley Montagu* (Oxford: Oxford University Press, 1999), p. 371.
42. *Common Sense: or, The Englishman's Journal*, no. 45 (10 December 1737).
43. See for example: 'I shall be told perhaps that in order to keep up to the Title of my paper I should offer some little Criticism of those of last Saturday; but I will take no notice of the stuff call'd Common Sense when ever it is either dull or unintteligible, and therefore I beleive I shall meddle with it very seldom' (Tuesday 27 December 1737, no. II, *Essays and Poems*, p. 112).
44. See especially nos V and VI, *Essays and Poems*, pp. 125–9, pp. 130–4.
45. Such attention includes a modern critical edition of the periodical, in *Selected Works of Eliza Haywood* Set 2, Vols II and III, ed. by Kathryn King and Alexander Pettit (London: Pickering and Chatto, 2001), and a collection of essays by a range of Haywood scholars, including King and Pettit, in *Fair Philosopher: Eliza Haywood and 'The Female Spectator'*, ed. by Lynne Marie Wright and Donald. J. Newman (Lewisburg: Bucknell University Press, 2006).
46. *The Female Spectator*, Book 1, *Selected Works* 2: II, 19. Hereinafter cited as *FS* by book, volume, and page number.
47. The poem was published in the *Gentleman's Magazine* for 8 December 1741.
48. Catherine Ingrassia, 'Eliza Haywood, Periodicals, and the Function of Orality', in *Fair Philosopher*, ed. by Wright and Newman, p. 151.
49. See Maurer, *Proposing Men*, p. 120.
50. Italia is an exception here. See *Literary Journalism*, p. 128.
51. See Juliette Merritt, 'Reforming the Coquet? Eliza Haywood's Vision of a Female Epistemology', in *Fair Philosopher*, ed. by Wright and Newman, pp. 176–92.
52. Alexander Pettit, 'The Pickering & Chatto *Female Spectator*: Nearly Four Pounds of Ephemera, Enshrined', in *Fair Philosopher*, ed. by Wright and Newman, p. 48.
53. For readings of this and other explicitly political aspects of *The Female Spectator*, including interactions with the abrasive correspondent 'Curioso Politico', see Rachel Carnell, 'It's Not Easy Being Green: Gender and Friendship in Eliza Haywood's Political Periodicals', *Eighteenth-Century Studies*, 32.2 (1998–99), 199–214; Kathryn King, 'Patriot or Opportunist? Eliza Haywood and the Politics of *The Female Spectator*', in *Fair Philosopher*, ed. by Wright and Newman, pp. 104–21; and Earla Wilputte, '"Too ticklish to meddle with": The Silencing of *The Female Spectator*'s Political Correspondents', in *Fair Philosopher*, ed. by Wright and Newman, pp. 122–140.
54. Ingrassia, 'Eliza Haywood', p. 151.
55. Ibid., p. 150.
56. Ricardo Miguel-Alfonso, 'Social Conservatism, Aesthetic Education, and the Essay Genre in Eliza Haywood's *Female Spectator*', in *Fair Philosopher*, ed. by Wright and Newman, p. 73.
57. Robert W. Jones, 'Eliza Haywood and the Discourse of Taste', in *Authorship, Commerce and the Public Scenes of Writing*, ed. by E.J. Clery et al. (Basingstoke: Palgrave Macmillan, 2002), pp. 103–9 (pp. 117, 109).

58. Eve Tavor Bannet, 'Haywood's Spectator and the Female World', in *Fair Philosopher*, ed. by Wright and Newman, p. 100.
59. King, 'Patriot or Opportunist?' p. 104. King's essay provides a detailed list of the periodical's numerous male contributors. See also Maurer, *Proposing Men*, pp. 212–31.
60. See Brean Hammond, *Imaginative Writing in England, 1660–1740: Hackney for Bread* (Oxford: Clarendon Press, 1997) and Catherine Ingrassia, *Authorship, Commerce and Gender in Eighteenth-Century England: A Culture of Paper Credit* (Cambridge: Cambridge University Press, 1998).
61. See Ros Ballaster, *Seductive Forms: Women's Amatory Fiction from 1684 to 1740* (Oxford: Clarendon Press, 1992).
62. See Karen Hollis, 'Eliza Haywood and the Gender of Print', *The Eighteenth Century: Theory and Interpretation*, 38.1 (1997), 43–63; and Ingrassia, *Authorship, Commerce and Gender*.
63. King, 'Patriot or Opportunist?', reads this discourse as explicit, Wilputte, ' "Too ticklish to meddle with" ', both in *Fair Philosopher*, ed. by Wright and Newman, as oblique. For a useful summary of the contemporary political context see Christine Blouch's introduction to *The Parrot*, in *Selected Works of Eliza Haywood*, Set II, Vol. 1, ed. by Christine Blouch, Alexander Pettit, and Rebecca Sayers Hanson (London: Pickering & Chatto, 2001), pp. 175–8.
64. King, 'Patriot or Opportunist?' p.111.
65. See Patrick Spedding, 'Measuring the Success of Haywood's *Female Spectator* (1744–46)', in *Fair Philosopher*, ed. by Wright and Newman, pp. 193–211.
66. As Italia writes, the periodical 'offers a free commerce between the sexes' as the female editor replaces the aristocratic salon hostess whose correspondents become in turn 'the learned men she patronizes by printing their contributions' (*The Rise of Literary Journalism*, p. 139).
67. Both in Eliza Haywood, *Selected Works. The Parrot*, ed. by Christine Blouch, Alexander Pettit, and Rebecca Sayers Hanson, Set II, Vol. 1; *The Young Lady*, ed. by Alexander Pettit and Margo Collins, Set 1. Vol. III.
68. See Jean Hunter, '*The Lady's Magazine* and the Study of Englishwomen in the Eighteenth Century', in *Newsletters to Newspapers: Eighteenth-Century Journalism*, ed. by Donovan Bond and W.H. McLeod (Morgantown: West Virginia University Press, 1977), pp. 103–17; Shevelow, *Women and Print Culture*, pp. 174–90; Ballaster et al., *Women's Worlds*, pp. 61–74.
69. Ballaster et al., *Women's Worlds*, p. 71.

10
Letters and Learning

Melanie Bigold

> Learning deny'd us, we at random tread
> Unbeaten paths, that late to knowledge lead;
> By secret steps break thro' th'obstructed way,
> Nor dare acquirements gain'd by stealth display.
> If some advent'rous genius rare arise,
> Who on exalted themes her talent tries,
> She fears to give the work, tho' prais'd a name,
> And flies not more from infamy than fame.
>
> (Catharine Trotter Cockburn)[1]

> I know not how it has happened that very many
> ingenious women of this nation, who were really pos-
> sessed of a great share of learning and have, no doubt,
> in their time been famous for it, are not only unknown
> to the public in general, but have been passed by in
> silence by our greatest biographers.
>
> (George Ballard)[2]

As the two epigraphs above attest, the plight of learned women in eighteenth-century Britain was neither easy nor widely acknowledged. Nevertheless, a number of their publications are remarkable: Anne Conway's Latin treatise on Platonist metaphysics; Mary Astell's seminal political, philosophical, and religious tracts; Damaris Masham's Lockean defences of practical religion; Catharine Trotter Cockburn's religious polemics and defences of John Locke and Samuel Clarke; Elizabeth Elstob's Anglo-Saxon translations; Elizabeth Carter's translations of Newtonian philosophy and *All the works of Epictetus*.[3] In an era when women, as Cockburn put it, '[b]y secret steps break thro' th'obstructed way, / Nor dare acquirements gain'd by stealth display', a significant contingent of 'advent'rous' women were nevertheless taking advantage of print culture to 'display' their political, religious, philosophical, and linguistic acumen if not always announcing their names in print.

However, publications in print are only a tiny fraction of what learned women produced. Margaret Ezell and Kathryn King have discussed the practice and importance of manuscript circulation as a form of publication for early modern women writers.[4] Their work has been crucial in detailing the extent to which women, and men, utilized manuscript circulation as a way of controlling the means of production, dissemination, and interpretation of their literary works. Until recently, much of the focus has remained on those works that are recognizably literary manuscripts (for example, poetry or prose fiction), but letters were also a significant means by which women engaged in philosophical, religious, and literary commentary and debate.

Hence, in addition to their printed works listed above, we might also mention the epistolary exchanges between Conway and the Cambridge Platonist Henry More (which has been called 'the first correspondence course in Cartesian Philosophy');[5] Astell's religious letters with John Norris; Masham's exchanges with Locke and Leibniz; Cockburn's with William Warburton, Edmund Law, Thomas Sharp, and her niece, Anne Arbuthnot; and Carter's with Catherine Talbot, Elizabeth Montagu, John Philip Baratier, and Isaac Hawkins Browne, to name only a few. While some of these manuscript correspondences 'survive(d)', and some have been published, many more have been lost.

The contingent nature of much epistolary evidence has been one of the major stumbling blocks for scholars seeking a sustainable argument for the importance of letter writing in the period. Letters have not been ignored – numerous scholars have acknowledged the pre-eminence of the form in the eighteenth century – but the dominance given to the idea of the private, conversational epistle has occluded our sense of its expansive possibilities, particularly in relation to authorial agency and the status of learned women in the Republic of Letters.[6] The ambiguity of the title, 'Women of Letters', is part of the problem. Like 'Men of Letters', the designation could embrace anyone with a dilettante interest in literary culture, but it could also refer to those who regularly contributed to literary journals or fashioned public careers as poets and philosophers. Unsurprisingly, many 'Women of Letters' have been relegated to the ranks of the former: scribblers who lack the sort of progressive literary career associated with the rise of professional authorship in the period.[7] In contrast, when we take into consideration the full range of their writings, whether in print or manuscript, familiar letter or poetic epistle, the picture changes in almost every case. Contextualizing women's correspondence shows that many women wrote intelligently and consistently on many contemporary issues, through varied and often more imaginative means than their male counterparts.

The types of letters literary women were writing and the varied correspondences in which they were engaging also suggests an important shift in the function and scope of letter writing in the eighteenth century. Many skilled letter writers were capable of writing the types of conversational missives Madame de Sévigné made famous and which are considered the hallmark of the eighteenth-century epistle. Women, in particular, were noted for such epistolary expertise.[8] This is an important and creative aspect of letter writing, but numerous women writers with literary and intellectual pretensions went beyond these tropes to embrace critical debate and commentary. Their letters are concerned with literary, philosophical, and religious topics, and function, as they did for Conway and More, as a type of intellectual correspondence course for their respective participants.

Contemporary interest in the subject of female education and the Enlightenment theories and modes of thought which supported these ideas were crucial factors in the rise of the learned woman. Arguments about the equality of the sexes gained ground in the seventeenth century; Cartesian duality, in particular, emphasized the cognitive equality of men and women, the mind or soul having 'no sex'.[9] While most English tracts did not go so far as to argue for true educational equality – most insisted that girls learn domestic skills and questioned their aptitude for the classical languages – they nevertheless encouraged a broadening of the subjects taught to women.

Learned women were also increasingly celebrated and supported in the late seventeenth and early eighteenth centuries. George Ballard's *Memoirs of Several Ladies* (1752) is probably the best known manifestation of this interest, but even before his posthumous commemoration, a number of learned women received financial and intellectual support from their contemporaries. Women's entry into the male-dominated realm of scholarship was often mediated by sympathetic male mentors: fathers, uncles, brothers, family friends, tutors, clergymen, and suitors.[10] Whether educating women, circulating their manuscript works, engaging with them in epistolary debate, posthumously printing their texts or arranging patronage connections, learned men were crucial figures in aiding women's integration into the early Republic of Letters.

Well-placed, intellectually minded women also supported other scholarly women. A number of aristocrats championed their learned female friends. Lady Catherine Jones, Anne, Countess of Coventry, and Lady Elizabeth Hastings played significant roles in the career of Astell. Lady Sarah Piers and the Churchills, the Duke and Duchess of Marlborough, helped Cockburn during her years as a dramatist. In tandem with these aristocratic patrons was a well-developed series of networks linking learned women themselves. Thus Elizabeth Burnet, already a friend of John Locke (and who also exchanged learned letters with him), introduced Locke to the work of his anonymous defender, Cockburn. As a result of Burnet's 'networking' on Cockburn's behalf, Locke sent Cockburn books and money. Astell herself encouraged Lady Mary Wortley Montagu to publish her letters and even wrote a manuscript preface for them; she was, however, unsuccessful in convincing Wortley Montagu to publish. Similar instances of gynocentric social networking can be identified in the writing lives of most early modern learned women.

Nevertheless, regardless of their aptitude or the support that they received, women were still excluded from 'some of the most critical settings for the acquisition of advanced education and participation in the exchange of enlightened ideas: universities, coffeehouses, cafés, and taverns'.[11] These spaces, according to Habermas, were the crucial sites where private subjects could engage in the 'rational-critical debate' which constituted/defined the modern subject.[12] However, women's exclusion from this situated public sphere did not preclude their exclusion from the modern formation of subjecthood which Habermas associates with 'public' discursive exchange. Indeed, as Anne Goldgar's study of the continental Republic of Letters has shown, many men who found themselves physically excluded from these discursive sites by virtue of their geographical obscurity, managed to participate in 'rational-critical debate', community, and modern subjectivity through the interconnected letter-writing networks of the scholarly world.[13]

Clare Brant affirms a similar degree of integration among British letter writers. She argues that Habermas's formulation of the public sphere as an 'ideal arena of discursive engagement' does not reflect 'the complexities of eighteenth-century communicative practice'.[14] Just as many male participants elected themselves to the world of letters by virtue of their interest in scholarly matters, so women could also join in the local, national, or international *commerce de lettres*, 'the purely literary correspondence', that constituted the primary mode of discourse in the Republic of Letters.[15] It is the existence of these 'purely literary correspondences' and the engagement with both Enlightenment thought and the scholarly endeavours of the Republic of Letters that truly distinguishes the erudite Woman of Letters.

Part of the reason women were able to participate and shape contemporary ideas in such compelling and influential ways was through their focus on language. In direct defiance of Milton's purported comment: 'one tongue is enough for a woman',[16] these women sought to expand their access to knowledge by learning the classical and modern languages; they also contributed to the introduction of 'new' languages (shorthand, for example), or the reintroduction of old ones (for example, Anglo-Saxon).[17] In order to explore the variety of ways in which women engaged or were excluded from the Republic of Letters, this chapter will briefly consider the writing lives of three different 'Women of Letters' in the period, paying particular attention to the ways in which their learning was presented to potential readers.

1 Contrasting careers: Elstob, Cockburn, Carter

Women may have been excluded from university membership, but this did not exclude them from the international world of learning nor from the production of scholarly works for a growing print market. In fact, a number of women became involved with debates associated with Oxford and Cambridge, and were routinely identified with these seats of higher learning by virtue of their learned accomplishments.

First among these women was Elizabeth Elstob (1683–1756). Elstob was encouraged in her studies by her brother, William, and was to become, like him, a valued member of George Hickes's circle of Anglo-Saxonists at Oxford. Elstob's first publication, a translation from the French of Madeleine de Scudéry's *Discours de la gloire* (1671), was followed by two groundbreaking works of Anglo-Saxon scholarship: *An English-Saxon Homily on the Birthday of St. Gregory* (1709) and *The Rudiments of Grammar for the English-Saxon Tongue* (1715). Scudéry was a notable choice; not only did this essay win a prize from the Académie Française, but she was also a theorist of letter writing.[18] Elstob's translation emphasizes gender from the outset. The title page announces that the author and translator are 'of the same Sex', it is dedicated to her aunt, 'Mrs. Elstob, at Canterbury', and it notes how much more appropriate Scudéry's text would have been had she had a female monarch, such as Queen Anne, for inspiration. Elstob also made significant contributions to works by other Anglo-Saxon scholars, including William Wotton, and was widely regarded as one of the foremost Saxonists of her time: Hickes referred to one of her works as 'the most correct I ever saw or read'.[19]

Elstob's work is unique for the importance it places on the vernacular, or the 'mother-tongue'. She wrote with the English reader in mind and stressed the role of Anglo-Saxon research as a means to better understanding the origins of the English language. In her *Rudiments of Grammar*, Elstob attacks Jonathan Swift's *Proposal for Correcting, Improving and Ascertaining the English Tongue* (1712), in which he suggests the establishment of an academy to police the English language. In contrast, Elstob presents a detailed history of the evolution of English, 'to shew the polite Men of our Age, that the Language of their Forefathers is neither so barren nor barbarous as they affirm'.[20] Swift's argument was largely dictated by his high cultural prejudices, whereas Elstob's was based upon scholarly research and a desire to elucidate a linguistic heritage based upon the 'mother-tongue'. The epigraph on her title page endorses her stance: '*Our Earthly Possessions are truly enough called a* PATRIMONY, *as derived to us by the Industry of our* FATHERS; *but the Language that we speak is our* MOTHER-TONGUE; *And who so proper to play the Criticks in this as the* FEMALES.'[21] Elstob's industry in this field helped to change the gender make-up of Britain's cultural inheritance; that is, she is significant as a female critic *and* her work emphasizes gender paradigms.

Despite these successes, Elstob failed to attain the financial support necessary to publish additional works of Anglo-Saxon scholarship.[22] Her inability to finance the printing of new works reminds us of the exclusive, because cost prohibitive, nature of print culture in the period. A further blow came with the deaths of Hickes and Elstob's brother William in 1715, leaving Elstob without intellectual support or an income. Under the strain of increasing debt, Elstob vanishes from view and does not reappear in the historical record until 1735, when Sarah Chapone and Ballard found her destitute, in ill health and teaching children in Evesham. Troubled by the pathos of the once great scholar teaching rudimentary skills in a country school, they found Elstob a more congenial post as governess to the Duchess of Portland's children.

During the period after 1735, Elstob re-emerges in the Republic of Letters through her correspondences with Ballard and other antiquaries of the mid-century. These letters, now in the Ballard Collection in the Bodleian, poignantly enact Elstob's rediscovery of the life of the mind. As her pecuniary cares become less pressing, and her scholarly networks start expanding, Elstob's letters become more engaging and engaged with intellectual and literary concerns. Her descriptions become more elaborate, efforts to reciprocate information prompt the sharing of translations, books, and coins, and copious queries are posed and answered.

Early antiquaries valued this type of exchange as much as the material objects that it helped to circulate. Their meticulous preservation of Elstob's letters and manuscripts, as well as those of many other scholars, reveals a culture that recognized the intellectual value of epistolary exchanges, and, therefore, sought to preserve those histories of the British Republic of Letters for future generations.

One of Elstob's contemporaries, Catharine Cockburn (1674?–1749), developed another sort of career in the Republic of Letters.[23] A dramatist, poet, philosopher, religious controversialist, and prolific writer of both fictional and familiar letters, Cockburn's writing life provides a complex, and therefore quite typical, example of the ways in which manuscript, print, learning, genre, and gender interface in the early eighteenth century.

Cockburn is probably best known as a dramatist, and there has been a tendency to divorce the literary author from the philosophical and theological one. However, her controversial publications overlap with her early dramatic career, while epistolary fictions and poetry appear in her later adversarial years. The mainstay throughout these two 'periods' is letter writing; more specifically, letter writing which is concerned with espousing a rationally-based theology and exploring the foundations of moral virtue. This interest is evident not only in Cockburn's posthumous *Works* (1751), which features a large selection of her polemical and familiar letters, but also in the many unpublished manuscript letters available in the British Library.

The status of familiar letters in the period could be quite fluid. Printed works which we might now designate as 'miscellaneous' tracts are often familiar letters that have simply been redesignated as 'Remarks' or 'Essay'; many even retain the original dates, superscriptions, and so on, though just as many 'hide' personal details with dashes or selective editing. On the other hand, letters which we might be inclined to classify as more learned and formal were routinely printed in volumes of familiar letters. What is instructive about this slippage between the seemingly private and personal, and the public and polemical, is the contemporary awareness of the multiple functions, tones, audiences, and textual lives that a letter could embrace.

In the second volume of Cockburn's *Works* and in her editor's manuscript compilations, the preliminary editorial arrangement and subsequent reshuffling of Cockburn's familiar and formal letters enact this generic ambiguity, revealing the multiple functions of the form. Thomas Birch, by virtue of editing Cockburn's letters was the first to recognize the multivalent tendencies of her letters, and it is useful to contrast a series of *manuscript* prose works that he designates as 'miscellaneous pieces' with the final arrangement in the *printed* edition.

In the preliminary manuscript transcription of the 'miscellaneous pieces', eleven manuscripts are bound together. In contrast, the printed version only includes ten entries. The eleventh piece in the manuscript version, Cockburn's 'Letter to her Niece upon Moral Virtue', does not make it into the published 'miscellaneous works', but turns up instead in the section entitled '*Letters between Mrs.* Cockburn *and several of her Friends*', later on in the same volume. Directly following the first eleven texts in the manuscript volume are more edited and original manuscript letters on similar themes to that expounded in the letter to her niece, which suggests that certain letters between Cockburn and her correspondents were being considered as part of a general section on philosophical and religious polemics. Thus, in addition to the letter to her niece, specifically placed and edited within the collection of 'miscellaneous pieces', are a number of other philosophical letters collected with the apparent purpose of highlighting Cockburn's morally and intellectually stimulating correspondence.

Why then was the letter to her niece moved? The most likely reason is that, once the 1751 edition became a posthumous document, Birch was able to collect together a fuller catalogue of Cockburn's private letters for inclusion in the *Works* and 'restored' the letter to its 'proper' place chronologically with the rest of the letters to her niece. However, the evolving constructions the letter went through in the editing process highlight the dual values accorded to works now universally relegated to biographical, if not marginal, status.

Cockburn's correspondence with Thomas Sharp was also moved, placed at the end of her familiar letters, just before her drama and poems. Sandwiched between such diverse pieces, these letters appear like a bit of an afterthought; for contemporary readers, however, they merited special attention. Cockburn's work on the foundations of morality and the moral sense was her most significant contribution to philosophical debate in the period. Specifically, it was her letters to Thomas Sharp and others on these issues that prompted admirers to push for the subscriber edition of her works, and it is those same letters to which Richard Price later drew attention in his own dissertations on the 'moral faculty'.[24]

Cockburn's letters to Sharp epitomize her lifelong interest in clarifying polemical discourse. When Sharp quibbled over points which divided advocates of Samuel Clarke and Daniel Waterland, Cockburn was unequivocal in her responses. Similar to her refutation and belittling of Thomas Burnet's critique of Locke, Cockburn's answers are structured as responses to another's arguments while advancing a moral philosophy that is distinctly her own.[25] For Cockburn, the important issue was establishing a non-voluntarist basis for moral obligation and, interestingly, it is precisely this argument which Price makes use of in his own discussions of moral philosophy.[26]

The letters also explore a number of other fraught terms and epistemological issues, but, throughout, Cockburn's skill at identifying, questioning, counter-subverting, and ultimately clarifying the use of those terms and the grounds of knowledge foregrounds her analytical and didactic abilities. This clarity and its pedagogical uses endeared Cockburn to theologians and philosophers eager to influence a wider market of readers. It also cemented her learned image for many of those later readers.

One of these readers was Elizabeth Carter, who was often characterized by her contemporaries as a college don or a 'university of ladies'.[27] This identification partly stemmed from her successful tutoring of her younger brother and nephew for entry into Cambridge and Oxford, but it was also a direct result of her scholarly publications and her status as one of the pre-eminent Women of Letters in the latter half of the eighteenth century. This chapter is about letters *and* learning, and Carter's learned image, though very much allied to an epistolary persona, was largely based upon her knowledge of the classical languages and her celebrated translations of Latin and Greek works.[28]

However, long before the financial success of her translation of *All the works of Epictetus* (1757/8), and suggestions of honorary doctorates,[29] Carter, like her friends Thomas Birch, Samuel Johnson, and Richard Savage, was trying to make a name for herself via Edward Cave's the *Gentleman's Magazine* (1731–1868). Carter contributed riddles, epigrams, and poems to Cave's magazine, but, like Birch and Johnson, also began to publish longer works of translation for him. These translations, *Sir Isaac Newton's Philosophy Explain'd for the Use of the Ladies* (1739), from the Italian of Francesco Algarotti, and *An Examination of Mr Pope's Essay on Man, From the French of M. Crousaz* (1739), signalled Carter's desire to forge a professional career in the Republic of Letters, and to participate in the mediation and exchange of Enlightenment ideas.[30]

Carter's decision to translate the Algarotti text was partially influenced by Birch, but the choice is nevertheless significant.[31] E.J. Clery points out that Carter's translations were not 'hack-work'; rather, they were important 'interventions in British intellectual and literary life through the indirect route of foreign commentary'.[32] That is, Crousaz's and Algarotti's texts were 'foreign' commentaries upon British intellectuals (Pope and Newton) and Carter was providing English readers with a translation, but also a critique of their works. In doing this, Carter was taking advantage of, or rather adapting herself to, a print market in which translations were increasingly in demand.[33] At the same time, she tailored the work to suit a still viable patronage network: she attempted to dedicate it, unsuccessfully, to the Countess of Hertford.[34]

Carter's choice of topic – an explication of the work of Britain's most revered Enlightenment figure – also reflects her lifelong interest in mathematics and astronomy. She visited William Haley in 1738, and engaged in a mathematical correspondence with the astronomer and mathematician Thomas Wright of Durham.[35] Both translations dealt with scientific matters and required specialist knowledge of Newton's theories as well as more general philosophical and literary expertise. For example, in her footnotes for the Algarotti translation Carter makes extensive use of historical and literary information from Pierre Bayle's *General Dictionary* (which Birch was translating and adapting). She also takes issue with some of Algarotti's generalizations on philosophy, as well as his use of translations of unidentified poetry.[36]

Of interest too, is the nature of the work itself. Algarotti intended to bring philosophy out of the 'solitary Closets and Libraries of the Learned [...and] into the Circles and Toilets of Ladies'.[37] Moreover, he was specifically engaging with a new breed of continental philosophers who were, in turn, engaging with Newtonian, as opposed to Cartesian, theories. Chief among these was the young Italian scholar Laura Bassi, one of the first women to be awarded a degree, the first to hold a university chair, and 'the advent of a new model of feminine learning – the professional scientist'.[38] Carter too was a professional, but in her case a professional Woman of Letters. She continued to engage in Enlightenment debates, becoming embroiled in anti-Trinitarian disputes with her *Remarks on the Athanasian Creed* (1752/3?). She also provided contemporaries with access to ancient philosophical theories with the first full English translation of the work of the Stoic Epictetus.

Carter also continued to write, circulate, and publish poetry, essays, and letters. Here again correspondence networks played an important role in shaping the nature of her work, but also in advancing her public career. As early as the Algarotti translation, Birch characterized Carter as an 'extraordinary Phaenomenon in the Republick of Letters'.[39]

Translation, learning, and letters were Carter's forte and, whilst space unfortunately prohibits a more expansive discussion of the links between her translations and familiar letters, there is fruitful work to be done in this area.[40]

An understanding of the complexity and versatility of letters as a mode of intellectual discourse, as well as a media of publication – whether scribal or print – reveals the adaptability of the form. Reassessing women's letter writing also makes it clear that the silences, or the marginalization, attributed to many women writers of this time is founded on an incomplete picture of authorship in the period. The letters of a select group of women writers are evidence of modern, progressive modes of thought similar to those identified as the hallmarks of Enlightenment thinking. If we take into account broader endeavours in the Republic of Letters, such as translation, the degree of women's involvement with the world of learning opens even farther. Perhaps more importantly for women's literary history, these women used their social and intellectual connections to maintain and advance a female Republic of Letters which would flourish in the salons, correspondences, and works of the Bluestockings in the latter half of the eighteenth century. 'It is no accident', Habermas argued, 'that the eighteenth century became the century of the letter.'[41]

Notes

1. 'Poem, occasioned by the busts set up in the Queen's Hermitage', written in 1732, first published in *Gentleman's Magazine*, 7 (May 1737), 308, and included in *The Works of Mrs. Catharine Cockburn*, 2 vols (London, 1751), II, 572–5.
2. George Ballard, *Memoirs of Several Ladies of Great Britain who have been celebrated for their writings or skill in the learned languages, arts and sciences* (London, 1752), p. 53.
3. Anon. [Anne Conway], *Principia philosophiae antiquissimae et recentissimae* (Amsterdam, 1690), translated into English as, *The Principles of the Most Ancient and Modern Philosophy* (1692); all Anon. [Mary Astell], *A Serious Proposal to the Ladies* (1694) and Part II (1697), *Letters Concerning the Love of God* (1695), *Some Reflections upon Marriage* (1700), *Moderation Truly Stated* (1704), *An Impartial Enquiry* (1704), *A Fair Way with the Dissenters* (1704), *The Christian Religion* (1705), and *Bart'lemy Fair* (1709); all Anon. [Damaris Masham], *A Discourse Concerning the Love of God* (1696) and *Occasional Thoughts in Reference to a Vertuous or Christian Life* (1705); Anon. [Catharine Trotter Cockburn], *A Defence of the Essay of Human Understanding, written by Mr. Lock* (1702). Anon. [Catharine Trotter Cockburn], *A Discourse Concerning A Guide in Controversies* (1707), Catharine Trotter Cockburn, *Remarks upon some Writers in the Controversy concerning the Foundation of Moral Virtue and Moral Obligation* (1743), Anon. [Catharine Trotter Cockburn], *Remarks upon the Principles and Reasonings of Dr. Rutherforth's Essay* (1747); Anon. [Elizabeth

Elstob], *An essay upon glory* (1708), *An English-Saxon Homily on the Birthday of St. Gregory* (1709), and *The Rudiments of Grammar for the English-Saxon Tongue* (1715); Anon. [Elizabeth Carter], *Sir Isaac Newton's Philosophy Explain'd for the Use of the Ladies*, 2 vols (1739), and *All the Works of Epictetus* (1757/8). This is, of course, only a selective list. All titles were published in London.

4. Margaret Ezell, *Social Authorship and the Advent of Print* (Baltimore and London: Johns Hopkins University Press, 1999), and Kathryn King, 'Elizabeth Singer Rowe's Tactical Use of Print and Manuscript', in *Women's Writing and the Circulation of Ideas: Manuscript Publication in England, 1550–1800*, ed. by George L. Justice and Nathan Tinker (Cambridge: Cambridge University Press, 2002), pp. 158–81. The practice extends well into the late eighteenth century.

5. Sarah Hutton, 'Anne Conway, Margaret Cavendish and Seventeenth-Century Scientific Thought', in *Women, Science and Medicine, 1500–1700: Mothers and Sisters of the Royal Society*, ed. by Lynette Hunter and Sarah Hutton (Gloucestershire: Sutton Publishing, 1997), pp. 218–34 (p. 219).

6. See *The Familiar Letter in the Eighteenth Century*, ed. by Howard Anderson, Philip B. Daghlian, and Irvin Ehrenpreis (Lawrence: University of Kansas Press, 1966); Clare Brant, *Eighteenth-Century Letters and British Culture* (Basingstoke: Palgrave Macmillan, 2006); Cynthia Lowenthal, *Lady Mary Wortley Montagu and the Eighteenth-Century Letter* (Athens, GA: University of Georgia Press, 1994); Bruce Redford, *The Converse of the Pen: Acts of Intimacy in the Eighteenth-Century Familiar Letter* (London: University of Chicago Press, 1986); and Keith Stewart, 'Towards Defining an Aesthetic for the Familiar Letter in the Eighteenth Century', *Prose Studies*, 5 (1982), 179–89. For a more theoretical discussion of the fictional aspects of the form see Janet Gurkin Altman, *Epistolarity: Approaches to a Form* (Columbus: Ohio State University Press, 1982). Brant notes that 'Between 1700 and 1800, more than twenty-one thousand items were published that used the word "Letter" or "Letters" in their title', p. 1.

7. I refer here primarily to those who did not publish novels.

8. Dena Goodman, 'Letter Writing and the Emergence of Gendered Subjectivity in Eighteenth-Century France', *Journal of Women's History*, 17.2 (2005), 9–37 (p. 11).

9. See Paula Findlen, 'Ideas in the Mind: Gender and Knowledge in the Seventeenth Century', *Hypatia: A Journal of Feminist Philosophy*, 17.1 (Winter 2002), 183–96.

10. See Susan Staves, 'Church of England Clergy and Women Writers', in *Reconsidering the Bluestockings*, ed. by Nicole Pohl and Betty A. Schellenberg (San Marino: Huntington Library, 2003), pp. 81–103. (Also published as vol. 65, nos. 1 and 2 of the *Huntington Library Quarterly*.)

11. Carla Hesse, 'Introduction: Women Intellectuals in the Enlightened Republic of Letters', in *Women, Gender and Enlightenment*, ed. by Sarah Knott and Barbara Taylor (Basingstoke: Palgrave Macmillan, 2005), pp. 259–64 (p. 260).

12. Goodman, 'Letter Writing', pp. 9–10.

13. Anne Goldgar, *Impolite Learning: Conduct and Community in the Republic of Letters, 1680–1750* (New Haven and London: Yale University Press, 1995), pp. 3–6.

14. Brant, *Eighteenth-Century Letters*, p. 5.

15. Goldgar, *Impolite Learning*, p. 15.

16. Thomas Birch, *An Historical and Critical Account of the Life and Writings of John Milton* (London, 1738), p. lxii. According to Birch, John Ward visited

Milton's youngest daughter Deborah shortly before her death, and she provided him with the quotation.

17. See Frances Teague, *Bathsua Makin, Woman of Learning* (Lewisburg: Bucknell University Press/London: Associated University Presses, 1998).
18. See her novel, *Clélie* (1654) and *Conversations nouvelles sur divers sujets* (1684).
19. Ballard MS Vol. 12, f. 203, Hickes to Arthur Charlett, 23 December 1712.
20. Elstob, *Rudiments of Grammar for the English-Saxon Tongue* (London, 1715), p. ii.
21. Ibid., p.A^r.
22. For a full account of Elstob's life and the many difficulties she experienced with print culture, see Sarah Collins, 'The Elstobs and the End of the Saxon Revival', *Anglo-Saxon Scholarship: The First Three Centuries*, ed. C.T. Berkhout and M. McC. Gatch (Boston, MA: G.K. Hall, 1982), pp. 107–18; Kathryn Sutherland, 'Editing for a New Century: Elizabeth Elstob's Anglo-Saxon Manifesto and Ælfric's St Gregory Homily', in *The Editing of Old English: Papers from the 1990 Manchester Conference*, ed. by D.G. Scragg and P.E. Szarmach (London: Boydell and Brewer, 1994), pp. 213–37; and Kathryn Sutherland, 'Elizabeth Elstob (1683–1756)', in *Medieval Scholarship: Biographical Studies on the Formation of a Discipline, Volume 2: Literature and Philology*, ed. by Helen Damico (New York and London: Garland Publishing, 1998), II, 59–73.
23. On the dating of Cockburn's birth, see Anne Kelley, *Catharine Trotter: An Early Modern Writer in the Vanguard of Feminism* (Aldershot: Ashgate, 2002), p. 1, n.1; 'Corrections to Thomas Birch (Ed.) The Works of Mrs. Catharine Cockburn', *Notes & Queries*, 47 (245), no. 2 (June 2000), 192–3; and 'Trotter, Catharine (1674?–1749)', *Oxford Dictionary of National Biography*, Oxford University Press, September 2004; online edition, October 2008 <http://www.oxforddnb.com/view/article/5768> [accessed 17 Sept 2009].
24. See Richard Price, *A Review of the Principal Questions and Difficulties in Morals* (London, 1758). The editors of Thomas Sharp's six-volume works likewise took advantage of Birch's edition, and reprinted Cockburn and Sharp's correspondence in volume two of *The Works of Thomas Sharp* (1763).
25. See Cockburn, *A Defence of the Essay of Human Understanding, written by Mr. Lock* (London, 1702), and Martha Brandt Bolton's excellent analysis, 'Some Aspects of the Philosophical Work of Catharine Trotter,' *Journal of the History of Philosophy*, 31.4 (October 1993), 565–78, reprinted in *Hypatia's Daughters: Fifteen Hundred Years of Women Philosophers*, ed. by Linda Lopez McAlister (Bloomington and Indianapolis: Indiana University Press, 1996), pp. 139–64.
26. See Richard Price, *A Review*, p. 17.
27. For her reading of Cockburn see, Elizabeth Carter, *A Series of Letters between Mrs. Elizabeth Carter and Miss Catherine Talbot, From the Year 1741 to 1770, To which are added, Letters from Mrs. Elizabeth Carter to Mrs. Vesey, Between the Years 1763–1787*, ed. by Montagu Pennington, 4 vols (London, 1809), II, 49. For her attribution as a 'university', see II, 186, 26 November 1754 and II, 351, Lambeth, 17 September 1760. Also see Edward Moore, *The World. By Adam Fitz-Adam*, Vol. III, new edition (1772), no. 131 (Thursday, 3 July 1755), 159–65.
28. In addition to *All the works of Epictetus*, Carter produced translations of Latin and Greek odes for the *Gentleman's Magazine* and for William Duncombe's

Works of Horace in English Verse. By Several Hands (London, 1757–59). She also assisted Isaac Hawkins Browne with his Latin poem, *De animus immortalitate* (London, 1754).

29. Elizabeth Montagu, quoting an unnamed newspaper article, writes that 'ye honour of a Doctors Degree had been more properly conferred on Mrs. Eliz Carter & Mrs. Montagu, than on a Parcel of Lords, Knights, and Squires, who are unlettered'. See Leonore Helen Ewert, 'Elizabeth Montagu to Elizabeth Carter: Literary Gossip and Critical Opinions from the Pen of the Queen of the Blues', PhD dissertation, Claremont Graduate School, 1968, p. 123.

30. Francesco Algarotti, *Sir Isaac Newton's Philosophy Explain'd for the Use of the Ladies*, trans. by Elizabeth Carter (London, 1739). Jean-Pierre de Crousaz, *An Examination of Mr Pope's Essay on Man, From the French of M. Crousaz*, trans. by Elizabeth Carter (London, 1739).

31. BL Add MS 4302, f. 104, Cave to Birch, 28 November 1738. Cave writes that Johnson suggested that Carter translate Boethius. She went with Birch's suggestion of Algarotti instead.

32. E.J. Clery, *The Feminization Debate in Eighteenth-Century England: Literature, Commerce and Luxury* (Basingstoke and New York: Palgrave Macmillan, 2004), pp. 76–7.

33. The Algarotti translation had two more London editions (1742 and 1772), and one in Glasgow (1765).

34. Judith Hawley, 'Carter, Elizabeth (1717–1806)', *Oxford Dictionary of National Biography*, Oxford University Press, September 2004; online edition, May 2009 <http://www.oxforddnb.com/view/article/4782> [accessed 17 September 2009].

35. Gwen I. Hampshire claims that Wright exchanged over one hundred letters with Carter, and Pennington states that she 'used to send him her schemes and solutions to be corrected'. Hampshire, 'An Edition of some Unpublished Letters of Elizabeth Carter, 1717–1806, and a Calendar of her Correspondence', B.Litt. dissertation, Oxford, 1972, p. xlvi, and Montagu Pennington, *Memoirs of the Life of Mrs. Elizabeth Carter* (London, 1807), p. 16. Hampshire's edition of Carter's letters is published as *Elizabeth Carter, 1717–1806: An Edition of Some Unpublished Letters*, ed. by Gwen Hampshire (Newark: University of Delaware Press, 2005).

36. See Algarotti, *Sir Isaac Newton's Philosophy Explain'd*, trans. by Carter, I, 22, 24, and 72.

37. Ibid., I, ii.

38. Hesse, 'Introduction', p. 261; also see Paula Findlen, 'Women on the Verge of Science: Aristocratic Women and Knowledge in Early Eighteenth-Century Italy', in *Women, Gender*, ed. by Knott and Taylor, pp. 265–87.

39. Thomas Birch, *History of the Works of the Learned*, Art XXXI (1 June 1739), p. 392.

40. See for example the letters she exchanged with Isaac Hawkins Browne regarding his Latin poem *De animus immortalitate*, in Trinity College Library, Cambridge, O.12.57²⁰, formerly classified as O.12.27²⁰ and Trinity R.4, p. 57.

41. Jürgen Habermas, *The Structural Transformation of the Public Sphere: An Inquiry into a Category of Bourgeois Society*, trans. by Thomas Burger (Cambridge, MA: MIT Press, 1994), p. 48.

Part IV
Worlds of Feeling

11
Religious Love

Jane Shaw

By the last decade of the seventeenth century, religious matters had been largely settled in England: a measure of toleration had been allowed to dissenters and Roman Catholics, with freedom of worship for dissenters granted in 1689; and the Latitudinarians were on the ascendant in the Church of England, with the promise of a 'reasonable' attitude to any religious controversy. This did not mean that women now shied away from the visionary or the political, which had been such a hallmark of women's writing in the conflicts of the mid-century, nor from an engagement with the New Philosophy, but it did mean that much religious writing took the form of the devotional. Women's writing became central to the shaping of an eighteenth-century *practical* Christianity that cut across denominations, and was as much concerned with ethics and morality as with theology; in turn, women's devotion became a crucial catalyst in their becoming writers. Furthermore, the cultivation of piety increasingly became the hallmark of virtuous femininity. For some women, their practice of piety instilled in them the habit of writing, as they kept spiritual diaries and autobiographies; for others, it was linked to learning, and gave them the means to acquire an education. Women employed many different literary forms to express their religious ideas: prose, poetry, hymns, letters – often published – as well as texts in epistolary form, philosophical arguments, short pamphlets, and polemical tracts.

1 Devotional writing and the cultivation of piety

In 1694, Mary Astell published the first part of *A Serious Proposal to the Ladies* (Part II was published in 1697). Astell's serious proposal was for a female monastery, or 'religious retirement', where women could develop

189

their spiritual life and devote themselves to learning.[1] Twenty-first century feminist readers have been shaped by a narrative that asserts the need for a room of one's own to *write*; for Astell, the main aim of her all-female space was *religious devotion*. It was to be a retreat – 'such a Paradise as your mother Eve forfeited' – in which Anglican piety might be cultivated and the fasts and feasts of the church observed (Astell was a High Churchwoman). Astell's proposal was made primarily on religious grounds: it was for the love of God rather than man, but it had a secondary purpose; it would not only be a 'Retreat from the World' but also 'an institution and previous discipline, to fit us to do the greatest good in it'. It could be 'a seminary to stock the Kingdom with pious and prudent ladies: whose good example it is to be hop'd will so influence the rest of the sex, that women may no longer pass for those little useless and impertinent Animals, which the ill conduct of too many, has caus'd them to be mistaken for'.[2] And to be 'pious and prudent' women had to be educated. Astell stood in a long line of female writers in Europe who saw education or, rather, the lack of it, as the reason for women's unequal position in society (see Chapter 1 above, 'Woman's Place'). In making her proposal Astell set a pattern for many women writers in the late seventeenth and eighteenth century: their purpose in writing was religious, but in the very act of that religious practice, they became writers.

This was as true of the nonconformists as it was of the Anglicans, as the career of Elizabeth Singer Rowe illustrates. Whilst for Astell the space from which women might write was an imagined female monastery (and it remained imaginary, for the plan was deemed too 'papist' by leading churchmen, despite emotional and financial support from many quarters[3]), for Rowe, the place from which she actually wrote was the provincial town of Frome in Somerset, where she spent her time engaged in philanthropic activity and supporting the Rooke Lane Independent Congregation. The nonconformist world that was so central to her daily life provided her both with literary and educational networks and the impulse to write, actively enabling her career as a writer.[4] Even when Rowe was writing passionate poetry under the pseudonym of Philomela in the 1690s, much of it was being published in the *Athenian Mercury*, run by John Dunton, who was of a Whiggish sensibility, and in sympathy with the nonconformist position.

Some of Rowe's writing was distinctly nonconformist: her poems on theological themes, such as 'A description of Hell in imitation of Milton', poetry written on biblical figures and texts, such as 'The Translation of Elijah' and 'Revelation Chap xvi', and many hymns that garnered the admiration of Isaac Watts. But her primary theme was love. She wrote exuberantly about divine love:

> Swallow'd in pleasure and divine surprise,
> I view thy love's unbounded mysteries:
> In all thy wond'rous paths I gladly trace
> Indulgent goodness and stupendous grace.[5]

And divine love was the source of human love as she had experienced it, passionately with her husband Thomas Rowe, in this world. There is a fine line between divine and human love, as she expressed it in one of her poems entitled 'On Love':

> Venus, the beauteous offspring of the day,
> From thy bright orb doth spring one propitious ray;
> Awake the gentlest passions in my breast,
> And be thy pow'r through all my soul confest.[6]

While she addressed theological themes in her work, she most frequently did so in terms of love, praise, and beauty, as, for example, in 'On the Creation':

> Hail mighty maker of the universe!
> My song shall still thy glorious deeds rehearse:
> Thy praise, whatever subject others chuse,
> Shall be the lofty theme of my aspiring muse.[7]

The model of a woman's piety as the guiding force of her writing life continued to be influential throughout the century. The Anglican Elizabeth Carter modelled her early career on Rowe.[8] The daughter of a learned clergyman in Kent, who educated his daughters as well as his sons, she was proficient in nine languages, including Greek, Latin, Italian, and French, and translated and published the work of Epictetus, the first-century Greek Stoic philosopher.[9] She was part of London literary society and a close friend of Dr Johnson, but the guiding force in her life was her religion, 'her constant care and greatest delight'. Her piety was 'the most distinguishing feature of her character. It was indeed the very piety of the Gospel, shewn not by enthusiasm, or depreciating that of others, but by a calm rational and constant devotion, and the most unwearied attention to acquire the temper, and practice the duties of a Christian life' wrote her equally pious clergyman biographer.

She read the Bible every day, 'and no person ever endeavoured more, and few with greater success, to regulate the whole of their conduct by that unerring guide'. But she had a particular dislike for 'controversial divinity' and 'advised her friends never to read books adverse to the scriptures, or raising objections to them'.[10] This concern with orthodoxy dictated her reading habits. Of Voltaire, she wrote to a friend: 'I have not seen any of his late writings, nor from the character of them, do I ever design it. I should as soon think of playing with a toad or a viper, as of reading such blasphemy and impiety as I am told are contained in some of his works.'[11]

By contrast, the Calvinistic Baptist, Anne Dutton, writing at just about the same time as Elizabeth Carter but moving in very different circles, was not afraid to address divisive theological issues. While for Carter, the cultivation of piety was the mainstay of her life (much discussed in her letters with friends) which enabled her to write and translate, for Dutton, the very act of writing about theology was, she believed, her vocation from God. She wrote in her spiritual autobiography, a classic account of herself as a sinner and of God's 'special providences' in dealing with her: 'the Lord that call'd me to feed his Lambs has extended my Usefulness to many at a great Distance by Writing and Printing, far beyond what I thought of!' This sense of her own calling was balanced over and against the evangelical sense of utter human depravity, as she asked of God: 'Wash thy vile worm, and my Polluted Service in thy Precious Blood.'[12] Brought up by Congregationalist parents, she became a Calvinistic Baptist in her youth and married a Baptist minister.

Anne Dutton was a thoroughly biblical theologian. *A Narration of the Wonders of Grace* (1734), her six-part theological tract on the nature of the Trinitarian God, salvation, and the second coming of Christ, written in verse, had the relevant biblical verses printed in the margins, with a different biblical verse on almost every line. Her theological perspective reflected the usual concerns of evangelicals: human sin and depravity, conversion and justification. She participated in the theological controversies of the day, writing against John Wesley's notion of perfection, which, as a Calvinist who believed in the elect, she found abhorrent.[13] The theme of predestination is woven throughout her works, even her poetry:

> The spirit keeps election in his eye,
> And knows exactly for whom Christ did die;
> [...] And thus he seeks, and finds the chosen sheep
> The father gave the shepherd Christ to keep;

And though along the fallen world they lie;
He comes resolved that there they shall not die.[14]

This put her on the side of the Calvinistic George Whitefield in the clash between Whitefield and John Wesley. He became her patron and spiritual adviser, and introduced her to a wider circle of evangelicals, but he also harnessed her writing energy to help him in his ministry, urging her to write to his followers in North America. She thus exercised her own ministry through letters, becoming well known in Georgia and South Carolina from her correspondence.

As an evangelical, Dutton took the biblical texts about the place of women seriously. How could she write and publish, when Paul had instructed Timothy that women should not teach, nor usurp authority over man (1 Timothy 2:12), and had told the Corinthian church that women should remain silent in church (1 Corinthians 14: 34, 35)? Dutton justified her many published works, as well as her voluminous correspondence on religious subjects, by arguing that all her teaching and instruction was private, and she used a different Pauline text in her defence:

> It is commanded, Rom, xiv, 19. *Let us therefore follow after the Things which make for Peace and Things wherewith one* (any one, Male or Female) *may edify another.* If it is the Duty of Women to seek the Edification of their brethren and sisters; then it is their Duty to use the Means of it, whether it be in speaking, writing or printing: Since all these are private, and proper to the Sphere which the Lord has allotted them. Thus any Believer, Male or Female, that is gifted for, and inclin'd to publish their Thoughts in Print, about any Truth of Christ, for the private Instruction and Edification of the Saints; is permitted, yea commanded, so to do.[15]

Dutton might have called herself a 'vile worm' but she had a strong sense of her gifts, a fierce longing to be active in the Church, and a deep conviction of her vocation as a writer.[16]

2 Theology: engaging with the New Philosophy

In 1693, Mary Astell (who had not by then published *A Serious Proposal*) wrote to John Norris, the rector of Bremerton near Salisbury, about his *Practical Discourses Upon Several Divine Subjects*, published that year.[17] She had an objection to Norris's argument, based on an inconsistency she had spotted: namely, that if 'GOD *is the only efficient Cause of all our Sensations'* (pain as well as pleasure), then surely he is not just 'the only Object of our Love' as the cause of our pleasure, as Norris had asserted, but also must be the object 'of our Aversion' as the cause of our pain?[18] Just as we tend to move away from pain and towards pleasure, then surely, too, we will both move from and towards God? The letter was written in a spirit of encouragement for Norris's position, rather than attack, and was received as such. Norris took up Astell's line, and came to the conclusion that we should love God not because he is the author of our pleasure but because he is the author of our Good (and that Good may include our pain, and God's curing of our pain). So began a correspondence that stretched over a year, consisted of fifteen letters, and was published in 1695 as *Letters Concerning the Love of God*. It also heralded Astell's serious theological concerns with the nature of God, and an attempt to demonstrate how a proper understanding of God might be attained. This she partially worked out in the *Letters*, and more fully and maturely in *The Christian Religion* (1705).

By entering into a correspondence with John Norris, which was later published, Astell became part of a loose network of women who, by their engagement with theological ideas, were also responding to the New Philosophy. The translation of Descartes into English in the 1650s; the new experimental philosophy; a pressing desire to find a 'reasonable' theological position in the wake of a religiously conflicted civil war; questions of epistemology: these were all major intellectual influences on theology in the late seventeenth and early eighteenth centuries. Women, as well as men, participated in ongoing discussions about the nature of God, the universe and the soul; the individual's relationship with God; how knowledge about God was attained and its relationship to morality. Several sets of relationships were vital here – not only Astell and Norris, but also Anne Conway and Henry More, Damaris Masham and John Locke (and, earlier, Margaret Cavendish and Thomas Hobbes): all based on a sense of intellectual affinity, and built on the exchange of ideas.

Astell's concerns with how knowledge about God is attained meant that she was necessarily engaged in a debate with Locke's work. Locke had argued that all knowledge, even our knowledge of God, comes from our individual experiences; from the material world that we perceive through our senses. In the *Letters*, Astell and Norris made an implicit critique of a Lockean position, arguing that God is the sole cause of all events in this world through direct intervention, and asking to what extent the love of God involved a renunciation of the world. Devotion was a key part of their theological scheme. In 1696, the year after the *Letters* were published, their position was challenged in an anonymous text, *Discourse Concerning the Love of God*. The author characterized Norris as teaching 'that we do not love God as we ought, whilst we love any Creatures at all' and criticized Norris and Astell's position on the grounds that if God is the sole object of our love, then this may excuse us from loving God's creatures and thus provide no foundation at all for virtuous conduct, thereby destroying the duties and obligations of social life. The author was Damaris Masham, Locke's great friend and patron. For Masham, it is 'by the Existence of the Creatures that we come to know there is a Creator; so by their Loveliness it is that we come to know that of their Author, and to Love him'. Only by acquiring the idea of Love from God's creatures can we then apply that idea to the Creator. According to Masham, Norris and Astell had things backwards. She was also critical of their emphasis on devotion, and made a pointed charge against Astell when she proposed that such 'a Devout way of talking' would lead to 'Enthusiasm' 'which can End in nothing but Monasteries, and Hermitages; with all those Sottish and Wicked Superstitions which have accompanied them where-ever they have been in use'. Astell had, by now, published *A Serious Proposal*. It is revealing of both the temper of the age and the preoccupations of these female writers that a philosophical debate was infused with moral questions about how piety should be cultivated: through devotion and a renunciation of the world, or in service to others? Masham took a typically Latitudinarian position: 'To be always busy in the affairs of the World, or always shut up from them, cannot be born [sic]: Always Company, or Always Solitude, are Dangerous: And so are any other Extreams.'[19]

Masham was the daughter of Ralph Cudworth, one of the Cambridge Platonists, and had been brought up in an atmosphere of learning in which the *via media*, the reasonable approach, was sought. She had met Locke in 1682 when she was twenty-three years old, and they had become close friends. Locke had great respect for Masham's intellect: she was an important interlocutor and intellectual influence on him.[20] In turn she learnt from him and benefited from her association with him in the public world of letters. In 1691, Locke – who was poor, ill and back from exile in Holland – came to live with Masham and her husband on their estate in Essex, and remained there until his death in 1704. Both Astell and Norris thought Locke had written *Discourse*. When Astell published her mature theological tract, *The Christian Life*, in 1705, she made her critique of Locke explicit, taking on the language of the *Discourse* in sarcastic terms. She attacked Locke's Socinianism, and his refusal to subscribe to the Trinity in his *Reasonableness of Christianity* and she attacked his materialism.[21]

As this snapshot into a debate about knowledge of God indicates, women were fully engaged in the intellectual reception of the New Philosophy. Anne Conway had been one of the first readers of Descartes in England; in her *Principles of the Most Ancient and Modern Philosophy* (published anonymously and posthumously in 1690) she refuted Cartesian dualism, and presented a Platonist metaphysics, which anticipated Leibniz's idea of the monad. She also sought to provide an adequate theodicy – an account of how a loving God can allow suffering in the world – in the light of her own acute physical pain: she suffered for much of her life from incurable headaches. Astell criticized the sceptical Earl of Shaftesbury's attack on enthusiasm (*Letter Concerning Enthusiasm*) in her *Bart'lemy Fair* (1709). Masham challenged the deists, when proposing a thoroughly reasonable approach to religion in which reason, revelation, and faith were all held in balance, in *Occasional Thoughts in Reference to a Vertuous or Christian Life* (1705). The largely self-educated Catharine Trotter Cockburn (1679–1749) wrote in defence of both John Locke and Damaris Masham,[22] and her theological works included *A Discourse concerning a Guide in Controversies* (1707), which compared Protestant and Roman Catholic doctrines. This was interesting in light of the fact that she had been born into the Church of England, had converted to Roman Catholicism at an early age, converted back to Anglicanism in 1707 (the year this tract was published), and married an Anglican clergyman in 1708. Lady Mary Wortley Montagu took on the male deists' attitude to other religions – as like 'ours': good when monotheistic and rational, bad when polytheistic and irrational – when she wrote in her letters from Turkey and further travels in Europe about the religious customs she observed.[23] All of these women contributed to a fierce, ongoing debate about the place of reason and revelation in religion, the issue of epistemology in theology, and the related questions of piety and morality in society.

3 Visionary and apocalyptic texts

The impact of the New Philosophy and the turn to Reason did not witness the total eclipse of visionary writing. Many still believed in the power of the prophet, and the importance of divine revelation. Jane Lead and M. Marsin stand out as visionary writers who reconfigured key Christian ideas in gendered terms. Lead was concerned – like so many of her contemporary female writers – with leading a holy life. She also longed to live a contemplative life, and this became possible after 1670 when her husband died. Two months into her widowhood, she claimed that she began to receive visions and prophecies, which continued for the rest of her life. In 1674, she joined the spiritual household of John Pordage, the radical follower of the German mystic, Jakob Boehme, a community united by the spiritual quest for 'Divine Wisdom'. For Lead, Wisdom was feminine – 'Sophia'; the imminent second coming of Christ was also about the coming of Sophia. While writers such as Astell, Masham, and Cockburn all emphasized the role of reason in religion (albeit with different meanings), Lead believed that Divine Wisdom would restore that 'Virgin Nature, and Godlike Simplicity, that have been deflowered through the subtlety of Reason' for Wisdom 'is in Marriage-form with God's omnipotency'. Reason was not a part of the vision of the New Jerusalem, just as 'Rationality was not in Adam before his Lapse'.[24] Lead bypassed the prevailing debates about reason, knowledge, and morality and turned, instead, in her vision for godly and peaceful living, to an imaginative reading of biblical texts (especially Daniel and Revelation) fused with the knowledge from her daily prophecies, recorded in her spiritual diary *Fountain of Gardens*, which ran to 2500 pages (parts of it painstakingly reconstructed, first by Pordage and then by Francis Lee, as Lead had a habit of writing down her visions on slips of paper and giving them out to her followers and friends).

In 1694, Francis Lee, a former fellow of St John's College, Oxford, came to meet Lead: he had been living in the Netherlands where he had read her writings (which were then gaining a larger readership on the Continent than in England). He became a disciple, and married Lead's widowed daughter, Barbara, moving into their household. Soon afterwards, one of Lee's friends from St John's, a clergyman named Richard Roach, joined them. This spiritual household became the centre of the Philadelphian Church, a millenarian movement awaiting the coming of Divine Wisdom. Lead believed in universal salvation, the coming together of all peoples at the millennium; modelling this, the Philadelphian Church was open to all denominations, and Lead described the true Philadelphian as one who acted 'in the good of all his Brethren, that is, of all Mankind'.[25] Further, she believed in the restoration of the harmony of an original, pre-Lapsarian existence, as expounded in her third book, *The Enochian Walks with God* (1694). At the heart of all her theology was the notion of a compassionate God, incorporating both the feminine and the masculine, whose love for the suffering, groaning, travailing creation, will redeem it fully and wholly in the end. Lead published prolifically in the last two decades of her life, even as she lost her sight. The inspiration for her writing was, she believed, divine; the primary message of her theology, prophetic.

About M. Marsin, we know very little. What we have is a series of fifteen texts, both pamphlets and more substantial books, written over a few years (1696–1701) at the turn of the century. They were characteristically apocalyptic, interpreting the signs of the times for intimations of Christ's coming (especially in *The near approach of Christ's Kingdom*, 1696). They were innovative in their insistence on both woman's role in interpreting scripture correctly and Marsin's own distinctive role, as a woman, in interpreting God's word. Quite simply, men had got it wrong in the past: they had failed to understand God's Word and therefore God's purposes properly. Where scripture does not fit with her understanding of women – the Pauline injunctions against women exercising authority, for example – Marsin simply disregards it. This did not mean that she did not take scripture very seriously; she did. In *Good News to the Good Women* and *Two Remarkable Females of Womankind* (both 1701), she made her case that women had had a greater role in the revelation of God's word and purpose than men, highlighting women's roles and authority in the Old and New Testaments – especially the Virgin Mary, the first woman 'to be filled with the Holy Ghost'.[26] It was in the light of all the rest of scripture that she therefore believed Paul was in error about women's authority and teaching.

Like her contemporary Lead, Marsin also looked forward to the re-establishment of a pre-Lapsarian state at the millennium. For Marsin, that entailed the re-establishment of an original equality of the sexes, to a state where 'the Husband will not be above the Wife, nor the Wife above the Husband, but as they were in the first Creation, before Sin entred [sic] into the World'. For then, the 'Women in the Kingdom which is to come, should be restored to that perfect state Woman was in before the Fall'.[27] What is remarkable about Marsin's body of work is how rapidly and radically she developed a distinctive feminist position, in a series of tracts written over five years, and how sure she was of her own authority as inspired and given by God.[28]

Almost all of the female writers of this period who engaged with the subject of religion asked questions about their position *as women* in relationship to the Christian tradition. Astell proposed a female monastery in order to create a space in which women might learn and pray together, believing that women's souls were equal with those of men. Anne Dutton was, in theory, the most constrained by the scriptural injunctions against women's authority in teaching – but she found her way round them because she so fervently believed in her religious calling to write. Jane Lead had a vision of all things coming right in the New Jerusalem, led by the divine feminine and masculine combined. And the radical M. Marsin believed that only women were capable of interpreting scripture properly and thus following God's commands. An earlier generation of feminist scholars understandably looked at the 'feminist' (a term whose use in relation to this period has been debated) work of many of these women; two or three decades later, the significance of religion in this period has been newly emphasized by historians. A new generation of scholarship has therefore emphasized the primacy of religion in the writing lives of these women. Women wrote because it was a part of their call, their piety, their devotion and their longing for learning; in that process they became writers. But they were first and foremost devout.

Notes

1. *Mary Astell's A Serious Proposal to the Ladies: Parts 1 and II*, ed. by Patricia Springborg (Peterborough, Ontario: Broadview Press, 2002).
2. Ibid., I, 74; II, 73, 76.
3. The idea continued to be mooted as, for example, in Sarah Scott, *A Description of Millenium Hall* (London, 1762), a novel about a utopian female community committed to philanthropy.
4. Sarah Prescott, 'Provincial Networks, Dissenting Connections, and Noble Friends: Elizabeth Singer Rowe and Female Authorship in Early Eighteenth-Century England', *Eighteenth-Century Life*, 25.1 (2001), 29–42 and *Women, Authorship and Literary Culture, 1690–1740* (Basingstoke and New York: Palgrave Macmillan, 2003). See also Marjorie Reeves, 'Literary Women in Eighteenth-Century Nonconformist Circles', in *Culture and the Nonconformist Tradition*, ed. by Jane Shaw and Alan Kreider (Cardiff: University of Wales Press, 1999), pp. 7–25.
5. *The Miscellaneous Works in Prose and Verse of Mrs Elizabeth Singer Rowe*, 2 vols, 4th edn (London, 1756) I, 124.
6. Ibid., I, 105.
7. Ibid., I, 11.
8. Norma Clarke suggests that Elizabeth Carter imitated the young Elizabeth Singer by sending her poems to the leading periodical of her day, the *Gentleman's Magazine*, just as Singer had sent hers to the *Athenian Mercury*. Norma Clarke, 'Soft Passions and Darling Themes: from Elizabeth Singer Rowe (1674–1737) to Elizabeth Carter (1717–1806)', *Women's Writing*, 7.3 (2000), 353–71.
9. *All the works of Epictetus, which are now extant; consisting of his discourses, preserved by Arrian, in four books, the Enchiridion, and fragments*, trans. by Elizabeth Carter (Dublin, 1759).
10. Montagu Pennington, *Memoirs of the Life of Mrs Elizabeth Carter* (Boston, MA, 1809 [first American edition taken from the second English edition]), pp. 17, 18, 17.

11. Elizabeth Carter to Mrs Vesey, May 30, 1774, in *A Series of Letters Between Mrs. Elizabeth Carter and Miss Catherine Talbot, from the Year 1741 to 1770: To which are Added, Letters from Mrs. Elizabeth Carter to Mrs. Vesey, Between the Years 1763 and 1787; Published from the Original Manuscripts in the Possession of the Rev. Montagu Pennington* (London, 1809), p. 113.

12. Anne Dutton, *A Brief Account of the gracious dealings of God, with a poor, sinful, unworthy creature, in three parts* (London, 1750), pp. 163, 176

13. Anne Dutton, *Letters to the Reverend Mr John Wesley against Perfection As not attainable in this Life* (London, 1743) and *A Letter to the Reverend Mr John Wesley: In Vindication of the Doctrines of Absolute, unconditional Election, Particular Redemption, Special Vocation, and Final Perseverance* (London, 1743).

14. Anne Dutton, 'A Poem on the Special Work of the Spirit in the Hearts of the Elect', in *A Narration of the Wonders of Grace* (London, 1734), p. 45.

15. Anne Dutton, *A Letter to such of the Servants of Christ, who may have any Scruple about the Lawfulness of Printing any Thing written by a Woman* (London, 1743), p. 5.

16. On Anne Dutton, see Stephen J. Stein, 'A Note on Anne Dutton, Eighteenth-Century Evangelical', *Church History*, 44.4 (December 1975), 485–91.

17. Mary Astell and John Norris, *Letters Concerning the Love of God*, ed. by E. Derek Taylor and Melvyn New (Aldershot: Ashgate, 2005).

18. Ibid., pp. 69, 70.

19. *Discourse Concerning the Love of God* (London, 1696), pp. 119, 65, 120, 126.

20. See, for example, Jacqueline Broad, 'A Woman's Influence? John Locke and Damaris Masham on Moral Accountability', *Journal of the History of Ideas*, 67.3 (2006), 489–510.

21. For differing interpretations of Astell on Locke, see Patricia Springborg, *Mary Astell: Theorist of Freedom from Domination* (Cambridge: Cambridge University Press, 2005) and Mark Goldie, 'Mary Astell and John Locke', in *Mary Astell: Reason, Gender and Faith*, ed. by William Kolbrener and Michael Michelson (Aldershot: Ashgate, 2007).

22. Catharine Trotter Cockburn, *The Defence of Mr Locke's Essay of Human Understanding* (London, 1702); *A Letter to Dr. Holdsworth Occasioned by his Sermon* (London, 1726) – a defence of Locke's orthodoxy.

23. See Jane Shaw, 'Gender and the "Nature" of Religion: Lady Mary Wortley Montagu's Embassy Letters and their Place in Enlightenment Philosophy of Religion', *Bulletin of the John Rylands Library*, 80.3 (1998), 129–45.

24. Jane Lead, *The Heavenly Cloud now breaking; or the Lord-Christ's ascension ladder, now sent down*, 2nd edn (London, 1701), pp. 28, 12.

25. Jane Lead, *The Messenger of an Universal Peace: or A Third Message to the Philadelphian Society* (London, 1698), p. 72.

26. M. Marsin, *Good news to the good women, and to the bad women too that will grow better; the like to the men* (London, 1701), p. 11.

27. Ibid., pp. 6, 5.

28. On Marsin's feminist approach, see Sarah Apetrei, '"A Remarkable Female of Womankind": Gender, Scripture and Knowledge in the Writings of M. Marsin', in *Women, Gender and Radical Religion in Early Modern Europe*, ed. by Sylvia Brown (Leiden: Brill, 2007), pp. 139–59.

12
Erotic Love

Toni Bowers

In 1728, Jonathan Swift published a poem marking the birthday of a female scandal writer, Corinna. At her birth Apollo, god of poetry, 'endowed her with his art'; but, in echo of the fairy tale where an infant's future is darkened by an uninvited guest, 'Cupid' and 'a satyr' crept to the baby's side and bestowed upon her more ambiguous gifts.

> Then Cupid thus: "This little maid
> Of love shall always speak and write;"
> "And I pronounce," the satyr said,
> "The world shall feel her scratch and bite."[1]

Swift's *Corinna* was long understood to point to Delarivier Manley, the Tory dramatist, novelist, and pamphleteer with whom he sometimes collaborated. But critics now agree that Eliza Haywood seems also to be targeted:[2] the final stanza names two titles within Corinna's 'scandal [...] cornucopia', '*Atalantis*' (Manley's *Secret Memoirs and Manners of Several Persons of Quality of Both Sexes from the New Atalantis, an Island in the Mediterranean*, 1709) and '*Memoirs of the New Utopia*' (Haywood's *Memoirs of a Certain Island Adjacent to the Kingdom of Utopia*, 1724). Manley and Haywood are conflated in Corinna as targets of Swift's disdain – joint participants in the fierce 'scratch and bite' of early eighteenth-century partisan debate, interchangeable writers of the steamy erotic tales now often called 'amatory fictions'.

Swift's conflation of Manley and Haywood, like the bemused and contemptuous tone of *Corinna*, reveals much about how the early eighteenth-century's most famous authors of erotic fiction were perceived by their more respectable peers. But as Swift surely knew, Manley and Haywood were not in fact born on the same day. Manley (b. c.1670) was Swift's own contemporary, while Haywood (b. 1693) was more than twenty years younger. *Corinna*'s other suggestion is more accurate: as Swift implies, it is precisely through tales of erotic love that 'Corinna' – both Manley and Haywood – participated in the 'scratch and bite' of public debate. This chapter elaborates Swift's suggestion by delineating a key strategy common to Manley and Haywood's erotic fiction. At the same time, it challenges any easy conflation of Manley and Haywood by showing how their deployments of that shared strategy exhibit historically driven differences. Put as briefly as possible, Manley's uses of the strategy I shall describe tend to be programmatically Tory-partisan, while Haywood's tend to be more a function of what I call 'Tory-oriented' ideological assumptions and values. Using evidence from both well-known and comparatively obscure tales, I will suggest that Haywood's erotic fiction of the 1720s shows her to have been an attentive reader of Manley, one who both emulated and revised her predecessor's narrative strategies for comparable, though not identical, political purposes.

1 Delarivier Manley

Like Haywood after her, Manley began her career in the theatre and came to prose fiction relatively late, as part of her work as Tory propagandist in a Whig-dominated age. Manley's erotic tales, like her partisan pamphleteering, offered Tory interpretations of recent and contemporary political affairs and did much to clarify – indeed to determine – what 'Tory' meant in her day.[3] In the *New Atalantis*, Manley built powerful satire from a series of scandalous *ad hominem* exposés of recognizable Whig targets – politicians, aristocrats, military heroes, and partisan operatives among them. Politics is a feverishly sexual business in the *New Atalantis*, sexual encounters are always a form of partisan contest, and every insult is meant to be taken personally.

The *New Atalantis* appeared in April (vol. 1) and late October (vol. 2) 1709 – a crucial juncture. The Union of England and Scotland was less than two years old and still fragile, and a French-sponsored Jacobite rising, the abortive ''08', had taken place mere months before, probably while Manley was writing. Manley's scandalous partisan allegory erupted into this fraught context, bringing about measurable political results. Queen Anne's late, surprising change to a Tory ministry took place in 1710, less than a year after *Atalantis*'s first appearance and in significant part as a result of the novel's unprecedented influence on partisan affairs.[4]

Nor was Manley content to attack powerful Whigs. She also used *Atalantis* implicitly to defend the collusion, duplicity, and bad faith endemic to Tory experience in the wake of the 'Glorious Revolution' and to reinterpret recent Tory history – a history of capitulation and broken vows – as a record of virtue besieged yet still triumphant. Manley's reinterpretation of collusion as virtue was a crucial partisan intervention in the first decade of the eighteenth century, when Tories seeking participation in high-level government at that time had to struggle to define and project an identity distinct from that of their nemeses, the rebellious (and often Roman Catholic) Jacobites. Even when Tories did manage to discredit Whig insistence that they were merely Jacobites in masquerade, it remained difficult to clarify a positive Tory identity. Since the party's glory days in the early 1680s, what defined 'Tory' had become less a clearly decipherable, stable partisan platform than habits of compromise and dissimulation.

Atalantis's loosely structured narrative – in which a group of invisible divinities from 'the kingdom of the Moon' tours a fictional island, obviously suggestive of Britain, while being regaled with scandalous stories by their loquacious guide, 'Intelligence' – deploys and revises familiar plot lines, rhetorical patterns, and character types inherited from earlier seduction stories. (Among these are the innocent maiden, scheming seducer, and treacherous female friend; male pursuit, wavering or duplicitous female resistance; sexual transgression graphically depicted; letters exchanged and misdirected; sexual violence and/or coercion; female disgrace, retreat to the convent, and abandonment.) In the process, Manley implicitly redefines collusions structurally like those inescapable for publicly engaged Tories of her generation as practices of complicated virtue based in a moral superiority markedly less clear in the real experience of Tory-oriented subjects during the first decades of the eighteenth century.

Take the most famous interpolated seduction story in the *New Atalantis*, the story of an unnamed duke's affair with his young ward, Charlot.[5] The duke, a brilliant and ambitious statesman, has raised Charlot as one of his own children, confining her to 'diversions [...] most innocent and simple' that include walking ('but not in public assemblies'), music ('all divine'), and reading ('improving books of education and piety').[6] Most of all, the duke emphasizes, Charlot must never allow herself to feel desire for men. Indeed, he insists, 'the very first impressions' of love ought 'to be carefully 'suppressed', since it is 'shameful for a young lady ever so much as to think of any tenderness for a Lover, 'till he was become her husband', and desiring women come to 'inevitable ruin' (pp. 38–9).

All this prim advice backfires when the duke, to his own surprise, begins to feel overwhelming sexual desire for Charlot. In keeping with an ancient romance *topos*, he literally grows sick with love;[7] and in another familiar turn, he changes her reading material – the inevitable first step toward Charlot's fall. Where once Charlot was denied any writing like Manley's own – 'airy romances, plays, dangerous novels, loose and insinuating poetry, artificial introductions of love, well-painted landscapes of that dangerous poison' (p. 38) – now the duke assigns Ovid, Petrarch, and other literary 'poison' guaranteed to 'corrupt the Mind' (p. 45), until Charlot is ripe for capitulation.

> The Duke's pursuing Kisses overcame the very Thoughts of any thing, but that new and lazy Poison stealing to her Heart, and spreading swiftly and imperceptibly thro' all her Veins, she clos'd her Eyes with languishing Delight! deliver'd up the possession of her Lips and Breath to the amorous Invader.
>
> (p. 44)

Characteristically, Manley's narrator manages to be at once graphic and euphemistic. The duke and Charlot are only kissing here, but carefully chosen codewords ('Invader', 'possession', 'meltings') suggest to knowing readers that intercourse will inevitably take place – these words function in Manley's fiction like the fireworks, spouting hoses, and crashing strings in Hollywood films from the 1940s and 1950s – and make the declaration that she 'gave her whole Person into his Arms' almost redundant (p. 44).

But not quite. For the first scene of sexual intercourse between the duke and Charlot, also narrated at once explicitly and formulaically, finally brings into the open the violence latent in the duke's desire. The duke, we read, 'made himself a full amends for all those pains he had suffered for her' despite Charlot's 'prayers, tears', and 'strugglings' (p. 48). 'Thus was *Charlot* undone! thus ruin'd by him that ought to have been her Protector!' (p. 48) Intelligence cries in outrage. Yet, as so often in amatory fiction, sexual violence is immediately recuperated. A moment later, Charlot 'espous'd his Crime, by sealing his Forgiveness', and the two go on to make love all night, Charlot 'not at all behind-hand in Extasies and guilty Transports' (p. 48). The duke's violence provokes not rebellion but responsive desire, sexual collusion that, as much as the sex itself, seals Charlot's doom. Predictably, her life soon becomes 'one continu'd Scene of Horror, Sorrow, and Repentance' (p. 54).

Intelligence brings home the conventional lesson: Charlot stands as 'a true Landmark: to warn all believing Virgins from shipwracking [sic] their Honour upon [...] the Vows and pretended Passion of

Mankind' (p. 54). At the same time, though, Charlot's story hints at a heterodox suggestion: that a woman might continue virtuous even *after* unlawful sexual capitulation. We can perceive this shadowy possibility in the much-emphasized sincerity and faithfulness of Charlot's love for the duke, qualities that persist even after he abandons her. Charlot's ingenuous, disinterested, unchanging love is an indicator of virtue in the logic of the *New Atalantis*, and she retains it even after her 'fall'. It's true that she irretrievably loses her reputation with her virginity, and that her story ends in tragedy; yet there is an insistent suggestion, just below the surface, that Charlot remains different *in kind* from the duke, that she retains a species of virtue unknown to him. It would be up to Haywood (and, later, Samuel Richardson) to elaborate on that suggestion.

That virtue might exceed virginity, and remain even *after* collusive desire and capitulation, is insinuated again in an interpolated tale from *Atalantis's* second volume, the story of Elonora. Here, the heroine's irrational desire for an unworthy man leads her into a series of transgressions and errors, until eventually she finds herself in a lonely garden at night, with a man intent on rape. The divinities interrupt the rape-in-progress just in time, but they make no move, at first, to commiserate with or comfort Elonora; instead, their great concern is to determine how far she is responsible for her own predicament. 'Oh Heavens!' cries Intelligence,

> What do I see? The *Beautiful*, the *Innocent Elonora* at this midnight hour in such a *Solitude* as this, with a Man [...]. How did you agree to so criminal an *Assignation*? It has the Appearance of being *voluntary!* there was no such thing as bringing you to the *Tuilleries* alone, without your own Consent and Approbation.
>
> (pp. 186–7)

Once Elonora tells her tale, however, such questions entirely vanish. Intelligence assures Elonora that the nation's 'Graceful *Empress*' will give her 'the Reward due to your suffering *Vertue*' and exalt her 'in your proper *Sphere*', 'reverenced for *Goodness* and dear to the *Empress* for a thousand *Vertues,* so much of Kindred to her own!' (pp. 123–4). What is most remarkable is that this surprising reversal does *not* come about because Elonora has behaved entirely virtuously. On the contrary, as her own narration reveals, she has perversely desired a despicable ingrate; she has even kept secret assignations with him. She has committed tragic, irreparable errors, contributed to the death of a virtuous brother, gambled to excess – in short, has largely been the agent of her own lost reputation. Nevertheless, after hearing her compromising tale, the divinities agree that Elonora is a model of virtue. The goddess Virtue, normally silent, even volunteers that Elonora 'shall remain under our Care. We will not have her leave us till her Establishment [...]. I request she may have part in all our Affairs and, when it is found convenient, share our *Invisibility*' (p. 214). Elonora is uniquely rewarded, in other words, honoured beyond any other mortal in the book. She began her account as a suspect woman whose compromised position 'seems to have the appearance of being voluntary'; by the tale's end she is honoured and justified by the goddesses, has become equally part of the mortal world and the heavenly realm, and – most striking of all – is *still virtuous*. In Elonora's story, Manley imagines a female virtue that can encompass error, transgressive desire, and collusion.

One knowledgeable critic has argued that because there is 'no recognizable individual hidden behind the central character', the Elonora story is merely a 'romantic interlude' quite other in kind from Manley's 'political allegories'.[8] I am arguing that the Elonora story in fact *extends* the political reach of *Atalantis*'s allegorical method, obliquely defining and defending Tory sensibility, a sensibility that by 1709 had long been marked by collusion with Whig agendas, anxiety to distinguish itself from Jacobitism, and uncertainty. Elonora's tale demonstrates that even when it eschews its characteristic *ad hominem* method, *Atalantis* continues its partisan signification, and does so specifically in its revisionary suggestions about the persistent virtue of sexually compromised women.

2 Eliza Haywood

Ten years later, Eliza Haywood would take up Manley's suggestion and make it explicit in her successful first novel *Love in Excess*, a work that answers *Atalantis* in many ways. Haywood's 1719 novel touched a nerve in a political landscape that looked very different than it had in 1709. The Treaty of Union, recent and pregnable when Manley wrote, by 1719 had weathered significant challenges; its perpetuation seemed likely.[9] Britain had negotiated major commercial advantages at the Peace of Utrecht (1713–14).[10] George I had ascended in peace (1714), and though the Jacobites had been scheming for two generations, they had achieved little. Jacobitism could by no means be discounted in 1719, of course. Just one year before, Stuart supporters had mounted a serious challenge, 'the '18', which like the plots of 1708 and 1715 sobered supporters of the Protestant succession by coming perilously close to realization; and there would be many other invasion scares and attempts to restore the Stuarts. (Rebellions were planned in 1720–21, 1743–44, 1745, even as late as 1759.) Still, slowly but surely, the passage of time was putting the Protestant government on an increasingly strong footing.

It remained dangerous in 1719 to display sympathies that might be construed as Jacobite, of course. But perhaps equally debilitating for writers who shared to any significant extent ideological assumptions like those of Manley (whether nominally 'Tory' or not) was the accretion of thirty years' uneasy collusion, on the part of Tory spokesmen, with Whig agendas. The bad faith built into that history of complicity had been painfully exposed in 1714 by the arrests of Queen Anne's two most visible self-described Tory ministers, Oxford and Bolingbroke, both of whom were accused of abetting the planned Jacobite rebellion of 1715. Though the plot failed (and Oxford's implication remained uncertain), the catastrophe was the final nail in the coffin of Tory credibility with the new king, George I, and erased the gains Tories had made during Anne's last four years. Under the proscription that would shortly become law, it would be more necessary than ever for Protestant Tories to cooperate with Whig policies, if only to prove their distance from Jacobite resistance and the loyalty to the Church that was their constant boast. All this meant that Haywood's erotic fiction entered what was in many ways a less straightforward political climate than Manley's had. That fact goes far to explain what have been perceived sometimes as inconsistencies in her writing. Haywood joined Tory and 'Patriot' Whig contemporaries in opposition to Walpole's administration, but also wrote at least one pamphlet that leaves open 'the possibility that Haywood held Jacobite sympathies': the dissonance does less to mark her as a Jacobite, as is sometimes averred, than to suggest her fundamental ideological affinity with contemporary Tory principles and perplexities.[11]

The power of *Love in Excess* in 1719 had much to do with Haywood's ability to exploit and revise certain of Manley's earlier, Tory-coded narrative strategies – strategies on display not only in *Atalantis* but also in Manley's other works, which Haywood is likely to have known. *The Adventures of Rivella* (1714), for instance, suggestively reinforces *Atalantis*'s hint that female 'virtue' can encompass error, self-delusion, and complicit desire. Throughout *Rivella*, Manley indirectly defends her heroine's morality as superior to the conventional moralizing of the narrator, Lovemore, who fails to understand what readers perceive despite him: that Rivella retains true virtue even after transgressive sexual experience.[12] Something similar might be said about any

number of Manley's productions: again and again, her female prota-
gonists feel and act on their own sexual desire and nevertheless retain
a claim to 'virtue'.

When Haywood turned to writing fiction, it was this suggestion in
Manley's stories that she took up and exploited, pushing it farther
than Manley had done. The familial resemblance between Haywood's
seduction fiction and Manley's is plain, of course. But when Haywood's
heroines concede, collude, and capitulate, those practices are not merely
consistent with virtue, as in Manley, but virtuous *per se*. *Love in Excess*
follows Manley when it imagines virtuous resistance and compromising collusion as something other than mutually-exclusive alternatives,
and when it does so through the representation of female virtue under
sexual duress. What is new in Haywood is virtue's representation as
something actually constituted *in* compromise, not merely able to
survive it. In moving beyond the hyper-topical confines of the Manley-
style *roman à clef*, Haywood redefines virtue in terms broad enough to
encompass not only uncompromised purity but also hitherto disquali-
fying degrees of sexual complicity.[13] Melliora Frankville, the heroine
of *Love in Excess*, is at once a paragon of virtue *and* a collusive agent in
transgression. In Melliora, Haywood provided readers of the 1720s with
a model for reimagining complicity as a manifestation of virtue.

The thesis that underwrites Melliora's characterization – that virtue
and collusion may co-exist – was a thesis with clear ideological insinua-
tions in 1719. For Melliora's complex sexual agency is structurally much
like the uneasily collusive political agency that had marked subjects of
tory-oriented sensibility and Tory partisans alike for decades. By valorizing it, Haywood not only authorized a revised definition of female
virtue, but also offered a model for imagining collusion itself as more
than a sell-out. Compromise and complicity are fully acknowledged
in Melliora's characterization, yet, reassuringly, she remains virtuous,
a model of integrity. Haywood's representation of Melliora offered
compromised tory-oriented subjects a prototype for self-recuperation
after the debacles of 1715, not to mention thirty years of collusion with
Whiggish principles and practices that many could not fully subscribe
to, yet dared not oppose.

Haywood produced an immense number of seduction tales after *Love
in Excess*.[14] She refined the strategies of amatory fiction throughout
the 1720s, formulating a series of responses to Manley that included
homage, imitation, and historically necessary revision from the point
of view of a tory-oriented British subject. Chief among the strategies
Haywood employed was the redefinition of virtue to include certain

kinds and degrees of collusion. Consider two examples from late in the 1720s, *The Lucky Rape* (1727) and *The Padlock; or, No Guard Without Virtue* (1728).

Haywood's *The Lucky Rape* conjures again a young woman whose unquenchable desire is directed at an inappropriate man – this time her long-lost and unrecognized brother. Emelia is saved from committing incest with Henrique – just barely – by a disturbing *deus ex machina*: rape at the hands of another man. For her inconvenience, as it were, she is granted a dubious reward: marriage to the rapist. The tale seems to understand incest as the worst possible calamity and rape as a comparatively minor offence, easily rectified by the re-absorption of the tainted woman into patriarchal society via marriage. Indeed, the unnamed narrator claims that the rape was Emelia's 'greatest Good, since by it she was not only deliver'd from that manifest Danger of Incest she was falling into, but also gain'd a Husband'.[15] But there remains a nagging undertow of scepticism about how 'lucky' all this makes Emelia.

Subversion sounds, for instance, in Emelia's surprising response to the news that the man she loves is in fact her brother. 'The disconsolate Emelia', readers are informed, 'sigh'd at the Remembrance of what might have happened, had they remain'd ignorant of each other' (p. 94). Emelia longs to go back to the time when she could look forward to becoming Henrique's lover without guilt or impediment; she wishes she could return to the blissful ignorance that might have enabled an affair with Henrique *without loss of virtue*. When she mourns that lost ignorance, Emelia makes visible the possibility that ignorance of transgression might actually mitigate, perhaps even redefine, transgression itself. 'But recollecting herself as well as she cou'd', Emelia submits to the prospect of marriage to the rapist Alonzo, who promises 'what Reparation was in his Power' and overcomes the 'Foible' that made him kidnap and brutalize her (p. 94). The bitterly satirical language reveals the insufficiency of the patriarchal script: along with riches and respectability, marriage to Alonzo represents the permanent, legally sanctioned subordination of Emelia's desire and agency to a man who has already proven his contempt for both. Marriage and rape are mutually enabling, mutually recuperative, and similarly directed toward neutralizing Emelia's desire. By the story's end, readers are drawn less toward the narrative resolution (which we might call 'forced' in more senses than one) than toward the regret and lingering desire that Emelia momentarily reveals. Which is worse, Haywood leads us to wonder, incest, or marriage's glib claim to recuperate rape? The question reverberates, retroactively puncturing the tale's blithe title with irony.

Haywood's *The Lucky Rape* echoes and revises Manley's 1720 story *The Perjur'd Beauty*.[16] There, after Victoria eloped with Romeo from a convent where she had been unwillingly immured, both the affair and the lovers' lives were cut short by the revelation of consanguinity: Romeo, son of Count Rossano, turned out to be half-brother to Victoria, Rossano's secret 'Natural Daughter'.[17] In their own defence, Manley's lovers argued what Haywood's would suggest again in *The Lucky Rape*: that they were innocent 'because the Relation between them was unknown' (and, in *The Perjur'd Beauty*, because forced nun's vows conferred 'Innocence' on Victoria's later vows to Romeo (p. 368)). In Manley's tale, the ecclesiastical authorities assembled in judgement rejected both arguments, and the lovers were executed; but the questions they raised remained at the story's end, alive and festering, ready for Haywood to take up. 'Beat not our Hearts as high, were not our Kisses as sweet, our Delights as perfect, whilst we remained in the State of ignorance?' Victoria asked melodramatically. 'Our Innocence and Frailty [...] has offended only against the Laws of Man, without breaking Those of Nature, or [...] our Creator!' (pp. 366–7).

As long as it lasted, then, ignorance was bliss in Manley's *Perjur'd Beauty*, just as it is in Haywood's *Lucky Rape*. Both tales also question the inherent criminality of incest and expose patriarchal interests in its taboo. In *The Perjur'd Beauty* the crime was really not Victoria's or Romeo's anyway, but their *father*'s: Victoria informed Count Rossano that the story 'reflects back upon your Lordship only', and Romeo, even on the scaffold, 'accus[ed] his Father for his untimely Fall' (pp. 363, 368). In *The Lucky Rape*, patriarchal interests are explicitly linked with both rape and marriage – supposedly separate phenomena that, from Emelia's point of view, overlap. It is the *men* in Emelia's family who stand to gain from trading her to the wealthy Alonzo and protecting Henrique's political career – a career freighted, not incidentally, with the burden of redeeming his father's disgrace at Court. *The Lucky Rape* thus re-addresses questions raised in Manley's *Perjur'd Beauty* while recasting that earlier tale's most destabilizing suggestion: that transgressive desire may not be opposed to virtue per se, but only within the law's frame – a frame that serves primarily, in both stories, to protect hypocritical fathers.

Manley's seduction writing is once again invoked in Haywood's *The Padlock: or, No Guard Without Virtue*.[18] Despite this tale's brevity, it incorporates a considerable range of familiar conventions derived most immediately from Manley: a loveless, mercenary marriage, a secret lover, a looming monastery, disguise, transgressive desire, and a pivotal role for written correspondence. The story begins in familiar territory when a rich elderly bachelor, Don Lepidio, marries a 'young Beauty', Violante,[19] who is 'compelled' to the union 'by the Avarice of her Parents' (p. 57). Violante feels 'Aversion' for Lepidio, but 'Virtue and Discretion' lead her to make a choice opposite to the one Richardson's Clarissa Harlowe would make in a similar situation: she submits to the marriage and 'resolve[s] to be contented, if possible, and not by struggling render her Fetters uneasy' (p. 58). Thus virtuously complicit in her own violation, Violante assumes the self-abnegating femininity recommended in Augustan conduct literature: 'she conformed herself to his Humours, always acquiescing to what he said, and in every Affair of Life made his Will the sole Guide and Standard of her actions' (p. 58).

But Lepidio, 'conscious of his own Demerit', cruelly oppresses Violante, imprisoning her at home, denying visits even to her female relatives and her confessor. She can have no male servants 'but such whose Deformity made the Eye ake to look at', and is even 'oblig'd' to wear a chastity belt (p. 58). Unsurprisingly, all this makes Violante 'discontented'. Lepidio blames her for a 'Want of conjugal Affection'; sex becomes rape.

> It was only by Compulsion he enjoyed her as his Wife [...]. *Violante's* forc'd Love was now so much abated, that the Grave would be now more welcome than his Embraces [...] compell'd to aid the Rapture she detested, [...] all she did was forc'd [by] this Tyrant.
>
> (pp. 59–60)

The situation appears hopeless until, one day, Violante receives a letter – that frequent catalyst to plot developments. The sender turns out eventually to be a 'near Neighbor', Honorius Severinus, who has for years loved Violante from afar.

Here, remarkably, the narrator steps in to justify Violante's growing attraction to Honorius: he is well-born, she has heard he is handsome, and she believes she owes him 'gratitude' for such faithful love; 'nor can it well be call'd a falling off from Virtue, if with all these Enticements, joyn'd to the cruel Usage of *Lepidio*, she entertain'd a Desire of conversing more nearly' with him (p. 69). The statement is debatable, to say the least. Such an assignation most surely *would* have qualified as 'a falling off from Virtue' in the conduct literature after which Violante has patterned her wifely behaviour, and (as is shortly proven beyond doubt) in Lepidio's opinion. But what matters most about the narrator's defence of Violante is not its accuracy or inaccuracy; the more important point is that the tale continues to insist on Violante's undiminished 'virtue', despite the fact that she is moving toward adultery. And when, eventually, Violante and Honorius elope, Violante becomes 'the most contented Woman in the World', and 'there were but few who condemn'd her Flight'. Lepidio grants a divorce, a papal dispensation allows the lovers to be 'publickly married', and Honorius, 'to vindicate her Honour, and his own Choice', publishes an account of 'the whole Transaction' for national distribution. 'None who either heard or read the story', the narrator concludes, 'but what applauded a constancy so uncommon, and condemn'd the Jealousy of *Lepidio*, who, by his own Mis-management had depriv'd himself, not only of the most beautiful, but also most virtuous Women [sic] in the World' (pp. 77–9).

The most virtuous woman in the world? Haywood spins a tale of adultery, then not only lavishes on its transgressive heroine a trustworthy, doting, handsome, and rich lover, but imagines as well public disgrace for the abandoned husband, an ecclesiastically sanctioned remarriage, and the hearty approval of an entire nation of contemporaries. The overkill is obvious and purposeful. It marks the participation of *The Padlock*, with its depiction of a victimized wife who finds not only release but *virtue* in unfaithfulness, in a project of ideological recuperation closely related to Manley's partisan work in 1709, but going even farther toward the construction of a new conception of virtue.

Notes

1. *Jonathan Swift: The Complete Poems*, ed. by Pat Rogers (New Haven: Yale University Press, 1983), p. 120.
2. See Rogers's headnote (*Jonathan* Swift, p. 650); J.R. Elwood, 'Swift's "Corinna" *Notes and Queries*, 200 (1955), 529–30; David Oakleaf, 'Introduction', Eliza Haywood, *Love in Excess* (Peterborough: Broadview: 1994, 2000), p. 268.
3. For Manley's partisan journalism, see the four pamphlets given in vol. V, ed. by Ruth Herman of *The Selected Works of Delarivier Manley*, ed. by Rachel Carnell and Ruth Herman, 5 vols (London: Pickering and Chatto, 2005), V, 41–92. Compare also Ros Ballaster, 'Introduction', Delarivier Manley, *New Atalantis* (Harmondsworth: Penguin, 1992), pp. xvi–xvii.
4. See G.M. Trevelyan, *England under Queen Anne*, 3 vols (London: Collins, 1965) I, 194; II, 62; Gwendolyn B. Needham, 'Mary de la Riviere Manley, Tory Defender', *Huntington Library Quarterly*, 12 (1948–49), 255–89 (p. 263); Ruth Herman, *The Business of a Woman: the Political Writings of Delarivier Manley* (London: Associated University Presses, 2003), p. 70.
5. The story is echoed in a later text with a comparable ideological agenda, possibly by Haywood, *The Perjur'd Citizen: or Female Revenge* (London, 1732).
6. *The New Atalantis*, ed. by Rachel Carnell, vol. II of *The Selected Works of Delarivier Manley*, ed. by Rachel Carnell and Ruth Herman, 5 vols (London: Pickering

and Chatto, 2005), p. 38. All subsequent references are to this edition and are given parenthetically in the text.

7. See Marion A. Wells, *The Secret Wound: Love-Melancholy and Early Modern Romance* (Stanford: Stanford University Press, 2007).

8. Herman, *The Business of a Woman*, pp. 68–9, 94.

9. Daniel Szechi, *1715: The Great Jacobite Rebellion* (New Haven and London: Yale University Press, 2006), pp. 41–3, 72–3.

10. See Pat Rogers, *The Symbolic Design of Windsor-Forest* (Newark: University of Delaware Press, 2004); Heinz-Joachim Mullenbrock, *The Culture of Contention* (Munich: Fink, 1997).

11. For Haywood's anti-Walpole fiction, see *The Adventures of Eovaai* (1736), reprinted the year before Walpole's ouster as *The Unfortunate Princess, or the Ambitious Statesman* (1741). The 'Pretender pamphlet' is *Letter from H— G—, Esq* [...]. *To a Particular Friend* (London: 1750). For 'the possibility that Haywood held Jacobite sympathies', see Rachel Carnell, 'It's Not Easy Being Green: Gender and Friendship in Eliza Haywood's Political Periodicals', *Eighteenth-Century Studies*, 32.2 (1998–99), 199–214 (p. 207). Compare Kathryn King, 'Patriot or Opportunist? Eliza Haywood and the Politics of *The Female Spectator*', in *Fair Philosopher: Eliza Haywood and The Female Spectator*, ed. by Lynn Marie Wright and Donald J. Newman (Lewisburg: Bucknell University Press, 2006), pp. 104–21; Earla Wilputte, 'Parody in Eliza Haywood's *A Letter from H— G—, Esq*', *Eighteenth-Century Fiction*, 17.2 (January 2005), 207–30; Paula R. Backscheider, 'The Story of Eliza Haywood's Novels: Caveats and Questions', in *The Passionate Fictions of Eliza Haywood: Essays on her Life and Work*, ed. by Kirsten T. Saxton and Rebecca P. Bocchicchio (Lexington: University Press of Kentucky, 2000) esp. p. 28; Catherine Ingrassia, *Authorship, Commerce, and Gender in Early Eighteenth-Century England* (Cambridge: Cambridge University Press, 1998), pp. 124–5 and 'Additional Information about Eliza Haywood's 1749 Arrest for Seditious Libel', *Notes and Queries*, 44 (June, 1997), 202–4; Thomas Lockwood, 'Eliza Haywood in 1749: *Dalinda*, and Her Pamphlet on the Pretender', *Notes and Queries*, 36 (1989), 475–7.

12. See *The Adventures of Rivella*, ed. by Rachel Carnell, vol. IV of *The Selected Works of Delarivier Manley*.

13. For an expanded version of this argument, see Bowers, 'Collusive Resistance: Sexual Agency and Partisan Politics in *Love in Excess*', in *The Passionate Fictions of Eliza Haywood*, ed. by Kirsten T. Saxton and Rebecca P. Bocchicchio (Lexington: University Press of Kentucky, 1998), pp. 48–68.

14. See Patrick Spedding, *A Bibliography of Eliza Haywood* (London: Pickering and Chatto, 2004).

15. Eliza Haywood, *The Lucky Rape*, appended to *Cleomelia, or the Generous Mistress* (London, 1727), p. 94. Subsequent references are given parenthetically in the text.

16. Manley's tale first appeared in *The Power of Love in Seven Novels* (1720). The story responds to Behn's similarly named tale, *The Nun, or The Perjur'd Beauty* and perhaps also to *Love in Excess*.

17. 'The Perjur'd Beauty,' in *The Power of Love* (1720), ed. by Rachel Carnell, vol. IV of *The Selected Works of Delarivier Manley*, p. 231.

18. *The Padlock* was originally published as an appendage to the third edition of a better-known tale; see *The Mercenary Lover or, The Unfortunate Heiresses* [...] *To which is added The Padlock: Or, No Guard Without Virtue* (London, 1728), pp. 57–79.
19. Haywood's heroine shares her name with the jilted protagonist of Manley's *The Wife's Resentment*, a work from the 1720 collection *The Power of Love*. Manley's collection was based largely on William Painter's *Palace of Pleasure* (1566).

13
The Love of Friendship

Moyra Haslett

Reasons humbly offer'd to the Consideration of the Hon. Miss L. why the Treaty of Fern-Hill, concluded in the Year 1732, should be totally set aside; or remain to Posterity with the following Emendations.

Whereas it was provided by that Treaty, that *M. J.* of the *City of Oxford*, Spinster, in regard to the various Avocations, and important Affairs transacted by the said Hon. Miss *L.* should be obliged to furnish out two Letters, for every one of that Lady's:

And whereas the said *M. J.* has punctually observ'd the Contents of this Treaty for the space of two Years, and upwards; but finding it absolutely destructive of her real and natural Interests, she humbly conceives, that she can't in Honour and Conscience observe it a moment longer:

That her real and natural Interests are closely connected with, and absolutely depend upon the Frequency of the said Lady's Letters; and that it has always been esteem'd the highest degree of human Prudence, to trample upon Honour and Conscience, whenever they come in Competition with these:

That during this time, the said *M. J.* has been at vast expence of Brains, in furnishing out Blunders, Absurdities, quaint Conundrums, and starv'd Conceits, without having receiv'd the least Equivalent in return; but has constantly been put off from time to time, with nothing but Wit, Humour, and good Sense: [...]

That she is utterly unable to bear the Burthen of such an expensive Treaty any longer, unless the aforesaid contracting power shall graciously condescend to be witty, *as often* as her said Correspondent shall find her self under the necessity of being dull:

That it has always been a Rule, from time out of mind, for all and every Correspondent to reply *as often* as they receive; but that by this Treaty, the said *M.J.* has not only suffer'd in her natural Rights as a Correspondent, but has also been greatly abridg'd in those more inviolable ones, her Pleasures:

That not knowing her good Friend and Ally was in such a flourishing Condition, and had so much ready Wit always circulating thro' her Veins, she suffer'd her at the Time of this Treaty, out of her great Regard and Tenderness, to make what Terms she pleas'd; but finding her self no longer in a Condition to comply with them, she humbly proposes, That this Treaty may henceforth become null and void; or else remain among the Papers of this House, with the following Emendation, *viz*

That the said Hon. Miss *L.* out of her native Generosity, and without any regard to the Merits, how great soever, of the said *M. J.* has at length graciously resolv'd, That her *Inclination* to oblige shall, for the future, go hand in hand with her *Power* of doing so; and that *both* shall be mutually employed for the sole Benefit and Advantage of the said *M. J.*

Sign'd and seal'd as before.[1]

This letter, from Mary Jones to a female friend, demonstrates the light-hearted wit and inventiveness, even whimsicality, in the most entertaining writing between women of this period. It adopts the slightly mock-heroic effect of talking of their letters in the political and legalistic terms of treaties and emendations, of rights and responsibilities, as if the resolution was one presented to parliament. We can see Mary Jones using women's exclusion from the world of official legislature as a source of private joking, of wry amusement, and, as a result, of literary confidence.

1 Intimacies

Jones's mock-complaint about the inequalities of the correspondence strikes us as intimate in its register. Reading the letter feels like eavesdropping. Yet the letter was openly published, in Jones's *Miscellanies in Prose and Verse* (1750), when both its author and its original recipient were still alive. The generic, broad title of the book belies its almost complete focus on female friendship, both as a theme and as a mode of address, in poems and letters addressed to Jones's particular friends, Martha Lovelace and Charlotte Clayton. It immediately reminds us that one of the most striking aspects of women's writing on female friendship in our period is that women felt emboldened to deploy the registers and tones common to manuscript writing – being intimate, teasing, playful, and familiar – in the anonymous, open-ended, and somewhat unknowable world of public print.

Similarly playful conceits also abound in the poems of Jones's miscellany. In 'On one of her Eyes', Charlotte Clayton just happens to mislay an eye when she falls from her horse, on her way to drink tea with a friend at nearby Abingdon. Local people, even one famous astronomer, suggest that her eye has become a star. But Jones knows that Venus, jealous of Charlotte's beauty and of the many admirers she attracts, swapped it for one of her own (pp. 62–5). In 'The Spider', Jones uses sexual imagery to describe the spider's attraction to Charlotte – a potentially hazardous choice, here safely defused in the poem's light-heartedness. When just on the point of being murdered by Charlotte and her maid, the spider wisely marches away (pp. 71–4).

Such poems demonstrate how the intimacy of affectionate teasing and shared jokes which characterizes 'private' relationships can be voiced in print, particularly when articulated in poems and letters addressed to female friends. They reveal something of the possibilities of poetry and the familiar letter, as more 'autobiographical' genres than fictional narratives, although their rootedness in specific relationships should not blind us to their own kinds of fictive inventiveness. Such poems and letters emerge from traditions of manuscript composition and circulation. Mary Jones's poems were written and read by her friends long before their eventual publication in 1750. Similarly, Anne Finch, Countess of Winchilsea's most playful, whimsical, and personal poems addressed to female friends are to be found in the Wellesley collection of manuscript poems, which were first published only in 1998. Of the fifty-three poems contained in this collection, seventeen are either on the subject of female friendship or are addressed to female friends, and these are also arguably the most interesting and inventive poems of the collection, if not of Finch's career as a writer. They are also significant in the ways in which they anticipate several of Jones's poems to Charlotte Clayton, although Mary Jones could never have known of these manuscript poems. Several record particular visits to and afternoons spent with friends. 'After drawing a twelf cake at the Honourable Mrs Thynne's' praises Finch's friends by focusing on the mismatches between the figures they 'draw' or are bestowed with when the Twelfth Night cake is cut. Mrs Higgons, for example, first draws the king, but her excessive generosity would make her a poor sort of king, a ruler who would only bankrupt the nation. Mrs Thynne draws the fool, but 'She cou'd have found no title so unfit / Or such a foil to her establish't wit'.[2] In 'The white mouse's petition to Lamira', the figure of the mouse, like Jones's spider, sanctions a focus on her friend's body, lightly eroticized:

> When I receive her soft caresses
> And creeping near her lovely tresses
> Their glossy brown from my reflection
> Shall gain more lustre and perfection
> And to her bosom if admitted
> My colour there will be so fitted
> That no distinction cou'd discover
> My station to a jealous Lover
> Her hands whilst they're my food bestowing
> A thousand graces will be shewing
> And smiles enliven every feature
> Whilst I engage her youthfull nature
> To mind my little tricks and fancies
> My active play and circling dances.

(p. 62)

The mouse's tribute to 'Lamira', Lady Ann Tufton, is openly amorous, but the eroticism is diffused and deflated by the mouse's absurdly grandiose ideas of its own importance (the mouse will set off her beauty) and strained arguments for acceptance (the mouse's whiteness will permit Lamira to harbour a lover unnoticed on her lily-white breast). The bathos of the mouse's pretensions permits Finch to write a poem in praise of her friend which is both playful and serious. There is a sense of familiar intimacy in the teasing, light-hearted use of a mouse as portentous speaker. But the poem also pays sincere compliment to Tufton, not least because the persona of the mouse is held up as an obvious fiction, both in its outrageousness as a possible suitor and in the poem's final swerve from mouse to Finch:

> To her my life shall be devoted
> And I as her first captive noted
> Shall fill a mighty place in story
> And share in that ambitious glory
> To which so many hearts are growing
> Where loss of freedom shall be owing
> To her whose chain my value raises
> And makes me merit all your praises.
>
> (p. 62)

In mock-heroic strain, the mouse is suggestively presented as a comically self-deprecating persona for Finch, and then, surprisingly, suddenly, revealed as Finch herself, as the poem ends in the obvious familiarity of 'me' and 'you'. To compliment one's friends is also to ennoble the self, as the final line's gesture of reciprocity in friendship shows Finch meriting the affection of the lady who is so esteemed.

2 Reciprocities

Mary Jones's letter to Martha Lovelace also reveals this particular appeal of female friendship to the woman writer: the way in which the perfect reciprocity idealized in such friendship could also be used to expose writerly self-deprecation as a conscious pose, a deliberate fiction. Mary Jones's letter is, apparently, about the good sense, wit, and superiority of the letters written by her friend. Two letters by Mary Jones for every one by Martha Lovelace is a poor return for her own expenditure, especially as Martha Lovelace's letters have revealed her to have an abundant supply of wit. But letters of female friendship, like poems of compliment to female friends, reveal that the praise bestowed on one's friends is also a tribute to oneself. Mary Jones's best work, she claims, is inspired by the virtue, kindness, and generous condescension of her friends. That they inspire her work is modestly seen as a compliment to them, rather than as boasting of her own work. But friendship is necessarily reciprocal. No virtuous, kind or generous woman would choose an unworthy recipient as her companion.

The motif of reciprocity, then, is a potentially complex one. Compliments to the other often entail self-deprecation. This is particularly evident in poetry, in which the female poet adopts the pose of modesty and self-deprecation. In Anne Finch's manuscript poem, 'To Flavia', for example, the theme of friendship, she claims, is sincere, even if her poetry is poor. Catherine Fleming, the 'Flavia' of the poem, has encouraged Finch to write a poetic paraphrase of a chapter from *Ecclesiastes*, and Finch complies, but she prefaces that poem with this one ('To Flavia. By whose perswasion, I undertook the following Paraphrase'), as an excuse for its failings:

> Then Flavia, when you next wou'd urge the muse,
> (Which to your influence, nothing can refuse,
> Who strictly judge, yet kindly do excuse)
> Let suitable Attempts, employ the Art;
> Or, let my hand, in verse, describe my heart;
> On Tenderness Compose, and friendship, due
> For all those kind regards it meets from you;
> Whither, in secret Verse, or moving Prose,
> You those regards, and friendly thoughts disclose;
> Then, if I fail, th'appointed leaf to fill,
> Believe my sentiments exceed my skill,
> Pleased, and excused, I so, my Task shou'd end,
> And sacrifice the Poet to the friend,
> When you conclude, the motions of my breast
> Too warm for Verse, too Great to be exprest.
>
> (pp. 13–14)

A friend's desire for poetry cannot be resisted. To compliment a friend in poetry is only to return what is due. It may even, as this poem 'To Flavia' hints, be an act of collaboration: 'Whither [...] You those regards, and friendly thoughts disclose'. And if the poetry should fail or be inferior, then such failure testifies only to the strength of her feeling and the inadequacy of language to convey their friendship. Conversely, in a poem such as Mary Jones's address to Martha Lovelace ('On her attending Miss Charlot Clayton in the Small-Pox'), Jones writes of how Martha's virtue has inspired her poetry to become greater:

> Yet Thou [Charlot], whose worth might sweeter sounds inspire,
> Indulge these efforts of a youthful lyre;

No flatt'ring purpose has the Muse in view,
Tho' prompt to praise, wherever Praise is due;
Averse to flatter, cautious to commend,
Hardly she sooths the frailties of a Friend.
But sick of the insipid senseless train,
For Thee she feels the animated strain:
O be she sacred to the wise and good!
Nor prostitute her praises to the croud;
With whom less pleas'd than pain'd, her lyre unstrung,
Upon a neighb'ring willow useless hung;
Till gentle deeds, and corresponding Love
Impell'd the sympathetic strings to move
To Nature's harmony; while artless lays,
To HER and LOVELACE tun'd, grow music in their praise.

(p. 116)

We can see in such examples how the conventions and patterns in poems of friendship permit the woman poet to speak confidently and modestly, to be both assertive and self-deprecating. Such intriguing, poised paradoxes might be said to be typical of women's poetry in general, but they are certainly exemplified in countless poems by women written in our period.

3 Imitations

Poetry on female friendship remains, however, most closely associated in feminist literary criticism with the work of Katherine Philips, whose first authorized edition of poems was published posthumously in 1667. Despite this, there has been relatively little interest in the way in which female poems on friendship revise and renew the tradition so associated with Philips.[3] Women writers in the early eighteenth century certainly continue the tradition in which retirement is figured as the means by which the poet can turn her back on the corrupt worlds of politics or of fashion. Many of the women writers of this early century remained loyal to the Stuarts, and found their Jacobitism put them at odds with the world of the court or of the city. Mary Astell, Jane Barker, Anne Finch, are all prominent Tory writers. The idealized retreats they envision are not solitary ones. Finch's 'Petition for an Absolute Retreat', for example, is not so absolute. Such a retreat is an escape from gossiping, importunate company: 'No Intruders thither come! / Who visit, but to be from home', but the desire for an ideal retreat is also a desire for the company of a much-loved companion:

> Give me there (since Heaven has shown
> It was not Good to be alone)
> A *Partner* suited to my Mind,
> Solitary, pleas'd and kind;
> Who, partially, may something see
> Preferr'd to all the World in me.[4]

The stanza continues the evocation of Adam and Eve in a prelapsarian Eden, when the only two mortals spent their time in love, before the introduction of rage, jealousy, and hate. But if this section sets up the expectation that Finch will find her perfect retreat in marriage, this is subverted with the introduction of 'Arminda', the poetic pseudonym for Finch's friend Catharine, Countess of Thanet. The poem thus offers its political critique of contemporary England with its hints of a loyal, supportive pro-Stuart community, albeit a community of only two. It reminds us that the pastoral tradition of quiet retirement and reflection could be used as a metaphor of political waiting, and solidarity.

Katherine Philips might be read as a precursor here, in that while her poems to female friends do not explicitly evoke her political, royalist affiliations, their entrancement with idealized pastoral retreats suggests a politicized philosophy of retirement, a refusal of worldly corruption which finds consolation in the sympathies of friendship. But while a number of women writers invoke Katherine Philips as an enabling precursor (Mary Astell, Anne Finch, Sarah Fyge Egerton, Jane Barker, and Elizabeth Carter in particular), Philips's reputation as a poet of passionate, ardent female friendship is almost entirely a late twentieth-century construction. Eighteenth-century accounts of Philips usually focus on her plays, or, when they identify her with the theme of friendship, it is often in connection with her male friends and, in particular, her letters to Charles Cotterell, *Letters from Orinda to Poliarchus* (1705). Several eighteenth-century accounts of Philips do quote extensively from Jeremy Taylor's essay on friendship which was addressed to Philips and which explores the argument – contra such writers as Aristotle and Cicero – that women might have the capacity to be friends.[5] But even though more than half of her collected poems articulate Orinda's love for other women, there is little evidence that the poet of contemporary feminist criticism, the writer of sapphic, eroticized poems to female friends, would have been a recognizable figure to her eighteenth-century readers, or at least that this element of her work would have been openly endorsed.[6] We have seen that poems of friendship between women in our period could certainly contain playfully erotic suggestions (as in Finch's 'The white mouse's petition' and Jones's 'The Spider'). But in general, poetry and letters exchanged between female friends in this period are less passionately ardent than Philips's poems, although they might be seen to transfigure Philips's passionate intensity into the spheres of religion or social critique.

4 Desires

In her anthology, *The Literature of Lesbianism* (2003), Terry Castle includes only two poems by British women writers from our period (in contrast to five poems by Katherine Philips and two each by Aphra Behn and Anne Killigrew from the preceding period).[7] The two selected – Elizabeth Singer Rowe's 'Love and Friendship: A Pastoral' (1696) and Finch's 'Friendship between Ephelia and Ardelia' (1713) – articulate love between women but they do so within the convention of pastoral dialogue, and thus their arguments can be less directly attributed to their authors than the convention of poetic pen-names adopted by Philips for herself and her friends.[8] Recent work on lesbianism in the eighteenth century has agreed that the period after the mid-seventeenth century represented a transitional time in which idealized 'romantic friendships' between women became subject to more scrutiny and suspicion, as cultural awareness and anxiety concerning lesbianism arose. Female homoeroticism is openly suggested in such female-authored texts as Delarivier Manley's *The New Atalantis* (1709), *The Travels and Adventures of Mademoiselle de Richelieu* (1743; whose author is anonymous but which has a female narrator), and *A Narrative of the Life of Charlotte Charke* (1755).[9] But, as Catherine Craft-Fairchild has argued, all of these, like their male-authored counterparts, present highly ambivalent, indeterminate depictions of female desire for other women.[10] An equally indeterminate narrative is Jane Barker's tale of 'The Unaccountable Wife' in which a wife leaves her husband to live in poverty and share a bed with his mistress, refusing all offers even a pension from the queen in order to beg in the streets for her female friend. Although the story is presented matter-of-factly, Barker's narrative persona, Galesia, and the lady to whom she tells the story find such behaviour completely 'unaccountable'.[11] When the existence of lesbianism becomes an 'open secret', then the strategies with which sympathetic writers might represent female lovers becomes necessarily more elusive and oblique. As readers, then, we need to be sensitive to the possible disguises and codes with which female desire for women might be articulated, without overdetermining such texts, making of them what they are not, quite.[12]

If there is less passionate intensity in writing between women in the eighteenth century than that visible in, for example, Katherine Philips's poems to her female friends, this might only enable their work to become more political, even 'proto-feminist'. We might recall here Jones's parody of the language of official discourse in the letter which opened this chapter. While the tone is partly that of comic *jeu d'esprit*, behind the teasing joke lies a more serious point about female exclusion from parliament and the courts. Mary Astell gives us a powerful example of someone who deployed the language of female friendship in order to assert female rights to intellectual respect. In *A Serious Proposal to the Ladies* (1694, 1697), she envisages an exclusively female community in which supportive, nurturing friendships among women are pre-eminent. There is little eroticism in this work, in marked contrast to the male authors who would imitate her proposal (as Daniel Defoe did in his project for 'An Academy of Women', 1687) or who would satirize Astell herself (as Addison, Steele, and Swift did in *The Tatler*).[13] Rather, Astell's work presents a powerfully argued defence of female community and companionship, written by, as the first title-pages announced, a 'Lover of her Sex'. Astell explicitly writes as a friend, in an act of special affection for women in general. Her celebration of female friendship and, implicitly, intimacy and companionship, might be starkly juxtaposed with Mary Wollstonecraft's later aversion to female boarding schools, and the 'grossly familiar' way in which women live in intimacy with one another.[14] There is none of this physical squeamishness in Astell, although admittedly her female bodies are rather ethereal. There is something approaching rhapsody, if not quite ecstasy, in her celebration of friendship as a foretaste of the pleasures of Heaven:

> we shall have opportunity of contracting the purest and noblest Friendship; a Blessing, the purchase of which were richly worth all the World besides! For she who possesses a worthy Person, has certainly obtain'd the richest Treasure! A Blessing that Monarchs may envy, and she who enjoys is happier than she who fills a Throne! A Blessing, which next to the love of GOD is the choicest Jewel in our Caelestial Diadem, which, were it duly practic'd, wou'd both fit us for heav'n, and bring it down into our hearts whist we tarry here. For Friendship is a Vertue which comprehends all the rest; none being fit for this, who is not adorn'd with every other Vertue.[15]

Nowhere else in the two volumes of this work is there such a concentration of exclamations as in this eulogy to friendship between women.

For many women writers, female friendship is seen to anticipate the enjoyment of a sociable life in Heaven together, to give us a foretaste of immortality or to represent the best attempt to emulate God's love. (Marriage or heterosexual love, in contrast, is often tinged with sexual desire, possessiveness, or injustice. We might recall here the way in which Finch's 'Petition for an Absolute Retreat' replaces Adam with a female friend.) Mary, Lady Chudleigh's poems 'To Almystrea' and 'The Choice' (both 1703), and many of Elizabeth Carter's poems to female friends articulate this sense. Chudleigh's idealization of female friendship in her essay 'On Friendship' (1710) sees it as perfected in eternity. Although friendship in these poems and associated essays and works is undoubtedly idealized, the idealization is just as clearly conscious and deliberate. Astell confronts the charge openly in the conclusion of her *Serious Proposal*, as does the final paragraph of Chudleigh's essay:

> But alas! where are such Friends to be found. I may please my self with charming Idea's, Court Phantoms of my own creating, and from those Inclinations I find in my own Breast, those innate Propensities to Kindness, which seem to be interwoven with my Being, to be of a piece with my Soul, draw uncommon Schemes of Friendship, of something so fine, so pure, so noble, so exalted, so much beyond whatever the World has yet known of Love, so wholly intellectual, so entirely abstracted from Sense, that I must never hope on this side of Heaven to meet with any that will come up to so exact a Model, to so Angelick a Perfection, or at least that will think me worthy of so near a Relation, of such a free, generous, and entire Exchange of Thoughts.[16]

Yet these texts also range themselves against a tradition of anti-feminist satire, in which women are invariably competitive, jealous, and envious of one another.[17] Both Astell and Chudleigh insist that women are not naturally given to envy. What is striking about these prose meditations on friendship is how defences of female friendship frequently become defences of female education, and arguments for women's right to the pleasures of rational conversation. One anonymously authored work – *Thoughts on friendship. By way of essay; for the use and improvement of the ladies. By a well-wisher to her sex* (1725) – also exemplifies the way in which a vindication of woman's capacity for friendship could become a vindication of her intelligence and natural abilities.

5 Betrayals

In fiction, however, we often see darker views of female friendship, friendships betrayed or exploited, friendships pursued for selfish ends. In Haywood's fiction, women are as often rivals as friends. In *Love in Excess* (1719–20), for example, the Count D'Elmont is loved by all the women who encounter him and the numerous women of the narrative are most usually in conflict with one another. When Melliora berates the Count for his inconstancy and deceitfulness, the Count's wife thinks her motivated by friendship to herself and solidarity with wronged wives. But Melliora is jealous of the Count's lover. And Alovysa herself, the Count's wife, goes to such extraordinary lengths to learn the name of her rival and thus be revenged upon her, that she precipitates her own murder.[18] However, even treacherous friendships can raise moral ambiguities. In Haywood's later novel, *The History of Miss Betsy Thoughtless* (1751), Betsy's friendship with Miss Forward is, as their speaking names ominously prefigure, far from ideal. As a young girl, living in the country, Betsy helps her friend to pursue an intrigue with Sparkish, by lying on her behalf and diverting others from Miss Forward's absence. When she later resumes her friendship with Miss Forward in London, she finds her abandoned by a second lover, Mr Wildly, their illegitimate child dying at only three days old. Betsy's sympathy for Miss Forward is questioned when she is drawn into a world of prostitution and easy virtue. Mr Trueworth warns Betsy to avoid the company of Miss Forward, as her reputation as a virtuous woman will inevitably be tarnished by the association. But Betsy trusts her friend and refuses to believe she is as depraved as Trueworth hints. That Betsy fails to take Trueworth's advice is, in one reading, yet another example of her 'thoughtlessness'. But her loyalty to her friend and her refusal to listen to second-hand reports of her wickedness might also strike us as admirable, if unfortunate in their consequences. When Betsy ends the friendship, she writes to Miss Forward: 'If you had retained the least spark of generosity, or good-will towards me, you would rather have avoided than coveted my company, as you must be sensible that to be seen with you must render me, in some measure, partaker of your infamy, though wholly innocent of your crimes' and signs herself 'the much deceived, and ill-treated, B. Thoughtless'.[19] Whether we might ultimately sympathize with or judge Betsy, like much else in this novel, is left undecided.

Satirical poems can often articulate the scepticism about contemporary 'friendship' evident in fiction. Many poems by Mary Barber and Mary Leapor, for example, depict shallow, trivial 'friends' who talk only to hear themselves speak and who visit friends only so that, selfishly, they can be entertained or flattered. Similarly, fictional narratives can contain positive accounts of female friendship. Haywood's *The British Recluse* (1722) has two ladies swap stories of how they have been undone by love.[20] Given that women are as frequently rivals as friends in Haywood's fiction, the conclusion of this narrative puts their friendship under the severest test, as they come to realize that their perfidious lovers were actually the same man. Both women confess their continuing affection for this lover, but both also feel solidarity with each other. The possible tension between these impulses is teasingly suggested by Haywood: Cleomira anxiously asks if Belinda has met him recently, and while Belinda insists that she would now refuse any advances, her refusal is articulated in such complexly constructed terms as to throw the reader into momentary suspension ('No, on my Honour [...] he knows not of my being here, nor I dare swear thinks my Presence worth a Wish; but were I sure he did, nay were I convinced that, although false to all my Sex beside, to me he would be true; nay did his Life depend on my granting him one Interview, I protest, by all that I adore, I never would consent'). The narrator adds that Cleomira '*seemed* perfectly pleased with this Assurance' (my emphasis), but that she 'omitted nothing to strengthen her in his Resolution'.[21] The narrative ends, however, with Cleomira and Belinda sharing a bed and living in perfect amity together.

Although the plot of *The British Recluse* unfolds the developing friendship of its two heroines, the doubling of Belinda and Cleomira is crucial not just for the manner of narration, but for the act of narration itself. Although many of the most popular amatory fictions of the time revolve around plots of courtship and romance, and to that extent do not explicitly engage with the theme of female friendship, they are often structured around the telling of stories between female friends. Jane Barker's Galesia trilogy is particularly noteworthy in this regard. In *Love Intrigues* (1713), Galesia tells the story of her early life, and her unhappy on-off courtship by Bosvil, to her close friend Lucasia (with conscious echoes of Katherine Philips's friend). In both *A Patch-Work Screen for the Ladies* (1723) and *The Lining of the Patch-Work Screen* (1726), Galesia is encouraged by an aristocratic lady who befriends her to contribute to her patchwork with her narrative fictions, poems, autobiographical accounts, recipes, medicines, and other miscellaneous pieces of text. The female friends and auditors in these accounts do not merely frame the narrative, but frequently act as interlocutors, thus repeatedly reminding us of their presence and the ways in which they enable the tale's narration.

6 Contracts

On a fictional level, then, these texts describe friendship but also present themselves as acts of friendship. In doing so, they exemplify the significant ways in which women writers in this period address an explicitly female reader. Earlier women writers are often forgotten, or obscured, but in this period a clear sense of a female tradition emerges in texts which are about or are inspired by female friendship. Dedications, subscription lists, and prefatory statements, for example, frequently draw attention to the historical female friends who have enabled, supported or inspired the work. Mary Astell wrote a celebratory preface for Lady Mary Wortley Montagu's Turkish Embassy letters, which she clearly encouraged her friend to publish. And countless friendships between women writers and female patrons and companions sustained the act of writing. Lady Mary Chudleigh was the friend of fellow writers Elizabeth Thomas and Mary Astell. Mary Barber, Constantia Grierson, and Laetitia Pilkington, as members of Swift's Dublin coterie, all addressed poems to each other (and Grierson's poems were posthumously published in collections of Barber's work and in Pilkington's *Memoirs*). We know that Mary Chandler visited Elizabeth Rowe, Mary Barber, and the Countess of Hertford. Other significant networks of female patronage included Lady Hertford's support of Elizabeth Rowe's work, Bridget Freemantle's encouragement of Mary Leapor, and Martha Lovelace and Charlotte Clayton's promotion of Mary Jones. Indeed, the networks of female friendship are too many to enumerate here, but the very fact of their pervasiveness provides a significant context for those works which explicitly address not only a general reader beyond the known communities of friendships, coteries, and correspondences, but a general reader who is explicitly identified as female (as Astell's *Serious Proposal*, Chudleigh's *The Ladies Defence* and *Essays*, Mary Davys's *The Reform'd Coquet* and Barker's *Patch-work Screen* all do, for example). There is a continuum here between the address to a fictional friend, the address to a real friend, or to a wider circle of friends, and the address to the more anonymous female reader, who might be unknown to the author but who is still figured, to this extent, as a friend.

Notes

1. Mary Jones, *Miscellanies in Prose and Verse* (Oxford, 1750), pp. 308–10. Comparable letters in the collection include a mock-announcement of the public reception in Oxford for 'Melissa' when she is conferred with an honorary degree giving her the title 'Mistress of Arts', and leave not only to vote in convocation but 'also to have the Last Word' (pp. 159–64 (p. 162)), and

articles of a mock-treaty in which letters exchanged between Jones and Martha Lovelace are described in terms of an agreement between nations (pp. 286–8). Subsequent references to this miscellany are given parenthetically in the text.

2. *The Anne Finch Wellesley Manuscript Poems: A Critical Edition*, ed. by Barbara McGovern and Charles H. Hinnant (Athens, GA and London: University of Georgia Press, 1998), p. 60. Subsequent references to this collection are given parenthetically in the text.

3. Marilyn L. Williamson, *Raising their Voices: British Women Writers, 1650–1750* (Detroit: Wayne State University Press, 1990) traces the importance of Philips and Aphra Behn as alternative models for women's writing in the eighteenth century, but this argument is now seen to set up a 'false opposition' between these two precursors. See Carol Barash, *English Women's Poetry, 1649–1714: Politics, Community, and Linguistic Authority* (Oxford: Oxford University Press, 1999), p. 5n. For a more nuanced consideration of Philips's influence, particularly in a chapter specifically on 'friendship poems', see Paula Backscheider, *Eighteenth-Century Women Poets and their Poetry* (Baltimore: Johns Hopkins University Press, 2005). Mary Jones was openly compared to Philips in a review of *Miscellanies in Prose and Verse* which appeared in the *Monthly Review* (March 1752).

4. Anne Finch, 'Petition for an Absolute Retreat', in *Miscellany Poems, on Several Occasions* (London, 1713), pp. 34, 39.

5. The essay was entitled *A Discourse of the Nature, Offices, and Measures, of Friendship, with Rules of Conducting It, in a Letter to the Most Ingenious and Excellent Mrs. Katharine [sic] Philips* (London, 1657). It did not argue that women could be equal to men as friends, but the selective passages quoted in the eighteenth century suggested otherwise. For eighteenth-century excerpts from this essay, see George Ballard, *Memoirs of several ladies of Great Britain* (1752), pp. 291–3 and Robert Shiells, *The Lives of the Poets of Great Britain and Ireland*, 5 vols (London, 1753), II, 152–4. Shiells's account is the only text in the eighteenth century which singles out Philips as the author of poems on female friendship, in reprinting one of Philips's poems addressed to Lucasia (II, 157–8). There were twenty-one of these poems in all, and they are notable because they are especially ardent.

6. Jacob Tonson published an extensive volume of poems by Katherine Philips in 1710. For modern feminist responses to Philips, see, for example, Harriette Andreadis, 'The Sapphic-Platonics of Katherine Philips, 1632–1664', *Signs: Journal of Women in Culture and Society*, 15.1 (1989), 34–60; Dorothy Mermin, 'Women Becoming Poets: Katherine Philips, Aphra Behn, Anne Finch', *ELH*, 57 (1990), 335–56; and Arlene Stiebel, 'Subversive Sexuality: Masking the Erotic in Poems by Katherine Philips and Aphra Behn', in *Renaissance Discourses of Desire*, ed. by Claude Summers and Ted-Larry Pebworth (Columbia: University of Missouri Press, 1993), pp. 223–36. Stiebel argues that Andreadis and Mermin write sensuality out of these passionate poems.

7. Terry Castle, ed., *The Literature of Lesbianism: A Historical Anthology from Ariosto to Stonewall* (New York: Columbia University Press, 2003).

8. Rowe's poem was frequently anthologized in the early eighteenth century, in variant versions, but usually accompanied with Matthew Prior's poem of tribute to her, in which he teasingly questioned whether Rowe might be

identified with Sylvia, who argues in defence of friendship, or Amaryllis, the advocate of love. As Rowe's poem unfolds, it becomes clear that 'friendship' and 'love' are indistinguishable and that the debate is really between the merits of same-sex, as opposed to heterosexual, love. See *Poetical miscellanies: the fifth part. Containing a collection of original poems, with several new translations. By the most eminent hands* (London, Jacob Tonson, 1704), pp. 368–82 (where Rowe's poem appears as 'A Pastoral, Inscrib'd to The Honourable, Mrs —') and pp. 604–5 (where Prior's poem appears as 'To the Author of the Pastoral. Printed page 378').

9. Delarivier Manley, *New Atalantis*, ed. by Rachel Carnell, vol. II of *The Selected Works of Delarivier Manley*, ed. by Rachel Carnell and Ruth Herman, 5 vols (London: Pickering and Chatto, 2005); Charlotte Charke, *Narrative of the Life of Mrs. Charlotte Charke*, ed. by Robert Rehder (London: Pickering and Chatto, 1999).

10. Catherine Craft-Fairchild, 'Sexual and Textual Indeterminacy: Eighteenth-Century English Representations of Sapphism', *Journal of the History of Sexuality*, 15.3 (2006), 408–31.

11. Jane Barker, 'The Unaccountable Wife', in *A Patch-Work Screen for the Ladies* (1723), in *The Galesia Trilogy and Selected Manuscript Poems*, ed. by Carol Shiner Wilson (Oxford: Oxford University Press, 1997), pp. 144–9.

12. For important recent work on lesbianism in our period, see Emma Donoghue, *Passions between Women: British Lesbian Culture 1668–1801* (London: Scarlett Press, 1993); Susan S. Lanser, 'Befriending the Body: Female Intimacies as Class Acts', *Eighteenth-Century Studies*, 32 (1998–99), 179–98; Elizabeth Susan Wahl, *Invisible Relations: Representations of Female Intimacy in the Age of Enlightenment* (Stanford: Stanford University Press, 1999); Susan S. Lanser, 'Sapphic Picaresque, Sexual Difference and the Challenges of Homo-Adventuring', *Textual Practice*, 15 (2001), 251–68; Susan S. Lanser, '"Queer to Queer": The Sapphic Body as Transgressive Text' and Catherine Ingrassia, 'Eliza Haywood, Sapphic Desire, and the Practice of Reading', both in *Lewd and Notorious: Female Transgression in the Eighteenth Century*, ed. by Katharine Kittredge (Ann Arbor: University of Michigan Press, 2003), pp. 21–46, and pp. 235–57.

13. Daniel Defoe, *An Essay upon Projects* (London, 1697) and *The Tatler*, no. 32, 23 June 1709, and *The Tatler*, no. 63, 3 September 1709, both in *The Tatler*, ed. by Donald F. Bond, 3 vols (Oxford: Clarendon Press, 1987), I, 236–42; I, 431–4.

14. See for example, Mary Wollstonecraft, *A Vindication of the Rights of Woman* (1792; Harmondsworth: Penguin, 1992), p. 240: 'In short, with respect to both mind and body, [women] are too intimate. That decent personal reserve, which is the foundation of dignity of character, must be kept up between woman and woman, or their minds will never gain strength or modesty. [//] On this account also, I object to many females being shut up together in nurseries, schools, or convents.'

15. Mary Astell, *A Serious Proposal to the Ladies*, ed. by Patricia Springborg (Peterborough, Ontario: Broadview Press, 2002), p. 98.

16. Mary, Lady Chudleigh, *Essays upon Several Subjects in Prose and Verse* (London, 1710), 'Of Friendship', reprinted in *The Poems and Prose of Mary, Lady Chudleigh*, ed. by Margaret J.M. Ezell (Oxford: Oxford University Press, 1993), p. 351.

17. For this tradition, see Felicity Nussbaum, *'The brink of all we hate': English Satires on Women, 1660–1750* (Lexington: University Press of Kentucky, 1984).
18. Eliza Haywood, *Love in Excess,* ed. by David Oakleaf (Peterborough, Ontario: Broadview Press, 2000), pp. 146, 156–8.
19. Eliza Haywood, *The History of Miss Betsy Thoughtless,* ed. by Christine Blouch (Peterborough, Ontario: Broadview Press, 1998), pp. 243, 244.
20. Eliza Haywood, *The British Recluse,* in *Popular Fiction by Women 1660–1730: An Anthology,* ed. by Paula R. Backscheider and John J. Richetti (Oxford: Oxford University Press, 1996), pp. 153–226.
21. *Popular Fiction by Women, 1660–1730: An Anthology,* ed. by Paula R. Backscheider and John J. Richetti (Oxford: Oxford University Press, 1996), p. 223. Other amatory fictions which involve the narration of tales of seduction to a female listener include Mary Davys, *The Lady's Tale* (1725; ed. by Martha Bowden 1999); Eliza Haywood, *The Agreeable Caledonian,* 2 vols (London, 1728, 1729) and *Epistles to the Ladies,* 2 vols (1749–50; ed. by Christine Blouch in *Selected Works,* Set I, Vol. II); and Mary Collyer, *Felicia to Charlotte,* 2 vols (London, 1744–49). For a note on this tradition, see Ros Ballaster, *Seductive Forms: Women's Amatory Fiction from 1684 to 1740* (Oxford: Clarendon Press, 1992), p. 170. We can see something of the influence of this tradition in Frances Sheridan's early romance *Eugenia and Adelaide* (written in 1739; published posthumously in 1791).

Part V
Overview

14
Critical Review

Ros Ballaster

The profession of literary critic is a relatively modern one; it is only with the early twentieth-century establishment of university courses in vernacular English literature that we can begin to see published critical works as the medium for the formation of literary canons and judgements concerning the aesthetic or other merits of literary works. Prior to that date the piecemeal support by private publishing houses – motivated by the prospects for commercial gain or prestige – of biographical dictionaries, encyclopaedias of knowledge and learning or anthologies of writing are the major sources we consult for evidence of which literary works have been valued and why. The inclusion or exclusion of work by women in these endeavours is often a matter of opportunity, acquaintance or hearsay. However, we are not without material in this area. Margaret Ezell records that 'Between 1675 and 1875, there were at least twenty-five biographical encyclopaedias and anthologies devoted to chronicling the lives and labours of literary Englishwomen.'[1] Like the form in which it is newly chronicled – the relatively modern phenomenon of the accessible printed book – women's literary achievement tends to be seen as a novelty or curiosity rather than as an expected product of a civilized culture.

In this chapter we will endeavour to identify the patterns and lacunae in critical writing from the late seventeenth century to the present day concerning women's literary writing of the period 1690 to 1750. It is important to recognize that while this volume has made a case for the coherence of this sixty-year period in the history of women's writing it held no such visible coherence to the commentators who wrote about women's writing in the period immediately following our closing date. The most significant and most often cited models for the woman writer throughout the eighteenth century published their works before

1690: the poets and dramatists Katherine Philips (publishing in the mid-1660s) and Aphra Behn (publishing between 1667 and 1688). Orinda (Philips) and Astrea (Behn) are consistently contrasted as examples of the virtuous coterie and public libertine female practitioner.[2] Women poets of the early eighteenth century consistently sought identification with Philips rather than Behn: Jane Barker and Elizabeth Singer Rowe are the best known examples.[3] Writing that celebrated women's contribution to the novel of the early nineteenth century put centre stage those women who achieved financial and critical reward in the later eighteenth century – Frances Sheridan, Frances Burney, Elizabeth Inchbald, Maria Edgeworth – expressing admiration for their combination of moralism and realism, by contrast (if they are mentioned at all) with the improbable romance plots and steamy voyeurism of prose fiction by women earlier in the century.

Until the mid-eighteenth century critical comment about women's literary writing of the late seventeenth and early eighteenth centuries is largely satirical. Hence, in 1691 Robert Gould's *A Satyrical Epistle to the Female Author of a Poem Called Sylvia's Revenge* complained in print that 'whore' and 'poetess' had become equivalent terms and lamented the passing of the age of Philips who wrote to instruct as well as to please. *The Tatler* (1709–11), a periodical always careful to speak to and about women, gave short shrift to the two women writers with the highest political print profiles of the early eighteenth century: Mary Astell and Delarivier Manley. The former is mocked as a naive Platonist who allows a rake and his companions access to her all-female educational community because she believes them converts to her idealist system and the latter as a tutor in the military arts at Astell's college who engineers the death by poison of her enemies.[4] However, the example of the *Tatler* should alert us to the fact that criticism of women writers, although always couched in terms of a transgression of feminine norms, can often be driven by party rather than sexual political antagonism. The Whig commitments of the *Tatler*'s author-editors, Richard Steele and Joseph Addison, made necessary targets of the Tory scandal writer Delarivier Manley and the High Church Tory Astell, major antagonist of Addison's ideological touchstone, John Locke.

As these three earliest examples of critical evaluation show, women's writing has been judged by exacting standards of sexual morality that are not so insistently and consistently applied to the writing of men. This may be one reason why devotional writing remains by far the largest output from women – whether print or manuscript – because its ethics are underpinned by an unassailable Christian morality. It also explains the significant difference from the reception of writing by male contemporaries which is acknowledged as aesthetically successful even when its sexual ethics are dubious (John Wilmot, Earl of Rochester, favourite of male and female poets alike, is the obvious example, but later examples include Matthew Prior, Alexander Pope, and John Gay).

Neither is it the case that the attack on women's writing is always and necessarily to do with political differences. A fellow Whig, playwright Mary Pix, receives the sharp end of Richard Steele's pen in the later but also Whiggish periodical, *The Spectator*, where he describes her as, like Aphra Behn (always invoked as the model for lasciviousness and female playwriting), unlearned and skilled only 'in the luscious Way'.[5]

Nonetheless, until the mid-eighteenth century, poetic achievement for women (and poetry remains the highest of literary genres at this point) is understood to require a necessary admixture of or aspiration to 'masculine' qualities of force, wit, and persuasiveness. Several critics have observed that the 'androgyny' celebrated in both Katherine Philips and Aphra Behn by other writers gives way by mid-century to a sense that the woman writer proves her literary credentials by proving the difference of her femininity. Consistent though is the measurement by a sexual standard (that the 'good' woman writer is a moral as well as a literary paragon) as demonstrated by the two texts of the mid-1750s which launched the eighteenth-century's reputation for learned and creative women: antiquarian George Ballard's lengthy *Memoirs of Several Ladies of Great Britain* (1752) providing biographies of over sixty women from the Renaissance onward[6] and scholar John Duncombe's celebratory short poem *The Feminiad* (1754) arguing for the special talents of British women in 'the warbling lyre' and listing fifteen women poets of merit (dismissing along the way Delarivier Manley, Susanna Centlivre, Aphra Behn, Teresa Philips, Laetitia Pilkington, and Lady Frances Vane).[7] While Ballard's selection is on the basis of learning, Duncombe's concern is with female poets alone. Among the writers Ballard includes from our period are Mary Astell, Mary Lady Chudleigh, Mary Monck, Anne Finch Countess of Winchilsea, and Constantia Grierson. Duncombe lists Anne Finch, Catharine Trotter Cockburn, Elizabeth Singer Rowe, Frances Seymour Countess of Hertford, Anne Viscountess Irwin, Mehetabel Wright, Judith Madan, Mary Leapor, Elizabeth Carter, Martha Ferrar, and Elizabeth Pennington. In both works, women's individual literary achievement is celebrated as remarkable and unusual and is measured against the (more numerous) immoral attempts of contemporaries. However, both texts construct the canon of writers they celebrate in terms of the extent to which they match an ideal of womanhood. Margaret Ezell comments of Ballard that his antiquarian stance conceals 'a rhetorical stance and a didactic purpose which converts the text from a simple repository of facts into a tribute to ideal womanhood' and characterizes that ideal as 'modest, middle-class, well-read, pious, and charitable'.[8] Both also introduce a new element in the memorializing of women's literary achievement, seeing it as a measure of the advancement of national character. Ballard calls special attention to his inclusion of Irish and Scottish women as well as women who wrote and lived abroad, while Duncombe sees women's learning as developing their capacity to run their homes as small mirrors of the virtues of the English nation. With regard to Ballard's selection Harriet Guest observes 'the emphasis on national and gendered character, at the expense of the differences between those memorialised'.[9]

Richard Terry concludes his assessment of the formation of a canon of women poets in the eighteenth century thus:

> What the eighteenth century adds to female canon formation is essentially its feminization. An image of the canonical female author is engendered that circumvents the need to suggest that authorial success by women can only be arrived at through the adoption of masculine traits and the replication of masculine forms of literary prowess. But the price that is paid for understanding female literary success in essentially feminine terms is that women writers become identified with, and confined within, a canon seen as exclusive to their own sex [...][10]

Until the later eighteenth century, literary writing, whether by men or women, is almost wholly defined in terms of metrical verse. Anthologies and verse celebrations of literary achievement focus exclusively on poetic writing, whether manuscript or print. Elegant writing in prose, such as that of the Earl of Shaftesbury, Bishop Burnet, Robert Hume, is admired and imitated but does not receive the kind of canon-forming attention we have discussed above. However, from the mid-eighteenth century onwards – and the extraordinary success of Samuel Richardson in particular in elevating prose fiction to challenge the status of the poetic epic as a mode which simultaneously instructs and gives pleasure – women begin to figure in histories of the novel/romance. Here too the story is one of repudiating disreputable styles associated with sexual transgression in favour of celebrating a new moralism.

Thus, Clara Reeve in her 1785 *The Progress of Romance*, has her female spokesperson Euphrasia chart the transition from epic to romance to novel, citing Richardson as a major player in moralizing the novel and praising Eliza Haywood for repenting the content of her earlier fiction written under the immoral influence of Aphra Behn and Delarivier Manley. Here too, though the aesthetic quality of Haywood's writing is much less relevant than her moral status, Euphrasia concludes 'her wit and ingenuity were never denied. I would be the last to vindicate her faults, but the first to celebrate her return to virtue, and her atonement for them.' The male commentator, Hortensius, describes Richardson as a novelist with a special remit for women, terming him 'a novelist all your own'.[11]

Yet, as William B. Warner has charted, the novel's elevation to a literary form in the mid-century, largely through the aegis of Samuel Richardson and Henry Fielding, relied on the representation of the form as addressed to the 'general' rather than just the female reader.[12] Nevertheless, women's involvement in the development of the form is always acknowledged. Anthologies of the novel begin to appear in the last quarter of the eighteenth century and women feature prominently in them. Elizabeth Griffith had proved her credentials as a model for female writers and readers in her co-authored *A Series of Genuine Letters Between Henry and Frances*: an exchange of letters between herself and her suitor-later-husband, Richard Griffith, which were revised for publication between 1757 and 1770. In 1777 she began a monthly serial handsomely published by subscription entitled *A Collection of Novels, Selected and Revised by Elizabeth Griffith*. Only three of the projected twelve volumes appeared, possibly through lack of subscribers, and they included from our period fiction by Penelope Aubin and Eliza Haywood. Griffith promised to remove gross or indelicate material from her selected texts and excludes from Eliza Haywood's *Fruitless Enquiry* a story in which a heroine is repeatedly raped and a scene in another story in which the hero is castrated. Her introduction rehearses the familiar story of the novel's emergence in the Restoration, its succumbing to amorous nonsense and then return to sense by the mid-eighteenth century. In this process, Griffith is one of the earliest commentators to identify Penelope Aubin as a significant agent in the moralizing and elevation of the form. Women continued to act as anthologizers of the novel with the publication of Anna Laetitia Aikin Barbauld's fifty-volume set *The British Novelists* (1810), each volume prefaced with biographical-critical accounts. Her essay 'On the Origin and Progress of Novel-Writing' opens with a call to assign the form 'a higher rank than has been generally assigned it', although it also includes the requisite dismissive comments about Behn, Manley, and Haywood. Barbauld only selects seven novels published before 1755 and only one is by a woman (Charlotte Lennox's 1752 *The Female Quixote*). Women receive more generous treatment at the hands of the anthologizer in later volumes, especially Ann Radcliffe, Maria Edgeworth, and Frances Burney, once more on the grounds that 'it will not be said that either taste or morals have been losers by their taking the pen in their hands'.[13]

While the novel is enjoying new literary status – albeit that women's contribution is only celebrated in the shape of the newly moralized formal realism of the later eighteenth and early nineteenth century – women's involvement in poetry and drama continues to receive attention, if piecemeal. Mary Scott's *The Female Advocate, a Poem, occasioned by reading Mr Duncombe's Feminead* (1774) claims to be written to console a melancholy female mind by thinking back through women's achievement in Britain, and radically enlarges the 'canon' suggested by Duncombe especially through a series of celebratory footnotes. From the period 1690 to 1750, Scott cites Mary Monck, Mary Lady Chudleigh, Constantia Grierson, Mary Barber (paired as a Hibernian heroine with Grierson), Mary Jones, Mary Masters, Sarah Fielding, and Elizabeth Tollet. A surprising omission from this list for the modern reader is Anne Finch, Countess of Winchilsea. Winchilsea provides an interesting demonstration of the fact that critical reputations of women were not only made (or broken) by the critical endeavours of other women. William Wordsworth in his preface to his 1815 *Poems* drew attention to her nature poetry, asserting that with the exception of Pope's 'Windsor Forest' and Finch's 'Nocturnal Reverie', English poetry between *Paradise Lost* and James Thomson's *Seasons* did not present 'a single new image of external nature'.[14] Wordsworth sent at Christmas 1819 a manuscript collection of extracts from Lady Winchilsea and other writers to Lady Mary Lowther. Since Wordsworth's expression of interest, Winchilsea has (rightly) enjoyed a significant reputation as an accomplished poet. And it is striking to note that Wordsworth is one of the earliest commentators to uncouple aesthetic and moral judgement in the admiration of female literary achievement.

In accounts of the British theatre only one woman playwright of the period 1690 to 1750 achieves any measure of attention and then largely only for one play: Susanna Centlivre for *The Busie Body* (1709). When Eliza Haywood saw into the press the first volume of *The Dramatic Historiographer* (1735), Centlivre's play was the only one of the forty-six plot summaries to be included that was written by a woman.[15] Prefaces by the playwright Elizabeth Inchbald to one hundred and twenty-five plays appeared weekly along with the plays selected by her publisher

Longmans from 1806 and were then collected in a twenty-four volume set entitled *The British Theatre* (1810). *The Busie Body* took up the eleventh volume and the only other female-authored plays in the collection were those by Inchbald herself, which were included in the twenty-third volume. As with the selections of novels by Griffith and Barbauld there was a strong bias in this anthology toward selection from the later eighteenth century, with the exception of Shakespeare (who enjoys the honour of twenty-four plays given over five volumes). Centlivre's supremacy over an earlier and arguably much more successful and accomplished playwright, Aphra Behn, is an interesting phenomenon and seems to be, again, about the advocacy of a more conservative and constrained female sexuality in the former's comedies. Behn's male libertine contemporaries such as George Etherege and William Wycherley (who appear in both Haywood and Inchbald's theatrical histories) continued to be tolerated, but her reputation appears to have been too damaged for retrieval by the late eighteenth century. We should note however that patterns or intent are not always easy to identify nor do they tend to simple conclusions. Decisions about reprinting plays seem often to be about what materials publishers had available that could turn them a profit, and selection rarely derived from a perception of special literary quality or the construction of a canon.

In relation to women's literary posterity in general, Margaret Ezell is astute in observing that after 1860 very few women of the latter part of our period enjoyed new single editions of their work. She contrasts Elizabeth Singer Rowe (whose work fell out of print completely after 1860) and Lady Mary Wortley Montagu whose grandson Lord Wharncliffe saw a fine three-volume annotated edition of her letters and works into print in 1837: 'for women's literature, having a well-born, well-educated grandchild with a taste for literature may indeed have been more of a factor in survival and inclusion in the canon of women's literature than typicality or literary merit'.[16]

By the mid-nineteenth century the known 'canon' of female-authored literary texts from the late seventeenth and early eighteenth century had been radically reduced and inclusion was tested against new standards of what constituted feminine merit in the arts shaped by the work and reception of a more recent generation of female writers and writing: Maria Edgeworth and Jane Austen in the novel, Charlotte Smith and Felicia Hemans in lyric poetry, Elizabeth Inchbald and Hannah Cowley in drama. Nevertheless, the pursuit of respectability and aesthetic status by women writers in the nineteenth century more often than not entailed identification with powerful male forebears or contemporaries. Thus, in the novel, George Eliot calls on the example of Henry Fielding in *Middlemarch* (1871–72, Book Two, Chapter 15), and Elizabeth Barrett Browning and Christina Rossetti evoke Petrarch in their female-voiced sonnet sequences, *Sonnets from the Portuguese* (1850) and *Monna Innominata* (1881).

However, an enthusiasm for biography and the use of biography as an ideological tool for the promotion of domestic feminized virtue means that while women's literary achievement is rarely acknowledged in other *literary* works or anthologies, the lives of learned and virtuous women who wrote continue to be narrated in a series of biographical dictionaries and encyclopaedias, often however with little sense of the nature of the writing itself. Of women writers from the period 1690 to 1750, Anne Elwood's *Memoirs of the Literary Ladies of England, from the Commencement of the Last Century* (2 vols, 1843) includes Lady Mary Wortley Montagu, Mary Delany, and Elizabeth Carter; Louisa Costello's *Memoirs of Eminent Englishwomen* (4 vols, 1844) includes Anne Finch Countess of Winchilsea and Susanna Centlivre; Julia Kavanagh, *English Women of Letters: Biographical Sketches* (2 vols, 1863), overlooks them altogether, leaping from Aphra Behn to Sarah Fielding without a backward glance; Samuel Knapp, *Female Biography* (1846), includes Mary Astell, Lady Mary Wortley Montagu, and Elizabeth Rowe; and Jane Williams's *The Literary Women of England* (1861) includes Mary Lady Chudleigh, Mary Monck, Anne Finch Countess of Winchilsea, Susanna Centlivre, Delarivier Manley, Jane Brereton, Elizabeth Rowe, Catharine Trotter Cockburn, Frances Seymour Countess of Hertford and Duchess of Somerset, Elizabeth Tollet, Elizabeth Pennington, Anne Ingram Viscountess Irwin, and Elizabeth Carter. Although Williams provides by far the largest number of entries two premises cause particular trouble for her assessment of the 'poetesses' of the early eighteenth century: first, her statement that between Waller and Pope all 'our poetic streams are rendered more or less turbid by the impurity of their channels' and second that women's 'share in the national poetry is like their part in a concert, to which men's voices give fulsomeness and power, and of which men are the composers or directors'. Thus, Mary Lady Chudleigh's 'original poems are most of them sullied by the vicious habits of her time, which so obscured the moral perceptions of even the pure in heart as to permit the familiar use of indelicate allusions'. The strongest praise is still equivocal: Anne Finch Countess of Winchilsea enjoys long quotations from her poetry, and of 'Life's Progress' Williams comments 'Great experimental knowledge of human life and human feeling is shown in this poem.' Margaret Ezell concludes with regard to these biographical-critical endeavours as a whole that a pattern developed in 'the nineteenth century of focusing attention on women writers' domestic lives, with their texts being autobiographical revelations, and on the liabilities under which they wrote'.[17]

It was left to the early twentieth century and a combination of new factors to herald a return to interest in women's writing of earlier periods: the growing industry of literary criticism proved keen to uncover new material and the admission of women to universities and degrees gave women new access to and motives for tracing the history of the literary endeavours of earlier women scholars and writers, while the campaign for female suffrage prompted a new self-consciousness about commonality with other women and concomitant demands for proof of women's powers of judgement, reason, and articulacy if women were to be 'trusted' with the vote. Virginia Woolf, Alex Zwerdling assets, 'essentially established the currently fashionable way of thinking about women's writing as an independent tradition'.[18] Virginia Woolf's long-standing interest in the writing of other women, her injunction in *A Room of One's Own* that women writers should 'think back through our mothers' is not an eccentric or singular interest, and in fact many of her critical writings on those mothers are responses to the published works of others in the first decades of the twentieth century who were taking an interest in women's writing of earlier periods.[19] Her essay 'A Scribbling Dame' is a review essay in response to George Frisbie Whicher's 1915 *The Life and Romances of Eliza Haywood*; in it, she compliments Whicher's archival determination rather than Haywood's contribution to literature, concluding: 'in that long and very intricate process of living and reading and writing which so mysteriously alters the form of literature [...] Mrs Haywood plays no perceptible part, save that of swelling the chorus of sound'.[20] Laetitia Pilkington fares rather better in an essay in *The Common Reader* (1920) where Woolf describes requesting the little brown volume of Pilkington's *Memoirs* not consulted 'since early in the last century' and considers the 'obscure' life she encountered there worth rehearsing, although without mention of the many poems included in the memoirs or of their merits.[21]

Woolf's story in *A Room of One's Own* (1928) of women's failure to succeed in literary endeavour as a result of lack of material support and the burden that women carry of the concerns of the real world which outweighs opportunities to explore the world of imagination can be contrasted with a more positive perspective on women's engagement with the real in the burgeoning interest in the development of the novel and women's contribution to it in the decades after Woolf was writing. While they did not always embrace first-wave feminism women academics of the first half of the twentieth century began to identify and explore English women's writing: Joyce M. Horner's two volume *The English Women Novelists and their Connection with the Feminist Movement (1688–1797)* in 1929 and 1930 and Bridget (B.G.) MacCarthy's two-volume *The Female Pen: Women Writers and Novelists 1621–1818* in 1944 and 1947 indicate the drift of new academic attention to women's writing of earlier periods. Women's success in the nineteenth-century novel led to an assumption that their achievement was best – often only – measured in this genre.[22] MacCarthy saw 'realism' as the special interest and enthusiasm of women writers and judged their aesthetic merit on the extent of their mastery of realist technique; however, she also shows a marked preference for the energetic storytelling of Delarivier Manley and Eliza Haywood over the sentimentalism and didacticism she identified in the works of Elizabeth Rowe and Sarah Fielding.[23] Joyce Horner makes a similar distinction between energetic but superficial narrative (Manley, Haywood) and moral but dull narrative (Aubin, Rowe) in the early eighteenth century and both forms of writing by women before the mid-century fail to achieve the kind of psychological enquiry she considers the true preoccupation of the woman writer best manifested later in the century. These works mark a shift away from judging women's literary work on exacting grounds of sexual moralism and toward an aesthetics of social realism which consistently favours narrative and hence had nothing to say about women as poets. The fondness for the novel in mid-twentieth-century criticism told a history in which all works before 1740 were seen as partial or immature attempts to achieve the fullness, depth, and realist satisfactions of Samuel Richardson's *Pamela* (1740) on which his successors (Frances Burney, Jane Austen, George Eliot) would build so impressively. Women novelists of this earlier period were tarred with the same brush if considered at all.

Feminism of the second wave of the later twentieth century onward in Britain and America saw a decisive turn toward consideration of women's literary history in the academy with significant works such as Ellen Moers *Literary Women: the Great Writers* (1977), Elaine Showalter's *A Literature of their Own: British Women Novelists from Bronte to Lessing* (1977) and Sandra Gilbert and Susan Gubar's *The Madwoman in the Attic: the Woman Writer and the Nineteenth Century* (1979). All three however took their starting point for women's achievement in literature from the nineteenth century and saw fiction/the novel as the mode in which women excelled. Yet, the critical framework of these texts – which shared an argument that women writers in detailing the struggles of their heroines to think beyond the immediate constraints of their social and economic circumstances were also modelling their own desire for creative autonomy as writers – remained a significant one for considering the work of women in other genres and of earlier periods in literary history in the years that followed their publication. It should come as no surprise given the dominance of the association between women and the novel in preceding years, that, when the next generation of feminist critics sought to expand and develop 'gynocriticism' as Showalter termed it, it was the novel to which they turned to discover or uncover women's writing.

The late 1980s to the present day has seen a wealth of publication concerning women's writing of our period, commensurate with the wider flowering of feminist criticism and enthusiasm for the publication of earlier texts by women. A review such as this cannot take account of every work but aims rather to give a sense of significant changes, re-evaluations and new discoveries. I discuss below three areas which have seen activity and energetic debate: major editorial projects, biographies and new information, and critical works. These activities are not unrelated; perhaps most significant is to note how criticism has also led or prompted editorial and biographical activity in order to make available materials for study otherwise only accessible in copyright libraries. So this discussion also points to the fertile interaction of different kinds of exploration.

In the late 1980s and through the 1990s and on the heels of a vigorous challenge from those promoting new models of critical theory – Marxist, poststructuralist, feminist, the notion of the 'literary canon' in the academic study of literature – key studies brought a wealth of women's writing to the attention of other critics: in the novel Jane Spencer's *Rise of the Woman Novelist: From Aphra Behn to Jane Austen* (1986), Janet Todd's *Sign of Angellica: Women, Writing and Fiction 1600–1800* (1989), my own *Seductive Forms: Women's Amatory Fiction from 1684 to 1740* (1992);[24] in poetry Carol Barash's *English Women's Poetry 1649–1714* (1997), Donna Landry's *The Muses of Resistance: Laboring-Class Women's Poetry in Britain 1739–1796* (1990), and Germaine Greer's *Slip-Shod Sibyls: Recognition, Rejection and the Woman Poet* (1995);[25] in drama Jacqueline Pearson's *The Prostituted Muse: Images of Women and Women Dramatists 1642–1737* (1988).[26] Works with a stronger emphasis on women's place in book history and the commercial marketplace of publication were Cheryl Turner's *Living by the Pen: Women Writers in the Eighteenth Century* (1992) and Paula McDowell's *The Women of*

Grub Street: Press, Politics and Gender in the London Literary Marketplace 1678–1730 (1998).[27]

Alongside such surveys, works appeared in print in anthologies or series. A groundbreaking selection of plays edited by Fidelis Morgan under the title *The Female Wits: Women Playwrights of the Restoration* (1981), which included single plays by Mary Pix, Catharine Trotter, Delarivier Manley, and Susanna Centlivre, served academic courses and private interest for many years.[28] A much more scholarly enterprise was the work of Roger Lonsdale in a hugely influential anthology and companion volume to his *The New Oxford Book of Eighteenth-Century Verse* (1984) with *Eighteenth-Century Women Poets: An Oxford Anthology* (1989). Lonsdale undertook assiduous biographical and textual research into his subjects and gave substantial space to the poets before 1750. One hundred and fifty-three of the 323 poems included were written or published before 1750. Although Lonsdale concludes that women found it easier and more acceptable to publish verse as the century progressed, he expresses admiration for the 'intelligence and versatility' of Anne Finch Countess of Winchilsea and Lady Mary Wortley Montagu, and the 'spirit' of Elizabeth Thomas.[29] In prose fiction, Paula Backscheider and John J. Richetti produced an excellent course text entitled *Popular Fiction by Women 1660–1730: An Anthology* (1996) sampling complete short works by Eliza Haywood, Delarivier Manley, Penelope Aubin, and Mary Davys, and selections from Elizabeth Singer Rowe.[30]

Alexander Pettit, distinguished editor of a recent *Selected Works of Eliza Haywood*,[31] in considering the history of this 'feminist recovery project' usefully applies the distinction of 'practical texts' (minimal and swift production of texts only for reading), 'definitive editions' (carefully collated textual editions of major works), and 'critical editions' (works appearing with limited but sound application of principles of textual editing and additional critical material such as introductions, lists of variants, appendices to enable interpretation). Pettit concludes with a call to arms (or at least reflective scholarship) to editors and potential editors of women's writing for the commercial press:

> Responding to a commercial need for editions by women writers, presses incidentally authorize the production of editions that may be as rigorous or as opportunistic, as illuminating or obfuscatory, as the editor chooses. By taking charge themselves, scholars can produce responsible editions that will receive wider distribution, and appear in print more quickly, than full-scale critical editions. The

expansion of the canon offers a splendid opportunity to raise the quality of editing. Or, of course, to lower it.[32]

Publishers' lists in the last decades of the twentieth century increasingly included lists dedicated to early women's writing and at their best such lists pay attention to consistency of editorial principle and selection of works on grounds of aesthetic merit or critical significance across volumes. Pickering Women's Classics series ran from 1991 to 2002 and included my own edition of Delarivier Manley's *New Atalantis* (1992) and Robert Rehder's edition of the *Narrative of the Life of Charlotte Charke* (1999) in its spare list of thirteen titles. Oxford University saw into press fifteen volumes edited through the Brown University Women Writers project under the title 'Oxford's Women Writers in English, 1350–1850' including from our period the poems and prose of Mary Lady Chudleigh, edited by Margaret Ezell (1993); selected fiction and drama of Eliza Haywood, edited by Paula Backscheider (1998) and from her *Female Spectator*, edited by Patricia Meyer Spacks (1998); Jane Barker's Galesia trilogy of short fictions, edited by Carol Shiner Wilson (1997); and the prophetic writings of Eleanor Davies, edited by Esther Cope (1995). Kentucky University Press's series 'Eighteenth-Century Novels by Women' includes Peter Sabor's edition of Sarah Fielding's *David Simple* (1998), Jerry Beasley's edition of Haywood's *The Injur'd Husband* and *Lasselia* (1999), and Martha Bowden's edition of three novels by Mary Davys (1999). Women writers are increasingly included in lists not designed solely to publicize the work of women. For example, works by women form the backbone of the independent Canadian academic publisher Broadview's 'Restoration and Eighteenth-Century' list (23 volumes with named female authors and 14 with named male authors as of spring 2010).

Scholars new to the period will also encounter significant progress in works of reference which have advanced from the vision of individual women scholars to major multi-authored projects in digital form, including a *Dictionary of British Women Writers*, edited by Janet Todd (1989), Lorna Sage's *The Cambridge Guide to Women's Writing in English* (1999) and the *Feminist Companion to Literature in English*, co-edited by Isobel Grundy, Patricia Clements, and Virginia Blain (1990).[33] Grundy and Clements have gone on to design and launch with Susan Brown the 'Orlando Project', a collaborative scholarly history of women's writing in the British Isles published by subscription by Cambridge University Press Online in 2006: this modern online resource is updated at six-monthly intervals.[34]

The digital age has not, however, seen literary historians turn their back on working with and in the print and manuscript archive; indeed, digital resources have often enhanced the prospects of recovery and discovery. Some of the most distinguished scholarship into the writing of women has and is taking place through the work of biographers. Exceptional biographies of recent years which have alerted readers and historians to women's complex agency in the early modern period are Isobel Grundy's culmination of a lifetime's work on Lady Mary Wortley Montagu in *Comet of Enlightenment* (1999) and Kathryn King's archival work resulting in *Jane Barker, Exile* (2000).[35] New attribution and bibliographical work has been more spare, but mention must be made of the bibliographical achievement of Patrick Spedding with regard to the murky world of attribution of works to Eliza Haywood (2004).[36]

The most recent work of critical-archival authority, Susan Staves's *A Literary History of Women's Writing in Britain 1660–1789* is an unapologetic call for acts of evaluation and comparison in our interpretation of a much-expanded field. Staves rightly asserts that 'it cannot be a sin against feminism to find that some women wrote well and others badly'.[37] Staves makes a vigorous defence of writers who received less attention from a feminist criticism driven by models derived from the nineteenth-century novel and/or the theoretical frameworks of Marxism, psychoanalysis, and deconstruction, preferring the achievements of pious writers such as Elizabeth Rowe, republican wits such as Lady Mary Wortley Montagu, and Cartesian rationalists Damaris Masham and Mary Astell to the flashy sexual and partisan politics of Delarivier Manley and Eliza Haywood. Staves does not shrink from offering a historical narrative to guide her readers: she charts a shift from the primarily partisan writings of the early years of the restored Stuart monarchy to the exciting outbreak of Cartesian polemic in the service of asserting women's reason and educability in the 1690s; and a return to party polemic in the Hanoverian years, succeeded by a retreat into the domestic securities of association with literary families on the part of women in the mid-eighteenth century. The decisive turn to aesthetic judgement in recent critical work is endorsed in Paula Backscheider's *Eighteenth-Century Women Poets and their Poetry* (2005). Backscheider complains that 'It seems easier to get agreement that the eighteenth-century poetic landscape needs revision to include women poets than to identify the women who necessitate the revisions and are worthy of sustained study.'[38] Those writers who receive individual attention by Backscheider are selected on grounds of their agency in shaping or transforming distinctive poetic genres and in the production of a signature voice or style of their own rather than because they articulate a particularly vocal or representative female position in the period. Hence, from our period, while Anne Finch Countess of Winchilsea is a familiar inclusion, Elizabeth Singer Rowe and Elizabeth Carter are less obvious contenders for whose agency, influence, and achievement as poetic practitioners Backscheider makes a powerful case.

This volume has shared that insistence on the focus on the literary, selecting authors and privileging discussion which foregrounds the aesthetic qualities of writers and makes us aware of literary careers rather than individual texts. By necessity a collection of essays cannot offer the kind of powerful narrative line made possible by the single-authored critical study such as Susan Staves provides. It has other merits, however, in giving us a sense of the current state of play in the debate and the construction of literary history. And it makes us aware of the many and shared conversations that continue between scholars with shared interests. And it is the energy and nature of collaboration itself – an activity at the heart of the construction of this volume – which promises to become a lively new focus of critical interest in relation to the work of early women writers.

Notes

1. Margaret Ezell, 'The Tedious Chase: Writing Women's Literary History in the Eighteenth and Nineteenth Centuries', in *Writing Women's Literary History* (London and Baltimore: Johns Hopkins University Press, 1993), pp. 66–103 (p. 68).
2. See Paul Salzman, 'Katherine Philips and Aphra Behn', in *Reading Early Modern Women's Writing* (Oxford: Oxford University Press, 2006), pp. 176–218.
3. See Janet Todd, 'After Her Death', in *The Critical Fortunes of Aphra Behn* (London: Boydell and Brewer, 1998), pp. 18–42.
4. *The Tatler*, no. 32, 23 June 1709 in *The Tatler*, ed. by Donald F. Bond, 3 vols (Oxford: Clarendon Press, 1987), I, 237–42, (p. 240); and no. 63, 3 September 1709, *The Tatler*, ed. by Bond, I, 434–41 (pp. 439–40).
5. *The Spectator*, no. 51, 28 April 1711, in *The Spectator*, ed. by Donald F. Bond, 5 vols (Oxford: Clarendon Press, 1965), V, pp. 215–20 (p. 218).
6. George Ballard, *Memoirs of Several Ladies of Great Britain who have been celebrated for their writings or skill in the learned languages, arts and sciences* (London, 1752).
7. John Duncombe, *The Feminiad. A Poem* (London, 1754), l. 62, p. 9.
8. Ezell, 'The Tedious Chase', p. 88.
9. Harriet Guest, 'Chapter Two: The Female Worthies', in *Small Change: Women, Virtue, Patriotism 1750–1810* (Chicago: University of Chicago Press, 2000), esp. pp. 49–769 (p. 57).

10. Richard Terry, 'Making the Female Canon', in *Poetry and the Making of the English Literary Past 1660–1781* (Oxford: Clarendon Press, 2001), pp. 277–8.
11. Clara Reeve, *The Progress of Romance and the History of Charoba, Queen of England* (Colchester, 1785), pp. 122, 135.
12. See William B. Warner, 'Formulating Fiction for the General Reader', chapter 3 of his *Licensing Entertainment: The Elevation of Novel Reading in Britain, 1684–1750* (London and Los Angeles: California University Press, 1998), pp. 88–127.
13. 'On the Origin and Progress of Novel-Writing', extracted in *Women Critics 1660–1820: An Anthology*, ed. by the Folger Collective on Early Women Critics (Bloomington and Indianapolis: Indiana University Press, 1995), pp. 174–98 (pp. 175, p. 185). See also Claudia L. Johnson, ' "Let me make the novels of a country": Barbauld's *The British Novelists* (1810/1820)', *Novel*, 34 (2001), 163–79.
14. William Wordsworth, 'Essay, Supplementary to the Preface', *Poems* (1815), in *William Wordsworth: The Major Works including the Prelude*, ed. by Stephen Gill (Oxford: Oxford University Press, 2000), p. 651.
15. *The Dramatic Historiographer (the Companion to the Theatre, volume One)*, ed. by Christine Blouch, Alexander Pettit, and Rebecca Sayers, Vol. I of Set 2, *Selected Works* (London: Pickering and Chatto 2001).
16. Lady Mary Wortley Montagu, *The Letters and Works of Lady Mary Wortley Montagu*, ed. by W. Moy Thomas, Lord Wharncliffe, 3 vols (London, 1837).
17. Jane Williams, *The Literary Women of England* (London, 1861), pp. 141, 142, 144–5, 150; Ezell, 'The Tedious Chase', p. 103.
18. Alex Zwerdling, *Virginia Woolf and the Real World* (Berkeley, Los Angeles and London: University of California Press, 1987), p. 226.
19. See Paul Salzman, *Reading Early Modern Women Writers*, pp. 224–5 on the connections between Montague Summers, editor of Aphra Behn in 1915, Vita Sackville-West, author of a biography of Behn in 1927, and Woolf's famous comments on Behn as the first professional woman writer in chapter four of her 1928 *A Room of One's Own* (Harmondsworth: Penguin, 1975); she refers to thinking back 'through our mothers' on p. 76.
20. Virginia Woolf, 'A Scribbling Dame', in *The Essays of Virginia Woolf: vol. 2, 1912–1918*, ed. by Andrew McNellie (San Diego, New York, London: Harcourt Brace Jovanovich, 1918), pp. 22–6 (p. 25).
21. Virgina Woolf, 'Lives of the Obscure', in *The Common Reader* (London: the Hogarth Press, 1925), pp. 160–7.
22. See Brian Corman, *Women Novelists before Jane Austen: The Critics and their Canons* (Toronto: University of Toronto Press, 2008).
23. See B.G. MacCarthy, *The Female Pen: Women Writers and Novelists 1621–1818*, reissued with a preface by Janet Todd (Cork: Cork University Press, 1994).
24. Jane Spencer, *Rise of the Woman Novelist: From Aphra Behn to Jane Austen* (Oxford: Oxford University Press, 1986); Janet Todd, *The Sign of Angellica: Women, Writing and Fiction 1600–1800* (New York: Columbia University Press, 1989); Ros Ballaster, *Seductive Forms: Women's Amatory Fiction from 1684 to 1740* (Oxford: Oxford University Press, 1992).
25. Carol Barash, *English Women's Poetry, 1649–1714: Politics, Community and Literary Authority* (Oxford: Oxford University Press, 1997); Donna Landry, *The Muses of Resistance: Laboring-Class Women's Poetry in Britain 1739–1796*

(Cambridge: Cambridge University Press, 1990); Germaine Greer, *Slip-Shod Sibyls: Recognition, Rejection and the Woman Poet* (London: Viking, 1995).

26. Jacqueline Pearson, *The Prostituted Muse: Images of Women and Women Dramatists 1642–1737* (Hemel Hempstead: Harvester, 1988).

27. Cheryl Turner, *Living by the Pen: Women Writers in the Eighteenth Century* (London: Routledge, 1992) and Paula McDowell, *The Women of Grub Street: Press, Politics and Gender in the London Literary Marketplace 1678–1730* (Oxford: Clarendon Press, 1998).

28. *The Female Wits: Women Playwrights of the Restoration*, ed. by Fidelis Morgan (London: Virago, 1981); *The Female Wits: Women Dramatists on the London Stage, 1660–1720*, ed. by Fidelis Morgan, 2nd edn (London: Virago, 1988).

29. *Eighteenth-Century Women Poets: An Oxford Anthology*, ed. by Roger Lonsdale (Oxford: Oxford University Press, 1989, corrected and with additional notes, 1990), p. xlv.

30. *Popular Fiction by Women 1660–1730: An Anthology*, ed. by Paula Backscheider and John J. Richetti (Oxford: Oxford University Press, 1996).

31. Alexander Pettit, *Selected Works of Eliza Haywood*, 6 vols (London: Pickering and Chatto, 2000–01).

32. Alexander Pettit, 'Terrible Texts, "Marginal" Works, and the Mandate of the Moment: The Case of Eliza Haywood', *Tulsa Studies in Women's Literature*, 22 (2003), 293–314.

33. *Dictionary of British Women Writers*, ed. by Janet Todd (London: Routledge, 1989); Lorna Sage, *The Cambridge Guide to Women's Writing in English* (Cambridge: Cambridge University Press, 1999); and *The Feminist Companion to Literature in English*, ed. by Isobel Grundy, Patricia Clements, and Virginia Blain (New Haven and London: Yale University Press and Batsford, 1990).

34. *Orlando: Women's Writing in the British Isles from the Beginnings to the Present*, ed. by Susan Brown, Patricia Clements, and Isobel Grundy (Cambridge: Cambridge University Press Online, 2006) <http://orlando.cambridge.org/>.

35. Isobel Grundy, *Lady Mary Wortley Montagu: Comet of the Enlightenment* (Oxford: Oxford University Press, 1999) and Kathryn King, *Jane Barker, Exile: A Literary Career 1675–1725* (Oxford: Oxford University Press, 2000).

36. Patrick Spedding, *A Bibliography of Eliza Haywood* (London: Pickering and Chatto, 2004).

37. Susan Staves, *A Literary History of Women's Writing in Britain, 1660–1789* (Cambridge: Cambridge University Press, 2006), p. 439.

38. Paula Backscheider, *Eighteenth-Century Women Poets and their Poetry: Inventing Agency, Inventing Genre* (Baltimore and London: Johns Hopkins University Press, 2005), p. 24.

Works Cited

Manuscripts

Ballard, George, MS Vol. 12, f. 203. Bodleian Library
Barker, Jane, Magdalen College MS 343.
Carter, Elizabeth, Trinity College Library, Cambridge, O.12.57[20]
Montagu, Elizabeth, BL Add MS 4302.
Richardson, Samuel, Victoria and Albert Museum Forster Manuscripts, FM XI and XII

Print sources

Achinstein, Sharon, 'Romance of the Spirit: Female Sexuality and Religious Desire in Early Modern England', *English Literary History*, 69 (2002), 413–38.
——, '"Pleasure by Description": Elizabeth Singer Rowe's Enlightened Milton', in *Milton and the Grounds of Contention*, ed. by Mark R. Kelley, Michael Lieb, and John T. Shawcross (Pittsburgh: Duquesne University Press, 2003), pp. 64–87.
——, *Literature and Dissent in Milton's England* (Cambridge: Cambridge University Press, 2003).
Adburgham, Alison, *Women in Print: Writing Women and Women's Magazines from the Restoration to the Accession of Victoria* (London: Allen and Unwin, 1971).
Addison, Joseph and Richard Steele, *The Spectator*, ed. by Donald F. Bond, 5 vols (Oxford: Clarendon Press, 1965).
——, *The Tatler*, ed. by Donald F. Bond, 3 vols (Oxford: Clarendon Press, 1987).
Algarotti, Francesco, *Sir Isaac Newton's Philosophy Explain'd for the Use of the Ladies*, trans. Elizabeth Carter (London, 1739).
Anderson, Howard, Philip B. Daghlian, and Irving Ehrenpreis, *The Familiar Letter in the Eighteenth Century* (Lawrence: University of Kansas Press, 1966).
Anderson, Misty G., *Female Playwrights and Eighteenth-Century Comedy: Negotiating Marriage on the London Stage* (Basingstoke: Palgrave, 2002).
Andreadis, Harriette, 'The Sapphic-Platonics of Katherine Philips, 1632–1664', *Signs: Journal of Women in Culture and Society*, 15.1 (1989), 34–60.
Apetrei, Sarah, '"A Remarkable Female of Womankind": Gender, Scripture and Knowledge in the Writings of M. Marsin', in *Women, Gender and Radical Religion in Early Modern Europe*, ed. by Sylvia Brown (Leiden: Brill, 2007), pp. 139–59.
——, '"Call No Man Master Upon Earth": Mary Astell's Tory Feminism and an Unknown Correspondence', *Eighteenth-Century Studies*, 41 (2008), 507–23.
Arbuthnot, John, John Gay, and Alexander Pope, *Three Hours after Marriage*, ed. by Richard Morton and William M. Peterson (Painesville, OH: Lake Erie College Press, 1961).
Armitage, David, Armand Himy, and Quentin Skinner, eds, *Milton and Republicanism* (Cambridge: Cambridge University Press, 1995).

Astell, Mary, *A Serious Proposal to the Ladies, Part II: Wherein a Method is offer'd for the Improvement of their Minds* (London, 1697).

——, *The Christian Religion, As Profess'd by a Daughter of the Church of England* (London, 1705).

——, *Bart'lemy Fair, or a Enquiry after Wit* (London, 1709).

——, *Reflections upon Marriage*, in *The First English Feminist: 'Reflections upon Marriage' and other writings by Mary Astell*, ed. by Hilda Smith (Aldershot: Gower, 1986).

——, *Astell: Political Writings*, ed. by Patricia Springborg (Cambridge: Cambridge University Press, 1996).

——, *Reflections upon Marriage*, in *Astell: Political Writings*, ed. by Patricia Springborg (Cambridge: Cambridge University Press, 1996).

——, *Mary Astell's A Serious Proposal to the Ladies: Parts 1 and II*, ed. by Patricia Springborg (Peterborough, Ontario: Broadview, 2002).

—— and John Norris, *Letters Concerning the Love of God*, ed. by E. Derek Taylor and Melvyn New (Aldershot: Ashgate, 2005).

Aubin, Penelope, *A Collection of Entertaining Histories and Novels ... by Mrs. Penelope Aubin*, 3 vols (London, 1739).

Backscheider, Paula, 'The Shadow of an Author: Eliza Haywood', *Eighteenth-Century Fiction*, 11 (1998), 79–100.

——, 'The Story of Eliza Haywood's Novels: Caveats and Questions', in *The Passionate Fictions of Eliza Haywood*, ed. by Kirsten T. Saxton and Rebecca P. Bocchicchio (Lexington: University Press of Kentucky, 2000), pp. 19–47.

——, *Eighteenth-Century Women Poets and their Poetry: Inventing Agency, Inventing Genre* (Baltimore: Johns Hopkins University Press, 2005).

—— and John J. Richetti, eds, *Popular Fiction by Women, 1660–1730: An Anthology* (Oxford: Oxford University Press, 1996).

Ballard, George, *Memoirs of Several Ladies of Great Britain*, ed. by Ruth Perry (Detroit: Wayne State University Press, 1985).

Ballaster, Ros, 'Introduction', *New Atalantis by Delarivier Manley*, ed. by Ros Ballaster (Harmondsworth: Penguin, 1992), pp. v–xxvii.

——, *Seductive Forms: Women's Amatory Fiction from 1684 to 1740* (Oxford: Clarendon Press, 1992).

——, 'A Gender of Opposition: Eliza Haywood's Scandal Fiction', in *The Passionate Fictions of Eliza Haywood: Essays on Her Life and Work*, ed. by Kirsten Saxton and Rebecca Bocchicchio (Lexington: University of Kentucky Press, 2000), pp. 143–67.

——, 'Jonathan Swift, the *Stella* poems', in *A Companion to Eighteenth Century Poetry*, ed. by Christine Gerrard (Oxford: Blackwell, 2006), pp. 170–83.

——, Margaret Beetham, Elizabeth Fraser, and Sandra Hebron, *Women's Worlds: Ideology, Femininity and the Women's Magazine* (London: Macmillan, 1991).

Barash, Carol, *English Women's Poetry, 1649–1714: Politics, Community, and Linguistic Authority* (Oxford: Clarendon Press, 1997).

Barbauld, Anna Laetitia Aikin, *The British Novelists*, 50 vols (London, 1810).

Barber, Mary, *The Poetry of Mary Barber (?1690–1757)*, ed. by Bernard Tucker (Lewiston: Edwin Mellen, 1992).

Barbon, Nicholas, *A Discourse of Trade* (London, 1690).

Barchas, Janine, 'Chandler, Mary (1687–1745)', *Oxford Dictionary of National Biography*, Oxford University Press, 2004, <http://www.oxforddnb.com/view/article/5106> [accessed 16 September 2009].

Barker, Anthony D., 'Poetry from the Provinces: Amateur Poets in the *Gentleman's Magazine* in the 1730s and 1740s', in *Tradition in Transition: Women Writers, Marginal Texts, and the Eighteenth-Century Canon*, ed. by Alvaro Ribeiro and James G. Basker (Oxford: Clarendon Press, 1996), pp. 241–56.

Barker, Jane, *Poetical Recreations: Consisting of Original Poems, Songs, Odes &C. With Several New Translations* (London, 1688).

——, *The Galesia Trilogy and Selected Manuscript Poems*, ed. by Carol Shiner Wilson (Oxford: Oxford University Press, 1997).

——, *The Poems of Jane Barker: The Magdalen Manuscript*, ed. by Kathryn R. King (Oxford: Magdalen College, 1998).

Barker-Benfield, G.J., *The Culture of Sensibility in Eighteenth-Century Britain* (Chicago: Chicago University Press, 1996).

Barrell, John, *The Idea of Landscape and the Sense of Place 1730–1840* (Cambridge: Cambridge University Press, 1972).

Bataille, George, *The Accursed Share*, Vol. I of *Consumption*, trans. by H. Robert Hurley (New York: Zone Books, 1988).

——, *The Bataille Reader*, ed. by Fred Botting and George Scott) Oxford: Wiley-Blackwell, 1997).

Beal, Peter, compiler, *Index of English Literary Manuscripts*, 2 vols (London: Mansel, 1987–1993).

——, *In Praise of Scribes: Manuscripts and their Makers in Seventeenth-Century England* (Oxford: Oxford University Press, 1998).

Beauty's Triumph: or, The Superiority of the First Sex Invincibly Proved (London, 1751).

Belanger, Terry, 'Publishers and Writers in Eighteenth-Century England', in *Books and their Readers in Eighteenth-Century England*, ed. by Isabel Rivers (Leicester: Leicester University Press & New York: St Martin's Press, 1982), pp. 5–25.

Berg, Maxine and Elizabeth Eger, eds, *Luxury in the Eighteenth Century: Debates, Desires and Delectable Goods* (Basingstoke: Palgrave, 2002).

Berry, Helen, *Gender, Society and Print Culture in Late-Stuart England: The Cultural World of the 'Athenian Mercury'* (Aldershot: Ashgate, 2003).

Birch, Thomas, *An Historical and Critical Account of the Life and Writings of John Milton* (London, 1738).

——, *History of the Works of the Learned*, Art XXXI (1 June 1739), 392.

Blanchard, Rae, 'Richard Steele and the Status of Women', *Studies in Philology*, 26 (1929), 325–55.

Blouch, Christine, '"What Ann Lang Read": Eliza Haywood and her Readers', in *The Passionate Fictions of Eliza Haywood: Essays on her Life and Work*, ed. by Kirsten T. Saxton and Rebecca P. Bocchicchio (Lexington: University Press of Kentucky, 2000), pp. 300–26.

Bowers, Toni, 'Collusive Resistance: Sexual Agency and Partisan Politics in *Love in Excess*', in *The Passionate Fictions of Eliza Haywood*, ed. by Kirsten T. Saxton and Rebecca P. Bocchicchio (Lexington, Kentucky: University Press of Kentucky, 1998), pp. 48–68.

Bowyer, John Wilson, *The Celebrated Mrs. Centlivre* (Durham, NC: Duke University Press, 1952).

Boyd, Elizabeth, *The Happy-Unfortunate; or, the Female Page. A Novel, In Three Parts* (London, 1732).

——, *The Snail: or the lady's lucubrations. Being entertaining letters between a lady at St. James's, and her friend at Dover, ... By Eloisa* (London: Printed for E. Boyd, in Vine Street, 1745).

Bradford, Richard, 'Rhyming Couplets and Blank Verse', in *A Companion to Eighteenth-Century Poetry*, ed. by Christine Gerrard (Oxford: Blackwell, 2006), pp. 341–55.

Brandt Bolton, Martha, 'Some Aspects of the Philosophy of Catharine Trotter', *Journal for the History of Philosophy*, 31 (1993), 565–88.

Brant, Clare, *Eighteenth-Century Letters and British Culture* (Basingstoke: Palgrave Macmillan, 2006).

Brewer, John, *The Sinews of Power: War, Money and the English State, 1688–1783* (New York: Alfred Knopf, 1993).

——, *The Pleasures of the Imagination: English Culture in the Eighteenth Century* (London: HarperCollins, 1997).

Broad, Jacqueline, 'A Woman's Influence? John Locke and Damaris Masham on Moral Accountability', *Journal of the History of Ideas*, 67.3 (2006), 489–510.

Brooke, Frances, *The Old Maid. By Mary Singleton, Spinster* (Dublin, 1756).

Brown, Laura, *The Ends of Empire: Women and Ideology in Early Eighteenth-Century English Literature* (Ithaca and London: Cornell University Press, 1993).

——, *Fables of Modernity: Literature and Culture in the English Eighteenth Century* (Ithaca and London: Cornell University Press, 2001).

Browne, Isaac Hawkins, *De animus immortalitate* (London, 1754).

Burnet, Gilbert, *Bishop Burnet's History of His Own Time*, 2 vols (London, 1724, 1734).

Campbell, Colin, *The Romantic Ethic and the Spirit of Modern Consumerism* (Oxford: Basil Blackwell, 1987).

Carnell, Rachel, 'It's Not Easy Being Green: Gender and Friendship in Eliza Haywood's Political Periodicals', *Eighteenth-Century Studies*, 32.2 (1998–99), 199–214.

Carswell, John, *The South Sea Bubble* (London: Cresset Press, 1960).

Carter, Elizabeth, trans., Francesco Algarotti, *Sir Isaac Newton's Philosophy Explain'd for the Use of the Ladies* (London, 1739).

——, trans., Jean-Pierre de Crousaz, *An Examination of Mr Pope's Essay on Man, From the French of M. Crousaz* (London, 1739).

——, trans., *All the works of Epictetus, which are now extant; consisting of his discourses, preserved by Arrian, in four books, the Enchiridion, and fragments* (Dublin, 1759).

—— and Catherine Talbot, *A Series of Letters between Mrs. Elizabeth Carter and Miss Catherine Talbot*, ed. by Montagu Pennington, 4 vols (London, 1809).

Carter, Philip, *Men and the Emergence of Polite Society in Britain 1660–1800*, Women and Men in History Series (London: Pearson Education, 2001).

Castle, Terry, ed., *The Literature of Lesbianism: A Historical Anthology from Ariosto to Stonewall* (New York: Columbia University Press, 2003).

Centlivre, Susanna, *The Busie-Body*, Vol. III of *Eighteenth-Century Women Playwrights*, ed. by Jacqueline Pearson (London: Pickering and Chatto, 2001).

Champion, Justin, *Republican Learning: John Toland and the Crisis of Christian Culture, 1696–1722* (Manchester: Manchester University Press, 2003).

Chandler, Mary, *The Description of Bath. A Poem ... To which are added, Several Poems by the same Author*, 3rd edn (London, 1736).

Chapone, Sarah, *The Hardships of the English Laws in Relation to Wives* (London, 1735).

Charke, Charlotte, *Narrative of the Life of Mrs. Charlotte Charke*, ed. by Robert Rehder (London: Pickering and Chatto, 1999).

Chudleigh, Lady Mary, *The Poems and Prose of Mary, Lady Chudleigh*, ed. by Margaret J.M. Ezell (Oxford: Oxford University Press, 1993).

Cibber, Colley, *The Double Gallant* (London, 1707).

Claridge, Laura and Elizabeth Langford, eds, *Out of Bounds: Male Writers and Gender(ed) Criticism* (Amherst: University of Massachusetts Press, 1991).

Clarke, Norma, 'Soft Passions and Darling Themes: from Elizabeth Singer Rowe (1674–1737) to Elizabeth Carter (1717–1806)', *Women's Writing*, 7.3 (2000), 353–71.

——, *Queen of the Wits: A Life of Laetitia Pilkington* (London: Faber and Faber, 2008).

Clery, E.J., *The Feminization Debate in Eighteenth-Century England: Literature, Commerce and Luxury* (Basingstoke: Palgrave, 2004).

——, Caroline Franklin, and Peter Garside, eds, *Authorship, Commerce and the Public Scenes of Writing 1750—1850* (Basingstoke: Palgrave Macmillan, 2002).

Cockburn, Catharine Trotter, *A Defence of the Essay of Human Understanding, written by Mr. Lock* [sic] (London, 1702).

——, *A Discourse concerning a Guide in Controversies* (London, 1707).

——, *A Letter to Dr. Holdsworth Occasioned by his Sermon* (London, 1726).

——, *The Works of Mrs. Catharine Cockburn*, 2 vols (London, 1751).

——, *Catharine Trotter Cockburn: Philosophical Writings*, ed. by Patricia Sheridan (Peterborough, Ontario: Broadview Press, 2006).

Collins, Sarah, 'The Elstobs and the End of the Saxon Revival', in *Anglo-Saxon Scholarship: the First Three Centuries*, ed. by C.T. Berkhout and M. McC. Gatch (Boston, MA: G.K. Hall, 1982), pp. 107–18.

Collyer, Mary, *Felicia to Charlotte*, 2 vols (London, 1744–49).

Common Sense: or, The Englishman's Journal, no. 45, 10 December 1737.

Conway, Anne, *Principia philosophiae antiquissimae et recentissimae* (Amsterdam, 1690).

——, *The Principles of the Most Ancient and Modern Philosophy* (London, 1692).

Copeland, Nancy, *Staging Gender in Behn and Centlivre: Women's Comedy and the Theatre* (Aldershot: Ashgate, 2004).

Corman, Brian, *Women Novelists before Jane Austen: The Critics and their Canons* (Toronto: University of Toronto Press, 2008).

Cowan, Brian, *The Social Life of Coffee: The Emergence of the British Coffeehouse* (New Haven: Yale University Press, 2005).

Cowper, William, *The Task* (London, 1785).

Craft-Fairchild, Catherine, 'Sexual and Textual Indeterminacy: Eighteenth-Century English Representations of Sapphism', *Journal of the History of Sexuality*, 15.3 (2006), 408–31.

Crawford, Patricia, *Women and Religion in England, 1500–1720* (London: Routledge, 1996).

——, 'Katharine and Philip Henry and their Children: A Case Study in Family Ideology', in *Blood, Bodies and Families in Early Modern England* (London: Pearson, 2004), pp. 175–208.

——, 'Anglicans, Catholics and Nonconformists after the Restoration, 1660–1720', in *Women and Religion in Old and New Worlds*, ed. by Susan E. Dinan and Debra Meyers (London: Routledge, 2001), pp. 157–86.

Critical Remarks on Sir Charles Grandison, Clarissa, and Pamela, ed. by A.D. McKillop, Augustan Reprint Society No. 21 (Los Angeles: Williams Andrews Clark Memorial Library, 1950).

Davenant, Sir Charles, *An Essay on the India Trade* (London, 1697).

Davies, Eleanor, *Prophetic Writings of Lady Eleanor Davies*, ed. by Esther Cope (Oxford: Oxford University Press, 1995).

Davis Perry, Lori A., 'The Literary Model for Elizabeth Singer Rowe's *History of Joseph*', *Notes and Queries*, 52.3 (2005), 349–51.

Davys, Mary, *The Reform'd Coquet, Familiar Letters Betwixt a Gentleman and a Lady, and The Accomplish'd Rake*, ed. by Martha F. Bowden (Lexington, Kentucky: University of Kentucky Press, 1999).

Defoe, Daniel, *Essay on Projects* (London, 1697).

——, *More Short-Ways with the Dissenters* (London, 1704).

——, *The Shortest Way with the Dissenters* (London, 1704).

——, *Some Considerations upon Street-Walkers. With a Proposal for lessening the present number of them. In two letters to a Member of Parliament* (London, 1726).

——, *The Best of Defoe's Review: An Anthology*, ed. by William L. Payne (New York: Columbia University Press, 1951).

Denham, John, *Coopers-Hill* (London, 1642).

Dinan, Susan E. and Debra Meyers, eds, *Women and Religion in Old and New Worlds* (London: Routledge, 2001).

Docwra, Ann, *An Epistle of Love and Good Advice* (London, 1683).

Donoghue, Emma, *Passions between Women: British Lesbian Culture 1668–1801* (London: Scarlett Press, 1993).

Doody, Margaret, *A Natural Passion: A Study of the Novels of Samuel Richardson* (Oxford: Clarendon Press, 1974).

Doughty, Oswald, 'A Bath Poetess of the Eighteenth Century [Mary Chandler]', *Review of English Studies*, 1 (1925), 404–21.

Drake, Judith, *An Essay in Defence of the Female Sex* (London, 1696).

Duncombe, John, *The Feminiad. A Poem* (London, 1754).

Duncombe, William, *Works of Horace in English Verse. By Several Hands*, 2 vols (London, 1757–59).

Dunton, John, *The Athenian Mercury; or Casuistical Gazette* (London, 1691–97).

——, 'The Double Courtship', in *Athenianism: or, the New Projects of John Dunton* (London, 1710), pp. 1–61.

Dutton, Anne, *A Narration of the Wonders of Grace* (London, 1734).

——, *A Letter to such of the Servants of Christ, who may have any Scruple about the Lawfulness of Printing any Thing written by a Woman* (London, 1743).

——, *A Letter to the Reverend Mr John Wesley: In Vindication of the Doctrines of Absolute, unconditional Election, Particular Redemption, Special Vocation, and Final Perseverance* (London, 1743).

——, *Letters to the Reverend Mr John Wesley against Perfection As not attainable in this Life* (London, 1743).

——, *A Brief Account of the gracious dealings of God, with a poor, sinful, unworthy creature, in three parts* (London, 1750).

Dyer, Richard, *The Fleece* (London, 1757).

Eger, Elizabeth, 'Luxury, Industry and Charity: Bluestocking Culture Displayed', in *Luxury in the Eighteenth Century: Debates, Desires and Delectable Goods*, ed. by Maxine Berg and Elizabeth Eger (Basingstoke: Palgrave, 2002), pp. 190–204.

Egerton, Sarah Fyge, *Poems on Several Occasions, together with a pastoral* (London, 1703).

Eighteenth-Century Women Playwrights, 6 vols, general editor Derek Hughes (London: Pickering and Chatto, 2001).

Eisenstein, Elizabeth, ed., *The Printing Press as an Agent of Change: Communications and Cultural Transformations in Early Modern Europe*, 2 vols (Cambridge: Cambridge University Press, 1979).

Elstob, Elizabeth, *An English-Saxon Homily on the Birthday of St. Gregory* (London, 1709).

——, *Rudiments of Grammar for the English-Saxon Tongue* (London, 1715).

Elwood, Anne, *Memoirs of the Literary Ladies of England, from the Commencement of the Last Century*, 2 vols (London, 1843).

Elwood, J.R., 'Swift's "Corinna"', *Notes and Queries*, 200 (1955), 529–30.

Erickson, Amy Louise, *Women and Property in Early Modern England* (London: Routledge, 1993).

Erskine-Hill, Howard, *Poetry of Opposition and Revolution: Dryden to Wordsworth* (Oxford: Clarendon Press, 1996).

Ewert, Leonore Helen, 'Elizabeth Montagu to Elizabeth Carter: Literary Gossip and Critical Opinions from the Pen of the Queen of the Blues', PhD dissertation, Claremont Graduate School, 1968.

Ezell, Margaret J.M., *The Patriarch's Wife: Literary Evidence and the History of the Family* (Chapel Hill: University of North Carolina Press, 1987).

——, 'The *Gentleman's Journal* and the Commercialization of Restoration Coterie Literary Practices', *Modern Philology*, 89.3 (1992), 323–40.

——, *Writing Women's Literary History* (Baltimore: Johns Hopkins University Press, 1996).

——, *Social Authorship and the Advent of Print* (Baltimore: Johns Hopkins University Press, 1999).

Fairer, David, *English Poetry of the Eighteenth-Century 1700–1789* (London: Longman, 2003).

——, 'Mary Leapor: *Crumble Hall*', in *A Companion to Eighteenth-Century Poetry*, ed. by Christine Gerrard (Oxford: Blackwell, 2006), pp. 223–36.

—— and Christine Gerrard, eds, *Eighteenth-Century Poetry: An Annotated Anthology*, 2nd edn (Oxford: Blackwell, 2004).

Fara, Patricia, *Pandora's Breeches: Women, Science and Power in the Enlightenment* (London: Pimlico, 2005).

Fielding, Henry, *Tom Jones*, ed. by John Bender and Simon Stern (Oxford: Oxford University Press, 1996).

——, *Joseph Andrews and Shamela*, ed. by Douglas Brooks-Davies and Martin Battestin, revised edn, Thomas Keymer (Oxford: Oxford University Press 1999).

Fielding, Sarah, *Remarks on Clarissa* (London, 1749).

——, *The Adventures of David Simple and Volume the Last*, ed. by Peter Sabor (Lexington: Kentucky University Press, 1998).

Findlen, Paula, 'Ideas in the Mind: Gender and Knowledge in the Seventeenth Century', *Hypatia: A Journal of Feminist Philosophy*, 17.1 (Winter 2002), 183–96.

——, 'Women on the Verge of Science: Aristocratic Women and Knowledge in Early Eighteenth-Century Italy', in *Women, Gender and Enlightenment*, ed. by Sarah Knott and Barbara Taylor (Basingstoke: Palgrave Macmillan, 2005), pp. 265–87.

Forell Marshall, Madeleine, *The Poetry of Elizabeth Singer Rowe, 1674–1737* (Lewiston, ME: Edwin Mellen Press, 1989).

Fox, Christopher, *Locke and the Scriblerians: Identity and Consciousness in Early Eighteenth-Century Britain* (Berkeley: University of California Press, 1988).

Fowke, Martha [Sansom], *Clio: the Autobiography of Martha Fowke Sansom, 1687–1736*, ed. by Phyllis J. Guskin (London: Associated University Presses, 1997).

Fudge, Erica, Ruth Gilbert, and Susan Wiseman, eds, *At the Borders of the Human: Beasts, Bodies and Natural Philosophy in the Early Modern Period* (London: Macmillan, 1999).

Gallagher, Catherine, 'Embracing the Absolute: The Politics of the Female Subject in Seventeenth-Century England', *Genders*, 1 (Spring 1988), 24–39.

——, *Nobody's Story: The Vanishing Acts of Women Writers in the Literary Marketplace, 1670–1820* (Berkeley and Los Angeles, University of California Press, 1994).

Gay, John, *The Shepherd's Week. In Six Pastorals* (London, 1714).

Gentleman's Magazine, 8 December 1741.

Gerrard, Christine, *Aaron Hill: The Muses' Projector 1685–1750* (Oxford: Oxford University Press, 2003).

——, ed., *A Companion to Eighteenth-Century Poetry* (Oxford: Blackwell, 2006).

Gilbert, Sandra, 'Patriarchal Poetry and Women Readers: Reflections on Milton's Bogey', *PMLA*, 93 (1978), 368–82.

Golden, Morris, 'Public Context and Imagining Self in *Pamela* and *Shamela*', *ELH*, 53 (1986), 311–29.

Goldgar, Bernard, *Impolite Learning: Conduct and Community in the Republic of Letters, 1680–1750* (New Haven and London: Yale University Press, 1995).

Goldie, Mark, 'Mary Astell and John Locke', in *Mary Astell: Reason, Gender, Faith*, ed. by William Kolbrener and Michael Michaelson (Aldershot: Ashgate, 2007), pp. 65–81.

Goldsmith, M.M., '"The Treacherous Arts of Mankind": Bernard Mandeville and Female Virtue', *History of Political Thought*, 7 (1986), 93–114.

Goodman, Dena, 'Letter Writing and the Emergence of Gendered Subjectivity in Eighteenth-Century France', *Journal of Women's History*, 17.2 (2005), 9–37.

Graham, Walter, 'Thomas Baker, Mrs. Manley, and the "Female Tatler"', *Modern Philology*, 34.3 (1937), 267–72.

Greene, Richard, *Mary Leapor: A Study in Eighteenth-Century Women's Poetry* (Oxford: Clarendon Press, 1993).

Greer, Germaine, *Slip-Shod Sibyls: Recognition, Rejection and the Woman Poet* (London: Viking, 1995).

Griffin, Dustin, *Regaining Paradise: Milton and the Eighteenth Century* (Cambridge: Cambridge University Press, 1986).

Griffith, Elizabeth, *A Collection of Novels, Selected and Revised by Elizabeth Griffith*, 3 vols (London, 1777).

—— and Richard Griffith, *A Series of Genuine Letters Between Henry and Frances*, 6 vols (London, 1757–70).

Grundy, Isobel, 'The Politics of Female Authorship: Lady Mary Wortley Montagu's Reaction to the Printing of Her Poems', *The Book Collector*, 31 (1982), 19–37.

——, *Lady Mary Wortley Montagu: Comet of the Enlightenment* (Oxford: Oxford University Press, 1997).

——, 'Lady Mary Wortley Montagu, *Six Town Eclogues* and Other Poems', in *A Companion to Eighteenth-Century Poetry*, ed. by Christine Gerrard (Oxford: Blackwell, 2006), 184–96.

——, Pamela Clements, and Virginia Blain, eds, *The Feminist Companion to Literature in English* (New Haven and London: Yale University Press and Batsford, 1990).

Guest, Harriet, *Small Change: Women, Virtue, Patriotism 1750–1810* (Chicago: University of Chicago Press, 2000).

Gunn, J.A.W., *Beyond Liberty and Property: The Process of Self-Recognition in Eighteenth-Century Political Thought* (Kingston and Montreal: McGill-Queen's University Press, 1983).

Habermas, Jürgen, *The Structural Transformation of the Public Sphere: An Inquiry into a Category of Bourgeois Society*, trans. by Thomas Burger (Cambridge: Polity, 1989).

Hageman, Elizabeth H. and Andrea Sununu, '"More copies of it abroad than I could have imagin'd": Further Manuscript Texts of Katherine Philips, "the matchless Orinda"', *English Manuscript Studies*, 5 (1995), 127–69.

Hammond, Brean, *Imaginative Writing in England, 1660–1740: Hackney for Bread* (Oxford: Clarendon Press, 1997).

Hampshire, Gwen, 'An Edition of some Unpublished Letters of Elizabeth Carter, 1717–1806, and a Calendar of her Correspondence', B.Litt. dissertation, Oxford University, 1972.

——, ed., *Elizabeth Carter, 1717–1806: An Edition of Some Unpublished Letters* (Newark: University of Delaware Press, 2005).

Harth, Erica, *Cartesian Women: Versions and Subversion of Rational Discourse in the Old Regime* (Ithaca: Cornell University Press, 1992).

Hawley, Judith, 'Carter, Elizabeth (1717–1806)', *Oxford Dictionary of National Biography*, Oxford University Press, September 2004, online edn, May 2009 <http://www.oxforddnb.com/view/article/4782> [accessed 17 September 2009].

Haywood, Eliza, *The Fair Captive* (London, 1721).

——, *Letters from a Lady of Quality* (London, 1721).

——, *Idalia* (London, 1723).

——, *The Force of Nature* (London, 1724).

——, *Poems on Several Occasions*, in *The Works of Mrs Eliza Haywood*, vol. IV (London, 1724).

——, *The Rash Resolve* (London, 1724).

——, *A Spy Upon a Conjurer* (London, 1724).

——, *The Works of Mrs Eliza Haywood*, 4 vols (London, 1724).

——, *The Masqueraders*, 2 vols (London, 1724–25).

——, *Memoirs of a Certain Island Adjacent to the Kingdom of Utopia*, 2 vols (London, 1724–5).

——, *Secret Histories, Novels and Poems*, 4 vols (London, 1725).

——, *The Fruitless Enquiry* (London, 1727).

——, *The Lucky Rape*, appended to *Cleomelia: or the Generous Mistress* (London, 1727), 79–94.

——, *The Perplex'd Dutchess; or, Treachery Rewarded* (London, 1727).

——, *Irish Artifice* (London, 1728).

——, *The Padlock: Or, No Guard Without Virtue*, appended to *The Mercenary Lover or, The Unfortunate Heiresses* (London, 1728), pp. 57–79.

——, *Letter from H— G—, Esq* ... . *To a Particular Friend* (London: 1750).

——, *The History of Miss Betsy Thoughtless*, ed. by Christine Blouch (Peterborough, Ontario: Broadview, 1998).

——, *Selections from the Female Spectator*, ed. by Patricia Meyer Spacks (Oxford: Oxford University Press, 1998).

——, *The Adventures of Eovaai, Princess of Ijaveo: A Pre-Adamitical History*, ed. by Earla Wilputte (Peterborough, Ontario: Broadview, 1999).

——, *Lasselia; or, The Self-Abandon'd*, ed. by Jerry C. Beasley (Lexington: University Press of Kentucky, 1999).

——, *Selected Fiction and Drama of Eliza Haywood*, ed. by Paula Backscheider (New York and Oxford: Oxford University Press, 1999).

——, *Love in Excess*, ed. by David Oakleaf (Peterborough, Ontario: Broadview Press, 2000).

——, *Selected Works of Eliza Haywood*, general editor Alexander Pettit, 6 vols (London: Pickering and Chatto, 2000–01).

——, *Anti-Pamela*, in *Anti-Pamela and Shamela*, ed. by Catherine Ingrassia (Peterborough, Ontario: Broadview, 2004).

——, *Fantomina and Other Works*, ed. by Alexander Pettit, Margaret Case Croskery, and Anna C. Patchias (Peterborough, Ontario: Broadview Press, 2004).

—— and William Hatchett, *The Opera of Operas; or, Tom Thumb the Great* (London, 1733).

Herman, Ruth, *The Business of a Woman: The Political Writings of Delarivier Manley* (Newark: Delaware University Press, 2003).

Hesse, Carla, 'Introduction: Women Intellectuals in the Enlightened Republic of Letters', in *Women, Gender and Enlightenment*, ed. by Sarah Knott and Barbara Taylor (Basingstoke: Palgrave Macmillan, 2005), pp. 259–64.

Hollis, Karen, 'Eliza Haywood and the Gender of Print', *Eighteenth Century: Theory and Interpretation*, 38.1 (1997), 43–63.

Howsam, Leslie, *Old Books and New Histories: An Orientation to Studies in Book and Print Culture* (Toronto: University of Toronto Press, 2006).

Hughes, Derek, *English Drama 1660–1700* (Oxford: Clarendon Press, 1996).

Hundert, E.G., *The Enlightenment's Fable: Bernard Mandeville and the Discovery of Society* (Cambridge: Cambridge University Press, 1994).

Hunter, Jean, 'The Lady's Magazine and the Study of Englishwomen in the Eighteenth Century', in *Newsletters to Newpapers: Eighteenth-Century Journalism*, ed. by Donovan Bond and W.H. McLeod (Morgantown: West Virginia University Press, 1977), pp. 103–17.

Hutton, Sarah, 'Anne Conway, Margaret Cavendish and Seventeenth-Century Scientific Thought', in *Women, Science and Medicine, 1500–1700: Mothers and Sisters of the Royal Society*, ed. by Lynette Hunter and Sarah Hutton (Gloucestershire: Sutton Publishing, 1997), pp. 218–34.

Inchbald, Elizabeth, 'Prefaces', *The British Theatre*, 24 vols (London, 1810).

Ingrassia, Catherine, 'Additional Information about Eliza Haywood's 1749 Arrest for Seditious Libel', *Notes and Queries*, 44 (June, 1997), 202–4.

——, *Authorship, Commerce and Gender in Early Eighteenth-Century England: A Culture of Paper Credit* (Cambridge: Cambridge University Press, 1998).

——, 'Eliza Haywood, Sapphic Desire, and the Practice of Reading', in *Lewd and Notorious: Female Transgression in the Eighteenth Century*, ed. by Katharine Kittredge (Ann Arbor: University of Michigan Press, 2003), pp. 235–57.

——, 'Eliza Haywood, Periodicals, and the Function of Orality', in *Fair Philosopher: Eliza Haywood and 'The Female Spectator'*, ed. by Lynne Marie Wright and Donald Newman (Lewisburg: Bucknell University Press, 2006), pp. 141–56.

Israel, Jonathan I., *Enlightenment Contested: Philosophy, Modernity, and the Emancipation of Man, 1670–1752* (Oxford: Oxford University Press, 2006).

Italia, Iona, *The Rise of Literary Journalism in the Eighteenth Century: Anxious Employment* (London: Routledge, 2005).

Johnson, Claudia L., '"Let me make the novels of a country": Barbauld's *The British Novelists* (1810/1820)', *Novel*, 34 (2001), 163–79.

Jones, Mary, *Miscellanies in Prose and Verse* (Oxford, 1750).

Jones, Robert W., 'Eliza Haywood and the Discourse of Taste', in *Authorship, Commerce and the Public Scenes of Writing 1750–1850*, ed. by E.J. Clery et al. (Basingstoke: Palgrave Macmillan, 2002), pp. 103–9.

Jordan, Constance, *Renaissance Feminism: Literary Texts and Political Models* (Ithaca: Cornell University Press, 1990).

Justice, George L. and Nathan Tinker, eds, *Women's Writing and the Circulation of Ideas: Manuscript Publication in England, 1550–1800* (Cambridge: Cambridge University Press, 2002).

Kavanagh, Julia, *English Women of Letters: Biographical Sketches*, 2 vols (London, 1863).

Keeble, N.H., *The Literary Culture of Nonconformity in Later Seventeenth-Century England* (Athens, GA: University of Georgia Press, 1987).

Kelley, Anne, 'Corrections to Thomas Birch (ed.) *The Works of Mrs. Catharine Cockburn*', *Notes & Queries*, 47 (245), no. 2 (June 2000), 192–3.

——, *Catharine Trotter: An Early Modern Writer in the Vanguard of Feminism* (Aldershot: Ashgate, 2002).

——, 'Trotter, Catharine (1674?–1749)', *Oxford Dictionary of National Biography*, Oxford University Press, September 2004, online edn, October 2008 <http://www.oxforddnb.com/view/article/5768> [accessed 17 September 2009].

Kelley, Mark R., Michael Lieb, and John T. Shawcross, *Milton and the Grounds of Contention* (Pittsburgh: Duquesne University Press, 2003).

King, Kathryn R., *Jane Barker, Exile: A Literary Career, 1675–1725* (Oxford: Oxford University Press, 2000).

——, 'Elizabeth Singer Rowe's Tactical Use of Print', in *Women's Writing and the Circulation of Ideas: Manuscript Publication in England, 1550–1800*, ed. by George Justice and Nathan Tinker (Cambridge: Cambridge University Press, 2002), pp. 158–181.

——, 'Patriot or Opportunist? Eliza Haywood and the Politics of *The Female Spectator*', in *Fair Philosopher: Eliza Haywood and 'The Female Spectator'*, ed. by Lynne Marie Wright and Donald Newman (Lewisburg: Bucknell University Press, 2006), pp. 104–21.

——, 'Eliza Haywood, Savage Love, and Biographical Uncertainty', *Review of English Studies*, 59 (2008), 722–39.

Kittredge, Katharine, ed., *Lewd and Notorious: Female Transgression in the Eighteenth Century* (Ann Arbor: University of Michigan Press, 2003).

Klein, Lawrence, 'Gender, Conversation and the Public Sphere in Early Eighteenth-Century England', in *Textuality and Sexuality: Reading Theories and Practices*, ed. by Judith Still and Michael Worton (Manchester: Manchester University Press, 1993), pp. 100–15.

——, *Shaftesbury and the Culture of Politeness: Moral Discourse and Cultural Politics in Early Eighteenth Century England* (Cambridge: Cambridge University Press, 1994).

——, 'Gender and the Public/Private Distinction in the Eighteenth Century: Some Questions about Evidence and Analytic Procedure', *Eighteenth-Century Studies*, 29.1 (1996), 97–109.

Knapp, Samuel, *Female Biography* (London, 1846).

Knott, Sarah and Barbara Taylor, eds, *Women, Gender and Enlightenment* (Basingstoke: Palgrave Macmillan, 2005).

Kolbrener, William, 'Astell's "Design of Friendship" in *Letters* and *A Serious Proposal, Part I*', in *Mary Astell: Reason, Gender, Faith*, ed. by William Kolbrener and Michael Michelson (Aldershot: Ashgate, 2007), pp. 49–64.

Kolbrener, William and Michael Michelson, eds, *Mary Astell: Reason, Gender, Faith* (Aldershot: Ashgate, 2007).

Kowaleski-Wallace, Elizabeth, 'Milton's Daughters: The Education of Eighteenth-Century Women Writers', *Feminist Studies*, 12.2 (1986), 275–93.

——, *Consuming Subjects: Women, Shopping, and Business in the Eighteenth Century* (New York: Columbia University Press, 1997).

Kramnick, Isaac, *Bolingbroke and His Circle: The Politics of Nostalgia in the Age of Walpole* (Ithaca: Cornell University Press, 1992).

The Ladies' Diary: or Woman's Almanack (London, 1704–1841).

Landry, Donna, *The Muses of Resistance: Laboring-Class Women's Poetry in Britain, 1739–1796* (Cambridge: Cambridge University Press, 1990).

Langford, Paul, *A Polite and Commercial People: England 1727–1783* (Oxford: Oxford University Press, 1998).

Lanser, Susan S., 'Befriending the Body: Female Intimacies as Class Acts', *Eighteenth-Century Studies*, 32 (1998–99), 179–98.

——, 'Sapphic Picaresque, Sexual Difference and the Challenges of Homo-Adventuring', *Textual Practice*, 15 (2001), 251–68.

——, '"Queer to Queer": The Sapphic Body as Transgressive Text', in *Lewd and Notorious: Female Transgression in the Eighteenth Century*, ed. by Katharine Kittredge (Ann Arbor: University of Michigan Press, 2003), pp. 21–46.

Laqueur, Thomas, *Making Sex: Body and Gender from the Greeks to Freud* (Harvard: Harvard University Press, 1990).

Lead, Jane, *The Enochian Walks with God* (London, 1694).

——, *Fountain of Gardens* (London, 1696).

——, *The Messenger of an Universal Peace: or A Third Message to the Philadelphian Society* (London, 1698).

——, *The Heavenly Cloud now breaking; or the Lord-Christ's ascension ladder, now sent down*, 2nd edn (London, 1701).

Leapor, Mary, *The Works of Mary Leapor*, ed. by Richard Greene and Ann Messenger (Oxford: Clarendon Press, 2003).

Le Moyne, Pierre, *The Gallery of Heroic Women*, trans. by Marquesse of Winchester (London, 1652).

Lennox, Charlotte, *The Lady's Museum. By the Author of the Female Quixote*, 2 vols (London, 1760–61).

Locke, John, *An Essay Concerning Human Understanding*, ed. by Peter N. Nidditch (Oxford: Clarendon Press, 1975).

——, *Some Thoughts Concerning Education*, ed. by John and Jean S. Yolton (Oxford: Clarendon Press, 1989).

——, *An Essay Concerning Human Understanding*, ed. by Roger Woolhouse, Penguin Classics (Harmondsworth: Penguin, 1997).

Lockwood, Thomas, 'Eliza Haywood in 1749: *Dalinda*, and Her Pamphlet on the Pretender', *Notes and Queries*, 36 (1989), 475–7.

——, 'Subscription-Hunters and their Prey', *Studies in the Literary Imagination*, 34 (2001), 121–35.

Lonsdale, Roger, ed., *Eighteenth-Century Women Poets: An Oxford Anthology*, 2nd corrected edition with additional notes (1989; Oxford: Oxford University Press, 1990).

Lopez McAlister, Linda, ed., *Hypatia's Daughters: Fifteen Hundred Years of Women Philosophers* (Bloomington and Indianapolis: Indiana University Press, 1996).

Love, Harold, *Scribal Publication in Seventeenth-Century England* (Oxford: Clarendon Press, 1993).

Lowenthal, Cynthia, *Lady Mary Wortley Montagu and the Eighteenth-Century Letter* (Athens, GA: University of Georgia Press, 1994).

MacCarthy, B.G., *The Female Pen: Women Writers and Novelists 1621–1818*, 2 vols (Cork, 1944, 1947); reissued as 1 vol. with a preface by Janet Todd (Cork: Cork University Press, 1994).

McDowell, Paula, *The Women of Grub Street: Press, Politics, and Gender in the London Literary Marketplace, 1678–1730* (Oxford: Clarendon Press, 1998).

——, 'Enlightenment Enthusiasms and the Spectacular Failure of the Philadelphian Society', *Eighteenth-Century Studies*, 35.4 (2002), 515–33.

Mack, Phyllis, *Visionary Women: Ecstatic Prophecy in Seventeenth-Century England* (Berkeley: University of California Press, 1992).

——, 'Methodism and Motherhood', in *Culture and the Nonconformist Tradition*, ed. by Jane Shaw and Alan Krieder (Cardiff: University of Wales Press, 1999), pp. 26–42.

Makin, Bathsua, *An Essay To Revive the Antient Education of Gentlewomen in Religion, Manners, Arts, and Tongues* (London, 1673).

Mandeville, Bernard, *The Fable of the Bees*, ed. F.B. Kaye, 2 vols (Indianapolis, Liberty Fund, 1988).

——, *By a Society of Ladies: Essays in The Female Tatler*, ed. by M.M. Goldsmith (Bristol: Continuum, 1999).

Manley, Delarivier, *The Selected Works of Delarivier Manley*, ed. by Rachel Carnell and Ruth Herman, 5 vols (London: Pickering and Chatto, 2005).

Marshall, P.G., *The Financial Revolution in England: A Study in the Development of Public Credit 1688–1756* (London: Macmillan and New York: St Martin's Press, 1967).

Marsin, M., *The Near Approach of Christ's Kingdom* (London, 1696).

——, *Good news to the good women, and to the bad women too that will grow better; the like to the men* (London, 1701).

——, *Two Remarkable Females of Womankind* (London, 1701).

Marvell, Andrew, *The Poems of Andrew Marvell*, ed. by Nigel Smith, Longman Annotated English Poets (Harlow: Pearson Education, 2003).

Masham, Lady Damaris, *Discourse concerning the Love of God* (London, 1696).

——, *Occasional Thoughts in Reference to a Virtuous and Christian Life* (London, 1705).

——, *The Philosophical Works of Lady Damaris Masham*, ed. by James G. Buickerood (Bristol: Thoemmes Press, 2004).

Maslen, Keith, *Samuel Richardson of London, Printer: A Study of his Printing* (Dunedin: University of Otago Press, 2001).

Maurer, Shawn Lisa, *Proposing Men: Dialectics of Gender and Class in the Early English Periodical* (Stanford: Stanford University Press, 1998).

McKeon, Michael, *The Secret History of Domesticity: Public, Private and the Division of Knowledge* (Baltimore and London: Johns Hopkins University Press, 2005).

McLean, Gerald, Donna Landry, and Joseph Ward, eds, *The Country and the City Revisited: England and the Politics of Culture, 1550–1830* (Cambridge: Cambridge University Press, 1999).

'Medley', *Notes and Queries*, Series 8, xi (1 May 1897), p. 348.

Mermin, Dorothy, 'Women Becoming Poets: Katherine Philips, Aphra Behn, Anne Finch', *ELH*, 57 (1990), 335–55.

Merritt, Juliette, *Beyond Spectacle: Eliza Haywood's Female Spectators* (Toronto: University of Toronto Press, 2004).

——, 'Reforming the Coquet? Eliza Haywood's Vision of a Female Epistemology', in *Fair Philosopher: Eliza Haywood and 'The Female Spectator'*, ed. by Lynne Marie Wright and Donald Newman (Lewisburg: Bucknell University Press, 2006), pp. 176–92.

Messenger, Ann, *His and Hers: Essays in Restoration and Eighteenth-Century Literature* (Lexington: University Press of Kentucky, 1986).

Miguel-Alfonso, Ricardo, 'Social Conservatism, Aesthetic Education, and the Essay Genre in Eliza Haywood's *Female Spectator*', in *Fair Philosopher: Eliza Haywood and 'The Female Spectator'*, ed. by Lynne Marie Wright and Donald Newman (Lewisburg: Bucknell University Press, 2006), pp. 72–81.

Milhous, Judith and Robert D. Hume, 'Playwrights' Remuneration in Eighteenth-Century London', *Harvard Library Bulletin*, 47 (1999), 3–90.

Miller, Shannon, *Engendering the Fall: John Milton and Seventeenth-Century Writers* (Philadelphia: University of Pennsylvania Press, 2008).

Mills, Rebecca, '"That Tyrant Custom": The Politics of Custom in the Prose and Poetry of Augustan Women Writers', *Women's Writing*, 7 (2000), 391–409.

Milner, James, *Three Letters, Relating to the South Sea Company and the Bank* (London, 1720).

Mollineux, Mary, *Fruits of Retirement, or Miscellaneous Poems* (London, 1702).

Montagu, Elizabeth, *The Letters of Elizabeth Montagu, with Some of the Letters of Her Correspondents*, ed. by Matthew Montagu, 4 vols (London, 1809–13).

Montagu, Lady Mary Wortley, *Letters of the Right Honourable Lady M—y W—y M—e. Written during her Travels in Europe, Asia and Africa*, 3 vols (London, 1763).

——, *The Letters and Works of Lady Mary Wortley Montagu*, ed. by W. Moy Thomas, Lord Wharncliffe, 3 vols (London, 1837).

——, *The Nonsense of Common-Sense*, ed. by Robert Halsband (Evanston: Northwestern University Press, 1947).

——, *The Complete Letters of Lady Mary Wortley Montagu*, ed. by Robert Halsband, 3 vols (Oxford: Clarendon Press, 1966).

——, *Essays and Poems and 'Simplicity, a Comedy'*, ed. by Robert Halsband and Isobel Grundy (Oxford: Clarendon Press, 1977).

Moore, Edward, *The World. By Adam Fitz-Adam*, Vol. III, new edition (1772), No. 131, (Thursday, 3 July 1755), 159–65.

Morgan, Fidelis, ed., *The Female Wits: Women Dramatists on the London Stage, 1660–1720*, 2nd edn (London: Virago, 1988).

——, ed., *The Female Tatler* (London: Everyman, 1992).

Mullenbrock, Heinz-Joachim, *The Culture of Contention* (Munich: Fink, 1997).

Needham, Gwendolyn B., 'Mary de la Riviere Manley, Tory Defender', *Huntington Library Quarterly*, 12 (1948–49), 255–89.

North, Sir Dudley, *Discourses upon Trade* (London, 1691).

Nussbaum, Felicity A., *'The brink of all we hate'*: *English Satires on Women, 1660–1750* (Lexington: University Press of Kentucky, 1984).

——, *The Autobiographical Subject: Gender and Ideology in Eighteenth-Century England* (Baltimore: Johns Hopkins University Press, 1989).

O'Brien, Karen, 'Imperial Georgic, 1660–1789', in *The Country and the City Revisited*, ed. by Gerald McLean, Donna Landry, and Joseph Ward (Cambridge: Cambridge University Press, 1999), pp. 160–79.

——, *Women and Enlightenment in Eighteenth-Century Britain* (Cambridge: Cambridge University Press, 2009).

Orlando: Women's Writing in the British Isles from the Beginnings to the Present, ed. by Susan Brown, Patricia Clements, and Isobel Grundy (Cambridge: Cambridge University Press Online, 2006) <http://orlando.cambridge.org/>.

Osell, Tedra, 'Tatling Women in the Public Sphere: Rhetorical Femininity and the English Essay Periodical', *Eighteenth-Century Studies*, 38.2 (2005), 283–300.

Owen, Susan J., *Restoration Theatre and Crisis* (Oxford: Oxford University Press, 1996).

Pateman, Carole, *The Sexual Contract* (Stanford, CA: Stanford University Press, 1988).

Pearson, Jacqueline, *The Prostituted Muse: Images of Women and Women Dramatists 1642–1737* (Hemel Hempstead: Harvester, 1988).

Pennington, Montagu, *Memoirs of the Life of Mrs. Elizabeth Carter* (London, 1807).

Perdita Manuscripts: Women Writers 1500–1700, Adam Matthew Digital <http://www.amdigital.co.uk>.

The Perjur'd Citizen: or Female Revenge (London, 1732).

Perry, Ruth, *The Celebrated Mary Astell: An Early English Feminist* (Chicago and London: University of Chicago Press, 1986).

——, 'Mary Astell and the Feminist Critique of Possessive Individualism', *Eighteenth-Century Studies*, 23 (1990), 444–57.

——, *Novel Relations: The Transformation of Kinship in English Literature and Culture, 1748–1818* (Cambridge: Cambridge University Press, 2004).

Pettit, Alexander, 'Terrible Texts, "Marginal" Works, and the Mandate of the Moment: The Case of Eliza Haywood', *Tulsa Studies in Women's Literature*, 22 (2003), 293–314.

——, 'The Pickering & Chatto *Female Spectator*: Nearly Four Pounds of Ephemera, Enshrined', in *Fair Philosopher: Eliza Haywood and 'The Female Spectator'*, ed. by Lynne Marie Wright and Donald Newman (Lewisburg: Bucknell University Press, 2006), pp. 42–59.

Philips, John, *Cyder* (London, 1708).

Philips, Katherine, *Letters from Orinda to Poliarchus* (London, 1705).

——, *Poems by the most deservedly admired Mrs. Katherine Philips, the Matchless Orinda* (London: Jacob Tonson, 1710).

Pix, Mary, *The Innocent Mistress*, in *Eighteenth-Century Women Dramatists*, ed. by Melinda C. Finberg (Oxford: Oxford University Press, 2001).

Pocock, J.G.A., *The Machiavellian Moment: Florentine Political Thought and the Atlantic Republican Tradition* (Princeton: Princeton University Press, 1975).

——, *Virtue, Commerce and History: Essays on Political Theory and History, Chiefly in the Eighteenth Century* (Cambridge: Cambridge University Press, 1985).

Poetical miscellanies: the fifth part. Containing a collection of original poems, with several new translations. By the most eminent hands (London, 1704).

Pomfret, John, *The Choice, or Wish* (Edinburgh, 1701).

Pope, Alexander, *The Twickenham Edition of the Poems of Alexander Pope*, general editor John Butt, 11 vols, 3rd edn (London: Methuen, 1962).

—— and others, *Memoirs of the Extraordinary Life, Works, and Discoveries of Martinus Scriblerus*, ed. by Charles Kerby-Miler (New York: Russell & Russell, 1966).

Poulain de la Barre, François, *De L'Egalité des deux sexes, discours physique et morale où l'on voit l'importance de se défaire des préjugez* (Paris, 1674; reprint Paris: Fayard, 1984).

Powell, Manushag, 'The Performance of Authorship in Eighteenth-Century English Periodicals', PhD dissertation, University of California, Los Angeles, 2006.

Prescott, Sarah, 'Provincial Networks, Dissenting Connections, and Noble Friends: Elizabeth Singer Rowe and Female Authorship in Early Eighteenth-Century England', *Eighteenth-Century Life*, 25 (2001), 29–42.

——, *Women, Authorship and Literary Culture, 1690–1740* (Basingstoke: Palgrave, 2003).

——, and Jane Spencer, 'Prattling, Tattling, and Knowing Everything: Public Authority and the Female Editorial Persona in the Early Essay-Periodical', *British Journal of Eighteenth-Century Studies*, 23 (2000), 43–57.

Price, Richard, *A Review of the Principal Questions and Difficulties in Morals* (London, 1758).

Redford, Bruce, *The Converse of the Pen: Acts of Intimacy in the Eighteenth-Century Familiar Letter* (London: University of Chicago Press, 1986).

Reeve, Clara, *The Progress of Romance and the History of Charoba, Queen of England* (Colchester, 1785).

Reeves, Marjorie, 'Literary Women in Eighteenth-Century Nonconformist Circles', in *Culture and the Nonconformist Tradition*, ed. by Jane Shaw and Alan Krieder (Cardiff: University of Wales Press, 1999), pp. 7–25.

Rendall, Jane, *The Origins of Modern Feminism: Women in Britain, France and the United States, 1780–1860* (Basingstoke: Macmillan, 1985).

Richardson, Samuel, 'Preface', Penelope Aubin, *A Collection of Entertaining Histories and Novels*, Vol. I (London, 1739), pp. 2–9.

——, *Pamela; In her Exalted Condition* (London, 1741).

——, *The Selected Letters of Samuel Richardson*, ed. by John Carroll (Oxford: Clarendon Press, 1964).

——, *Clarissa or The History of a Young Lady*, ed. by Angus Ross (Harmondsworth: Penguin, 1985).

——, *Sir Charles Grandison*, ed. by Jocelyn Harris, Oxford World's Classics (Oxford: Oxford University Press, 1986).

——, *Pamela; or, Virtue Rewarded*, ed. by Thomas Keymer and Alice Wakeley (Oxford: Oxford University Press, 2001).

Rivers, Isabel, ed., *Books and their Readers in Eighteenth-Century England* (Leicester: Leicester University Press and New York: St Martin's Press, 1982).

——, *Reason, Grace and Sentiment: A Study of the Language of Religion and Ethics in England, 1660–1780*, 2 vols (Cambridge: Cambridge University Press, 1991, 2000).

Rochester, John Wilmot, Earl of, *The Complete Poems of John Wilmot Earl of Rochester*, ed. by David M. Veith (New Haven: Yale University Press, 1968).

Rogers, Pat, *The Symbolic Design of Windsor-Forest* (Newark: University of Delaware Press, 2004).

Rowe, Elizabeth Singer, *Poems on Several Occasions* (London, 1696).

——, *Friendship in Death, in Twenty Letters from the Dead to the Living* (London, 1728).

——, *Letters Moral and Entertaining*, 3 vols, 2nd edn (London, 1733–34).

——, *The History of Joseph. A Poem. In Eight Books* (London, 1736).

——, *The Miscellaneous Works in Prose and Verse of Mrs. Elizabeth Rowe*, ed. by Theophilus Rowe, 2 vols (London, 1739).

The Early Modern Englishwoman: A Facsimile Library of Essential Works: Vol. 7: Elizabeth Singer [Rowe], ed. by Jennifer Richards (Aldershot: Ashgate, 2003).

Rumbold, Valerie, *Women's Place in Pope's World* (Cambridge: Cambridge University Press, 1989).

——, 'Cut the Caterwauling: Women Writers (Not) in Pope's Dunciads', *Review of English Studies*, 52 (2001), 524–39.

Sage, Lorna, *The Cambridge Guide to Women's Writing in English* (Cambridge: Cambridge University Press, 1999).

Salzman, Paul, *Reading Early Modern Women's Writing* (Oxford: Oxford University Press, 2006).

Savage, Richard, ed., *Miscellaneous Poems and Translations. By Several Hands* (London, 1726).

Schiebinger, Londa, *The Mind Has No Sex? Women in the Origins of Modern Science* (Cambridge, MA: Harvard University Press, 1989).

Scott, Mary, *The Female Advocate, a Poem, occasioned by reading Mr Duncombe's Feminead* (London, 1774).

Scott, Sarah, *A Description of Millenium Hall* (London, 1762).

Shaftesbury, Lord Antony Ashley Cooper, *Characteristicks of Men, Manners, Opinions, Times*, 3 vols, 2nd edn corrected (London, 1714).

Shaw, Jane, 'Gender and the "Nature" of Religion: Lady Mary Wortley Montagu's Embassy Letters and their Place in Enlightenment Philosophy of Religion', *Bulletin of the John Rylands Library*, 80.3 (1998), 129–45.

—— and Alan Krieder, eds, *Culture and the Nonconformist Tradition* (Cardiff: University of Wales Press, 1999).

Sekora, John, *Luxury: The Concept in Western Thought, Eden to Smollett* (Baltimore: Johns Hopkins University Press, 1977).

She Ventures and He Wins [Ariadne] (London, 1695).

Sheridan, Frances, *Eugenia and Adelaide* (London, 1791).

Sherman, Sandra, *Finance and Fictionality in the Early Eighteenth Century: Accounting for Defoe* (Cambridge: Cambridge University Press, 1996).

Shevelow, Kathryn, 'Fathers and Daughters: Women as Readers of the *Tatler*', in *Gender and Reading*, ed. by Elizabeth Flynn and Patrocino Schweickart (Baltimore: Johns Hopkins University Press, 1986), pp. 107–23.

——, *Women and Print Culture: The Construction of Femininity in the Early Periodical* (London: Routledge, 1989).

Shiells, Robert, *The Lives of the Poets of Great Britain and Ireland*, 5 vols (London, 1753).

Smith, Hannah, 'English "Feminist" Writings and Judith Drake's *An Essay in Defence of the Female Sex'*, *Historical Journal*, 44 (2001), 727–47.

——, 'Mary Astell and the Reformation of Manners in Late Seventeenth-Century England', in *Mary Astell: Reason, Gender, Faith*, ed. by William Kolbrener and Michael Michaelson (Aldershot: Ashgate, 2007), pp. 31–47.

Smith, Tania, 'Elizabeth Montagu's Study of Cicero's Life: The Formation of an Eighteenth-Century Woman's Rhetorical Identity', *Rhetorica*, 26.2 (Spring 2008), 165–87.

Sombart, Werner, *Luxury and Capitalism* (1913; New York: Ann Arbor, 1967).

Spedding, Patrick, *A Bibliography of Eliza Haywood* (London: Pickering and Chatto, 2004).

——, 'Measuring the Success of Haywood's *Female Spectator* (1744–46)', in *Fair Philosopher: Eliza Haywood and 'The Female Spectator'*, ed. by Lynne Marie Wright and Donald Newman (Lewisburg: Bucknell University Press, 2006), pp. 193–211.

Spencer, Jane, *The Rise of the Woman Novelist: From Aphra Behn to Jane Austen* (Oxford: Oxford University Press, 1986).

——, *Aphra Behn's Afterlife* (Oxford: Clarendon Press, 2000).

Springborg, Patricia, *Mary Astell: Theorist of Freedom from Domination* (Cambridge: Cambridge University Press, 2005).

Staves, Susan, 'Church of England Clergy and Women Writers', in *Reconsidering the Bluestockings*, ed. by Nicole Pohl and Betty A. Schellenberg (San Marino: Huntington Library, 2003), pp. 81–103.

——, *A Literary History of Women's Writing in Britain, 1660–1789* (Cambridge: Cambridge University Press, 2006).

Stearns, Bertha Monica, 'The First English Periodical for Women', *Modern Philology*, 28 (1930), 45–59.

——, 'Early English Periodicals for Ladies (1700–1760)', *PMLA*, 48 (1933), 38–60.

Stecher, Henry F., *Elizabeth Singer Rowe, the Poetess of Frome: A Study in Eighteenth-Century English Pietism* (Bern: Herbert Lang, 1973).

Steele, Anne, *Miscellaneous Pieces in Verse and Prose, by Theodosia* (Bristol, 1780).

Stein, Stephen J., 'A Note on Anne Dutton, Eighteenth-Century Evangelical', *Church History*, 44.4 (December 1975), 485–91.

Stewart, Keith, 'Towards Defining an Aesthetic for the Familiar Letter in the Eighteenth Century', *Prose Studies*, 5 (1982), 179–89.

Stiebel, Arlene, 'Subversive Sexuality: Masking the Erotic in Poems by Katherine Philips and Aphra Behn', in *Renaissance Discourses of Desire*, ed. by Claude Summers and Ted-Larry Pebworth (Columbia: University of Missouri Press, 1993), pp. 223–36.

Stuurman, Siep, *François Poulain de la Barre and the Invention of Modern Equality* (Cambridge, MA: Harvard University Press, 2004).

Sutherland, Kathryn, 'Editing for a New Century: Elizabeth Elstob's Anglo-Saxon Manifesto and Ælfric's St Gregory Homily', in *The Editing of Old English: Papers from the 1990 Manchester Conference*, ed. by D.G. Scragg and P.E. Szarmach (London: Boydell and Brewer, 1994), pp. 213–37.

——, 'Elizabeth Elstob', in *Medieval Scholarship: Biographical Studies on the Formation of a Discipline*, ed. by Helen Damico, 3 vols (New York: Garland, 1995–2000), II, 59–73.

Swift, Jonathan, *Journal to Stella*, ed. by Harold Williams, 2 vols (Oxford: Clarendon Press, 1948).

——, *Jonathan Swift: The Complete Poems*, ed. by Pat Rogers (New Haven: Yale University Press, 1983).

——, *Jonathan Swift: Major Works*, ed. by Angus Ross and David Woolley (Oxford: Oxford University Press, 2003).

Szechi, Daniel, *1715: The Great Jacobite Rebellion* (New Haven and London: Yale University Press, 2006).

Tavor Bannet, Eve, 'Haywood's Spectator and the Female World', in *Fair Philosopher: Eliza Haywood and 'The Female Spectator'*, ed. by Lynne Marie Wright and Donald Newman (Lewisburg: Bucknell University Press, 2006), pp. 82–103.

Taylor, Barbara, *Mary Wollstonecraft and the Feminist Imagination* (Cambridge: Cambridge University Press, 2003).

Taylor, Jeremy, *A Discourse of the Nature, Offices, and Measures, of Friendship, with Rules Of Conducting It, in a Letter to the Most Ingenious and Excellent Mrs. Katharine [sic] Philips* (London, 1657).

Teague, Frances, *Bathsua Makin, Woman of Learning* (Lewisburg: Bucknell University Press/London: Associated University Presses, 1998).

Terry, Richard, *Poetry and the Making of the English Literary Past 1660–1781* (Oxford: Clarendon Press, 2001).

Thomas, Elizabeth, *Miscellany Poems on Several Subjects* (London, 1722).

Thomson, James, *The Seasons* (London, 1730).

Thoughts on friendship. By way of essay; for the use and improvement of the ladies. By a well-wisher to her sex (London, 1725).

Todd, Janet, *The Sign of Angellica: Women, Writing and Fiction 1600–1800* (New York: Columbia University Press, 1989).

——, ed., *Dictionary of British Women Writers* (London: Routledge, 1989).

——, *The Critical Fortunes of Aphra Behn* (London: Boydell and Brewer, 1998).

Toland, John, *Letters to Serena* (London, 1704).

Tomaselli, Sylvana, 'The Enlightenment Debate on Women', *History Workshop Journal*, 20 (1985), 101–24.

Trevelyan, G.M., *England under Queen Anne*, 3 vols (London: Collins, 1965).

Trill, Suzanne, 'Religion and the Construction of Femininity', in *Women and Literature in Britain 1500–1700*, ed. by Helen Wilcox (Cambridge: Cambridge University Press, 1996), pp. 46–51.

Trotter, Catharine, *The Revolution of Sweden*, Vol. II of *Eighteenth-Century Women Playwrights*, ed. by Anne Kelley (London: Pickering and Chatto, 2001).

Turner, Cheryl, *Living by the Pen: Women Writers in the Eighteenth Century* (London: Routledge, 1992).

Vanbrugh, Sir John, *The Provok'd Wife, A Comedy* (London, 1697).

Vieth, David M., *Attribution in Restoration Poetry: A Study of Rochester's Poems in 1680* (New Haven: Yale University Press, 1963).

Voltaire, François-Marie Arouet de, *Eléments de la Philosophie de Newton* (Paris, 1738).

von Maltzahn, Nicholas, 'The Whig Milton, 1667–1700', in *Milton and Republicanism*, ed. by David Armitage, Armand Himy, and Quentin Skinner (Cambridge: Cambridge University Press, 1995), pp. 229–53.

Vries, Jan de, 'Luxury in the Dutch Golden Age in Theory and Practice', in *Luxury in the Eighteenth Century: Debates, Desires and Delectable Goods*, ed. by Maxine Berg and Elizabeth Eger (Basingstoke: Palgrave, 2002), pp. 41–56.

Wack, Mary Frances, *Lovesickness in the Middle Ages: the Viaticum and Its Commentaries* (Philadelphia: University of Pennsylvania Press, 1990).

Wahl, Elizabeth Susan, *Invisible Relations: Representations of Female Intimacy in the Age of Enlightenment* (Stanford: Stanford University Press, 1999).

Waller, Edmund, *St James Park* (London, 1661).

Warner, William, *Licensing Entertainment: The Elevation of Novel Reading in Britain, 1684–1750* (Berkeley and Los Angeles: University of California Press, 1998).

Watson, J.R., *The English Hymn: A Critical and Historical Study* (Oxford: Clarendon Press, 1997).

Watt, Ian, 'Robinson Crusoe as Myth', in *Robinson Crusoe*, Norton Critical Edition (New York: Norton, 1975), pp. 311–31.

——, *The Rise of the Novel: Studies in Defoe, Richardson and Fielding* (1957; Harmondsworth: Pelican, 1976).

Watts, Michael, *The Dissenters: From the Reformation to the French Revolution* (Oxford: Clarendon Press, 1999).

Weil, Rachel, *Political Passions: Gender, The Family and Political Argument in England, 1680–1714* (Manchester: Manchester University Press, 1999).

Wells, Marion, *The Secret Wound: Love-Melancholy and Early Modern Romance* (Stanford: Stanford University Press, 2007).

The Whisperer (1709), reprinted in *Contemporaries of the 'Tatler' and 'Spectator'*, ed. by Richmond P. Bond, Augustan Reprint Society No. 47 (Los Angeles: Williams Andrew Clark Memorial Library, 1954).

White, Cynthia, *Women's Magazines 1693–1968* (London: Michael Joseph, 1970).

Williams, Jane, *The Literary Women of England* (London, 1861).

Williamson, Marilyn L., *Raising their Voices: British Women Writers, 1650–1750* (Detroit: Wayne State University Press, 1990).

Wilputte, Earla, 'Parody in Eliza Haywood's A Letter from H— G—, Esq', *Eighteenth-Century Fiction*, 17.2 (January 2005), 207–30.

——, ' "Too ticklish to meddle with": The Silencing of *The Female Spectator's* Political Correspondents', in *Fair Philosopher: Eliza Haywood and 'The Female Spectator'*, ed. by Lynne Marie Wright and Donald Newman (Lewisburg: Bucknell University Press, 2006), pp. 122–40.

Winchilsea, Anne Finch, Countess of, *Miscellany Poems, on several occasions* (London, 1713).

——, *The Poems of Anne Countess of Winchilsea*, ed. by Myra Reynolds (Chicago: University of Chicago Press, 1903; reissued New York: AMS Press, 1974).

——, *The Anne Finch Wellesley Manuscript Poems*, ed. by Barbara McGovern and Charles H. Hinnant (Athens, GA and London: University of Georgia Press, 1998).

Wiseman, Susan, 'Monstrous Perfectibility: Ape-Human Transformations in Hobbes, Bulwer, Tyson', in *At the Borders of the Human: Beasts, Bodies and Natural Philosophy in the Early Modern Period*, ed. by Erica Fudge, Ruth Gilbert, and Susan Wiseman (London: Macmillan, 1999), pp. 215–38.

Wittreich, Joseph, *Feminist Milton* (Ithaca: Cornell University Press, 1987).

——, ' "John, John, I blush for thee": Mapping Gender Discourse in *Paradise Lost*', in *Out of Bounds: Male Writers and Gender(ed) Criticism*, ed. by Laura Claridge and Elizabeth Langford (Amherst: University of Massachusetts Press, 1991), pp. 42–3.

Wollstonecraft, Mary, *A Vindication of the Rights of Woman* (Harmondsworth: Penguin, 1992).

Woman Not Inferior to Man: or A Short and Modest Vindication of the Natural Right of the Fair-Sex to a Perfect Equality of Power, Dignity, and Esteem, with the Men. By Sophia, A Person of Quality (London, 1739).

Woman's Superior Excellence over Man: or, A Reply to the Author of a Late Treatise (London, 1740).

Women Critics 1660–1820: An Anthology, ed. by Folger Collective on Early Women Critics (Bloomington and Indianapolis: Indiana University Press, 1995).

Woolf, Virginia, *The Common Reader* (London: The Hogarth Press, 1925).

——, *The Essays of Virginia Woolf: vol. 2, 1912–1918,* ed. by Andrew McNellie (San Diego, New York, London: Harcourt Brace Jovanovich, 1986).

Wootton, David, 'Pierre Bayle, Libertine?' in *Oxford Studies in the History of Philosophy,* ed. by M.A. Stewart, 2 vols (Oxford: Oxford University Press, 1997), II, 197–226.

Wordsworth, William, *Poems and Extracts Chosen by William Wordsworth for an Album presented to Lady Mary Lowther, Christmas 1819,* ed. by Harold Littledale (London: H. Frowde, 1905).

——, *William Wordsworth: The Major Works including the Prelude,* ed. by Stephen Gill (Oxford: Oxford University Press, 2000).

Wright, Lynne Marie and Donald J. Newman, *Fair Philosopher: Eliza Haywood and 'The Female Spectator'* (Lewisburg: Bucknell University Press, 2006).

Yearsley, Ann, 'Clifton Hill', in *Poems on Several Occasions* (London, 1785), pp. 127–47.

Zach, Wolfgang, 'Mrs. Aubin and Richardson's Earliest Literary Manifesto (1739)', *English Studies,* 62 (1981), 271–85.

Zinsser, Judith P., *La Dame D'Esprit: A Biography of the Marquise du Châtelet* (New York: Viking, 2006).

Zook, Melinda, 'Contextualising Aphra Behn: Play, Politics and Party, 1679–89', in *Women Writers and the Early Modern Political Tradition,* ed. by Hilda L. Smith (Cambridge: Cambridge University Press, 1998), pp. 75–94.

Zwerdling, Alex, *Virginia Woolf and the Real World* (Berkeley, Los Angeles and London: University of California Press, 1987).

Index

CPSIA information can be obtained at www.ICGtesting.com
Printed in the USA
LVOW102149070313

323266LV00015B/143/P